Zongmi on Chan

TRANSLATIONS FROM THE ASIAN CLASSICS

Translations from the Asian Classics

Zongmi on Chan

Jeffrey Lyle Broughton

COLUMBIA UNIVERSITY

NEW YORK

Columbia University Press
Publishers Since 1893
New York   Chichester, West Sussex

Sponsored by the Chiang Ching-kuo Foundation for International Scholarly Exchange.

The author thanks Abbot Aoki of Kumida-dera in Osaka for kind permission
to reproduce the portrait of Zongmi used as this book's frontispiece.
Thanks to Yoshioka Nobuko for her kind assistance in securing permission from Kumida-dera
and Stephen M. Strasen for his kind assistance in digitizing the image. *Source*: Portrait of
Guifeng Zongmi (Keihō Shūmitsu; 780–841). Hanging scroll. Ink with color on silk.
95 × 53 cm. Late fourteenth to early fifteenth centuries. One of a set of four portraits of
Kegon school patriarchs in the possession of Kumida-dera in Osaka prefecture.

Library of Congress Cataloging-in-Publication Data
Broughton, Jeffrey L., 1944–
Zongmi on Chan / Jeffrey Lyle Broughton.
p. cm.—(Translations from the Asian classics)
Includes English translations of Chinese texts.
Includes bibliographical references and index.
ISBN 978-0-231-14392-9 (cloth : alk. paper)—ISBN 978-0-231-51308-1 (e-book)
1. Zongmi, 780–841.   2. Zen Buddhism—China—Doctrines.   I. Title.
BQ8249.T787B76 2009
294.3'9270951—dc22   2008040358

Columbia University Press books are printed on permanent and durable acid-free paper.
This book is printed on paper with recycled content.
Printed in the United States of America
c 10 9 8 7 6 5 4 3 2 1

To Elise Yoko Watanabe

LAMENTING CHAN MASTER ZONGMI

A precipitous path where only birds can go with snow on the
    ridges and peaks,
The master is dead—who will go up there to do Chan sitting?
Dust on his writing table has piled up since he extinguished.
The colors of the trees have changed since he was alive.
His tiered stupa faces pines rustling in the wind.
His footprints remain beside the neglected spring.
I just sigh over the tiger that used to listen to his sutra chanting,
Arriving on time at the side of his dilapidated hermitage.

    —Jia Dao (779–843) (*Quan Tangshi* [*Complete Tang Poems*],
        17:573.6669; see glossary under Jia Dao)

CONTENTS

TRANSLITERATION SYSTEMS

CHINESE: HANYU PINYIN

I have adhered to the "Basic Rules for Hanyu Pinyin Orthography" found in John DeFrancis, *ABC Chinese-English Comprehensive Dictionary* (Honolulu: University of Hawai'i Press, 2003), 1341–49. The general guideline there is to take the word (*ci*) as the unit of spelling. Thus, structures of two or three syllables that express an integral concept are written together as one word, but there will always be ambiguous cases. Note that this differs from the Library of Congress system's general principle of separation of syllables (see "Library of Congress Pinyin Conversion Project: New Chinese Romanization Outlines," http://www.loc.gov/catdir/pinyin/romcover.html).

JAPANESE: MODIFIED HEPBURN

See Watanabe Toshirō, Edmund R. Skrzypczak, and Paul Snowden, eds., *Kenkyusha's New Japanese-English Dictionary*, 5th ed. (Tokyo: Kenkyūsha, 2003), *Rōmaji tsuzuri hōhyō* [Romanization Spelling Chart].

KOREAN: MCCUNE-REISCHAUER

See http://www.loc.gov/catdir/cpso/romanization/korean.pdf.

SANSKRIT: IAST (INTERNATIONAL ALPHABET
FOR SANSKRIT TRANSLITERATION)

However, Sanskrit terms that appear in the list of Roger Jackson, "Terms of Sanskrit and Pāli Origin Acceptable as English Words," *The Journal of the International Association of Buddhist Studies* 5, no. 2 (1982): 141–42, appear without italicization or diacritical marks. Names of Indian patriarchs other than disciples of the Buddha, treatise masters, translators, and deities, such as Dhrtaka, Simha, Nagarjuna, Asanga, Bhavaviveka, Kumarajiva, Gunabhadra, Divakara, Siksananda, Ucchusma, etc., also appear without diacritical marks.

TIBETAN: WYLIE

See Turrell Wylie, "A Standard System of Tibetan Transcription," *Harvard Journal of Asiatic Studies* 22 (December 1959): 261–67.

ABBREVIATIONS

CBETA	Chinese Buddhist Electronic Text Association: http://www.cbeta.org
CHAN CANON	Zongmi's lost collection of Chan literary materials entitled *Chanyuan zhuquanji* (*Collection of Expressions of the Chan Source*)
CHAN LETTER	Text formed from Zongmi's answers to questions about Chan sent in letter form to him by Pei Xiu. It has been known by various titles such as *Zhonghua chuanxindi chanmen shizi chengxi tu* (*Chart of the Master-Disciple Succession of the Chan Gate that Transmits the Mind Ground in China*), *Pei Xiu shiyi wen* (*Imperial Redactor Pei Xiu's Inquiry*), etc.
CHAN NOTES	Zongmi's notes on Chan houses embedded in the third fascicle of his thirteen-fascicle subcommentary entitled *Yuanjuejing dashu chao* (*Extracts from the Great Commentary on the Perfect Awakening Sutra*)
CHAN PROLEGOMENON	Zongmi's magnum opus on Chan, entitled *Chanyuan zhuquanji duxu* (*Prolegomenon to the Collection of Expressions of the Chan Source*)

DAIZŌKYŌ · Kamata Shigeo and others, eds. *Daizōkyō zen-kaisetsu daijiten*. Tokyo: Yūzankaku shuppan, 1998. Descriptive dictionary of texts in the *Taishō Canon*

EXCERPTS · *Pŏpchip pyŏrhaeng nok chŏryo pyŏngip sagi* (Chinul's *Excerpts from the Separately Circulated Record of the Dharma Collection with Inserted Personal Notes*)

HIRAKAWA · Hirakawa Akira, ed. *Bukkyō Kan-Bon daijiten/ Buddhist Chinese-Sanskrit Dictionary*. Tokyo: The Reiyūkai, 1997

ISHII (1–10) · Enbun 3 (1358) Gozan edition of the *Chan Prolegomenon* with a modern Japanese translation in ten parts: Ishii Shudō and Ogawa Takashi. "*Zengen shosenshū tojo* no yakuchū kenkyū (1)." *Komazawa daigaku Bukkyō gakubu kenkyū kiyō* 52 (March 1994): 1–53

——. "*Zengen shosenshū tojo* no yakuchū kenkyū (2)." *Komazawa daigaku Bukkyō gakubu kenkyū kiyō* 53 (March 1995): 37–125

——. "*Zengen shosenshū tojo* no yakuchū kenkyū (3)." *Komazawa daigaku Bukkyō gakubu kenkyū kiyō* 54 (March 1996): 19–55

——. "*Zengen shosenshū tojo* no yakuchū kenkyū (4)." *Komazawa daigaku Bukkyō gakubu ronshū* 27 (October 1996): 39–73

——. "*Zengen shosenshū tojo* no yakuchū kenkyū (5)." *Komazawa daigaku Bukkyō gakubu kenkyū kiyō* 55 (March 1997): 19–39

——. "*Zengen shosenshū tojo* no yakuchū kenkyū (6)." *Komazawa daigaku Bukkyō gakubu ronshū* 28 (October 1997): 81–110

——. "*Zengen shosenshū tojo* no yakuchū kenkyū (7)." *Komazawa daigaku Bukkyō gakubu kenkyū kiyō* 56 (March 1998): 67–86

——. "*Zengen shosenshū tojo* no yakuchū kenkyū (8)." *Komazawa daigaku Bukkyō gakubu ronshū* 29 (October 1998): 17–56

——. "*Zengen shosenshū tojo* no yakuchū kenkyū (9)." *Komazawa daigaku Bukkyō gakubu kenkyū kiyō* 57 (March 1999): 51–113

——. "*Zengen shosenshū tojo* no yakuchū kenkyū (10)." *Komazawa daigaku Bukkyō gakubu ronshū* 30 (October 1999): 59–97

KAMATA	Kamata Shigeo, ed. and trans. *Zengen shosenshū tojo.* Zen no goroku 9. Tokyo: Chikuma shobō, 1971. Wanli 4 (1576) Korean edition of the *Chan Prolegomenon* and the *Manji zokuzō* (ZZ) *Chan Letter* discovered in 1910 at Myōken-ji in Kyoto
MIND MIRROR	*Zongjinglu* (Yongming Yanshou's *Record of the Axiom Mirror* [=*Zongjianlu/Record of the Axiom Mirror*= *Xinjinglu/Record of the Mind Mirror*]; Taishō no. 2016)
QTW	*Quan Tangwen.* 20 vols. Imperial edition, 1814. Reprint, Taipei: Datong shuju, 1979. *Complete Tang Prose*
SHINPUKU-JI	Ishii Shudō. "Shinpuku-ji bunko shozō no *Hai Kyū shūi mon* no honkoku." *Zengaku kenkyū* 60 (1981): 71–104. Kamakura (Ninji 2 [1241]) manuscript of the *Chan Letter* discovered at Ṣhinpuku-ji in Nagoya
SHŪMITSU	Kamata Shigeo. *Shūmitsu kyōgaku no shisō-shi teki kenkyū.* Tokyo: Tokyo daigaku shuppankai, 1975
T	Takakusu Junjirō and Watanabe Kaigyoku, eds. *Taishō shinshū daizōkyō.* 100 vols. Tokyo: Taishō issaikyō kankōkai, 1924–34
UI	Ui Hakuju, ed. and trans. *Zengen shosenshū tojo.* 1939. Reprint, Tokyo: Iwanami shoten, 1943. *Manji zokuzō* (ZZ) 1601 *Ming Canon* edition of the *Chan Prolegomenon* and the ZZ *Chan Letter* discovered in 1910 at Myōken-ji in Kyoto
XIXIA	Solonin, K. J. "Hongzhou Buddhism in Xixia and the Heritage of Zongmi (780–841): A Tangut Source." *Asia Major* 16, no. 2 (2003): 57–103
YANAGIDA I	Yanagida Seizan, ed. and trans. *Shoki no Zenshi I.* Zen no goroku 2. Tokyo: Chikuma shobō, 1971
YANAGIDA II	Yanagida Seizan, ed. and trans. *Shoki no Zenshi II.* Zen no goroku 3. Tokyo: Chikuma shobō, 1976
ZZ	*Dai Nippon zoku-zōkyō* (*Manji zokuzō*). 150 cases. Tokyo: Zōkyō shoin, 1905–12

Zongmi on Chan

Introduction

This book [Zongmi's *Chan Prolegomenon*] is not only a means for coming to know of matters related to Zen; it is also a book that is valuable for coming to know Buddhism in general.
—Ui Hakuju, *Zengen shosenshū tojo* (1939)

Modern Japanese Zen has tended to foster a rather one-dimensional characterization of the Chan/Zen school's slogan "mind-to-mind transmission; no involvement with the written word [*yi xin chuan xin bu li wenzi*]." For Japanese Zen it is common to imply that textual learning (*gakumon*) in Buddhism in general and personal experience (*taiken*) in Zen are separate realms. For instance, Yamamoto Genpō (1866–1961), the most famous Rinzai Zen master of early Shōwa Japan and sometimes called the second coming of Hakuin Ekaku (1685–1768), said that the crucial requirement for a Zen monk is the "mind of the Way" (*dōshin*), and that adding learning (*gakumon*) to this is like making a ferocious demon hold a metal cudgel (*oni ni kanabō*). Supplying a cudgel is like adding superfluous strength to a demon that is already strong.[1] Even in Zen scholarship such a dichotomy between Zen mind and the word shows up. The *Great Dictionary of Zen Studies* (*Zengaku daijiten*), a multivolume Zen dictionary published by the Sōtō Zen school in Japan in the 1970s, begins its entry for "no involvement with the written word" with the following:

The slogan "no involvement with the written word; a separate transmission outside the canonical teachings" is spoken of as a special characteristic of the Zen school. Scholars of the teachings took as the main thing only the written words and theories of the sutras and treatises and thereby lost the true spirit of Buddhism. In the Zen school, the true dharma as real Buddhism does not depend upon the mere written word and the sutra teachings but is something transmitted from mind to mind. And so, valuing personal experience [*tai-ken*], Zen advocated the slogan "no involvement with the written word; a separate transmission outside the canonical teachings."[2]

The career and writings of the Tang dynasty Chan master Guifeng Zongmi (780–841) serve to undermine the foundational assumptions of this commonly accepted model of the separateness of Zen mind and canonical word. Zongmi, a renowned Chan master as well as one of China's greatest scholars of the Buddhist scriptures, with many years of rigorous Chan practice at his mountain hermitage, held that the first patriarch of Chan in China, Bodhidharma, propagated the slogan "a mind-to-mind transmission; no involvement with the written word" in order to inform his Chinese audience, bogged down in Buddhist writings, that the moon does not lie in the finger pointing at the moon (*Chan Prolegomenon*, section 11). Zongmi explained Bodhidharma's silent mind transmission as a silent pointing to "Knowing" (*zhi*),[3] the very substance of mind, but held that Bodhidharma did not eschew all words (*Chan Prolegomenon*, section 30):

It was just because this land [of China] was deluded about mind and grasped the written word, took the name for the substance, that Bodhidharma's good skill [in teaching devices] was to select the phrase "transmission of mind." He raised this term ("mind" is a term), but was silent about its substance (Knowing is its substance). . . . To the very end, [Bodhidharma] did not give others the previously mentioned word "Knowing." He simply waited for them to awaken of their own accord and then, for the first time, said: 'That is how it really is [*fang yan zhenshi shi*]!' Only when they had personally realized the substance [*qin zheng qi ti*] did he seal them, cutting off remaining doubts. This is why [his teaching] was called "silent transmission of the mind seal [*mo chuan xinyin*]." The word "silent" means only that he was silent about the word "Knowing," not that he did not say anything [*fei zong bu yan*].

Zongmi cogently and persuasively argued that Chan realizations are identical to the teachings embedded in canonical word and that one who transmits Chan must use the sutras and treatises as a standard (*Chan Prolegomenon*, section 13). In fact, the teachings serve as *precedents* that *legitimize* the Chan realizations (*Chan Prolegomenon*, section 49). He strongly favored the model of all-at-once (sudden) awakening (to Knowing) followed by step-by-step (gradual) practice found in the *Perfect Awakening Sutra (Yuanjuejing)*. But Japanese Rinzai Zen has, since the Edo period, marginalized the sutra-based Chan of sudden awakening–gradual practice propounded in Zongmi's *Chan Prolegomenon* and continued in its successor text, the *Mind Mirror (Zongjinglu)* of Yongming Yanshou (904–976), favoring instead the rhetorical and iconoclastic Chan found in such texts as the *Record of Linji (Linjilu)* and the *Extensive Record of Yunmen (Yunmen guanglu)*. In the rhetoric of the *Record of Linji* the sutras are just old toilet paper. Many modern Rinzai Zen masters, including Yamamoto Genpō mentioned above, have thoroughly immersed themselves in the *Record of Linji* (Genpō, in fact, vowed to read it one hundred times), and modern Rinzai scholarship has produced a stream of translations and studies of this text (leading to a stream of translations into English, French, and German). Since the West, because of developments in modern East Asian history, has received its overall impression of the Chinese Chan tradition from Japanese Zen, the Western perspective as now constituted reflects the emphases, shadings, deletions, and blindspots of its Japanese informant.

The first step toward reevaluating the history of Chan in East Asia as a whole is to read Zongmi (and Yanshou) and then look afresh at the Chinese Chan of the Song, Yuan, and Ming dynasties, as well as regional traditions such as Korean Sŏn, Tangut/Xixia Chan, and the neglected Five Mountains Zen of Ashikaga Japan (a text-based form of Rinzai Zen not emphasized in the modern Rinzai Zen genealogy). The outcome of such a reevaluation is likely to be a growing realization that Zongmi-style sutra-based Chan was much more normative in East Asia than we have been led to believe. In time this approach would surely lead to a revised version of Chan history that has less shouting, hitting, tearing up of the sutras, scatological sayings, and so on, and more sober sutra study combined with a highly ritualized practice gradually carried out over time. This introduction will examine Zongmi's career, the content of his theoretical works on Chan, and his effects on Chinese Chan, Tangut/Xixia Chan, Korean Sŏn, and Japanese Five Mountains Zen. Following this introduction are complete translations of his three surviving Chan works.

BIOGRAPHICAL SKETCH OF GUIFENG ZONGMI: AN ERUDITE CHAN MONK

In the context of Tang Chan masters, two aspects of Zongmi's biography stand out: his enrollment in his twenties at an elite academy where the curriculum was based on the classics; and, after becoming a Chan monk, his attainment of a high level of erudition in Buddhist literature as a whole. Such a career trajectory does not fit the usual profile. Tang Chan masters as a rule in their youth did not attend academies in preparation for the examination system. Rather, they typically began their contact with the Buddhist monastic world in childhood or during their early teens. Also, during their Chan careers they did not function as learned exegetes and commentators on the Buddhist sutra and treatise literature. The biography of Zongmi breaks down into six phases.[4]

BIRTH AND YOUTHFUL CLASSICAL EDUCATION (780–804)

Zongmi was born in 780 into a provincial elite family of wealth and power, the He, in Guozhou, Xichong county (present-day Sichuan province).[5] From the age of six to fifteen or sixteen he worked at typical classical studies, and from seventeen to twenty or twenty-one, perhaps because of the death of his father, he studied some Buddhist texts. From twenty-two to twenty-four he was enrolled at the nearby Righteousness Learning Academy.[6] There he surely deepened his exposure to such books as the *Classic of Poetry, Changes, Zhou Rites, Analects, Mencius, Xunzi,* Sima Quian's *Shiji,* and so forth, building up a substantial memory corpus. Later he fused this corpus based on the core works of Chinese learning with an enormous one based on Buddhist learning.

A YOUNG MAN'S COMMITMENT TO CHAN PRACTICE (804–810)

In 804, at the age of twenty-four, Zongmi's career path took an abrupt turn. In Suizhou, the site of the Righteousness Learning Academy and the Dayun Monastery, he happened to meet Chan Master Daoyuan of the Dayun. Zongmi promptly left home, training under Daoyuan for two or three years until he received "the sealed mind" from Daoyuan in 807.[7] It was also during this phase that he encountered a copy of the apocryphal *Perfect Awakening Sutra (Yuanjuejing),* a sutra whose very structure is built on the model of sudden awakening followed by gradual practice, and had an awakening experience.[8] The *Perfect Awakening* always remained his favorite sutra. Zongmi traced his Chan lineage as follows:

Huineng, the sixth patriarch
↓
Heze Shenhui, the seventh patriarch
↓
Cizhou Zhiru
↓
Yizhou Nanyin (=Weizhong)
↓
Suizhou Daoyuan

Zongmi's claim of Heze descent has been questioned in modern scholarship, but, in fact, the confusion lies with Yizhou Nanyin's self-presentation, not Zongmi's. During his career Nanyin had contact with two different Shenhuis: the one associated with the Heze Monastery in the eastern capital Luoyang listed above (probably through his disciple Cizhou Zhiru); and Jingzhong Shenhui, a pillar of the Jingzhong (Pure Assembly) lineage of Chan that flourished around the Jingzhong Monastery in the city of Chengdu, Sichuan. Zongmi sometimes referred to the latter Shenhui as Yizhou Shi, probably to make clear the distinction between these two Shenhuis. Nanyin first trained under Heze Shenhui or his disciple Cizhou Zhiru before going to Sichuan and becoming one of Jingzhong Shenhui's important disciples.

Nanyin was installed as abbot of Shengshou Monastery in Chengdu in 807, the same year in which Zongmi obtained the sealed mind from Nanyin's disciple Daoyuan. Shengshou was nominally a branch of the Jingzhong school, but Nanyin must have stressed his connection to Heze. As the American scholar Peter Gregory states: "The identification of the Sheng-shou tradition with Ho-tse Shen-hui [Heze Shenhui] did not originate with Tsung-mi [Zongmi]."[9] In other words, Daoyuan continued his master's emphasis on Heze rather than Jingzhong and passed this emphasis on to his student Zongmi. Thus, we could call Zongmi's Chan Shengshou Chan or Sichuanese Heze Chan.

INHERITANCE OF CHENGGUAN'S HUAYAN (810–816)

In 810 Zongmi left Sichuan for good, passing through Xiangyang in Hubei and the eastern capital of Luoyang before proceeding on to the western capital Chang'an. He speaks of these events in a letter to Qingliang Chengguan (738–839) sent in the autumn of 811.[10] Zongmi had been studying Chengguan's Huayan commentaries, some of the most intricate commentarial literature of scholastic Buddhism, and he begged the great Huayan exegete of Chang'an to accept him as an apprentice. Once accepted, he went to Chengguan and studied under him for two years (812–813), later remaining in consultation with him. It was a case of a practicing Chan monk taking up the in-depth study of difficult texts under the foremost Buddhist pandit of the day.

And the staggeringly erudite Chengguan recognized the talent of the newcomer. Of the myriad students around Chengguan, only Zongmi and a Sengrui are said to have penetrated to the inner sanctum of the master's teachings.[11] Chengguan, who wrote voluminous commentaries on the *Huayan Sutra*, had some experience with Chan and incorporated Chan into the vast edifice of Huayan.[12] Zongmi's masterpiece, the *Chan Prolegomenon*, uses some key elements from the works of Chengguan and Fazang to discuss Chan and identifies the *Huayan Sutra* (as well as the *Perfect Awakening Sutra*) with the highest level of Chan. Chengguan, of course, considered Huayan higher than all forms of Chan.

PRODUCTION OF TECHNICAL BUDDHIST EXEGESIS (816–828)

Zongmi took up residence on Mt. Zhongnan, southwest of the imperial capital Chang'an in Shaanxi, eventually settling at Caotang Monastery at the foot of one of the peaks of Zhongnan, Guifeng. Hence he acquired the name Guifeng Zongmi. From the north face of Mt. Zhongnan, the metropolis of Chang'an was visible. Centuries earlier Caotang had been the site of Kumarajiva's translating activities, and it became Zongmi's base. In 828 he was summoned to the court of Emperor Wenzong, where he received such honors as the purple robe and the title Great Worthy (*dade*). During this phase Zongmi produced many technical Buddhist works; this makes him unique among major Chan masters of the Tang. A list of extant and lost exegetical works that can be dated with some certainty to this period includes:

1. Commentary on the *Awakening of Faith in the Mahayana*
2. Commentary on the *Thunderbolt-Cutter Perfection of Wisdom Sutra*
3. Abridged commentary to the *Perfect Awakening Sutra*
4. Subcommentary to the above abridged commentary
5. Procedural manual on conditions for praxis, methods of worship, and cross-legged dhyana sitting according to the *Perfect Awakening Sutra*
6. Commentary on the *Perfect Awakening Sutra*
7. Subcommentary to the above commentary
8. Essay on the *Huayan Sutra*
9. Commentary on the *Dharmagupta-vinaya*

10. Compilation of passages from commentaries to the *Perfect Awakening Sutra*

11. Commentary and subcommentary on Vasubandhu's *Thirty Verses on Consciousness Only.*[13]

I could add to this list a commentary on the *Nirvana Sutra* that may be datable to this phase. Amazingly, this list is just a portion of Zongmi's total oeuvre.[14]

ASSOCIATION WITH LITERATI AND PRODUCTION OF CHAN WORKS (828–835)

At this time Zongmi was in contact with many literati and politicians, sometimes answering their queries on Buddhist topics, and some of this material was gathered together in a collection or in various collections after his death. By far the most famous layman mentioned in connection with Zongmi was the poet Bai Juyi (772–846), with whom Zongmi socialized during a visit to the eastern capital Luoyang in 833. But the absolutely central figure around Zongmi was his slightly younger disciple and personal friend Pei Xiu (791–864). Until the master's death in 841, Pei and Zongmi were exceptionally close, with Pei writing prefaces to a number of Zongmi's works as well as his funerary inscription.[15]

Zongmi wrote a preface to Pei Xiu's *Encouraging the Production of the Thought of Awakening (Quan fa putixin wen)* in which he mentions their long association in the practice of the Buddhist way: "In the end period [of the dharma] people are of little faith. At this time there is Mr. Pei of Hedong, a superior scholar of the Confucian gate, who faces this with humaneness. Pei and I have been intertwined in the buddha path for a long time."[16] I imagine that Pei, until the end of his life, in spite of contact with numerous other Buddhist masters, considered Zongmi his foremost teacher. And I also imagine that Zongmi considered Pei his foremost student.

The *Old Tang History (Jiu Tangshu)* biographical entry for Pei portrays a fusion of active and competent official, accomplished man of letters, outstanding calligrapher, and fervent Buddhist practitioner:

[Pei was] good at the literary arts, excelled at letter writing, and formed his own unique style in the art of calligraphy. His family had for generations embraced Buddhism. Xiu was even deeper into Buddhist books. Taiyuan [in Shanxi] and Fengxiang [in Shaanxi] are near famous mountains with many Buddhist monasteries. On the pretext of sightseeing he would wander on walks through the mountains and forests, carrying on discussions with Buddhist monks learned in the Buddhist doctrinal systems in search of the principles of Buddhism. After his middle years he did not eat garlic, onions, and meat, always observing the precepts of vegetarianism, and he put aside lustful desires. Incense burners and precious [Buddhist] books were always about his study. He took songs and chants of praise as music of the dharma. Both he and President of the Department of Affairs of State He Ganzhi took dharma names. People of the time respected his high purity but scorned his excessiveness [in matters Buddhist]. Many told stories ridiculing him, but Xiu did not consider these things something from which to deviate.[17]

Zongmi's major Chan works took shape during this phase of his career, and the timing is significant since it suggests that these works were in some way connected to the influential elite of the capital and court. He was broadcasting Chan to a very important metropolitan audience. The *Chan Letter*, known under various titles, the most common in modern scholarship being *Chart of the Master-Disciple Succession of the Chan Gate That Transmits the Mind Ground in China* (*Zhonghua chuanxindi chanmen shizi chengxi tu*), is a short text consisting of Zongmi's answers to questions about Chan sent in letter form to him by Pei Xiu, whose sophistication in Buddhist matters would be hard to overestimate. The *Chan Canon* or *Collection of Expressions of the Chan Source* (*Chanyuan zhuquanji*) was an enormous repository of Chan lore, a collection of extracts (and perhaps whole works) drawn from the literatures of all the Chan houses. We can assume that during this phase Zongmi was absorbed in compiling the *Chan Canon*, but it is possible that well before this time he had been engaged in assembling and copying all sorts of Chan materials for his collection. The *Chan Canon* is lost, but we do have his comprehensive introduction to its content, the *Chan Prolegomenon* or *Prolegomenon to the Collection of Expressions of the Chan Source* (*Chanyuan zhuquanji duxu*). Without question, the surviving *Chan Prolegomenon* stands as Zongmi's magnum opus. In this work he brings together all the themes of his career in a masterly presentation.

THE SWEET DEW INCIDENT AND RETIREMENT (835–841)

In 835, through his friendship with the politician Li Xun, a chief minister, Zongmi became implicated in a failed attempt, dubbed the Sweet Dew Incident, to oust the eunuchs from power at the court of Emperor Wenzong.[18] In the midst of the debacle, the plotter Li Xun sought refuge from the inevitable eunuch counterattack in the mountains at Caotang Monastery, and Zongmi was willing to secrete him as a shaven-head Buddhist monk. For this Zongmi was arrested but eventually released; apparently his forthright testimony and personal courage in the face of possible execution impressed a general of the eunuch forces. The Chan master passed his last years in obscurity, perhaps forced retirement. He died in cross-legged sitting posture at the Xingfu Monastery's Stupa Compound, which was in the northwest sector of Chang'an, not far from the imperial residence, on the sixth day of the first month of Huichang 1 (February 1, 841); on February 17 his body was returned in a coffin to Guifeng and on March 9 cremated.[19] In 853 Emperor Xuanzong awarded Zongmi the posthumous title "Concentration-Wisdom Chan Master," and a "Stupa of the Blue Lotus" was erected to hold his remains.[20]

ZONGMI'S FOUR WORKS ON CHAN

CHAN NOTES

SEVEN HOUSES OF CHAN

The earliest of Zongmi's Chan works is the text I have dubbed the *Chan Notes*, an untitled set of reports on seven Chan houses that is embedded in the third fascicle of his enormous thirteen-fascicle subcommentary on the *Perfect Awakening Sutra*, entitled *Extracts from the Great Commentary on the Perfect Awakening Sutra (Yuanjuejing dashu chao)*. These seven houses of Chan are:

1. Northern lineage (*Beizong*), active mainly in the Luoyang and Chang'an areas before Zongmi's time (actually, this school called itself "East Mountain Dharma Gate" and never used the designation "Northern," which was laid upon it by its opponents)[21]
2. Jingzhong, located in Sichuan
3. Baotang, located in Sichuan
4. Hongzhou, originally based in Jiangxi but in Zongmi's time represented in various locales
5. Oxhead (*Niutou*), originally based in Jiangsu and Zhejiang
6. South Mountain Buddha-Recitation Gate Chan Lineage (*Nanshan nianfomen chanzong*), located in Sichuan
7. Zongmi's own Heze, based in the Luoyang and Chang'an areas and represented in Sichuan

Presumably, since the *Extracts from the Great Commentary on the Perfect Awakening Sutra* is datable to the years 823 and 824 while the *Chan Letter* and *Chan Prolegomenon* are products of his literati period from 828 to 835, the material in the *Chan Notes* was compiled about a decade earlier than the *Chan Letter* and *Chan Prolegomenon*. Given that Zongmi chose to insert the *Chan Notes* into a technical work of sutra exegesis, it seems reasonable to assume that this fascinating sketch of the Chan houses was not particularly aimed at a lay audience outside the Buddhist cloister. For each of seven Chan houses the *Chan Notes* gives Zongmi's observations.

TWO ASPECTS TO EACH CHAN HOUSE: IDEA AND PRACTICE

The *Chan Notes* is the starting point of Zongmi's project in Chan studies, and in this first draft he focuses on supplying data on the genealogies, teachings, and practices of the Chan houses, engaging in little in the way of critical assessments or ranking the houses, a theme which he subsequently takes up in his *Chan Letter*. But one of the most striking innovations of the project as a whole is already present in this early foray: the bifurcation of each Chan house into two aspects, idea (the underlying Mahayana view or theory) and praxis.[22]

No one before or since has applied this sort of idea-and-practice template to Chan, though such a template is not unknown outside Chinese Buddhism. For instance, Tibetan Buddhist scholastics applied a virtually identical formula to the three turnings of the wheel of dharma, that is, the texts of the three teachings of Buddhism from a Mahayana perspective. They divided the texts of each of the three teachings into two parts, view and praxis.[23] For example, in the case of the texts of Mainstream Buddhism, the so-called Hinayana teaching, the scholastic treatises called *abhidharma* that organize the doctrinal terms of the sutra literature into orderly categories are regarded as the *view*, and the monastic disciplinary code, the vinaya, is regarded as the *practice*. Zongmi's application of an idea-and-practice template to Chinese Chan should probably be viewed in this sort of context. In fact, Zongmi's classification work on Chan should be viewed simultaneously from the perspective of pan-Mahayana taxonomy and the perspective of Chan studies.

A SLOGAN FOR EACH CHAN HOUSE

In the *Chan Notes* Zongmi distills the idea and practice of each house into a pithy six-to-eight-character slogan. An account of the house's genealogy and a fairly extensive description of its idea and practice usually accompany the slogan. A good example is the Hongzhou slogan (section 4): "Everything is the Dao and give free rein to mind [*chulei shi dao er renxin*]." Part of the phrasing probably comes from the famous work on literary theory and criticism entitled *Literary Mind and the Carving of Dragons* (*Wenxin diaolong*) by Liu Xie (c. 465–522). Liu's treatise compares the writer who plies the art of good literary composition to the artful player of chess (*weiqi/go*), who pursues to the limit strategic and tactical calculations. The writer who abandons technique and trusts to luck is like a *weiqi* player who simply follows the whims of his own mind: "To discard art/skill/technique and give free rein to mind [*qishu renxin*] is like a *weiqi* player who hopes for an accidental victory by chance."[24] Zongmi likewise favored art/skill/technique over trusting to luck. He links the first half of this slogan to the *Lanka Descent Sutra*'s buddha-in-embryo (tathagatagarbha) idea and the second half to the practice of "stopping karma and nourishing the spirit":

> The [Hongzhou] idea is in line with the *Lanka Descent Sutra* when it says: "The buddha-in-embryo is the cause of good and non-good, having the potentiality to create all the beings everywhere in the rebirth paths, the receptor of suffering and joy, synonymous with cause." Also, [the chapter entitled] "The Mind Behind the Words of the Buddhas" [of that sutra] also says: "A buddha land, a raising of the eyebrows, a movement of the eyeballs, a laugh, a yawn, [a ringing of a Buddhist] bell, a cough, or a swaying, etc., are all buddha events." Therefore, [I characterize the Hongzhou idea as] *everything is the Dao. Give free rein to mind* [*renxin*] is their practice gate of *stopping karma and nourishing the spirit* [*xiye yangshen*] (sometimes [they use] *stopping spirit and nourishing the path* [*xishen yangdao*]). This means that you do not stir your mind to cut off bad or cultivate good. You do not even cultivate the path. The path is mind. You should not use mind to cultivate [the path in] mind. The bad is also mind. You should not use mind to cut off [the bad in] mind. When you neither cut off nor create, but just give free rein to luck and exist in freedom [*renyun zizai*], then you are to be called a liberated person. You are also to be called a person who surpasses the measure. There are no dharmas to be caught up in, no buddhas to become. Why? Outside the mind nature there is not one dharma to be apprehended. Therefore, [I say of Hongzhou]: "*Just giving free rein to mind* is their practice."

Zongmi is not saying that Hongzhou itself cited the *Lanka Descent Sutra* as canonical support for its teaching. Rather, Zongmi the taxonomist has determined that the Hongzhou idea rests on the basis of or is in line with the *Lanka Descent* passage. But elsewhere in this summary there is at least the possibility that he is indeed accurately reproducing Hongzhou phrasing. For instance, the slogan *"stopping karma and nourishing the spirit,"* for which he even gives an alternate wording (as if he heard two variants), and the phrase *"give free rein to luck"* could be actual Hongzhou lines. The upshot is that we cannot call him a historian of Chan in the modern scholarly sense, but he does have something of the disposition of a born investigator or comparativist, as he himself recognized and commented upon in the *Chan Letter* (section 13): "I, Zongmi, have an innate disposition toward checking and verifying [*kanhui*], and so I visited [the Chan houses] one after the other and found each of their purports to be thus."

CHAN LETTER

POSTHUMOUS ZONGMI COLLECTIONS AND THE ORIGINAL TITLE OF THE *CHAN LETTER*

The *Chan Letter* began as a literary correspondence between a disciple and a Chan master. A vexing problem with the text that emerged from this correspondence has been the confusion over its original title, though there may never have been one. In East Asia the *Chan Letter* has circulated under many titles and has also circulated as a part of a posthumous collection (or in various collections) of Zongmi's writings (also under various titles).[25] For instance, a woodblock-printed edition of a *Posthumous Collection of Guifeng* (*Guifeng houji*) containing the *Chan Letter* was in circulation in both the North and South during the Northern Song period (around 1010 through 1030). In any case, sorting out the details that are known in an attempt to determine an original title is surely not a profitable endeavor. Long ago the Japanese scholar Ui Hakuju suggested that this short treatise was a correspondence by letter, and hence originally there was no title.[26] I have chosen to use the title *Chan Letter*.

PEI XIU'S QUESTIONS AND ZONGMI'S ANSWERS WITH A CHAN GENEALOGICAL CHART

The *Chan Letter* consists of six questions and answers between Pei Xiu and Zongmi. Pei's opening question (section 1) requests that Zongmi compose a short essay on the Chan lineages to serve Pei as a guidebook to the world of Chan. Zongmi replies that he will lay out the branch and the mainline master-disciple transmissions, with his own Heze house of Chan, of course, as the central or orthodox line of descent down from the first Chan patriarch of China Bodhidharma, and will discuss the relative depths of their teachings, that is, provide critiques. He supplies a very lengthy genealogical chart of all transmissions (section 7), consisting of a total of seventy-four names and one title. This is the earliest extant Chan genealogical chart to trace all lineages descending from Bodhidharma.

The remaining five questions (sections 5, 20, 21, and 22) are specific and elicit focused responses from Zongmi. At some point an editor must have deleted the epistolary format, the dating, polite formalities, and so forth, to produce a compact treatise. That editor could have been Zongmi himself or perhaps the editor(s) of one of the posthumous collections of his writings. Zongmi does not hold back in his wide-ranging references to Buddhist technicalities, indicating he considered Pei virtually on the level of a trained monastic in formal Buddhist discourse.

The *Chan Letter* is a continuation and deepening of Zongmi's Chan project begun with the *Chan Notes* a decade earlier. The analytical bifurcation by the *Chan Notes* of the Chan houses into idea and practice is maintained in the *Chan Letter*, though the latter enhances the vocabulary for the first half of that dichotomy.[27] The *Chan Letter* represents a significant advance by expounding point-by-point critical appraisals of four Chan houses. Though the *Chan Notes* does have a short set of evaluations (at the end of section 5), this passage is little more than the seed of a fully elaborated set of critiques.

FOCUS ON FOUR CHAN HOUSES

The *Chan Letter* treats only four Chan houses (Northern, Hongzhou, Niutou, and Heze), deleting the three Sichuanese houses covered in the *Chan Notes*. This deletion on Zongmi's part is probably attributable to two factors. First, at the time of writing the *Chan Letter*, Zongmi was residing in the capital and its environs, and the distant Sichuanese Chan houses would not have been well known to a general capital audience. Second, for Pei Xiu's edification he desired to narrow down the Chan field so as to showcase a comparison of Hongzhou and his own Heze. Zongmi probably felt that his disciple was in need of nuanced guidance in making a choice between Heze and its main competitor of the time, Hongzhou, which did have representatives at the capital Chang'an (see *Chan Letter*'s chart, section 7), even though its original base was in distant Jiangxi in south-central China.

THE SIMILE OF THE WISHING JEWEL

The *Chan Letter*'s critiques culminate in what is perhaps the most effective of Zongmi's many similes, the thought gem (*moni zhu*=*cintāmaṇi*), a fabulous jewel that grants wishes or satisfies all desires (sections 16–19). The wishing jewel, in the form of a flaming ball pointed at the top, is a staple of Buddhist iconography, often found in the hand of a buddha or bodhisattva. Drawing this jewel simile from the *Perfect Awakening Sutra*,[28] Zongmi adapts it to the task of critically assessing each of the four Chan houses. The jewel stands for the one mind (*yi lingxin*) and the jewel's brightness for void and calm Knowing (*kongji zhi*). The jewel utterly lacks any color characteristics, just as Knowing lacks all discriminations. When the color black is placed before the jewel and it appears black all the way through, it is like the mind of Knowing in the common person, full of delusion, stupidity, passion, and desire. The views of the four Chan houses are illustrated in terms of their attitudes to the jewel when it is facing a black object, reflecting black ignorance.

The view of the Northern lineage (section 16) shows belief in the jewel's brightness, but Northern followers assert that the jewel is wrapped in obscurity by the black color. They try to wipe it clean to eliminate the blackness. Only when they succeed in making the brightness reemerge do they say that they see a bright jewel. Obviously, Zongmi has inherited Heze Shenhui's distortions of "Northern" Chan. The Hongzhou lineage (section 17) points out that the blackness itself *is* the bright jewel and that the substance of the bright jewel is never to be seen, indeed, cannot be seen. When they see a jewel that is not facing any colors, one that is just bright and pure, they put up a deep resistance and fail to recognize it, fearing being limited to the one characteristic of brightness. The Niutou lineage (section 18) holds to the view that the colors on the jewel are unreal and that it is devoid of substantial reality (*svabhāva-śūnya*) all through; they deduce that the bright jewel is nothing but this voidness (sunyata) and beyond apprehension. Hence, the Niutou view is not awakened to the realization that the locus wherein the color characteristics are all void is precisely the non-void jewel.

The view of the Heze lineage (section 19) is:

> Just the perfect brightness of jade-like purity [*yingjing yuanming*] *is* the jewel substance [*zhuti*]. . . . The black color, up to and including all the other colors, such as blue and yellow, etc., are unreal. . . . When one truly sees the color black, the black from the outset is not black. It is just the brightness. The blue from the outset is not blue. It is just the brightness, up to and including, all the [other colors], such as red, white, yellow, etc., are like this. They are just the brightness. If, at the locus of the color characteristics, one after the other you just see the perfect brightness of jade-like sparkling purity, then you are not confused about the jewel. . . . If you are just free of confusion about the jewel, then black is non-black; black *is* the bright jewel, and so on with all colors. This is freedom [from the two extremes of] existence and

non-existence. The brightness and the blackness are in fusion. How could there be any further obstacle?

If one were to select a single passage in Zongmi's Chan writings to sum up his own Chan, this would certainly be a good candidate: on the one-mind jewel with its variegated flashing colors and forms the adept sees only a lustrous jade-like purity emitting sparkling rays of light (Knowing). Having suddenly seen that lustrous purity (sudden awakening), he then continues in a long-term course of rigorous practice rooted in its sparkling rays. Clearly, Zongmi implies a ranking of Chan reactions to the blackened jewel, with his own Heze at the top and Northern at the bottom. The *Chan Letter*'s high evaluation of Heze is clearly an attempt to bring Pei Xiu over to Heze.

CRITIQUE OF HONGZHOU

Zongmi's critique of Hongzhou is prominent in the *Chan Letter*. First, it is necessary to ascertain more precisely the target of this critique:

1. The target is not the Hongzhou founder, Hongzhou Ma, that is, Mazu Daoyi. On the contrary, Zongmi describes Ma admiringly as a lofty ascetic who wandered widely performing austerities and practicing cross-legged Chan sitting (section 6).
2. Zongmi says (section 17) that Hongzhou teachings mislead the stupid ones into mistaking the colors reflected on the jewel for the bright jewel itself and identifies these stupid ones as *that lineage's junior trainees (bi zong houxue)*.
3. The time frame is the Hongzhou of the *present (jin)*. Since Zongmi wrote the *Chan Letter* around the early 830s, *present* presumably refers roughly to the early ninth century.

When we assemble the above pieces, the best guess is that Zongmi is talking about Hongzhou teachers residing in local Chang'an monasteries in the early ninth century and their younger students. The teachings of this milieu would certainly have come to the notice of the collector Zongmi. The genealogical chart of his *Chan Letter* (section 7) lists two Hongzhou masters who fit the description: Zhangjing Huaihui, who resided in the Zhangjing Monastery outside the Tonghua Gate of Chang'an's east wall and Xingshan Weikuan, who resided in Chang'an's Xingshan Monastery.[29] Zongmi arrived on the Chang'an scene in 812 when these two were teaching there; they died a few years later (816 and

817, respectively). Their successors could be the junior trainees of Hongzhou that Zongmi mentions.

The critique of Hongzhou in the *Chan Letter* was originally aimed by Zongmi at an audience of one, Pei Xiu, who clearly is already sympathetic to Hongzhou teachings. The *Chan Letter* points out to Pei the limitations of Hongzhou vis-à-vis Heze. The partisan tone of the *Chan Letter* is absent in the *Chan Prolegomenon*, a treatise aimed at a broad clerical and lay audience, embodying a highly inclusive vision of Chan. In the *Chan Prolegomenon* (section 24) Zongmi, rather than criticizing Hongzhou from a Heze point of view, stresses that both Hongzhou and Heze are "of the same single axiom" (*tongyi zong*). Whereas the *Chan Letter*'s overall tone is advocatory, the *Chan Prolegomenon*'s tone is ecumenical, promoting the oneness of the all the Chan factions. But even the *Chan Letter* (section 22) closes with a statement to the effect that "whatever the [Chan] lineages say [*zhuzong suoshuo*] is always the teachings of the buddhas."

This difference between Zongmi's two works is rooted in the Mahayana strategem of skill in expedients—Zongmi tailored his two presentations to different audiences. But, after Zongmi's time, the *Chan Letter* came into circulation in xylograph format and hence was read by a much wider audience than originally intended. By Song times its claim for Heze as the central/orthodox line of descent within the Southern lineage of the sixth patriarch Huineng and its relegation of Hongzhou to collateral status were outdated assertions, but its exposition of the Heze teaching of Knowing was still attractive to many readers. For instance, in the thirteenth century the Korean teacher Chinul put the *Chan Letter*'s section on the Heze teaching of Knowing at the very beginning of his magnum opus entitled *Excerpts*, but explicitly discarded any claim for Heze as the orthodox line of descent.

The *Chan Letter*'s theoretical criticism of Hongzhou (section 21) can be summarized as follows: Pei Xiu argues that Hongzhou does use terms such as "spiritual awakening" (*lingjue*) and "mirror illumination" (*jianzhao*) that seem to be indistinguishable from Heze's "Knowing" (*zhi*). Zongmi answers that these Hongzhou terms do not apply to deluded beings, neutral states of mind, etc., while Knowing pervades all sentient beings in all states of mind. Hongzhou and Niutou hold up "sweeping away traces" (*fuji*) as the pinnacle. In so doing they have gotten the intention behind the negative teaching, true voidness, but are still missing the intention behind the teaching that reveals, excellent existence. In other words, they have gotten the substance, but missed the functioning. Pei counters that the Hongzhou teaching that the potentiality to talk, act, and so on *is* your buddha nature,[30] in fact, does reveal the mind nature, and, hence, Hongzhou is not deficient with respect to the functioning aspect. Zongmi replies that the true mind has two types of functioning: the intrinsic, original functioning (*zixing benyong*) and the conditioned, responsive functioning (*suiyuan yingyong*). The Hongzhou teaching is just the conditioned, responsive functioning and misses the intrinsic. Also, the revealing teaching has two types of revealing, by inference and by direct perception. Hongzhou teaches that the potentiality for action allows us to infer the existence of the buddha nature, which cannot be directly perceived. Heze, on the other hand, reveals the mind substance by teaching that *Knowing is mind*. This is the revealing by direct perception omitted by Hongzhou.

The ethical critique of Hongzhou (section 22) is worth quoting in full:

Present-day Hongzhou's just saying that every type of passion, hatred, precept [holding], or concentration [samadhi] is the functioning of the buddha nature fails to distinguish between the functioning of delusion and awakening, perverted and correct. Their idea lies in [the assumption that] the mind nature of thusness is free of stupidity, and, therefore, they are not selective. [They hold that], in terms of the true nature, from the outset there is no verbalization, and so who [could possibly] say "different" or "same?". . . . Hongzhou constantly says: "Passion, hatred, friendliness, and good are all the buddha nature. What distinctions exist?" This is like a person who just discerns that wetness from beginning to end is undifferentiated but does not realize that the merit of supporting a boat and the fault of overturning it are widely divergent. Therefore, even though that lineage is near to the gate of all-at-once awakening, it has yet to hit the bull's-eye. In the matter of the gate of step-by-step practice [Hongzhou] makes the mistake of completely deviating from it.

Altogether Zongmi makes six points to Pei Xiu:

1. Hongzhou's holding that the potentiality for speech and action must be the buddha nature is merely pointing to the conditioned functioning (the reflections on the surface of a bronze mirror) and from that deducing the existence of the buddha nature (the bronze metal of the mirror itself). This inferential approach misses the intrinsic functioning (the reflectivity of the bronze). The subtext here is that Heze has what Hongzhou lacks.
2. Hongzhou merely infers the existence of the mind substance, that is, the buddha nature, and thus exhibits only revealing by inference, lacking revealing by direct perception. (These are two of the three Buddhist sources of knowledge, the third being buddha word.) Once again Heze has what Hongzhou lacks.

3. Hongzhou fails to distinguish between precept holding and precept breaking, between mental concentration and mental distraction, and between perverted views of reality and correct views.

4. Hongzhou fails to recognize the difference between merits and faults. (The merit-and-fault vocabulary of the boat metaphor of undifferentiated wetness that can either support the boat or overturn it is not Buddhist. It reflects the ethical vocabulary of the larger society of Zongmi's time. For instance, the Tang histories mention books used for recording the merits and faults of officials, which served as the basis for rewards and punishments.)[31]

5. Hongzhou is only "near to the gate of all-at-once awakening and has yet to hit the bull's-eye."

6. Hongzhou "makes the mistake of completely deviating" from step-by-step practice. This is Zongmi's real complaint about Hongzhou, and what he is most concerned with getting across to Pei.

Even though Zongmi asserts that Hongzhou fails to differentiate between the wholesome and the unwholesome, nowhere does he suggest that Hongzhou pursued the (antinomian) implications of this position. For example, he never says that Hongzhou even rhetorically encouraged the breaking of Buddhist precepts or advocated indulging in the depravities of greed, anger, and stupidity in the spirit of a slogan such as "the depravities are awakening." And he never associates Hongzhou with anticonventional or iconoclastic behavior, such as kicking disciples or burning buddha images, though this is the image of Hongzhou that holds sway in Song Chan books and in much modern scholarship. (And he does mention unconventional behavior elsewhere, in the case of the Baotang house [*Chan Notes*, section 3]). In other words, the Hongzhou that Zongmi pictures for Pei Xiu is not marked by any radical departure from the usual or traditional in the currents of contemporary Chan.[32]

So the question remains: What made Zongmi so uneasy about Hongzhou? He was trying to wean Pei from his attraction to Hongzhou, and that attraction may have bothered the master. But is Zongmi's uneasiness really rooted in a perception that his own Heze house was losing out to Hongzhou in the early 830s? If that is the case, the above is not much more than a thinly disguised polemic designed to stave off the triumph of Hongzhou over Heze. But such an explanation is not entirely convincing. An exchange between the poet Bai Juyi and the previously mentioned Hongzhou master Weikuan gives us an example of a style of Hongzhou rhetoric that might have come to the attention of Zongmi and caused him to become uneasy: "[Bai] asked another question: 'Since there are no discriminations, why should one cultivate mind?' The master

[Weikuan] answered: 'Since mind from the outset is undamaged, why would you have to fix it [*he yao xiuli*]?'"[33] Weikuan is using what Zongmi calls the rhetoric of "showing the original nature," but not following it up with what Zongmi calls the rhetoric of "reliance on this nature to practice dhyana," and maybe this was typical of Hongzhou. The *Chan Prolegomenon* (section 20) says:

> In a master-student transmission, [the master] must know the medicine [for each and every] disease. This means that all instructional teaching devices inherited from the past *first show the original nature* [*kaishi benxing*] *and then require reliance on this nature to practice dhyana* [*yixing xiuchan*]. In most cases, when the nature is not easily awakened to, it is due to the grasping of characteristics. Thus, if [a master] wants to reveal this nature, he must first eradicate grasping [on the part of the student]. In [the master's] teaching devices for eradicating this grasping, he must [employ a type of rhetoric in which] common person and noble one are both cut off, merits and faults are both gotten rid of, in the precepts there is neither violation nor observance, in dhyana there is neither concentration nor distraction, the thirty-two marks [of a buddha] are all like flowers in the sky, and the thirty-seven parts of the path are all a dream or illusion. The idea is that, if [the master] enables [the student] to have a mind free of attachment, then [the student] can practice dhyana. [But] junior trainees and those of shallow knowledge *just grasp these* [Chan] *phrases* [*of the rhetoric of showing the original nature*] *as the ultimate path* [*jiujing dao*]. Furthermore, as to the gate of practice [*xiuxi zhi men*], because most people are self-indulgent and indolent, [masters] further speak a great deal of taking joy [in the path] and wearying [of this world]. They criticize passion and anger and commend diligence, regulation of the body and regulation of breath, and the sequence of coarse and subtle [characteristics]. *When novices hear this* [rhetoric of diligent gradual practice], *they become deluded about the function of original awakening and single-mindedly grasp characteristics.* Only those [trainees] of great ability and fixed will serve their masters for the full course [of training]. They then attain the purport of [both] awakening and practice. [Trainees] of a light, shallow nature, *upon hearing only one idea* [i.e., either the original nature or gradual practice], *say that they already have had enough* [*ji wei yi zu*].

Perhaps Zongmi feared that Hongzhou leaned too far toward the rhetoric of showing the original nature, while shortchanging the rhetoric of the subsequent gradual practice grounded in that original nature. This might have led Hongzhou students to mistakenly grasp Hongzhou sayings, which were intended to reveal the nature, *as the ultimate path itself* and to prematurely conclude that they were already finished with the Chan endeavor. Zongmi assumed that Chan transmitters in their teaching should employ a judicious combination of the rhetoric of the original nature and the rhetoric of gradual practice, leading students first to an initial instantaneous recognition of having been awakened to the original nature all along (original awakening) and then to a subsequent long, arduous cultivation (which is really a non-cultivation). Zongmi himself was shown the original nature by his teacher Daoyuan and only subsequently spent ten years in the mountains outside the capital involved in a highly ritualized practice that included obeisance to the three treasures of the buddha, dharma, and community; asking pardon; regulation of food intake, sleep, and so forth; engagement in the cross-legged sitting posture; regulation of the body, breathing, and thoughts; and so on. It seems that, in Zongmi's eyes, Hongzhou discourse did not always adequately cover both bases, and he wanted to make sure Pei Xiu understood this.

THE CRITIQUE OF HONGZHOU AND ZHU XI'S CRITIQUE OF BUDDHISM

Some have pointed out that Zongmi's critique of Hongzhou foreshadows the neo-Confucian critique of Buddhism as a whole.[34] The Song neo-Confucian Zhu Xi (1130–1200) charged that the Buddhist conception of the nature lacks any inherent moral standard by which to make distinctions, which, on the surface at least, sounds like Zongmi's critique of Hongzhou. For Zhu Xi, the nature (by which he means *human nature* and not *mind nature* or *buddha nature*) is full of humanity, righteousness, propriety, and wisdom, and what the Buddhists call the nature is what Confucians call the (morally indeterminate) mind.[35]

Zhu Xi charges Buddhism with (in Zongmi's phrasing) giving free rein to the mind (*renxin*), that is, trusting the whims of one's own mind, and for Zhu Xi the mind can go either in the direction of moral principle or in the direction of human desires. Peter Gregory states: "The similarities in their respective theories of the fundamental nature of man operate on the level of structure."[36] But this structural parallel should not obscure for us the fact that Zongmi's categories are formulated in terms of the Buddhist triad of precepts, concentration, and wisdom, while Zhu Xi's are formulated in the Mencian terms of compassion for others, feeling ashamed at one's bad acts, the observance of ritual forms that express giving way or yielding to others, and knowing right from wrong. Indeed, Zongmi is not a crypto-Confucian, and Zhu Xi is not a crypto-Buddhist.

CHAN LETTER VERSUS PEI XIU'S *ESSENTIALS*
OF THE DHARMA OF MIND TRANSMISSION
AND *WANLING RECORD*

Zongmi's *Chan Letter* has a formal and classical air to it, deriving not only from its theoretical and analytical content, which looks backward over the whole Chan tradition, but also from its elegant and terse classical literary language (*wenyan*). Both aspects bring to mind a contrasting work compiled by the junior participant in the dialogue of the *Chan Letter*, Pei Xiu. Shortly after Zongmi's death in 841 Pei held official posts in the Yangtze River area and at those times transcribed formal talks by the Hongzhou master Huangbo Xiyun and question-and-answer sessions between himself and Xiyun.[37] From these encounters with one of the most important masters of the Hongzhou line, Pei, with editorial assistance from some of Xiyun's disciples, produced the two-part Chan book known as *Essentials of the Dharma of Mind Transmission* (*Chuanxin fayao*) and *Wanling Record* (*Wanlinglu*). Pei did go on from the *Chan Letter* to study Hongzhou, but this does not imply his repudiation of Zongmi. Pei simply pursued every opportunity to study Buddhism.

Whereas Zongmi's *Chan Letter* surveys and analyzes Chan's Tang dynasty past, the schools and teachings of the eighth and early ninth centuries, Pei's record is a harbinger of the Song-dynasty future of Chan. The *Chan Letter* tells of the Northern lineage (in effect a figure of speech by the time of the *Chan Letter*), the Niutou lineage (still active), the Hongzhou lineage (spreading throughout China), and the Heze lineage (faded by the Five Dynasties and Song except perhaps in the northwest around Zongmi's base and in the state of Xixia where Guifeng Chan lived on). But Pei's record foreshadows what is to come during the Song, a Linji Chan claiming descent from the Hongzhou master Huangbo Xiyun and the publication of a Chan literature couched to a high degree in the vernacular-based literary language, old *baihua* (*gu baihua*).[38]

The *Chan Letter* is almost exclusively in the classical literary language, but Pei's record, particularly in its question-and-answer sections, is to a considerable extent in old *baihua*. This aspect of Pei's record sets it off from the preceding early Chan literature as an example of a new stage in language style. By contrast, in terms of both content and language style, Zongmi's *Chan Letter* and *Chan Prolegomenon* belong firmly to early Chan literature, and, in fact, *constitute a summa of early Chan*. "Early Chan literature" refers to the Chan texts that first circulated during the eighth century, most of which are known to us through twentieth-century discoveries in the various deposits of Dunhuang manuscripts now scattered throughout Europe and East Asia.[39] Zongmi drew from this sort of corpus in creating his description and analysis of Chan, and extracts from such texts surely filled the pages of his *Chan Canon*. Zongmi's surviving Chan writings and these Dunhuang Chan manuscripts, once integrated, form the framework of a portal onto Tang-dynasty Chan. So many other Chan sources come to us filtered through Song-dynasty editors. The *Record of Linji*, for instance, in the form we have it from a Song editor, is stylistically a Song book, not a Tang book.

Some of these early Chan texts from Dunhuang do contain *baihua* elements, but in no case do those elements reach a critical mass that would enable us to label the text in question an old *baihua* text. Pei's record is the earliest extant text to approach such a threshold and thus can be said to mark the closing of the early Chan literature period and the opening of the age of Chan texts in old *baihua*. Chan texts from the tenth century onward are actually cast in a mixture of old *baihua* and elements of the classical literary language, with the former growing stronger over time. Old *baihua* clearly shows similarities to the modern *baihua* of the twentieth century, particularly in pronouns, suffixes, the tendency toward longer sentences that are closer to actual speech patterns, and so forth. Another genre of old-*baihua* texts of this period is the transformation texts (*bianwen*), narrative treatments of Buddhist and secular subjects intended for oral performance.[40]

Some time after the composition of Pei Xiu's record the old-*baihua* component in Chan literature moved into a phase of accelerated expansion. A representative example is the *Extensive Record of Yunmen* (*Yunmen guanglu*), which is the record of a Chan master active in the first half of the tenth century, though our earliest extant edition dates to the early eleventh century.[41] Yunmen's record is cast in a very pronounced old-*baihua* style. Zongmi's *Chan Letter* and *Chan Prolegomenon* remained virtually untouched by this shift in Chan literature, which is part of a sea change at both the popular and elite levels. Zongmi's production of Chan works falls within what some literary historians designate as Late Tang (roughly 827 onward). His Chan works exhibit the elegance and refinement of the last years of Tang court culture, just preceding the ascendancy of a Chan literature closer to the everyday speech patterns (*suyu*) of outlying regions of China, particularly in the southeast.[42]

CHAN CANON

WHAT DID THE *CHAN CANON* LOOK LIKE?

The *Chan Canon* is not extant. We know it was enormous, one-hundred or more rolls in length.[43] For Pei Xiu its sheer novelty and gargantuan size justified calling it a "Chan basket," by which Pei meant that it was nothing less than a new section to the tripartite Buddhist canon, a Chan addition to the traditional three baskets.[44] Scholars have hunted far and wide for some surviving trace of this Chan basket, but we seem to have no explicit quotation from it anywhere in all East Asian Buddhist literature.[45] It seems to have disappeared.

What did it look like? The following is a tentative reconstruction based on statements in the *Chan Prolegomenon* (sections 57–58). The *Chan Canon* opened with a transcription of Bodhidharma's *Two Entrances and Four Practices*.[46] This was followed by about ninety rolls of the miscellaneous writings of the Chan houses, probably both lengthy excerpts and whole works. Even though the content of some of these Chan writings made him uneasy, Zongmi did not edit or revise them to conform more closely to his own preferences. He included them as is. We can guess that many of these Chan titles overlapped with the titles found by modern scholars among the Dunhuang Chan manuscripts.

The Chan writings were arranged into perhaps seven houses, and at the beginning of each of the seven or so sections there was a note providing a synopsis of the house's idea, perhaps similar to the synopses of the *Chan Notes*. These synopses served to introduce a veritable sea of primary source materials. The *Chan Canon* also contained some sort of record of the names of the followers of the various Chan lineages, perhaps a Chan genealogical chart like that of the *Chan Letter*. In turn all this was followed by ten rolls of lengthy sutra excerpts, including many of the same sutras quoted in the *Chan Prolegomenon*. These sutra excerpts sealed or authenticated the preceding Chan materials.

Zongmi viewed the *Chan Canon* as a gigantic vault containing the teaching devices of the noble ones useful for the treatment of an infinite variety of diseases of delusion—all the teaching devices of the Chan houses assembled into one gigantic teaching device (*yi dai shanqiao*; *Chan Prolegomenon*, section 12). His two similes for the relationship between the *Chan Canon* and the *Chan Prolegomenon* derive from everyday life: the *Chan Prolegomenon* is like the headrope (*gang*) by which the *Chan Canon* net (*wang*) is hauled up from the sea with its enormous catch; the *Chan Prolegomenon* is like the collar (*ling*) of the *Chan Canon* garment, which is grasped by the wearer in order to put the garment on. The *Chan Prolegomenon* is the activator, the *Chan Canon* the activated. The former is the rule that ties everything in the latter together. Those training alone did not need to study the entirety of the *Chan Canon*—only those intending to become teachers were to master the whole of it, in order to arm themselves with a vast repertoire of teaching devices for leading students on the Chan path. Had the *Chan Canon* survived, it might now be our biggest fishing net for catching early Chan literature.

DID FRAGMENTS OF THE *CHAN CANON*
SURVIVE IN THE *MIND MIRROR*?

A passage in the *Chan Prolegomenon* (section 8) suggests that at least a draft copy of the *Chan Canon* was in existence during the time Zongmi was composing the *Chan Prolegomenon*. In that passage an anonymous questioner opens with a remark about his current browsing through the content of the *Chan Canon*: "But as I *now browse through the collected Chan writings of the various houses,* [I find that] most of them are [cast in the form of] an unrelenting succession of questions [asked of the preceptor by a disciple, which are either] abruptly affirmed or abruptly repudiated [by the preceptor]" (emphasis mine). Beyond whatever conjectures can be generated from this line, we actually know nothing about the status of the *Chan Canon* in Zongmi's time and immediately thereafter.

One guess is that the *Chan Canon* was indeed copied out from the original Chan and sutra sources but later lost in the chaos of the late Tang, and this is certainly plausible. On the other hand, there is at least the possibility that some of its Chan content was rescued by being siphoned off into another compendium, the massive *Mind Mirror* (*Zongjinglu*) of the Five Dynasties Chan figure Yongming Yanshou (904–976).[47] Yanshou in his *Mind Mirror* does not identify with a particular Chan house of his day, presenting himself as a follower of Bodhidharma Chan as a whole. However, he is invariably pictured by modern scholarship as the third patriarch of the Fayan house.[48] *Yanshou's actual role in Chan was as the conservator of the legacy of Chan inclusiveness found in Zongmi's* Chan Prolegomenon (section 12):

> Essentially speaking, if one considers [the Chan houses] individually, then they are all wrong. If one brings them together, then they are all right [*hui zhi ji jie shi*]. I will use buddha word to illustrate the intention behind each of them, to select the strong points of each of them, to unify them into three axioms, and to juxtapose these to the three canonical teachings. [Without this approach,] how could they be brought together into one substitute skillful teaching device, and how could they all become the essential dharma gate? If each [of these Chan houses] would forget its feelings, they would all flow back into the sea of wisdom.

Three characteristics of Yanshou's *Mind Mirror* suggest a possible link to the lost *Chan Canon*:

1. The *Mind Mirror* continues the *Chan Prolegomenon's* fundamental orientation and methodology (assuming Chan and the teachings are

identical; championing Bodhidharma Chan as a whole; paring down voluminous sources to their essence, and so on). The *Mind Mirror,* which echoes the *Chan Prolegomenon's* exquisitely balanced classical literary style, contains numerous chunks of quotations, paraphrases, and terminological borrowings from the *Chan Prolegomenon.*[49]

2. The tripartite structure of the *Mind Mirror* may echo the tripartite structure of the *Chan Canon.*[50]

3. The size of the *Mind Mirror,* one hundred fascicles, is comparable to what we know of the size of the *Chan Canon,* which various sources record as from one hundred to one-hundred-sixty fascicles in length.[51]

The moment we read the opening sentence of the *Mind Mirror* we know we are in the land of Zongmi:

Speaking meticulously, the [Chan] patriarchs designate the principles of Chan [*chanli*], transmitting the correct axiom [*zhengzong*] of silent coinciding, and the buddhas extend the gate of the teachings [*jiaomen*], setting up the great purport of the explanations. As a consequence, what the former worthies received in transmission the junior trainees have as a refuge. Therefore, I first lay out the *Designating-the-Axiom Section.* Because of doubts there are questions. To resolve the doubts there are answers. Because of questions, feelings of doubt can come into the open. Because of answers, excellent understanding arises from a latent state. This means that this perfect axiom [of mind/one mind/true mind] is difficult to believe in and difficult to understand. It is the number-one formulation, prepared for [beings of] the highest disposition. If we do not provisionally set up verbal explanations, there is no way to wash away the grasping of feelings. Because of the finger [pointing at the moon], one apprehends the moon. It is not a gate without teaching devices. One gets the rabbit and forgets the net.[52] It is spontaneous union with the path of the heavenly real. Next I set up the *Questions-and-Answers Section.* Merely because the times are of the end period [i.e., the end time of the dharma], one seldom encounters [a being of] great disposition and [instead] gazes upon the inferiority of shallow minds, floating faculties, and tiny knowledge. Even though knowing the axiom purport is truly a refuge, questions and answers resolve doubts and gradually eliminate the obstructions of confusion. Wishing to solidify faith power, I must borrow testimonials. So I will widely quote the sincere words of the [Chan] patriarchs and buddhas that secretly coincide with the great path of perfection and constancy. Everywhere I will pluck the essential purports of the sutras and treatises, so as to perfectly complete the true mind of resolution. Lastly, I arrange the *Quotations-to-Authenticate Section.* Taking these three sections to join together into a single outlook, they search out, collect, cover, and embrace everything about the profound.[53]

Perhaps Yanshou was using what he learned of the lost *Chan Canon* from its brief description at the end of the *Chan Prolegomenon* as a blueprint for the construction of his own collection.

We know that a manuscript of Zongmi's *Chan Prolegomenon* in the hand of his closest disciple, Pei Xiu, a masterly calligrapher renowned in his own time for his unique style, made it from Zongmi's base in the northwest to Yanshou's base in the coastal area at the mouth of the Yangtze River, where copies were made.[54] When Yanshou came into possession of a *Chan Prolegomenon*, he may have inherited along with it some portion of the Chan materials of the *Chan Canon*. In that scenario fragments of Zongmi's lost Chan basket survived into Song times by being embedded by Yanshou in his *Mind Mirror*.

CHAN PROLEGOMENON

A SUMMA OF CHAN AND THE TEACHINGS

The culmination of Zongmi's Chan project is his preface to the *Chan Canon*, the *Prolegomenon to the Collection of Expressions of the Chan Source* (*Chanyuan zhuquanji duxu*), which dates to sometime around 833. Calling a theoretical treatise of twenty-one thousand Chinese characters a "preface" is probably a serious misnomer. If we are forced to find some genre niche for Zongmi's greatest work, it can best be described as a "prolegomenon," a formal essay or critical discussion serving to introduce and interpret an extended work. That extended work, of course, is the *Chan Canon*. The *Chan Prolegomenon* is characterized by an all-inclusiveness with regard to Chan. All the houses without exception are accepted as valid expressions of Chan. The modern reader is struck by this vision of the oneness of Chan, along with the allusiveness and intricacy of the work. The *Chan Prolegomenon* has no predecessor text in the lineage chart of Chan literature, though it does have a successor text—Yanshou's *Mind Mirror*.

The *Chan Prolegomenon*'s theme is the interlocking relationship between varieties of Chan and the Indian Buddhist teachings. Zongmi, as mentioned above, thought of this essay as the headrope to the *Chan Canon* net, the collar to the *Chan Canon* garment. In other words, the function of the *Chan Prolegomenon* for Zongmi was to activate the vast *Chan Canon* for the reader, to serve as a sort of lever by which the reader could easily access the massive amount of Chan poetic sayings (*juji*) stored in the *Chan Canon*. The *Chan Prolegomenon* assumes that the poetic Chan material in the *Chan Canon* scoops up an abridgement (*cuolue*) of the broad and virtually boundless Indic sutra-treatise corpus and, as an abridgement of those voluminous Indic texts, is geared to Chinese sensibilities (section 7). Zongmi remarks that while the dis-cursive sutra-treatise corpus is difficult for Chinese to rely upon, the succinct Chan poetry is easy for them to access.

The *Chan Prolegomenon* is conceptually far beyond both the *Chan Notes*, which sketches out the Chan lines of the day, and the *Chan Letter*, an imagina-tive treatment of four Chan lineages and teachings concerned primarily with showing Pei Xiu the superiority of Heze over Hongzhou. The *Chan Prolegom-enon* subsumes Zongmi's summa of Chan into a summa of all the Indian Bud-dhist teachings known in Tang China (with the exception of the esoteric teach-ings). The Indic patina found in the *Chan Prolegomenon* is an integral part of Zongmi's agenda, for he is showing the rightful stations of Chinese Chan teachings within the ascending levels of an Indian Mahayana habitat.

In terms of textual learning Zongmi was simultaneously a Buddhist pandit (like his teacher Chengguan) learned in the Indic-language corpus in Chinese translation, including the vast ancillary literature composed in Buddhist Chi-nese, and a Chinese literatus with a solid education in the indigenous classics and histories, on equal footing with the likes of the talented calligrapher and prose stylist Pei Xiu. Only such a "Confucian monk" (*ruseng*) could have com-posed the truly elegant *Chan Prolegomenon*, which should be considered not just a Buddhist treatise but a notable piece of classical Chinese literature as well. As a Buddhist treatise it is probably unsurpassed in literary value in the history of Chinese Buddhist literature. As for including it within the domain of classical Chinese literature, students of that literature generally find Buddhist works opaque, alien, rhythmically deficient, and thus automatically ineligible for inclusion in the literary canon.

THE MASTER METAPHOR: THE *FU* OR TALLY FIT

The master metaphor of the *Chan Prolegomenon* is the tally (*fu*). A well-known example from Chinese history is the tiger tally in use from the Warring States period down to the Sui. The tiger tally was an authenticating object given by the imperial center to authorize troop movements. In the shape of a tiger with an inscription on the back, in the beginning it was made of jade, but later of bronze. The tiger was cut into two parts, half remaining at the center, the impe-rial court, and half given to the regional official or general in charge of the troops. When it was time to implement a troop movement, the court sent an official carrying the center's half to check whether it fit into the other half. If the two portions tallied, the army could be activated.

In Tang times in matters of state a fish tally came into use, and a *fu* for ordinary contractual purposes was usually made of bamboo or wood. The word *fu* also refers to magical drawings employed by Daoist adepts and Buddhist tantric masters to cure pain and sickness, attain intelligence and long life, control fires and floods, and so forth.[55] All these associations (tally with or coincide; true fit; authorization; bona fides; signet; magical charm/talisman) hover over the master metaphor of the *Chan Prolegomenon*. Zongmi mentions eight pairs of *fu* halves, and each pair fits together seamlessly to form a whole:

Three types of teachings	Three axioms of Chan
All-at-once teaching	Chan all-at-once gate
Step-by-step teaching	Chan step-by-step gate
What the Chan masters say	The Buddha's intention
Intentions of the Chan patriarchs	Buddha mind
Chan texts	The Buddha sutras
All-at-once awakening	Step-by-step practice
Original awakening/real	Non-awakening/unreal[56]

The first six (sections 9 and 6) have to do with Chan and the Buddha, the last two (sections 19 and 52) with the stages of the path. Since there is redundancy in the case of the Chan-and-the-Buddha tallies, I need only discuss the first three.

THE THREE TEACHINGS OF THE BUDDHIST CANON

According to the *Chan Prolegomenon*, the three types of canonical teachings are:

1. The teaching of cryptic meaning that relies on (dharma) nature to speak of characteristics (section 25)
2. The teaching of cryptic meaning that eradicates characteristics to reveal (dharma) nature (section 27)
3. The teaching that openly shows that the true mind is (dharma) nature (section 29)[57]

To say that the first two teachings are of cryptic meaning (*miyi*) indicates that their meaning is not clear, plain, obvious, manifest, and explicit; to say that the third openly shows means that it expressly, overtly, clearly, and plainly shows its content.

Within the first teaching, the *Chan Prolegomenon* (section 25) sets up three subdivisions:

a. The karmic cause-and-effect teaching that allows rebirth as a human or a god
b. The Hinayana teaching of the cutting off of the depravities and the extinguishing of suffering, eventually leading to the fruit of arhat (the four *Āgamas* and the Hinayana treatises discuss a and b)[58]
c. The teaching that takes consciousness to eradicate sense objects, found in such sutras as the *Unraveling the Deep Secret* and in Yogācāra treatises[59]

Only c., the third subdivision of the first teaching, constitutes half of a tally with a Chan axiom. (Hereafter, for the sake of simplicity, c. is referred to as the first teaching.) The other two, the teaching of karmic recompense and the Hinayana, have no Chan correlates in the *Chan Prolegomenon* and hence play no role in Zongmi's tally schema.

The *Chan Prolegomenon* summarizes the first teaching as follows: In each sentient being eight types of consciousness have existed spontaneously from without beginning. Within these, the eighth, the storehouse consciousness (*zangshi=ālaya-vijñāna*), is fundamental. This storehouse consciousness suddenly transforms into the organ body, the external world, and the karmic seeds. As this root consciousness revolves, its turnings produce the seven active consciousnesses, each of which has the potentiality to manifest its own objective supports (*suoyuan=ālambana*). For instance, the eye consciousness (the first of the five sense consciousnesses) takes forms (shape and color) as its objective supports, and the seventh consciousness (the consciousness of intellection that is always accompanied by the depravities of self-ignorance, self-view, self-pride, and self-love) takes the seeing part of the storehouse consciousness as its objective support. The eighth, the storehouse consciousness, takes as its objective supports the organ body, the karmic seeds, and the external world. Outside these eight consciousnesses there are no real dharmas.

Because of the power of fumigating habit energy (*xunxi=vāsanā* from past lives) that discriminates between between self and dharmas, when the consciousnesses arise, they transform into a seeming self and dharmas. Because two consciousnesses—the sixth, which makes discriminations/judgments after the sense perceptions of the five sense consciousnesses, and the seventh, which constitutes the defiled locus of self—are covered by ignorance (*wuming=avidyā*), they take this seeming self and dharmas as objective supports and grasp them as a real self and real dharmas. Thus, the organ body and external world are just consciousness transformations. Having awakened to the realization that there has never been a self and dharmas, that only mind (*weixin=citta-mātra*) has existed, one then relies on this insight to practice. Step-by-step one extinguishes the hindrances and realizes truth. The bodhisattva stages fill up completely, flipping over the five sense consciousnesses and the sixth, seventh, and eighth consciousnesses, so they become respectively the four awakening knowledges. Zongmi refers to this teaching (Yogācāra) as the characteristics (*lakṣaṇa*) axiom (*xiangzong*).

The second teaching, the teaching that eradicates characteristics to reveal dharma nature, is based on the *Perfection of Wisdom Sutras* and Madhyamaka treatises.[60] The *Chan Prolegomenon* summarizes this teaching of eradicating characteristics as follows: All dharmas are dependent on causes and conditions (*zhongyuan=hetu pratyaya*) and thus have no nature of their own, no essential or inherent property (*wu zixing=asvabhāva*). Since there has never been a dharma that did not arise from conditions, all dharmas are void (*kong=śūnya*), that is, devoid of a nature of their own. In voidness (*kongzhong=śūnyatā*) there are no eyes, ears, nose, tongue, body, mind; no eighteen psycho-physical constituent elements of the personality; no twelve members of the chain of causation; no four truths; no knowledge and no attainment; no karma and no retribution; no practice and no realization; no samsara and no nirvana. Practice is being unsupported, not established anywhere, not fixed in anything (*bu zhu yiqie*). Zongmi sometimes refers to this second teaching (Madhyamaka) as the voidness axiom (*kongzong*).

The third teaching, which openly shows that the true mind is dharma nature, finds its support in such sutras as the *Huayan, Secret Array, Perfect Awakening, Buddha Top-knot* (=*Heroic Progess Samadhi*),[61] *Śrīmālā, Buddha-in-Embryo, Lotus,* and *Nirvana* and in such treatises as the *Ratnagotra, Buddha Nature, Awakening of Faith, Ten Stages, Dharma Sphere,* and *Nirvana.*[62] The *Chan Prolegomenon* summarizes the third teaching as follows: This teaching points directly to the realization that one's own mind (*zixin=svacitta*) is the true nature (*zhenxing=tattva*). It does not discuss characteristics, nor does it negate characteristics. It does not involve teaching devices or a hidden, cryptic meaning. This teaching says that all sentient beings possess the true mind (*zhenxin*) of voidness and calm that is intrinsically pure from without beginning—bright and never darkening, it is a clear and constant Knowing (*zhi=jñāna*).[63] The true mind/Knowing is called by various names such as buddha nature, buddha-in-embryo, mind ground, and so forth. From beginningless time, thought of the unreal (*wangxiang=abhūta-vikalpa*) forms a screen over the true mind/Knowing so that, never self-realized, it sinks into the suffering sea of the rebirth process. The buddhas, feeling sadness at this, appear in the world to say that all the dharmas are devoid of substantial reality and to show openly that this true mind is identical to all the buddhas. Zongmi often refers to this third teaching as the nature axiom (*xingzong*), an abbreviation of dharma-nature (*dharmatā*) axiom (*faxing zong*).

THREE AXIOMS OR "REALIZATIONS" OF CHAN

Zongmi assumes that Chan teachings are initially oral teachings, given by word of mouth (*chanmen yanjiao*), which are transcribed as poetic sayings. The *Chan Prolegomenon* (section 9) postulates the realization of three *ideas* of Chan, which are referred to as the three *zongs* of Chan (*san zong*).[64] It is important to note that the *Chan Prolegomenon* employs the term "*zong*" in two separate meanings: (1) a Chan genealogical line tracing itself back to the same Chan ancestor, rendered in the following translations by *lineage*; (2) an equivalent of the Sanskrit term *siddhānta* ("axiom/established conclusion").[65] The three *zongs* of Chan are the three *siddhāntas* (axioms) of Chan, not the three *lineages*. Zongmi knows of eight lineages/houses of Chan.

"*Zong*"="*siddhānta*" is the first part of Zongmi's name ("Zongmi" means "the *siddhānta* is secret") and has its locus classicus in the *Lanka Descent Sutra*, where it refers to "awakening on one's own to the axiom that is beyond words," as opposed to theory/teachings, which includes all verbal expressions of *siddhānta* in the Buddhist canon and all teaching devices. The Gunabhadra translation of the *Lanka Descent Sutra* says:

> The Buddha said to Mahāmatī: 'All the hearers, private buddhas, and bodhisattvas have two types of penetration characteristics: axiom penetration and theory penetration [*zongtong ji shuotong* = *siddhānta-naya deśanā*]. Mahāmatī! Axiom penetration means, because one on his own attains superior advance and is free of speech, the written word, and thought of the unreal, he goes to the untainted realm, the self-awakening stage, the own mark. He is free of all awareness of the unreal and subdues the Evil Ones of all the external [non-Buddhist] paths. Because self-awakened, he goes to where the radiance of the sun's rays issue forth, and this is called the characteristic of axiom penetration. What about the characteristic of theory penetration? It means the various teachings spoken of in the nine sections of the canon, free of the characteristics of difference, non-difference, existence, non-existence, and so forth. Taking skillful teaching devices to accord with sentient beings, one speaks dharma as appropriate to them and enables them to cross over to liberation. This is called the characteristic of theory penetration.[66]

This distinction is the *Chan Prolegomenon*'s fundamental distinction between *zong* and *jiao* (the teachings). In the *Chan Prolegomenon*, the followers of the Chan houses through their own practice realize or awaken to various "house *siddhāntas*" (my term), and Zongmi distills these *siddhāntas* down to just three, which are identical to the three teachings of characteristics, voidness, and nature. But, a bit confusingly, Zongmi sometimes uses *zong* to refer to the three teachings, calling them the characteristics *siddhānta*, the voidness *siddhānta*, and the nature *siddhānta*. It is useful here to bring in a pan-Buddhist perspective—the three *zongs* of the *Chan Prolegomenon*, whether referring to the three Chan *siddhāntas* or the three teachings (they are identical, in any case) are parallel to the structure of the four *siddhāntas* into which the Tibetans classify Indian Buddhism (*siddhānta* = Tibetan *grub mtha'*): the difference *siddhānta* and the sutra *siddhānta* (two Mainstream/Hinayana schools); the mind-only *siddhānta* (Yogācāra); and the middle *siddhānta* (Madhyamaka).[67]

The last two of the four Tibetan *siddhāntas*, the Mahayana *siddhāntas* of mind only and the middle, are identical to: (1) Zongmi's two teachings of characteristics and voidness, the first two of his three teachings; and (2) the first two of his three Chan *siddhāntas* discussed below. Zongmi's ranking order is the same as that of the Tibetan schema, that is, with the voidness teaching ranked higher than the characteristics teaching. The reason for this congruence is that the Tibetan schema and the first two levels of Zongmi's schema ultimately derive from the same source—the classification work of Indian Madhyamaka exegetes such as Jnanaprabha (Zhiguang), a pandit at Nālandā Monastery around 600. Zongmi probably received information about Jnanaprabha's taxonomy from the writings of the Huayan teacher Fazang, who reported that Jnanaprabha had set up a three-tiered existence-voidness progression of teachings:[68]

1. The Buddha at first at Deer Park for the sake of those of small faculties, spoke the Hinayana of the four truths, clarifying that *mind and sense objects are both existent.*

2. Next, in the middle period, for the sake of those of medium faculties, he spoke the dharma-characteristics Mahayana, clarifying the consciousness-only principle in which *sense objects are void but mind is existent.*

3. In the third period, for the sake of those superior faculties, he spoke the no-characteristics Mahayana, in which *mind and sense objects are both void.*[69]

Zongmi, working from this sort of structure, created his tripartite system showing the identity of *jiao* and *zong*, the teachings and Chan. His system, in ascending order, is: characteristics, voidness, and nature (the complete teaching of the *Huayan Sutra*, *Perfect Awakening Sutra*, and so forth). The innovation of the *Chan Prolegomenon* (sections 21–24) was to extend Indian-style taxonomizing into the realm of Chan by stipulating the three equivalent Chan axioms, or perhaps we should call them three Chan "axiom realizations":

1. (Realizing) the axiom of stopping thought of the unreal and cultivating mind (only)
2. (Realizing) the axiom of cutting off and not leaning on anything
3. (Realizing) the axiom of directly revealing the mind nature[70]

In the *Chan Prolegomenon* the first (cryptic) teaching of taking consciousness to eradicate sense objects (=the characteristics axiom) forms a tally with the first Chan axiom of stopping thought of the unreal and cultivating mind only (section 26); the second (cryptic) teaching of eradicating characteristics to reveal dharma nature (=the voidness axiom) forms a tally with the second Chan axiom of cutting off and not leaning on anything (section 28); and the third teaching of openly showing that the true mind is dharma nature (=the nature axiom) forms a tally with the third Chan axiom of directly revealing the mind nature (section 29). Anything that can be said about one of the three teachings can equally be said about its corresponding Chan axiom, for in the *Chan Prolegomenon the Chan axioms and the teachings are utterly identical* (sections 28–29). According to the tally metaphor, the three axiom realizations of Chan and the three levels of Mahayana sources merge into oneness as they are inserted into each other, becoming a single, coherent "text."

CHAN OF INCOMPLETE MEANING
AND CHAN OF COMPLETE MEANING

The *Chan Prolegomenon* apportions eight Chan houses of middle-late Tang times into these three Chan axioms. For instance, it places the Jingzhong, Northern, Baotang, and South Mountain Buddha–Recitation Gate houses within the first Chan axiom of stopping thought of the unreal and cultivating mind only (section 22).[71] The Shitou house, about which Zongmi provides no information in any of his three surviving Chan works, and the Niutou house are inserted into the second Chan axiom of cutting off and not leaning on anything (section 23). At the pinnacle of the Chan tower, the Heze and Hongzhou houses are inserted into the third Chan axiom of directly revealing the mind nature (section 24). Zongmi is not asserting the existence of historical connections between individual Chan houses and the text-based schools of Chinese Buddhism. He is engaged in taxonomizing, making his distinctions on the basis of whether

a given Chan house negates just sense objects or both sense objects and consciousness, whether it analyzes characteristics or eradicates them, and so forth.
In other words, his criteria are the traditional classification criteria of Mahayana
exegetics.

The second Chan axiom goes beyond the first Chan axiom in the same way
the second teaching goes beyond the first teaching; that is, whereas the first
Chan axiom negates only sense objects, the second Chan axiom negates both
sense objects and consciousness, holding that both are void, that is, devoid of a
nature of their own. The third Chan axiom, in this vein, goes beyond the first
two Chan axioms in the same way the third teaching goes beyond the first two.
Thus, the third Chan axiom neither speaks in terms of characteristics nor
eradicates characteristics, and, with no cryptic or hidden intention, directly
reveals the mind nature. The first two Chan axioms are of the cryptic type.

This translates to the following in terms of houses of Tang Chan: Heze and
Hongzhou are Chan of clear, explicit, definite, complete meaning, of meaning
that can be taken as it stands (liaoyi-nītārtha). One does not have to deduce
their intention. The other six Chan houses (Jingzhong, Northern, Baotang,
South Mountain Buddha–Recitation Gate, Shitou, and Niutou) are Chan with
a meaning that is incomplete (buliaoyi-neyārtha). Since in a Mahayana framework a text of explicit meaning is recommended as a guide in preference to one
that is of incomplete meaning, there is the implication that Heze and Hongzhou Chan are to be preferred as guides. But Zongmi states explicitly (section
12) that no Chan house is heterodox (xiepi).

THREE PRAXIS PROGRAMS OF THE CHAN HOUSES

By inserting the Jingzhong, Northern, Baotang, and South Mountain Buddha–
Recitation Gate houses into the slot of the first Chan axiom, the Chan Prolegomenon is equating the praxis program of these four Chan houses with the
Yogācāra program of the first teaching. Yogācāra in its foundational Indian texts
lays out the path for the elimination of thought of the unreal, the basis or locus
of the duality of grasped and grasper, and it is worth noting that Zongmi wrote
a commentary and subcommentary (not extant) on a seminal Yogācāra text,
Vasubandhu's Thirty Verses on Consciousness Only. The Chan Prolegomenon
(section 22) tells us that trainees in these Chan houses are, in fact, executing the
Yogācāra program under the tutelage of their Chan masters: "They must, relying on the oral teachings of the masters, turn away from sense objects and view
mind, extinguishing thought of the unreal [wangnian]." The Chan Prolegomenon equates the praxis program of the Niutou and Shitou houses with the

Madhyamaka praxis program of the second teaching: being unsupported, not established anywhere, not fixed in anything (*buzhu yiqie*). In the *Chan Letter* (section 12) Zongmi describes Niutou practice as "forgetting feelings" (*wangqing*), a route to the implementation of the Madhyamaka program of being unsupported or unfixed.

As for the praxis programs of Heze and Hongzhou, the *Chan Prolegomenon* (section 31) says that the practice of the basic axiom and basic teaching, that is, the third Chan axiom and the third teaching, is the one-practice concentration (samadhi), and this one-practice concentration is not really a practice in the usual sense of the term: "Grounded in substance, one produces practice; one cultivates and yet it is a non-cultivation."[72] The *Chan Letter* (section 14) describes the Heze version of this practice of non-practice as "merely getting the mind of no mindfulness" and the Hongzhou version (section 11) as "merely giving free rein to mind."[73] With the telltale word "merely" in both cases Zongmi is suggesting that, for Heze and Hongzhou, that is all there is to it. Judging solely by the wording of these catchphrases, Heze practice was the attaining of an absence and Hongzhou practice the abandoning of technique. They converged in the third Chan axiom.

TALLY OF THE STEP-BY-STEP TEACHING AND THE CHAN STEP-BY-STEP GATE

The next two tallies are the tally of the all-at-once teaching of the Buddha and the Chan all-at-once gate and the tally of the step-by-step teaching of the Buddha and the Chan step-by-step gate (section 6). The *Chan Prolegomenon* (section 45) defines the step-by-step teaching of the Buddha as follows: For the sake of those beings of medium and inferior karmic faculties, the Buddha spoke the humans-and-gods teaching, the Hinayana, the dharma-characteristics (mind-only) teaching, and the eradication-of-characteristics (voidness) teaching. These are step-by-step. Thus, the step-by-step dharma-characteristics (mind-only) teaching, the first teaching, and the step-by-step eradication-of-characteristics (voidness) teaching, the second teaching, together form a tally with the Chan step-by-step gate, that is, the first and second Chan axioms.

Northern, which belongs to the first Chan axiom, according to the *Chan Letter* (section 22) "is just step-by-step practice and is completely lacking in all-at-once awakening," and presumably the same can be said of the other houses of the first axiom, though Zongmi does not explicitly say so. The same passage in the *Chan Letter* says Niutou, the representative of the second Chan axiom, "half-understands the gate of all-at-once awakening" and "has no deficiency with respect to the gate of step-by-step practice." Niutou, in other words, is not wholly the Chan step-by-step gate as we might expect from a mechanical interpretation of the tally.

TWO TYPES OF ALL-AT-ONCE TEACHING

There are two types of all-at-once teaching (section 45), the all-at-once of the Buddha's responding throughout his teaching career to beings of the highest disposition and the all-at-once of the Buddha's rite of transforming beings at the site of his enlightenment.[74] The latter refers to the single occasion immediately after the Buddha attained awakening beneath the tree. On this one occasion, for the sake of those of superior faculties, he preached that causes suffuse the sea of effects, that when one first raises the thought of awakening, one attains awakening, that effects penetrate to the source of causes, and so forth. This is only one sutra of the vast *Huayan* collection, the "Chapter on Entrance Into the Dharma Sphere," and the *Commentary on the Ten Stages*, a commentary on the "Ten-Stages Chapter" of the *Huayan*.[75] No other sutras or treatises record this all-at-once teaching of the rite of transforming beings.

By contrast, the all-at-once of responding to beings of the highest disposition refers to those occasions peppered throughout the Buddha's long teaching career when, having met a being of superior faculties and sharp intellect, he directly showed the undiluted dharma described above. As soon as this being heard the Buddha speak, he awakened all at once and gained the identical fruit of a buddha. This all-at-once of responding to beings of the highest disposition is "one part" (*yi fen*) of the *Huayan Sutra* (probably referring to the *Huayan Sutra* line "When one first raises the thought of awakening, one attains unexcelled, perfect awakening")[76] and such sutras as the *Perfect Awakening*, the *Buddha Top-knot* (=*Heroic Progress Samadhi*), the *Secret Array*, the *Śrīmālā*, and the *Buddha-in-Embryo*.[77] Whenever the Buddha encountered a being of receptive disposition, he spoke this teaching; it is not restricted either to the first or last portion of his teaching career.

This all-at-once teaching of responding to beings of the highest disposition and the Chan all-at-once gate make a tally. In other words, the undiluted teaching of true mind that the Buddha delivered from time to time throughout his career to beings of superior faculties is identical to the third Chan axiom, that is, identical to both Heze and Hongzhou Chan. The parity of Heze and Hongzhou in this formulation reflects the impartial modus operandi of the *Chan Prolegomenon*, as contrasted to the critical modus operandi of the *Chan Letter*. In the *Chan Letter* (section 22), even on the question of all-at-once awakening,

Zongmi takes a slightly critical tone toward Hongzhou, saying that Hongzhou is only "near to the gate of all-at-once awakening and has yet to hit the bull's-eye."

TALLY OF ALL-AT-ONCE AWAKENING
AND STEP-BY-STEP PRACTICE

Next is the tally of all-at-once awakening and step-by-step practice (section 19). At first glance, all-at-once awakening and step-by-step practice appear to be completely contradictory, for the former implies that the depravities have never existed, and thus there is no need for any sort of practice to cut them off, and the latter implies that the depravities have not been fully cut off and hence practice is incomplete. This tally is really explained by the *Chan Prolegomenon*'s chart (section 54), which I discuss below, but in section 46 Zongmi provides a series of metaphors to hint at how it works. The sun rises all at once, but frost melts step-by-step. A baby is born all at once, but the art of proper conduct is perfected step-by-step. A fierce wind blowing over the water stops all at once, but the waves on the water stop step-by-step. Intelligence emerges all at once, but ritual and music are learned through a series of progressive steps (*li yue jian xue*). This last metaphor highlights Zongmi's "Confucian" sensibility—the Confucian *Book of Rites* says that "the teachings of ritual and music discipline human feelings."[78] For Zongmi, Chan practice in general is analogous to the role of ritual and music in the Confucian vision, for he says in the opening section of the *Chan Prolegomenon*: "Forgetting feelings [*wangqing*] and coinciding with [the principle of Chan] is Chan practice." *Zongmi's gradual practice consists of subjecting the feelings to discipline* (leading to *forgetting* those feelings or escaping their sway).

TALLY OF ORIGINAL AWAKENING/REAL
AND NON-AWAKENING/UNREAL

The last tally, original awakening/real and non-awakening/unreal (section 52) is another way of expressing the previous all-at-once awakening and step-by-step practice tally and is worked out in the chart (section 54). This tally is concerned with the practice and realization that come after awakening (section 52). Note that here "awakening" refers to understanding awakening (*jiewu*), intellectual comprehension of the teachings, and "realization" to realization awakening (*zhengwu*), the enlightenment (bodhi) of a buddha. This gradual practice consists of a sequence of levels of awakening to the unreal and returning to the real, the adept cutting off each successive level of delusion in a progression along the path. The awakening sequence works backward from the end of the delusion sequence, overturning and eradicating one by one the ten levels of delusion, but there is a discrepancy (explained below) involving the first level of the awakening sequence and the first two levels of the delusion sequence. Here are the ten levels of awakening:

1. All-at-once awakening to original awakening
2. Producing the three minds of compassion, wisdom, and the vow to cross oneself and others over to the other shore of nirvana
3. Cultivating the five practices of giving, precepts, forbearance, striving, and stopping-viewing
4. Opening up of the three minds: straight mind, deep mind, and mind of great compassion
5. Realizing self is void
6. Realizing dharmas are void
7. Mastery over forms
8. Mastery over mind
9. Divorcing from thoughts
10. Becoming a buddha

The ten levels of delusion are:

1. [Original awakening]
2. Non-awakening
3. Thoughts arise
4. Seer [subject] arises
5. Sense objects appear
6. Grasping of dharmas
7. Grasping of self
8. Three poisons of passion, hatred, and stupidity
9. Creation of karma
10. Receiving of recompense—rebirth in one of the six paths

The adept's all-at-once awakening in the first level of the awakening sequence to the original awakening of the first level of the delusion sequence and overturning the non-awakening of the second level of the delusion sequence *constitutes the first level.* Awakening no. 2 then overturns delusion no. 10; awakening no. 3 overturns delusion no. 9; awakening no. 4 overturns delusion no. 8; awakening no. 5 overturns delusion no. 7; awakening no. 6 overturns delusion no. 6; awakening no. 7 overturns delusion no. 5; awakening no. 8 overturns delusion no. 4; and awakening no. 9 overturns delusion no. 3. At level no. 10 of awakening, becoming a buddha, the buddha one becomes is just initial awakening (*shijue*), overturning delusion no. 2, non-awakening (*bujue*), and combining with delusion no. 1, original awakening (*benjue*). Thus, initial awakening and original awakening are non-dual. Zongmi calls this a mysterious tally (*mingfu*) and ends with a Huayan line and two sutra quotations: "At level one causes suffuse the sea of effects; at level ten effects penetrate to the source of causes. The *Nirvana Sutra* says: 'The two, raising the thought [of awakening] and the ultimate, are not separate.' The *Huayan Sutra* says: 'When one first raises the thought [of awakening], one attains unexcelled, perfect awakening.'"[79] In other words, the mental attitude one arouses when aspiring to become a buddha *is* the attainment of buddhahood.

Zongmi's intention, as always, was to preserve the gradual cultivation that follows all-at-once (understanding) awakening and precedes realization awakening. The chart is the bare outline of a gradualist-practice program that is simultaneously sudden. Probably, the chart originally consisted only of terminological labels in red and black ink with text captions beneath (mostly quotations from the *Awakening of Faith*). Zongmi says (section 53) that categories of purity are in red (*zhuhua*) and categories of impurity in black (*mohua*). It seems that some time after Zongmi, a graphic dimension in the form of an arcane set of circles was inserted into his chart. In that addition the awakening process, for instance, is illustrated by a sequence of circles resembling phases of a waxing moon and the delusion process by a sequence of circles resembling phases of a waning moon. With the inclusion of the circles the chart comes to evoke a Daoist or tantric *fu* drawing.

INFLUENCE OF THE *CHAN PROLEGOMENON* AND *CHAN LETTER* IN SONG CHINA, THE KINGDOM OF XIXIA, KORYŎ KOREA, AND KAMAKURA-MUROMACHI JAPAN

NO COLLECTION OF RECORDED SAYINGS FOR ZONGMI

The Song dynasty (960–1279) is the age of woodblock-printed books, often products of subtle refinement and beauty admired and imitated throughout East Asia. Some Chan followers worked to assemble what remained of the Tang manuscript tradition of Chan books. Over time an extensive printed Chan literature came into wide circulation, including intact Tang texts (such as the

Chan Prolegomenon and Pei Xiu's *Essentials of the Dharma of Mind Transmission*), Tang materials reworked and burnished by Song editors (such as the *Record of Linji*), and new Song books (such as the *Record of [Pure Talk] in the Forest [Linjianlu]*). Zongmi's influence on Chan in Song times was not as a speaking and acting Tang Chan master who sprang to life from the pages of a Song xylograph of his sayings record. It was the orientation, theoretical structures, and striking similes of his *Chan Prolegomenon* and *Chan Letter* that exerted the influence on Song Chan. And our view of post-Tang Chan has failed to take that influence into account.

Part of the reason for that failure may lie in the fact that no Chan record of Zongmi's sayings and activities was compiled or published during the Song. In a sense, a Chan sayings record created its Chan master, rather than the other way around. The editors of the *Patriarchal Hall Collection* (*Zutangji*) of 952, for instance, unequivocally state that they have been unable to find any such record for Zongmi and so cannot relate a typical Chan career for him.[80] And the Zongmi entry in the *Jingde Era Record of the Transmission of the Lamp* (*Jingde chuandeng lu*) of 1004 is little more than a pastiche of quotations from the *Chan Prolegomenon* and works related to Zongmi, containing no Zongmi sayings or anecdotes.[81]

So far as I have been able to determine, we have but one Zongmi saying, found buried in Yanshou's *Mind Mirror* (exactly where we would expect it), and in its Buddhist allusion and literary language it is utterly different from the earthy and colloquial Chan utterances so admired in Song Chan: "Preceptor Caotang says: 'Well, Indra's net is not yet stretched out, so how can we see the thousands of jewel ornaments [at each of the myriad knots]? Suddenly the grand headrope of the net is activated, and ten thousand eyes spontaneously open up.' "[82] This saying is based on a Huayan simile for the layer-on-layer inexhaustibility of the Buddhist causation formula, origination by dependence. At each of the knots of the god Indra's jewel net, which hangs from the ceiling of his palace, a jewel is attached. Each jewel reflects all the other jewels, and the jewels in the reflections also reflect.

THE MIND MIRROR AS CONDUIT TO THE SONG FOR THE CHAN PROLEGOMENON

Yanshou's *Mind Mirror* served as a channel through which the ideas and models of Zongmi's *Chan Prolegomenon* were widely disseminated to the Song world. During the Yuanfeng era (1078–1085) of the Northern Song, a woodblock-printed edition of the *Mind Mirror* was carried out and distributed to various monasteries.[83] Another edition was executed during the Yuanyou era (1086–1093) at the Song capital Kaifeng, and before long Yanshou's collection was included in the *Song Canon* (the *Chan Prolegomenon* was not). Many xylograph copies of the *Mind Mirror* circulated during the Song, and many compilations of extracts and catalogues of it were published.[84] The range of its influence was exceptionally broad, extending to Buddhism outside the Chan orbit, and even to non-Buddhist Song learning.

The *Mind Mirror* conveyed to Song Chan the most fundamental elements of Zongmi's *Chan Prolegomenon*, sometimes in Zongmi's wording or close paraphrases: (1) the necessity for Chan transmitters to rely upon the sutras and treatises as the definitive standard or norm; (2) the true mind of clear and constant Knowing that is the substance of all the teachings and Chan; (3) the assumption that the nature axiom is the pinnacle of the teachings; (4) the use of the terminological pair *zong-jiao* or a synonym to denote the dichotomy of Chan and the word, and (5) the championing of the model of all-at-once awakening followed by step-by-step practice. We see every one of these themes in the following scattered passages from the *Mind Mirror*:

Question: An ancient worthy said: "If you make me set up an axiom and establish a fixed purport [*li zong ding zhi*], it is like looking for hair on a tortoise or seeking horns on a rabbit." A *Lanka Descent Sutra* verse says that all dharmas are non-arising and you should not establish any axiom. So why do you give this [first] chapter [of your *Mind Mirror*] the title *Designating-the-Axiom Section* [*biaozong zhang*]? Answer: The words [of my title are designed to] dispel [misunderstandings]. In the case of the [Chan] axiom that is a non-axiom [*wuzong zhi zong*], axiom and theory [*zong shuo*] merge without impediment. The Chan axiom opens the path of singularity. You must not grasp at the teaching devices [of the sutras and treatises] and miss the great purport [=the Chan axiom]. But you also must not discard those teaching devices, cutting off the later explanations [of the teachings]. . . . This is the substance of the minds of all sentient beings. It is a spiritual Knowing that never darkens [*lingzhi bumei*], quiescent and illuminating without omission. It is not just the Huayan axiom—it is the substance of all the teachings. . . . Take the noble words [of the sutras and treatises] as the definitive source of knowledge, for the false is difficult to remove. Use the best teachings as your guidebook, a standard to be relied upon [*yiping you ju*]. Therefore, Preceptor Guifeng [in section 11 of the *Chan Prolegomenon*] says: "The first patriarch of all the [Chan] lineages is Śākyamuni. The sutras are buddha word, while Chan is the intention of the buddhas. The mouth and mind of the buddhas cannot possibly be contradictory." . . . The true mind [*zhenxin*] in its self substance is inexpressible by words. It is clear like limitless space. It is a mirror of purity with a jade-like perfect brightness. . . . What is discussed at present

in this *Mind Mirror* is not the setting up of existence of the dharma characteristics [teaching]. Nor is it the reversion to voidness of the eradicating characteristics [teaching]. It merely clarifies correct principle in accordance with
the perfect teaching [*yuanjiao*] of the nature axiom [*xingzong*]. . . . The true
mind is clear, quiescent, and illuminating. It does not arise from sense objects.
It is empty and gives free rein to conditions. It has never involved mental activity. It is bright and never darkening, a clear and constant Knowing. . . . This
[treatise, the *Mind Mirror*,] discusses seeing the nature and clarifying mind. It
does not widely divide up [Chan] axioms and judge teachings. It solely holds up
direct entrance into all-at-once awakening and perfect practice. It does not seek
a liberation free of the [fish] traps and [rabbit] nets, nor does it ever grasp the
written word and become deluded about the basic axiom [=the nature axiom].[85]
When it relies on the teachings [*yijiao*], it is Huayan,[86] showing the broad, great
texts of the one mind. When it relies on the axiom [*yizong*], it is Bodhidharma
[Chan], the purport of *directly revealing* sentient beings' *mind nature* [using the
wording of Zongmi's third Chan axiom]. . . . Therefore, the *Mind Mirror* in
summary has two ideas: the first is all-at-once awakening to the axiom of
Knowing [*dunwu zhi zong*], and the second is perfectly cultivating the [grad-
ual] work. . . . One must first get an original awakening into the non-arising
non-disappearing of one's own true mind as cause and after that take this non-
arising purport to [gradually] cure everything everywhere.[87]

The scholar of Song Chan Albert Welter has said that by Song times the
zong-jiao terminology had become a commonplace—to the point where monasteries were officially designated as either one or the other.[88] He has also argued
that in the early Song two contrasting styles of Chan, "moderate" (Yanshou)
and "rhetorical" (centering on the Linji house), represented "the poles between
which a potential interpretation of Chan swung. . . . [This polarity is] indicative
of the range of possibilities for interpretation available to all Chan masters." As
far as labels go, I prefer "sutra- and treatise-based Chan" (or perhaps "nature-
axiom Chan") for the Guifeng-Yanshou orientation. It is unfortunate that treatments of Yanshou seldom emphasize how much he owes to the Zongmi of the
Chan Prolegomenon (as opposed to the *Chan Letter*).[89] *Zongmi was the Tang
dynasty grandfather of Yanshou Chan.*
      This Guifeng-Yanshou style of Chan, sometimes called canonical written-
word Chan (*wenzi chan*), advocated the nature axiom and sudden awakening–
gradual practice of the *Perfect Awakening Sutra* and the *Heroic Progress Samadhi Sutra* (=*Buddha Top-knot Sutra*). These two sutras, both apocryphal (at least
in part for the latter), are built on the sudden awakening–gradual practice
model.[90] Zongmi's *Chan Prolegomenon* designates these sutras as (1) sutras of
the nature axiom/third teaching (tallies with the third Chan axiom) and

(2) expressions of the all-at-once teaching of the Buddhas's responding throughout his teaching career to beings of the highest dispositon (tallies with the Chan all-at-once gate). They are thus quintessential Chan sutras. Yanshou's *Mind Mirror* repeatedly quotes both of them.[91]

The rhetorical pole of Song Chan gave this written-word Chan the pejorative label "kudzu Chan" (*geteng chan*). The kudzu is a tendrilled vine, used as a metaphor for things that become entangled and thus for the utter complexity, confusion, and futility of the word. We see the rhetorical pole's stance reflected in the *Extensive Record of Yunmen*, the collected sayings of one of the rhetorical pole's favorite literary figures:

> [The Master Yunmen said:] "If *this matter* [*ci ge shi*] lay in words—the three vehicles and the twelve divisions of the teachings are most definitely not lacking for words—for what reason would there be the slogan *separate transmission outside the teachings* [*jiaowai biechuan*]?" . . . [The Master] ascended the hall and said: "Just at the moment a single word is raised and the thousand differentiations fall [nicely] into place, drawing in every minute dust mote, it is *still* [nothing but] a verbal explanation/theory of the teachings approach [*huamen zhi shuo*]. What is a patch-robed Chan monk to do?" . . . Question: "What is the body of Śākyamuni like?" Answer: "A cylinder of dried shit [*ganshijue*]." . . . [The Master] ascended the hall and said: "Vasubandhu Bodhisattva for no reason transforms into a chestnut-wood staff." Then with his staff he drew a line on the ground and said: "The buddhas, numberless as dust motes or grains of sand, are all in here speaking kudzu [*shuo geteng*]." He then got down from his seat. . . . [The Master] ascended the hall and said: "Today I am going to speak kudzu with you: 'Shit, ash, piss, fire, muddy pigs, scabby dogs.' Not knowing what to love and what to detest, you are making your livelihood in a shit pit [*shikeng li*]."[92]

For Yunmen *"this matter"* is a separate transmission outside the thousands upon thousands of words in the three vehicles and the twelve divisions of the Buddhist canon. *The Record of Linji*, which has an old-*baihua* style akin to that of the *Extensive Record of Yunmen* (they had the same Song editor), says "the three vehicles and twelve divisions of the teachings are old toilet paper that wipes away filth" and describes an exchange between Linji and a specialist in the three vehicles and twelve divisions of the teachings in which the lecture specialist is driven into silence and rudely rebuked.[93]

Not only did the *Mind Mirror* pass on the central ideas of the *Chan Prolegomenon* to the Chan enclaves of Song dynasty China; it performed the same function for Korea and Japan. Welter speaks of moderate Chan's "persistent influence over Chan and the spread of Chan throughout East Asia, to Korea, Japan, and Vietnam, in spite of the persistent claims of contemporary [Japanese] Rinzai [Zen] orthodoxy to the contrary."[94] Setting aside the question of what role Rinzai Zen has played in shunting the *Mind Mirror* with its Zongmi assumptions into the historical shadows and elevating the rhetorical style of texts like the *Record of Linji* and *Extensive Record of Yunmen* to prominence, it is more than fair to say that the *Mind Mirror* was highly influential in Koryŏ Korea and Kamakura-Muromachi Japan.

For example, in Korea a Koryŏ king saw a copy of the *Mind Mirror* (*Chonggyŏng nok*) and dispatched messengers bearing gifts to obtain it.[95] And the Chan works of Chinul, the dominant figure in the Chan of the later Koryŏ period (ca. 1200–1400), extensively quote the *Mind Mirror*.[96] In Chinul's Chan, Zongmi's Chan works and Yanshou's *Mind Mirror* went hand in hand, and Chinul was nothing less than instrumental in the formation of the entire Korean Sŏn tradition. The *Mind Mirror* was included in the famous *Koryŏ Canon* of 1251,[97] but the *Chan Prolegomenon* was not, just as was the case with the *Song Canon* in China.

In the case of medieval Japan we find the *Mind Mirror* (*Sugyōroku*) at the very beginnings of Kamakura-period Zen, the Daruma lineage, which spread in the Nara and Kyoto areas during the late 1100s. Its founder, Dainichi Nōnin, is said in a biographical notice to have fielded questions about important passages in the *Mind Mirror* at one of his assemblies, and a key work of the Daruma lineage, the *On Perfect Awakening* (*Jōtōshōgakuron*), is heavily based upon chunks from the *Mind Mirror*.[98] In fact, quotations of the Great Master Nichi, Dainichi Nōnin himself, in *On Perfect Awakening* are actually material from the *Mind Mirror*. Nōnin's interest in the *Mind Mirror* was not a singularity in Kamakura Zen. Two major Zen figures in the Tendai esoteric mold, Myōan Yōsai (1141–1215) and Enni Ben'en (1202–1280), used the *Mind Mirror*. Yōsai's apologia *Propagate Zen and Protect the Country* (*Kōzen gokoku ron*) repeatedly cites the *Mind Mirror*, and Enni had a reputation among his contemporaries as an expert on Yanshou's treatise.[99] In short, the *Mind Mirror* was very much present in Kamakura Zen.

In the subsequent Ashikaga period, the *Mind Mirror* circulated widely in Five Mountains (Gozan) Zen circles. Five Mountains was one of the great eras of printing in Japan, mainly reprints of Song and Yuan dynasty editions but including works by Japanese authors. In content, Gozan editions consisted mainly of Chinese Chan books plus Tang and Song poetry and prose collections, Chinese rhyme books, Chinese classics and histories, and so on. The central Gozan figure Shun'oku Myōha (1311–88) early in his career studied printing operations, as well as poetry styles and musical chanting of sutras, under the expatriate Chinese master Zhuxian Fanxian (Jikusen Bonsen; 1292-1348).[100] Myōha, who carried on Bonsen's emphasis on publishing, arranged in Enbun 3 (1358) for a woodblock printing of the *Chan Prolegomenon* and in Ōan 4 (1371) commissioned an edition of the *Mind Mirror*. Of note is the fact that the number of skilled woodblock carvers involved in the latter project was the greatest number recorded for any Five Mountains edition.[101] Such a concentration of resources suggests the great prestige of the *Mind Mirror* at the time. And just over a century later in 1480, the Rinzai monk Ikkyū Sōjun (1394–1481) received as a gift a precious xylograph copy of the *Mind Mirror,* presumably Myōha's edition, from a prominent layman in return for writing out the single character "no" (*muji*), quite a big present (about 800,000 characters) in return for such a tiny courtesy.[102]

THE KINGDOM OF XIXIA: TANGUT TRANSLATIONS OF THE CHAN PROLEGOMENON AND CHAN LETTER

In the history of Inner Asia for romantic aura there are few cultures that surpass that of Xixia, a multiethnic state located in the Ordos and Gansu corridor in the northwest from the eleventh to thirteenth centuries. Known almost universally by the Chinese name Xixia ("Western Xia"), its Tibeto-Burman language and people are always designated as Tangut, originally a Mongol term.[103] Its population included Tanguts, Hans, Tibetans, and Uighurs. After a number of campaigns, in 1227 Chinggis khan's Mongol forces utterly extinguished this state. Today there is a small reminder of this brilliant culture in the current name for the region, the Ningxia Hui Autonomous Region.

But the self-designation of this people was Mi or Mi-nia, and they called their state the "State of White and High" or "Great State of White and High," the meaning of which has eluded scholars for some time.[104] The Chinese scholar Nie Hongyin has suggested that the answer may lie in two native Mi-nia (Tangut-language) poems.[105] In an epic poem on the origins of the Mi-nia, "white" indicates the West as the birthplace of the Mi-nia nationality; in a set of verses on the creation of the Mi-nia script, "high" indicates the highlands in the west in contrast to the Chinese lowlands in the east. Thus, the name of the state in the Mi-nia language probably meant the "Great State on the Highlands in the West."

In 1908 an expedition of the Imperial Russian Geographical Society led by Peter Kuzmitsch Kozlov discovered the remains of an outpost of the Great State on the Highlands in the West at Khara-khoto in present-day Inner Mongolia, about fifty miles northeast of Dunhuang, and brought a massive corpus of Mi-nia (Tangut) woodblock-printed books and manuscripts back to St. Petersburg.

This collection shows that the Great State on the Highlands in the West was a sophisticated Buddhist kingdom with a fascinating orthography of its own making. In 1036, to commemorate the official announcement of the indigenous script the era name was changed.[106] Two years later, the Mi-nia began to translate the entire Chinese Buddhist canon, and this project was completed in 1090.[107]

The Buddhism of the Great State on the Highlands in the West was based on Mi-nia (Tangut) translations of a wide spectrum of Chinese and Tibetan Buddhist texts: Mahayana sutras and treatises, tantric manuals and dharani works, Chan and Huayan works (particularly those of Zongmi), and so forth. The Russian collection contains multiple fragments of the *Chan Prolegomenon* and the *Chan Letter*; commentaries on the *Chan Prolegomenon*; a record of Chan encounters by Zongmi's disciple Pei Xiu; and a strange text that synthesizes Hongzhou Chan and Guifeng Chan from the perspective of the latter.[108] The last two are unknown to the Chinese Chan tradition as we have it.

The Russian scholar K. J. Solonin cautions that, as of now, all we have is random glimpses of Tangut Buddhism, the general nature of which is unclear:

> Since the known Tangut texts comprise neither a systematic library nor a canon, thus [*sic*] glimpses of a Tangut Buddhist tradition come merely through various, discrete texts. We cannot as yet determine their basic or entire meanings, nor place them in a general framework. These texts represent occasional "things at hand," mainly those placed inside the Khara-Khoto stupa on the eve of the Mongol occupation of this remote outpost of Tangut civilization on the Mongolian steppe. . . . Study of the extant Tangut Buddhist materials reveals that the Xixia state was a safe haven for Huayan Buddhism, even after this tradition had supposedly disappeared in China. What the term "Huayan" implies is not only the classic Chinese school of Fazang (643–712), but also a heterogeneous tradition of the late-Tang master Guifeng Zongmi (780–841), many of whose works are to be found among the Khara-Khoto texts. The continued existence of Zongmi's tradition is attested by several presumably primary Tangut texts (that is, those for which no Chinese version can be located or even deduced).[109]

Solonin surmises that Zongmi's lineage had not been interrupted after the Huichang Suppression of foreign religions in the 840s, as has generally been assumed, but continued developing in northwestern China and prospered in the Great State on the Highlands in the West at least until the middle of the twelfth century.[110] His speculation on the affinity between the Tanguts and Zongmi is also worth quoting:

The most interesting problem is to explain the apparent affection the Tanguts held for Zongmi. This is perhaps best discussed in terms of cultural geography rather than religious studies: the center of Zongmi's tradition at the Straw Hut Temple (Caotang si) near Chang'an was probably one of the few Chinese Buddhist centers known to the Tanguts in this period. . . . Several accounts suggest that the Straw Hut Temple was active all through the period of Jin rule (1115–1234), and even later. Therefore, the impact of this temple on the formation of Tangut Buddhism may well have been considerable and continuous.[111]

There is a distinct possibility that *Mi-nia (Tangut) Chan was a direct continuation of the Guifeng Chan of China*, that is, the Chan of Zongmi centered at Caotang Monastery in North China in the period after his death in 841. At least three Tangut-language texts may in time shed light on Guifeng Chan both in the Great State on the Highlands in the West and in China after the time of Zongmi:

1. *The Mirror*
2. *Record of the Hongzhou Axiom with Commentary and Clarification*
3. *Meaning of the Perfectly Enlightened Mind of the Ultimate One Vehicle*[112]

The Mirror sets up three teachings:

1. *Nature origination*=the teaching of one mind or true mind
2. *Mind calmness*=Bodhidharma's wall viewing (sudden awakening)
3. *Generating practice*=Bodhidharma's four practices (gradual practice)

This text of Mi-nia Buddhism, which is deeply rooted in the orientation of Guifeng Chan, in its opening section quotes the *Chan Letter* on the topic of one mind:

[The *Chan Letter*, section 9, says:] "Delusion produces all the depravities, but even these depravities are not divorced from this mind [=the first teaching of *nature origination*].[113] Awakening produces limitless, excellent functions, but even these excellent functions are not divorced from this mind [*ci xin*]. Even though in terms of merits and demerits the excellent functions and the depravities are different, in awakening and in delusion, this mind remains undifferentiated. If you desire to seek the buddha path, then you must awaken to this mind. Therefore, down through the generations, the patriarchal lineage has just transmitted this." . . . Further, Chan Master Guifeng said: "If you intend to attain the fruit of wisdom, knowledge of causes and conditions is necessary. If [the knowledge of] causes and conditions is false, the fruit will be false as well."[114] . . . Further, Master Ming of Kaiyuan[115] said: "If you strive to attain the fruit with a fundamentally unenlightened mind, that produces the same exhaustion as squashing sand to get oil or burning your house during the cold season [to keep warm]." . . . The *Awakening of Faith* says: "All dharmas from the outset are free of the characteristics of speech, free of the characteristics of the written word, free of the characteristics of objective supports of mind, ultimately sameness, without change, and indestructible. Because it is just one mind [*yixin*], we call it thusness."[116] . . . In Huangbo's *Mind Transmission* it is said: "All the buddhas and all sentient beings are just one mind [*wei shi yixin*], and there is no other dharma. This mind from without beginning has neither arisen nor disappeared."[117] . . . In the *Chan Prolegomenon* [section 4] it is said: "If one's practice is based on having all-at-once awakened to the realization that one's own mind is from the outset pure, that the depravities have never existed, that the nature of the wisdom without outflows is from the outset complete, that this mind is buddha [*ci xin ji fo*], that they are ultimately without difference, then it is dhyana of the highest vehicle. This type is also known by such names as tathagata-purity dhyana, etc." . . . The second teaching is that of *mind calmness*.[118] Bodhidharma said: "Quieting mind is wall viewing."[119] . . . Bodhidharma's doctrine of *mind calmness* is the foundation and source of the multitude of doctrines of *mind calmness*. . . . The seventh patriarch [Shenhui in his *Platform Talks*] said: "The mindfulness of no mindfulness is being mindful of thusness."[120] . . . The *Perfect Awakening Sutra* says: "All the bodhisattvas and sentient beings of the end period, [relying on this practice, are thus capable of] being eternally free of illusions."[121] . . . The third is the teaching of *generating practice*.[122] Bodhidharma said: "*Generating practice* is the four practices."[123] . . . Further, Chan Master Shiye in the *Commentary on the Perfect Awakening Sutra* had also expounded the three teachings.[124] His explanations generally coincide with the above descriptions, though retaining minor differences. . . . In such an awakening, one's own mind eliminates deluded elements, and the perfect, true mind, possessing spontaneous Knowing [*zizhi*],[125] is attained. . . . Actually, it was Bodhidharma himself who propagated the *three teachings of nature origination, mind calmness, and generating practice*. [These three] resemble the three legs of a tripod.[126] If one is missing, the whole ceases to exist. . . . When the three ways are completed, miraculous perfection is attained. Question: Earlier it was said that in the way of *nature origination* originally there are no defilements, and the nature is awakened in itself. If there are no defilements, then why should they be removed? Answer: The Great Master Guifeng

[Zongmi] once said[127]: "Even though this truth is realized directly in its completeness, nevertheless defiled mind-perception is difficult to remove . . ."[128]

The *Record of the Hongzhou Axiom with Commentary and Clarification* begins by attributing the slogans "everything is the real" and "everything is the Dao" to the founding master of Hongzhou, Hongzhou Ma.[129] But both of these sayings appear in Zongmi's *Chan Notes* (section 4) and *Chan Letter* (11 and 13), and they are almost certainly encapsulations of Hongzhou coined by Zongmi rather than Hongzhou sayings picked up by Zongmi. This heavily layered text, which consists of a root text entitled *Teachings and Rituals of the Hongzhou Lineage Masters* accompanied by commentary and subcommentary, takes as its main theme a threefold division of Chan. The first two divisions are none other than the *Chan Prolegomenon's zong* (realizing the *siddhānta*) and *jiao* (the *siddhānta* in words), and the third is a synonym of the wish-fulfilling gem of Knowing:

1. Chan beyond words/phrases
2. Chan in conformity with words/phrases
3. Great Ancient Treasure Seal[130]

Here, the root text is in boldface, and for the sake of clarity the two commentaries are blurred:

The master said: The essence of my teaching. . . . These are words of the founding master of Hongzhou . . . **is that everything is the real** . . . **everything is the Dao.** . . . **Chan Master Juehui awakened in his mind.** He realized *what is beyond words* but did not realize *what is in conformity with words.* He became attached to *what is beyond words* and did not intend to attain *that which is in conformity with words.* He opened his right eye and closed the left eye.[131] He did not realize *both what is in conformity with words and what is beyond words.* This is a mistake, because one part is missing. Among the people who are attached to this, none can be said to have complete Knowing. **And immediately** [Juehui] **said: The Great Master Bodhidharma transmitted from mind to mind with no involvement with the written word.** . . . Daji [that is, Hongzhou Ma] said: **Do not speak like that.** If there is the substance [*ti* = what is beyond words], but there is no functioning [*yong* = what is in conformity with words], this is not the true substance. . . . **In compliance with the substance, functioning appears, and all the words** [of the teachings] **are in accord.** . . . Juehui attained the ultimate awakening, awakening to *the non-duality of what is beyond words and what is in conformity with* *words.* . . . When the non-duality of what is in conformity with words and what is beyond words is realized, the *Chan of the Great Ancient Treasure Seal* is complete. . . . When we talk about the completeness of the tripartite Chan, this is to say that each of them must be realized.[132]

This is consistent with the *Chan Prolegomenon* (section 44):

The three teachings and the three Chan axioms are the dharma of one taste. Therefore, one must first, according to the three types of buddha teachings [=what is in conformity with words], realize the Chan minds of the three axioms [=what is beyond words],[133] and only after that will both Chan and the teachings be forgotten, both mind and buddha calmed [=the non-duality of what is beyond words and what is in conformity with words=the Great Ancient Treasure Seal]. When both are calmed, then thought after thought all is the buddha; there will not be a single thought that is not buddha mind. When both are forgotten, then line after line all is Chan; there will not be a single line that is not Chan teaching.

In the *Record of the Hongzhou Axiom with Commentary and Clarification* we have Hongzhou Ma defending the Zongmi position and rebuking an otherwise unknown Hongzhou follower, Juehui, for erroneously taking the Bodhidharma slogan "no involvement with the written word" to mean that just awakening to what is beyond words is sufficient for liberation. Juehui eventually advances to realize both the Chan beyond words and the Chan in conformity with words, attaining ultimate awakening, the Great Ancient Treasure Seal. Here Guifeng Chan subsumes Hongzhou Chan.

In the Tangut finds we have nothing less than *the literary remains of a hitherto unknown non-Han regional variant of the Chan tradition.* Who was behind such Tangut-language Chan texts as *The Mirror* and *Record of the Hongzhou Axiom with Commentary and Clarification*? We do not know as of now. The former, which is full of quotations from Zongmi's *Chan Prolegomenon* and *Chan Letter*, Chengguan's writings, and Zongmi's favorite sutras and treatises, is a restatement of his *Chan Prolegomenon*'s true-mind teaching and sudden awakening–gradual practice. The latter is an imaginative treatment of the *Chan Prolegomenon*'s tally fit (*fu*) of Chan and the teachings. Everything suggests that Mi-nia Chan was, in the broadest sense, directly traceable to Guifeng Chan. A parallel to Mi-nia Chan that immediately comes to mind is far away from Xixia, which was located on the northwest fringe of the Chinese periphery: Korea, on the northeast fringe.

KORYŎ KOREA: CHINUL AND CHONGMIL (ZONGMI)

Zongmi found his most receptive environment, with the possible exception of Xixia, almost four hundred years after his time, on the Korean peninsula. The key Korean inheritor of Zongmi's orientation was Chinul (1158–1210), also known by the posthumous name National Teacher Puril Pojo. Chinul never traveled to China but nevertheless absorbed the Chan works of Zongmi (Korean Chongmil) in both letter and spirit. Chinul's magnum opus of 1209, *Excerpts from the Separately Circulated Record of the Dharma Collection with Inserted Personal Notes* (*Pŏpchip pyŏrhaeng nok chŏryo pyŏngip sagi*) is a guidebook designed by Chinul for the Sŏn sitters gathered around him.[134] This work, which was to have such a momentous influence on the overall outlook of Korean Buddhism, is an expression of sutra-based sudden awakening– gradual practice Guifeng Chan. First, its opaque title requires more than a little explanation.

Dharma Collection refers to one of the collections of Zongmi's miscellaneous pieces that circulated in China and Korea. Another title for the same sort of collection was *Posthumous Collection of Guifeng* (*Guifeng houji*). These collections seem to have consisted primarily of Zongmi's answers to questions submitted to him, and the *Chan Letter*, which consists of Zongmi's answers to Pei Xiu's questions, was one component of such collections. *Record* refers to the *Chan Letter* itself. When excerpting the *Chan Letter*, Chinul's *Excerpts* introduces the quotation as "the *Record* says" or "the text says" (and sometimes with no introduction at all). *Separately Circulated* indicates that the *Chan Letter* has been extracted from the collection and thereby converted into an independent work that circulates on its own. *Inserted Personal Notes* refers to Chinul's interspersed comments and many other quotations, from Zongmi's *Chan Prolegomenon*, a Chengguan commentary on the *Huayan Sutra*, Yanshou's *Mind Mirror*, the *Sayings Record of Dahui* (*Dahui yulu*), and so on. In his comments Chinul sometimes refers to himself as Moguja, Oxherder.

Chinul's *Excerpts* essentially rests on two foundation stones, blocks of quotations from the *Chan Letter*, the centerpiece of which is Guifeng Chan's Knowing (Korean *chi*), and, toward the end, blocks of quotations from the *Sayings Record of Dahui* on Dahui's method of gazing-at-the-topic (Korean *kanhwa*). The Dahui method consists of holding up to attention ("gazing at") twenty-four hours a day a single word or short phrase (the *huatou* or topic) from a Chan case (*gong'an*), and this is continuously carried out over time. In Chinul's schema the sudden awakening is awakening to Guifeng Chan's Knowing, and the gradual practice is cultivation of Dahui's method of gazing-at-the-topic. The *Excerpts* stands as a creative hybrid of these two. Chinul's preface says:

> Moguja says: Heze Shenhui was a teacher of the view of Knowing. Although he was not the direct successor of [the sixth patriarch] Caoqi [note that Chinul has jettisoned the *Chan Letter's* championing of Heze as the orthodox line], his understanding-awakening was high and bright and his distinctions clear. Because Master [Zong]mi received the purport of his lineage, within this *Record* [=*Chan Letter*] he extended and clarified it so that it could be clearly seen. Now, for the sake of those who rely on the teachings to awaken to mind [*inkyo osim*], I have pruned [the *Chan Letter*] down and produced a summary of excerpts. This will serve as a model for the practice of viewing. *I note that mind cultivators of the present fail to rely on the written word as a guide, but just take [Chan] transmissions with a hidden meaning* [*milŭi sangchŏn ch'ŏ*] *as the path.* In murkiness they take useless pains to do cross-legged sitting while dozing off. Sometimes in the midst of the practice of viewing they lose their minds in a mixed-up confusion. *Therefore, they must rely on [Master Zongmi's] oral teachings concerning things as they really are* [*ŭi yŏshil ŏnkyo*] *to make distinctions about the whole course of awakening and practice.*[135] Taking [these teachings] to mirror their own minds, they will at all times engage in viewing-illumining and not pervert their efforts. Also, as to the content of the *Record* [as Zongmi arranged it], the various lineages, such as that of Shenxiu and so on, are at the beginning. The reason is that [Zongmi] was distinguishing [which lineages] hit the bull's-eye and which miss it, proceeding from shallow to profound. Now I am putting the extracts from the Heze lineage [section of the *Chan Letter*] at the beginning, essentially to enable those engaged in the practice of viewing first to awaken to the realization that their own mind, whether in delusion or awakening, is a spiritual Knowing that never darkens [*yŏngji pulmae*] and is intrinsically immutable. Only afterwards will they successively peruse the [excerpts from the *Chan Letter* dealing with the teachings and practices of the] various lineages and realize that their purports all are deep in good skill [in teaching devices] with respect to the gate of people [of varying dispositions]. If at the beginning [trainees] do not apprehend the source [=the "Source" in the title of the *Chan Prolegomenon*=the Knowing of Heze Chan], then, with respect to purports of the other lineages, they will follow after verbal traces and falsely produce thoughts of seizing and rejecting. How then will they be able to fuse with understanding and take refuge in their own minds? *Also, I fear that practitioners of viewing who are not yet capable of forgetting feelings and being empty and bright, [after suddenly awakening to Knowing] will stagnate on the theoretical expression [of Knowing], and, therefore, toward the end [of*

my text] *I provide brief excerpts from sayings on the shortcut gate* [of practicing gazing-at-the topic] *by a master who was the real thing* [Dahui Zonggao]. *This is essentially to enable* [those practitioners] *to eliminate diseases* [that may arise] *connected to Knowing* and come to know the live road of escape from self.[136]

Chinul reprimands contemporary Korean practitioners for focussing exclusively on Chan transmissions of cryptic meaning while neglecting the guidance of the written word (of complete meaning). His antidote is *reliance on Chongmil's teachings to outline the correct program of awakening and practice.* Chinul's program is Chongmil's program—with the addition of Dahui's method. In the body of his *Excerpts* Chinul argues that sudden awakening followed by gradual practice is the appropriate model for Chan followers of high aspiration during the present age.[137] His slightly earlier work, the *Formula for Cultivating Mind* (*Susim kyŏl*) of 1203–1205, has three formulas: (1) enlightened mind seeks the Buddha; (2) sudden awakening and gradual practice; and (3) void and calm spiritual Knowing.[138] On the second theme it states:

> As the [*Heroic Progess Samadhi*] *Sutra* says: "As to principle, one all-at-once awakens; riding this awakening, [thoughts of the unreal] are merged into annulment. But phenomena are not all-at-once removed; [only] by a graduated sequence are they exhausted."[139] Therefore, Guifeng [Zongmi] deeply clarified *the principle of first awakening and later practice* [*sŏno husu*]. . . . As to sudden awakening [*tono*], when the ordinary being is deluded, [he assumes that] the four elements are his body and thought of the unreal is his mind. He is unaware that his self nature is the true dharma body. He is unaware that his own empty Knowing [*hŏji*] is the the true Buddha. He seeks the Buddha outside mind and is on a constant run. Suddenly entrance to the road is pointed out to him by a good guide. For one moment he retraces the light and sees his own self nature. The ground of this nature from the outset is free of the depravities; [it is] the no-outflows knowledge nature complete from the outset, not the slightest bit different from all the buddhas. *Therefore, we speak of sudden awakening. As for gradual practice* [*chŏmsu*], *having suddenly awakened to the realization that the original nature is no different from the buddhas, the beginningless habit energy is difficult to eliminate finally, and, therefore, he relies on this awakening to practice. The results of this gradual perfuming mature, nourishing the sagely embryo. After a long time, he becomes a noble one, and, therefore, we speak of gradual practice.*[140]

It would be hard to exaggerate the importance of Chinul's *Excerpts* and *Formula for Cultivating Mind* as well as Zongmi's *Chan Prolegomenon* (*Sŏnwŏn jejŏnjip tosŏ*) and *Chan Letter* (submerged in the *Excerpts*) in the history of Korean Buddhism. The *Chan Prolegomenon*, for instance, has gone through a remarkable number of woodblock-print editions in the monasteries of Korea.[141] A specialist in old Korean books, Kuroda Ryō, remarked: "In Korea the *Chan Prolegomenon* was one of the Buddhist books with the highest number of woodblock printings, done at frequent intervals at the monasteries in all the various regions."[142] In contrast to Japan, where the *Chan Prolegomenon* was neglected within the Zen fold after around 1500, in Korea it regularly emerged from the monastic printing establishments and was studied all over the peninsula. The Japanese Kegon scholar Kamata Shigeo has said that the *Chan Prolegomenon* "is one of the most highly regarded books in Korean Buddhism."[143]

Chinul's later heirs in his Guifeng orientation were Kihwa (1376–1433) and Hyujŏng (1520–1604). Guifeng Chan has been at the center of the curriculum of Korea's Chogye school since about 1700 in the form of the *Fourfold Collection* (*Sajip*): *Letters of Chan Master Dahui Pujue* (*Dahui Pujue chanshi shu*); *Chan Master Gaofeng Yuanmiao's Essentials of Chan* (*Gaofeng Yuanmiao chanshi chanyao*); *Chan Prolegomenon*; and Chinul's *Excerpts*.[144] Of all the Buddhist cultures on China's periphery that produced woodblock-printed editions of the *Chan Prolegomenon*—the Khitans of the Liao state (907–1125),[145] the Mi-nia (Tanguts) of the Great State on the Highlands in the West (Xixia), the Koreans, and the Japanese—none surpassed the firmness of the Koreans in embracing all dimensions of Guifeng Chan.

KAMAKURA JAPAN: SHŌJŌ'S KEGON AND SHŪMITSU (ZONGMI)

During the first half of the thirteenth-century Chinese Chan of the Song dynasty was just beginning to stream into Kamakura Japan from the continent, and it was initially perceived by many Japanese as exceedingly newfangled and alien. The Chan works and sutra commentaries of Zongmi (Japanese Shūmitsu) found a reception within Kegon studies. Kegon was one of the schools of the so-called old Kamakura Buddhism, a term referring to those forms of Buddhism that had arrived much earlier than the Kamakura period (the Nara schools plus Tendai and Shingon). Because of the effect of the work of the Japanese medieval historan Kuroda Toshio, we now generally call this Buddhism "exoteric-esoteric Buddhism" (*kenmitsu Bukkyō*) and assume that it still remained the dominant form of Buddhism during the Kamakura period, in spite of the rise of the Pure Land, Zen, and Lotus (Nichiren) movements. For the initial transmission of Zongmi's Chan works in this exoteric-esoteric Buddhist milieu, two key figures are the Shingon monk Kōben (also known as Myōe Shōnin; 1173–1232), who was deeply immersed in Kegon studies, and his disciple Shōjō (1194–?).

In the winter of 1223 Myōe transmitted to Shōjō a set of secret judgments (*hiketsu*) on Zen, perhaps involving the handing over of the *Chan Letter* and the *Chan Prolegomenon* (*Zengen shosenshū tojo*). This was an esoteric oral transmission (*kuden*) in the Shingon style. Shōjō gave literary form to this secret transmission in his 1255 *Outline of the Zen Axiom* (*Zenshū kōmoku*), which folds Zen into the Kegon system, using Zongmi's *Chan Letter* as the tool for the job.[146] *Outline of the Zen Axiom* is a sort of Japanese exoteric-esoteric Buddhist analogue of Chinul's use of the *Chan Letter* in his *Excerpts*. The two works are roughly contemporaneous; they both are based, to a considerable extent, on the *Chan Letter*; and they both advocate Guifeng Chan's Knowing teaching and sudden awakening–gradual practice. We might say that both are reflections of the influence of the *Chan Letter* in Song China.

Shōjō's work does not focus on contemporary Japanese developments in Zen but solely on the four lineages of Chan found in Zongmi's *Chan Letter*. The *Outline of the Zen Axiom* opens with Shōjō's responding to a request from laymen that is almost identical to the one Pei Xiu makes of Zongmi at the beginning of the *Chan Letter*. Shōjō's preface states:

I have in Buddhism for a long time specialized in listening to Kegon [from my master Myōe]. On the side I have received consultation [from him] on the Zen gate [note that Zen is subsidiary in this exoteric-esoteric Buddhist context]. Now, as I am currently in contact with lay people, in passing my hand over the elephant it is difficult to discriminate [what part of the elephant I am touching]. I am no different from a lost sheep. Here two or three people who know me have secretly sounded me out: "The Zen gate of the present time is in a confused state, with many principles of right and wrong. We wish you would show us a guide and resolve our net of doubts." Suddenly I was moved by these words, as if there were a karmic connection from a past birth. Accordingly, I do not calculate the transmission [of Zen] that I received as superficial, and I will imperfectly record what I previously heard. It is not the case that this must become an ornamental form on my ankle; my only desire is to anticipate a karmic connection in a future life. Truly, in opening this *Outline of the Zen Axiom* I will briefly differentiate five gates. The first is to distinguish sameness and difference between the teachings and Zen. The second is to clarify separate transmission outside the teachings. The third is to reveal seeing the nature and becoming a buddha. The fourth is to show step-by-step and all-at-once in awakening and practice. The fifth is to relate the views of the various streams of Zen.[147]

The building materials for *Outline of the Zen Axiom* come largely from the *Chan Letter*, though there are many quotations from Chengguan's commentaries and some from Yanshou's *Mind Mirror* (once again showing the wide circulation of that compendium all across East Asia). Shōjō's conclusions under the five rubrics are as follows:

1. The all-at-once teaching, the fourth of the five teachings of the Kegon schema (with Kegon as the fifth and perfect teaching), and the Zen axiom of Bodhidharma are essentially the same, though there are some differences—in other words, Zen is compatible with exoteric-esoteric Buddhism

2. *Separate transmission outside the teachings; no involvement with the written word* refers to the awakening on one's own to the axiom (*siddhānta*) that is beyond words of the *Lanka Descent Sutra*—in other words, these slogans are grounded in canonical written word

3. *See the nature and become a buddha* refers to Shenhui's teaching of Knowing as transmitted by Zongmi

4. Taking awakening in the sense of intellectual-understanding awakening, Zen belongs to the gate of all-at-once awakening and step-by-step practice (Zongmi's model)

5. In discussing the views of the various streams of Zen, Shōjō completely follows the *Chan Letter*

Perhaps part of Shōjō's agenda was to domesticate Chan for the Japanese exoteric-esoteric Buddhist scene. Once given its subordinate niche in the Kegon spectrum of five teachings, it could not become threatening in the manner of the slightly earlier Daruma lineage of Zen of Dainichi Nōnin or the radical Pure Land teachings that were gaining ground at the time under the banner of the exclusive *nenbutsu*, exclusive reliance on simple oral recitation of the name of Amida Buddha. Shōjō's master, Myōe, was much alarmed at exclusive *nenbutsu*, which discarded all the traditional teachings and practices, and he tried to counter such a development with a competitive simplification rooted in exoteric-esoteric Buddhism. In this unstable situation (note that in the *Outline of the Zen Axiom* passage above it is mentioned that "the Zen gate of the present time is in a confused state") it would be natural for representatives of exoteric-esoteric Buddhism to frame Zongmi as "a patriarchal master of the Kegon lineage."

FIVE MOUNTAINS (GOZAN) ZEN OF THE ASHIKAGA PERIOD: SHŪMITSU AS PROTOTYPE FOR SHUN'OKU MYŌHA AND KIYŌ HŌSHŪ

During the Ashikaga period from about 1300 to 1500, Five Mountains Zen, the Zen of the metropolitan Rinzai monasteries of Kyoto and Kamakura, was the engine of elite Japanese culture. This Five Mountains Zen, which in the past has often been dismissed as a sort of decadent, secularized Zen, a falling away from pure Zen, is only beginning to receive the positive reevaluation it deserves. Just as Zongmi had worked to broadcast Chan in a polished format to the literati and politicians of the court of Emperor Wenzong of the Tang dynasty, Five Mountains Zen monks in Japan during the Ashikaga era were broadcasting a Zen imbued with much contemporary elite Chinese culture to the military men and aristocrats of Kyoto's shogunal and imperial courts. Given the similarity in audience composition and interests, it should come as no surprise that the two styles of presenting Chan and Zen show points of convergence.

The following description of Five Mountains Zen could be applied, without too much revision, to Guifeng Chan:

> Japanese Five Mountains Zen . . . was not radical socially, since it took the form virtually of a state religion; it was clearly not iconoclastic in its reverence for the sages of several Zen lineages as well as of Chinese poetry and painting; it emphasized textual and literary study; and it practiced a highly allusive and indirect mode of producing meaning. . . . [Five Mountains Zen] writings might better be described as highly allusive and complex texts which assume a common knowledge of a broad range of intellectual, religious, and aesthetic treatises. . . . Finally, the Muromachi Five Mountains monks certainly provide us with still more evidence useful in rethinking characterizations of Zen as radically antitextual, individualistic, anti-institutional, paradoxical or mystical, and iconoclastic. For these Japanese monks, Zen Buddhist religious insight is inseparable from textual study, written expression in prose or poetry, cultural appreciation, and the mainstream social and institutional context for these behaviors.[148]

The *Chan Prolegomenon*'s elegant literary style, broad erudition, allusiveness, and complexity meshed with the Chinese literary temperament of Five Mountains Zen. The *Chan Prolegomenon*'s successor text, Yanshou's *Mind Mirror*, fit in nicely for the same reasons.

As mentioned earlier, the powerful and influential Rinzai Zen figure Shun'oku Myōha in 1358 arranged for a printing of the *Chan Prolegomenon* and in 1371 for a printing of the *Mind Mirror*.[149] And there is a striking parallel between an incident in Myōha's early career and Zongmi. Myōha's record, the *National Teacher Chikaku Fumyō's Sayings Record*, says:

> The Patriarch [Musō Soseki] frequently interrogated him [Myōha] with [stories of the] ancient worthies' [responding to the varying] dispositions [of disciples] and the karmic conditions [of the encounters]. The Master [Myōha] was supposed to answer like an echo. The Master repeatedly presented his [level of] understanding and repeatedly met with a scolding: 'Your inclinations are not poor, but it is just that your understanding is obstructed.' Because of this [the Master] did not engage in literary pursuits with the writing brush, but just followed the patriarch's [instructions] in singlemindedly applying himself to cross-legged sitting, not allowing his ribs to touch the mat. One day, as he was reading the *Perfect Awakening Sutra*, he arrived at [the first of the four items in the 'Purity Bodhisattva Chapter' that says] 'wherever they are at any time, they do not produce false thoughts'[150] and suddenly 'got it' [*kotsuzen utoku*]. He composed two verses and presented them to the Patriarch. The Patriarch nodded.[151]

This incident exactly echoes Zongmi's sudden awakening upon encountering the *Perfect Awakening* at a vegetarian banquet. One can easily imagine Myōha at a later stage in his career sitting in his study one afternoon perusing Zongmi's *Chan Prolegomenon* with all its sutra quotations and its *Perfect Awakening* assumptions. Myōha's editions of the *Chan Prolegomenon* and *Mind Mirror* allowed wide access in Kyoto's Zen precincts to these classics of sutra-based Zen. This "classical Buddhist" aspect of Five Mountains Zen is often overlooked by its modern critics, who stress that the "secular" pursuits of these Five Mountains Zen monks, particularly the composition of Chinese poetry, squeezed the Buddhism out of their Zen. But Myōha's edition of the *Chan Prolegomenon* (sections 1, 7, and 9) informed its Five Mountains readers that Chan texts, which tally with the sutras, are in some sense a form of Chinese poetry (*juji*).

Of the major Five Mountains Zen monks, one of the most learned in both the canonical sutra-treatise literature and Zen texts was Kiyō Hōshū (1361–1424), who, to use standard Buddhist parlance, was a sort of magical-creation body (nirmanakaya) of Zongmi.[152] This erudite Rinzai Zen master, who was much attracted to Zongmi's works, was close to the shogun Ashikaga Yoshimitsu, was a teacher of the syncretist thinker Ichijō Kanera, and even had contact with the Nō dramatist and theoretician Zeami Motokiyo. Kiyō wrote a piece on

Zongmi containing an outline of Zongmi's biography and encapsulating his Zen style with the following aphorism: "No Zen separate from the teachings; no teachings separate from Zen."[153] This slogan shows that Kiyō had assimilated what Zongmi was saying in the *Chan Prolegomenon*. Even Kiyō's reputation as the first in Japan to propagate Zhu Xi's commentaries on the Confucian *Four Books* echoes Zongmi's accommodating attitude toward the Confucian tradition.

The Ōnin War of 1467 through 1477 ravaged Kyoto and accelerated the dispersion of Five Mountains Zen culture outside the capital. But after the waning of Five Mountains Zen in Kyoto, study of the *Chan Prolegomenon* seems to have languished in Japan. Though there were two woodblock-printed editions done around the Genroku era in the late seventeenth century,[154] Zongmi's text appears to have remained in relative obscurity until the modern period. The situation began to change only in 1939 when Ui Hakuju, an Indologist-Buddhologist who had trained in Sanskrit in Europe, published his edition and translation of both the *Chan Prolegomenon* and the *Chan Letter*.[155] As the epigraph at the beginning of this chapter illustrates, Ui was struck by the sophisticated way Zongmi's great work integrated Zen and Buddhism in its entirety. By "Buddhism in general" (*Bukkyō ippan*), Ui meant the Indic sutras and treatises, the titles of which are sprinkled throughout the *Chan Prolegomenon*. Since the publication of Ui's pioneering book, the world of Zen studies in Japan has gradually taken up study of the texts of Guifeng Chan.[156]

GUIFENG CHAN: AN ASSESSMENT

GUIFENG-YANSHOU CHAN MARGINALIZED AS A SYNCRETISM

I consider Zongmi's primary persona to be a Chan persona, and there is evidence that such was the case for Zongmi himself and among his contemporaries, particularly his closest disciple and confidant Pei Xiu. At the end of the *Chan Prolegomenon* (section 58), a work Zongmi wrote at the peak of his powers, he expresses his joy at how fortunate he is to be the thirty-eighth-generation successor in the Chan mind transmission. Pei Xiu, the person who knew Zongmi best, states in the *Stele Inscription for Chan Master Guifeng*: "The Great Master was the fifth generation from Heze, the eleventh generation from Bodhidharma, the thirty-eighth generation from Kāśyapa—this was the series of his dharma lineage."[157] Pei's funerary inscription makes little of Zongmi's exposure to Chengguan's Huayan, mentioning only that Zongmi visited Chengguan and quoting Chengguan's praise of the young Chan monk.[158] But Zongmi's

Chan persona and his influence on the later development of Chan are often seriously underplayed.

In Japan, when Zongmi is the topic, his Chan persona is not at center stage. He has usually been cast as the Kegon patriarchal master following Chengguan in the Kegon line and as the fountainhead of a syncretic type of Chan called the "union of the teachings and Zen" or "Kegon Zen," with little made of the historical influence of Guifeng Chan on various developments in East Asian Chan.[159] Such marginalizing of Zongmi *as Chan master* extends to his putative successor, Yanshou, who is usually presented not as a pure Chan figure but as a syncretist of the dual practice of Chan and recitation of Amida Buddha's name (*nenbutsu*), in spite of the fact that Yanshou's magnum opus, the *Mind Mirror*, explicitly says that buddha-recitation is just for those who lack faith in the Chan slogan "one's own mind is the Buddha" and rush around seeking on the outside.[160] The assumption is that such "syncretisms" are on the outskirts of the "pure Zen" precincts.[161]

This shunting of Zongmi and Yanshou to the periphery of Chan has had negative effects for the study of Chan in the West, contributing to the West's skewed assessment of the East Asian Chan tradition as a whole. Too often we have read East Asian Chan through Japanese Zen since the Edo period. This has led to our present lack of knowledge concerning the collective impact of Zongmi and Yanshou in China and Korea and hence to thinking of Chan and textual study as more or less mutually exclusive. A byproduct has been a consuming preoccupation with Chan's antitextual, antinomian, and iconoclastic rhetoric.

SUDDEN AWAKENING AND GRADUAL PRACTICE OF THE PERFECT AWAKENING SUTRA AND HEROIC PROGRESS SAMADHI SUTRA AS NORMATIVE IN EAST ASIAN CHAN

The *Chan Prolegomenon* designates the *Perfect Awakening* and the *Heroic Progress Samadhi* as expressions of one of the two types of the Buddha's sudden teaching (*dunjiao*), the suddenness of his responding to beings of superior disposition (*zhuji dun*) after his enlightenment beneath the tree. Whenever during his long preaching career the Buddha encountered a being of superior faculties he suddenly revealed the true mind (*zhenxin*). However, as the very structure and content of both sutras illustrates, the beings who received this true-mind teaching, after suddenly awakening, still had to engage in practice in order gradually to rid themselves of the habit energy (*xunxi*) inherited from past births. According to the *Chan Prolegomenon,* these two sutras are a tally fit (*fu*) with the sudden gate (*dunmen*) of Chan. The *Perfect Awakening* and *Heroic Progress Samadhi* were widely read in Chan circles during the Song and Ming dynasties, and *their orientation of sudden awakening to the nature axiom followed by gradual practice runs right through the middle of Song and Ming Chan, as well as the Chan of Xixia, Koryŏ Korea, and Ashikaga (Five Mountains) Japan.* This sutra-based picture of East Asian Chan is most certainly not Chan as presented by modern Japanese Rinzai Zen, which does not stress the sutra-based Rinzai Zen of the Five Mountains in its genealogy. Rinzai Zen today transmits an image of Zen framed by the *Record of Linji*— wherein the real teacher boldly "discards the teachings of the Buddhist canon."[162]

We can begin a cursory tracing of the evidence for the normative nature of the sudden awakening–gradual practice model of the *Perfect Awakening* and *Heroic Progress Samadhi* with the single most important Chan figure of the Song dynasty, Dahui Zonggao (1089–1163). In the *Letters of Chan Master Dahui Pujue,* Dahui strongly exhorts one of his correspondents never to forget the gradual practice that comes after sudden awakening, quoting as canonical support the *Heroic Progress Samadhi*:

This matter most definitely is not easy. You must produce a feeling of shame. Often people of sharp faculties and superior intellect *get it* [*de zhi*] without expending a lot of effort. *They subsequently produce easy-going thoughts* [*rongyi xin*] *and do not engage in* [post-awakening] *practice* [*bian bu xiu-xing*]. In any case, they are snatched away by sense objects right in front of them and cannot act as a master subject. Days and month pass, and they wander about without coming back. Their Dao power cannot win out over the power of karma, and the Evil One gets his opportunity. They are surely grabbed up by the Evil One. On the verge of death they do not have effective power [*bu de li*]. By all means remember my words of previous days. [*As the* Heroic Progress Samadhi Sutra *says:*] "*As to principle, one all-at-once awakens; riding this awakening,* [thoughts of the unreal] *are merged into annulment. But phenomena are not all-at-once removed;* [only] *by a graduated sequence are they exhausted.*"[163] Walking, standing, sitting, and lying, you must never forget this. As to all the various sayings of the ancients beyond this, you should not take them as solid, but you also should not take them as empty. *If you become practiced over a long period of time* [*jiujiu chunshu*], spontaneously and silently you will coincide with your own original mind. There is no need for separately seeking anything outstanding or unusual.[164]

Dahui's *Letters*, in other words, assumes the sudden awakening–gradual practice paradigm. And in the *Letters* the gradual-practice component is Dahui's new method of gazing-at-the-topic (the topic word or phrase of a case). In another letter Dahui speaks of this gradualistic method as analogous to the conditioning of a work animal:

> In both still places and noisy places constantly lift up [to awareness the topic] *cylinder-of-dried-shit. Days and months will pass, and the water buffalo will spontaneously become more practiced [zi chunshu].* More than anything else the thing you must not do is project another doubt onto something else. When the doubt on top of [the topic] *cylinder-of-dried-shit* is eradicated, then doubts as numerous as the sand grains of the Ganges River will simultaneously be eradicated.[165]

In Ming-dynasty Chan, the nature axiom/true mind and sudden awakening–gradual practice orientation of the *Perfect Awakening* and *Heroic Progress Samadhi* are prominent in the teachings of Hanshan Deqing (1546–1623), one of the most important Chan masters of the late Ming. Deqing in his *Old Man Hanshan's Dream Roving Collection (Hanshan laoren mengyouji)* states:

> You must not have your mind wait for awakening. Because our wonderful, perfect true mind [*miaoyuan zhenxin*], which from the outset transcends all oppositions, is congealed by thought of the unreal, and mind, sense organs, and sense objects stand in confrontation with it, for this reason, there is the arising of the depravities and the creation of karma. *The practitioner in the now merely at one moment lays down the body-mind and world* [=sudden awakening] *and only lifts up this one moment to face forward.*[166] He absolutely must not bother about whether he is awakened or not awakened. *Just moment after moment, step after step, he keeps on going*[167] [=gradual practice]. . . . The true mind from the outset is pure. Because it is stained by thought of the unreal, before long suffering and the depravities arise. The buddha body is originally one's own mind. Because it is screened by ignorance, its radiance does not manifest. Mind is buddha. One's own mind makes a buddha.[168]

Deqing, in fact, wrote commentaries on both the *Perfect Awakening* and the *Heroic Progress Samadhi.*[169] In summing up the first three chapters of the *Perfect Awakening*, he argues that, during the final phase of dharma, sudden awakening and gradual practice is the appropriate model for all beings except those of extra-superior faculties, who are few and far between:

The previous Mañjuśrī chapter [of the sutra] directly says: "One knows these [illusory] flowers in the sky [*zhi shi konghua*], and so there is no wheel-turning [in samsara] and no body-mind to undergo that birth-and-death." The Samantabhadra chapter says: "When you know illusion [*zhi huan*], you are free, without creating teaching devices. Freedom from illusion *is* awakening, and there are no gradual steps." *These [first two chapters] are the one mind of all-at-once awakening. On the spot one [attains] all-at-once realization, without wading through a course and without relying on practice.* [These two chapters] are just the one character "Knowing" [*dan yi zhizi*] and that is all. These [two chapters] are so that those of extra-superior faculties can awaken. But what about [all those beings referred to in this sutra as] "sentient beings of the end period"? *Those of extra-superior faculties are few, but those of medium and inferior faculties are numerous. If [the latter] do not practice, they will forever be in birth-and-death. If there are no correct teaching devices for practice, they will have no method by which to enter. If there are no gradual steps [wu jianci], it is* even difficult to achieve all-at-once awakening.[170]

In the case of Xixia Chan, the Tangut-language text called *The Mirror*, which has a Guifeng Chan structure of nature axiom, sudden awakening, and gradual practice, quotes both the *Heroic Progress Samadhi* and *Perfect Awakening*.[171] The Korean Sŏn master Chinul's *Excerpts* cites both the *Heroic Progress Samadhi* and *Perfect Awakening* and argues for sudden awakening–gradual practice as the best approach for the present era; his *Formula for Cultivating Mind* also quotes the *Heroic Progress Samadhi* in support of sudden awakening–gradual practice.[172] In Ashikaga Japan, beyond the examples of Shun'oku Myōha's sudden awakening upon reading a line in the *Perfect Awakening* and Kiyō Hōshū as a second coming of Zongmi, we can look to the archetypal Five Mountains Zen master Gidō Shūshin (1325–1388), a junior contemporary of Myōha, and Zekkai Chūshin (1336-1405), a student of Myōha widely considered the greatest poet of all the Five Mountains Zen poet-monks. Gidō, who propounded the identity of the sutras and Zen, in his diary mentions both the *Perfect Awakening* and the *Heroic Progress Samadhi* many times, in fact, far more times than any other sutra, and also mentions his reading the *Mind Mirror* and copying out passages. Chūshin's record mentions that he lectured on both of these sutras, and his year-by-year biography informs us that they constituted part of his daily curriculum.[173] Though Gidō lectured on the nature axiom and sudden awakening–gradual practice paradigm of these sutras frequently, this "classical Buddhist" aspect of Gidō's Zen is never emphasized. Treatments of Gidō highlight instead his literary side, the many poems he left behind and his lectures on the Song collection of Tang poetry entitled *Poems in Three Styles* (*Santai shi*). Chūshin, known almost exclusively for his poems in Chinese, has a quatrain dedicated to Zongmi in which he calls Zongmi the "the old man in the *nāga* [mythological serpent=the Buddha] samadhi."

GUIFENG CHAN: BUDDHA WORD
AND WHAT IS BEYOND WORDS

Lest we conclude that Zongmi put too much stock in the written word, the buddha word of the *Perfect Awakening Sutra* with its sudden awakening–gradual practice model, we should recall the passage in the *Chan Prolegomenon* (section 8) where he says Chan enables people to realize dark understanding, which always requires *getting the idea and forgetting the words*, an allusion to the Daoist classic *Zhuangzi*. When Zongmi was speaking in this *Zhuangzi* mode, he could sound a bit like a master of rhetorical Chan:

> The instructions of the [Chan] masters lie in liberation in the here and now. The intention [of the Chan masters] is to enable people to realize dark understanding, and dark understanding necessarily entails forgetting words [*xuantong bi zai wangyan*]. Therefore, if at once [the Chan trainee] does not retain any traces [*yanxia bu liu qi ji*], the traces are cut off at his mind ground, and principle appears at his mind source [*li xian yu xinyuan*], then faith, understanding, practice, and realization are not acted upon, and yet they are spontaneously achieved. *The sutras, rules of discipline* [vinaya], *treatises, and commentaries are not rehearsed* [*bu xi*], *and yet they are spontaneously understood in a mysterious way.*

If the Chan adept attains this dark understanding, he penetrates the voluminous sutras, detailed disciplinary codes, profound scholastic treatises of the great bodhisattvas, and endless commentaries of the Buddhist canon *without any rehearsal*. Zongmi himself did this. This is what he meant when he wrote in an autobiographical comment that, upon first encountering the *Perfect Awakening Sutra* as a young Chan monk under his master Daoyuan, the teachings of the sutra at once "became clear and bright like the heavens."[174] The principle of that sutra "appeared at his mind source."

Without missing a beat, Zongmi was capable of pivoting from this rhetoric of Chan's "sudden" dark understanding and asserting that buddha word is absolutely necessary as a *standard* or norm for Chan transmitters. His simile for this standard (*Chan Prolegomenon*, section 13) was a tool found among skilled woodworkers, the inked marking line. The craftsman on the job uses this tool to mark correctly the wood:

The sutras are like an inked marking string [*shengmo*], serving as a model by which to establish the false and the correct. The inked marking string is not the skill itself; a skillful craftsman must use the string as a standard [*wei ping*]. The sutras and treatises are not Chan; one who transmits Chan must use the sutras and treatises as a norm [*wei zhun*].

But in using the sutras and treatises as a norm or criterion, the Chan transmitter must never become enmeshed in the words on the page and fail to come to an understanding of mind. That will lead to formal knowledge of the written word of the sutras and treatises but never to awakening. Zongmi's example for this negative scenario is the Buddha's disciple Ānanda (*Chan Prolegomenon*, section 8), who memorized every word the Buddha spoke throughout his long preaching career but in the end, at the Buddha's complete nirvana, had not yet achieved awakening. If there is a problem, it is always with the reader and never with the sutras:

> If a seeker of the buddha path merely grasps at the terms in the teachings without understanding his own mind [*bu liao zixin*], then he will come to know the written words and [be able to] read the sutras, but never realize awakening. He will wear down the texts in explaining their principles, but kindle only passion, hatred, and false views. [The Buddha's disciple] Ānanda heard everything the Buddha said and held it in his memory, but grew old without ascending to the fruit of a noble one. If you stop objective supports and return to illumination, after a short time, you will realize non-arising. Then you will know that there is a reason behind each of the bequeathed teachings and each of the approaches to crossing people over [to nirvana]. You should not place the blame on the written words [*bu ying yu wenzi er ze ye*].

How then can we sum up Guifeng Chan's balancing act between Chan's dark understanding and written canonical norms? Perhaps one of the recently discovered Chan texts of the kingdom of Xixia, the Tangut-language *Record of the Hongzhou Axiom with Commentary and Clarification*,[175] is our best bet: In Guifeng Chan the Chan adept *must realize both what is in conformity with words (sutra) and what is beyond words (Chan siddhānta)*, and only then is the Great Ancient Treasure Seal (the wish-fulfilling gem of Knowing) complete. In the monocular/binocular simile of that text, awakening to what is beyond words (Bodhidharma's "no involvement with the written word") while failing to awaken to what is in conformity with words (the sutras as an authoritative norm) is like opening the right eye and closing the left. *Guifeng Chan is binocular Chan that has depth perception (stereopsis)*. By using two images of the same scene obtained from slightly different angles, Guifeng Chan can accurately triangulate the distance to the Great Ancient Treasure Seal/Knowing. Monocular Chanists and monocular sutra exegetes are at a disadvantage.

ZONGMI AND THE BODHIDHARMA SLOGAN

The slogan "mind-to-mind transmission; no involvement with the written word" is certainly not traceable to Bodhidharma. In fact, the only plausible candidate for a Bodhidharma saying in all of early Chan literature is one that appears in the Dunhuang manuscript *Bodhidharma Anthology* and in Yanshou's *Mind Mirror*: "When deluded, the person pursues dharmas; when understanding, dharmas pursue the person."[176] Heze Shenhui's *Platform Talks* (*Tanyu*) of the early eighth century says that Shenhui's master Huineng "had a mind-to-mind transmission because he separated from the written word [*yi xin chuan xin li wenzi gu*]."[177] This appears to be the prototype of the Bodhidharma slogan as we know it. The familiar form of the slogan and its attribution to Bodhidharma may have begun with Zongmi. Predictably, Zongmi held that for Bodhidharma the slogan was a matter of revealing the mind axiom, not a matter of freedom from the written word as an end in and of itself. According to Zongmi, Bodhidharma felt that Chinese practitioners of his day were not using sutra word and the exegesis of the scholastic texts to illumine their minds but were letting them stagnate on the page, and his slogan was a timely antidote for that particular disease (*Chan Prolegomenon*, section 11):

> Bodhidharma received dharma in India and personally brought it to China. He saw that most of the scholars of this land had not yet obtained dharma, that their understanding was based merely on scholastic nomenclature and numerical lists, and that their practice was concerned only with phenomenal characteristics. Because his desire was to inform them that the moon does not lie in the finger [pointing at the moon] and that dharma *is* our mind, he just [raised the slogan] "a mind-to-mind transmission; no involvement with the written word." *To reveal his [mind] axiom and eradicate grasping he had this saying. It is not that he was preaching a liberation [consisting] of freedom from the written word.*[178]

Yanshou's *Mind Mirror* quotes this last line to counter the objection of a Chan advocate of the "separate transmission outside the teachings." The critic insists that Chan, the single sword that identifies the target and fiercely advances straight towards it (similar to the Japanese *sumō* ideal of coming out straight ahead [*mae ni deru*] at the initial charge), demands the cessation of the complexities and ambiguities of canonical study:

Question: From of old the [Chan] axiom vehicle's sole decree has been that one cease [canonical] study—*the single sword that goes right in [dan dao zhi ru], the separate transmission outside the teachings.* Why would you rely on wisdom, much learning, and extensive discussion of nature and characteristics? The words [of the canonical texts] are complex and their principles hidden; the water moves, and the pearl [of mind] is obscured. Answer: [Study of canonical word] *reveals the [mind] axiom and eradicates grasping [xianzong pozhi].* The road of study, which is an expedient [*upāya*] to sweep away [traces], investigates the purport [=Chan axiom] to be understood. *Fusion penetration [of that purport/axiom] is a not a liberation [consisting] of freedom from the written word [rongtong fei li wenzi jietuo].*[179]

The poet Bai Juyi says much the same thing in a heptasyllabic regulated verse composed during Zongmi's visit to Luoyang in 833. In this verse, entitled "Presented to the Superior Man Caotang Zongmi," Bai touches upon Zongmi's dual nature as simultaneously a transmitter of all sections of the Buddhist canon and one torch in the unbroken line of torches of the Chan mind transmission. Bai observes that Chan people who take Bodhidharma's slogan "no involvement with the written word" too far into extremism are missing the middle path of Buddhism. In a more technical Buddhist formulation, they have fallen into the trap of seeing the becomings of the world in the light of the nihilistic extreme of is-not-ness, losing the middle path that is free of both is and is not. While the goal of the Mahayana is not to be fixed in anything (*bu zhu yiqie*), anti-word Chan champions of "the single sword that goes right in" are fixed in mere absence (*chang zhu xukong*):

My master's path is conjoined with the Buddha.
Moment after moment the unconditioned, dharma after dharma
    potentiality,
His mouth storehouse transmits the twelve sections of the canon.
His mind platform illumines like a hundred-thousand torches.
Utter freedom from the written word is not the middle path.
To be forever fixed in empty space [ākāśa] is the Hinayana.
Few are those who know the coursing of the bodhisattva.
The world only values "eminent monks."[180]

1 *Translation of the* Chan Letter

CHART OF THE MASTER-DISCIPLE SUCCESSION OF THE CHAN GATE THAT TRANSMITS THE MIND GROUND IN CHINA[1]

ZONGMI, THE MONK [OFFICIATING AT MEMORIAL] SERVICES AT THE INNER PRACTICE SITE[2] [WITHIN THE IMPERIAL PALACE], ANSWERS MINISTER PEI'S INQUIRY

[ALTERNATE TITLE: IMPERIAL REDACTOR PEI XIU'S INQUIRY[3]]

The layman Pei Xiu sends a letter to Zongmi asking the master for a statement on the Chan lineages. Pei requests synopses of their genealogical histories; expositions of their teachings; and a critical ranking. Zongmi answers that it is necessary, first of all, to know which Chan transmissions are collateral, that is, branch offshoots [*bang*], and which one is the central/orthodox line [*zheng*]. Each Chan house has compiled a genealogical record that illustrates only its one line of descent, without paying attention to the other lines. Once the houses are ranked, Pei will see that the direct inheritor of the mind teaching of Bodhidharma is the Heze lineage.

1. Minister Pei Xiu inquires: The Chan dharma is widely practiced. The followers of each lineage are different and slander one another. They are unwilling to

merge into identity. It is urgently necessary to distinguish their origins and his-tories [that is, genealogies] and come to know which are profound and which shallow. Even though I have devoted attention to this, I have not yet attained clarity. I dread making a mistake when composing a record [of Chan].[4] I re-spectfully hope that you will compose a brief piece on a few sheets of paper that will differentiate the various histories and in broad terms arrange in order the Northern lineage, the Southern lineage, the Heze and Hongzhou lineages within the Southern lineage, the Niutou lineage, and so forth. It would fully treat the essentials, that is, which are shallow and which profound, which all-at-once and which step-by-step, and which hit the mark and which miss it. It would serve me as a tortoise or mirror [that is, a divination guidebook] until the end of my life. Xiu bows a second time.[5]

Chan Master Zongmi answers: What Bodhidharma transmitted from the outset was a dharma of non-duality. Because of changes [introduced by later] followers, there seem to be different roads [in Chan]. If you close the locking bar on the gate to this, then all [the roads] are wrong. If you understand this, then they are all correct. Transmission records[6] compiled by our predecessors just discuss [their own] single line of direct descent. If you wish to distinguish the succession of masters in the various lineages, then you must come to know which are collateral [that is, collateral offshoots] and which is central/orthodox. Now, I will present the collateral and orthodox master-disciple [transmissions], but when I later relate the relative depth of their oral teachings,[7] you will spontane-ously see that the mind of Bodhidharma [that is, his teaching of the intrinsically pure mind or buddha-in-embryo] has flowed down to the Heze [lineage].

The Niutou lineage is a separate lineage outside the Northern-Southern dichotomy. Its founder, Huiyong (also read Huirong), was a student of voidness (sunyata) teach-ings who was sanctioned by the fifth patriarch, Hongren. This house is now in its sixth generation.

2. The Niutou lineage is a collateral offshoot from the fourth patriarch [Daoxin].[8] At its root there is Chan Master Huiyong [also read Huirong],[9] whose nature was lofty and divine wisdom [prajna] sharp. As a result of having previously studied the various sections of the [*Perfection of*] *Wisdom* [*Sutras*] for many years, he had already awakened to the realization that all dharmas from the outset are void and that deluded feelings are grasping of the unreal. Later he encountered the fourth patriarch [Daoxin], who sealed his understanding of the principle of voidness [sunyata]. Because he dwelt in the locus of voidness and yet openly showed the nature of excellence of the non-void, his awakening-understanding was clear without the need of lengthy training. The fourth patriarch told him: "This dharma from ancient times has been entrusted to only one

person [at each generation]. I have already handed it over to my disciple Hong-ren *(that is, the fifth patriarch)*. You may set yourself up separately." Subsequently, [Huiyong] set up a separate lineage on Mt. Niutou [in the southern outskirts of Jinling, that is, Nanjing] and served as its first patriarch. It has unfolded up to and including the sixth generation. *(Later, the fifth patriarchal master, Zhiwei,*[10] *had a disciple, Masu.*[11] *Su had a disciple, Daoqin, that is, Jingshan.*[12]*)* This particular lineage has no connection at all with the Southern and Northern lineages. The Southern and Northern lineages derive from disciples of the fifth patriarch [Hongren]. Before the fifth patriarch, the designations Southern and Northern did not even exist.

The Northern lineage is a collateral house coming down from the fifth patriarch. In the generation after Shenxiu, one of the major disciples of the fifth patriarch, it called itself the "Bodhidharma lineage."

3. The Northern lineage is a collateral offshoot from the fifth patriarch. It is said that there were ten people, including Shenxiu, who were equally disciples of the fifth patriarch, the Great Master [Hong]ren. Because the Great Master sanctioned each of them as worthy to be the master of one direction [that is, as a regional teacher], the people of the time said: "Ren produced ten sons."[13] *(Preceptor [Hui]neng was the direct, legitimate successor. He is not among these ten.)* Among them [Shen]xiu, Lao'an and Zhishen were the best known for their virtue, and they were all revered as masters by Emperor Gaozong [r. 649–683]. Their heirs [continue] unbroken down to the present. Among them, the transforming work of Xiu's disciple Puji was even more flourishing [than that of his master].[14] He became the "Dharma Ruler of Two Capitals" and "Master of Three Emperors." It just called [itself] the "Bodhidharma lineage" and did not use the designations "Southern" and "Northern."

The Southern lineage is the basic lineage deriving from the sixth patriarch, Huineng. It gained its name in opposition to the flourishing of Shenxiu's gradualist teaching in the North. I will now give the story of Huineng's transmission to Shenhui according to the *Patriarch Lineage Transmission Record.*

4. The Southern lineage is the basic lineage that has transmitted the robe and dharma [of Bodhidharma] for generation upon generation since the Great Master Caoqi [Hui]neng received Bodhidharma's spoken purport. Later, in opposition to Shenxiu's great dissemination of the step-by-step teaching in the North, it came to be called the "Southern lineage." Because the history of this transmission is known throughout the world, I will not present it. Later, when [Huineng] was about to die, he handed the dharma seal over to Heze and made him

his successor. I have in the past presented a version of the story of this succession.[15] However, it is very incomplete, and now that I have received your inquiry, I will expand it somewhat, in conformity with the *Patriarch Lineage Transmission Record* inherited from the past.[16] In the midst of the Preceptor Neng section presented in the *Transmission* it says: "There was a monk of Xiangyang, Shenhui. His family name was Gao, his age fourteen. *(That is, Heze. Heze is the name of the monastery [in Luoyang] where he was dwelling when he transmitted dharma.)* He came to visit Preceptor [Huineng]. The Preceptor asked: 'Good friend, you come from afar. You have suffered greatly. Did you bring the fundamental thing or not?' He answered: 'I have brought it.' [Huineng said:] 'If you have the fundamental thing, then you should truly know the master element.' He answered: 'I, Shenhui, take non-abiding as the basis. Seeing is the master element.' The Great Master [Huineng] said: 'How dare this novice make such a grandstand play!'[17] He immediately took his staff and thrashed him. Beneath the staff, Shenhui meditated: 'Through successive eons it is hard to meet a great, good friend. Now that I have managed to encounter one, how can I begrudge my life?' The Great Master was testing [Shenhui], having recognized that the conditions for [Shenhui's] deep awakening had arrived *(like Yao's coming to know Shun through testing him in various difficulties[18])*." At the end of [the Neng section of] the *Transmission*, it further says: "When Preceptor [Neng] was about to enter nirvana, he silently conferred a secret oral transmission [*miyu*] upon Shenhui. The words were: 'From the past within our transmission it has been fixed that one hands over only to one person. Within, I transmit the dharma seal and thereby seal your own mind. Without, I transmit the robe and thereby mark the axiom purport. However, I almost lost my life several times for the sake of this robe.'" *(That the robe was stolen several times by the Northern lineage appears in the first portion of this* Transmission. *At present I cannot record [these incidents].)* [The *Transmission* continues: "Huineng said:] 'The Great Master Bodhidharma made a prediction: "After six generations, a life will be like a dangling thread." You are the one.'" *(This [Bodhidharma] saying [also] appears in the* Transmission, *where it presents Bodhidharma.)* "'Therefore this robe should be kept in the mountains. Your karmic nexus will be in the North, and so you must cross over the mountain range. After twenty years you will spread this dharma and widely cross over sentient beings.'[19] When Preceptor [Neng] was on the verge of death, his disciples, Xingtao, Chaosu and Fahai[20] asked: 'To whom will the Preceptor hand over his dharma?' The Preceptor said: 'The one to whom I have entrusted it will spread it in the North after twenty years.' They asked: 'Who is it?' He answered: 'If you wish to know him, catch him with a net on Mount Dayu.'" *(The* Transmission *says: "The mountain range is 'gao/high.' Heze's family name was Gao. Therefore it cryptically indicates him.")*

The central/orthodox line of descent within the Southern lineage of Huineng is known as the Heze lineage, a name that distinguishes it from the collateral offshoot from Huineng, known as the Hongzhou lineage. Emperor Dezong in 796 sent down an imperial proclamation making Heze Shenhui the seventh patriarch.

5. The Heze lineage is nothing but the dharma of Caoqi [Huineng] with the purport of no other teaching [mixed in]. It was given this additional lineage designation in opposition to the collateral offshoot Hongzhou. The history of this transmission has already been discussed above. However, after Preceptor Neng died, the step-by-step teaching of the Northern lineage was greatly practiced *(also as presented above)*. Therefore, it constituted a hindrance to the propagation of the all-at-once gate. Because the inscription of the Caoqi tradition was effaced and [another] substituted for it, for twenty years the axiom teaching was hidden. *(The myriad hardships that the Great Master encountered are all like that in the abbreviated* Transmission *presented above. They are given at length in the original* Transmission. *On another day I will present the details.)* At the beginning of the Tianbao era [742–755], Heze [Shenhui] entered [the eastern capital of] Luo[yang] and greatly spread this [all-at-once] gate. He then revealed that the lineage of [Shen]xiu's disciples was collateral and that their dharma gate was step-by-step. Since the two lineages were being practiced side by side, and the people of the time wanted to differentiate them, the labels "Southern" and "Northern" began from this time.

[Pei Xiu] asks: Since Heze became the seventh patriarch, why was an eighth, up to and including a ninth and tenth, not set up? They were not set up later. What prevented relying on the transmission robe as a standard [of proof]? It just stopped at the sixth.

[Zongmi] answers: According to the real truth, names and numbers are cut off from the outset. If even [the number] one does not exist, how can you speak of [the numbers] six and seven? Now, [if you speak] in conformity with the worldly truth, the transmission from patriarch to disciple within the context of worldly dharmas does have a table of [transmission]. It is like a state's setting up seven temples.[21] Burial is in the seventh month.[22] Seven generations wear mourning garments. There are seven patriarchs of good luck. *(They are the same for Daoism and Buddhism.)* The sutras speak of the seven buddhas.[23] The number of circuits in holding to the buddha-recitation,[24] [the number of] people on an [ordination] platform,[25] [the number of] devices for [monastic] forms,[26] [the number of] bows to and circumambulations of a buddha,[27] and the limit to the [number of] monks invited [by a donor to a Buddhist feast], all stop at seven. If they go beyond this, it is twice seven, up to and including seven times seven, but it does not stop at six or go on to eight or nine. At present, the ritual forms transmitted to us accord with the world and produce faith. What is there to

doubt about them? Therefore, the Emperor Dezong in Zhenyuan 12 [796] ordered the crown prince to assemble all the Chan masters, set in order the axiom
purport of the Chan gate, and inquire into which transmissions are collateral
and which is central/orthodox.[28] Subsequently, an imperial proclamation came
down setting up the Great Master Heze as the seventh patriarch. The inscription [installed] within Shenlong Monastery can be seen [today]. Furthermore,
an encomium to the seventh-generation patriarchal master in the imperial
hand circulates in the world.[29]

Daoyi is the fountainhead of the Hongzhou lineage. He was originally a disciple of
the Korean Preceptor Kim (Musang/Wuxiang) of the Jingzhong lineage in Sichuan.
Daoyi was a fervent sitter who wandered far and wide practicing sitting. Upon meeting Huairang, a collateral student of the sixth patriarch and solitary practitioner,
Daoyi came to honor him. In Jiangxi Daoyi spread Huairang's teachings.

6. Initially the Hongzhou lineage is a collateral offshoot from the sixth patriarch. There was a Chan master with the family name Ma, given name Daoyi.
Previous to this, he had been a disciple of Preceptor Jin/Kim [Korean reading
Kim] of Jiannan [Sichuan].[30] *(The origin of Kim's lineage was Zhishen. [This
lineage] was neither Southern nor Northern.)* He was lofty in the extremities of
the path. He traveled performing austerities. Wherever he was, he practiced
cross-legged Chan sitting, up to and including Nanyue [that is, Mt. Heng in
Hunan], where he encountered Chan Master [Huai]rang. They had a dialogue
concerning the axiom of the teaching, and [Daoyi's] principle did not measure
up to that of Rang. It was then that [Daoyi] realized that Caoqi was the legitimate successor who had received the transmission of the robe and dharma, and
so he had a change of heart and came to honor [Rang.] [Daoyi] then dwelled in
Chuzhou [in Zhejiang] and Hongzhou [in Jiangxi]. In both the mountains and
towns he widely practiced worship and guided path followers. Later, at Kaiyuan
Monastery in Hongzhou, he widely transmitted the spoken purport of Rang.
Therefore, the people of the time referred to it as the "Hongzhou lineage."
Rang was a collateral offshoot from Caoqi. *(Caoqi had over a thousand of such
[disciples].)* He was a fellow trainee of Heze. He just practiced alone and from
the outset did not open a dharma [that is, did not teach]. Because Preceptor Ma
greatly disseminated his teaching, Ma has come to be [considered] the founder
of a particular lineage, [the Hongzhou].

The above narration of genealogies may lead to confusion, so I will provide a chart.

7. The foregoing has presented in brief the masters of the various lineages. Such
is the overall picture. However, because the collateral and the central/orthodox,
the horizontal and the vertical, are intertwined in confusion, and are thus difficult to record, I will now draw a chart. I hope that with one glance no doubts

will linger in your mind. Be careful to connect the sequences. [Zongmi's chart follows immediately in the original. See figure 1.1, pages 76–84, for the chart and its notes.—Trans.]

From here onward I will provide critiques of the oral teachings of the various houses of Chan. Since Chan aims at an inner illumination beyond the spoken and written word, I am ambivalent about writing this. However, I must do so.

8. Above I have presented the masters and disciples of the various lineages. Now I will next make distinctions concerning the levels of profundity inherent in the oral teachings[31] they have transmitted. However, the purport of the Chan gate lies in inner illumination. It is not something the writing brush can relate, nor is it susceptible to verbal exposition. Although it is beyond the verbal, I am still compelled to speak of it. Being beyond the writing brush, it is difficult for me to lower my brush [to the paper]. In this instance I must not stop but [am compelled to] write. I hope you will let it illumine your mind and not stagnate on the page.

Bodhidharma brought a mind dharma from the West, and this mind is what Bodhidharma Chan has handed down. Here "mind" means "original awakening." However, the dispositions or temperaments of some Chan adepts have not been in tune with this teaching, and, hence, they have fallen into idiosyncratic interpretations. This is the origin of the questionable theories of some Chan houses.

9. Bodhidharma came from the West and just transmitted a mind dharma. Therefore, he himself said: "My dharma is a mind-to-mind transmission; no involvement with the written word."[32] This mind is the pure original awakening[33] of all sentient beings. It is also called the buddha nature. Some call it spiritual awakening. Delusion produces all the depravities, but even these depravities are not divorced from this mind. Awakening produces limitless, excellent functions, but even these excellent functions are not divorced from this mind. Even though in terms of merits and demerits the excellent functions and the depravities are different, in awakening and in delusion, this mind remains undifferentiated. If you desire to seek the buddha path, then you must awaken to this mind. Therefore, down through the generations, the patriarchal lineage has just transmitted this. Thus, when [the master and disciple] have coincided in a mutual response, then, even though one torch [or master] has transmitted [its flame] to a hundred-thousand torches[34] [or disciples], there has been no difference between any two torches. When the dispositions [of the disciples] have not been geared to the [mind-dharma] teaching, then, even though the dharma has been proclaimed with one sound, each and every [disciple] has followed his own understanding of it.[35] This is how the questionable theories of [Chan] lineages have been passed on to later people.[36] Now, I will present each of the lineages and after that[37] judge their mistakes and correct points.

FIGURE 1.1

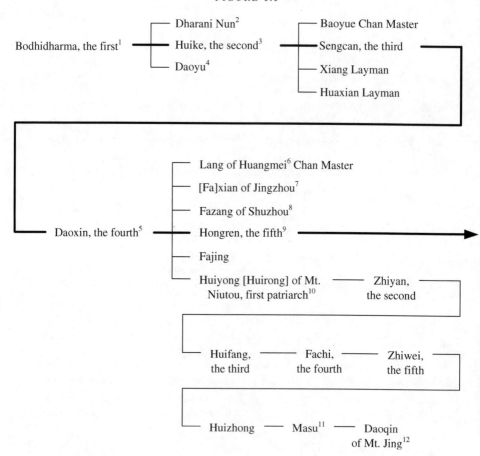

Faru of Luzhou[13]

Tong of Xiangzhou[14]

Shenxiu[15] —— Puji[16] (seventh) —— Cheng of Zhangjing Monastery,
of the Northern north of the western capital
lineage (sixth) mountains;[17] and Gan of Tongde
[Yi]fang of Yuezhou[18] Monastery of the eastern capital

Xuanshi of Guo[zhou] and Lang[zhou][19]

Huineng, the sixth[20] ——————————————————→

Fa of Yezhou[21]

[Zhi]shen of Zizhou[22] —— Chuji —— Kim —— Shi of Yizhou
of of [= Jingzhong
Chi of Jiangning[26] Zizhou[23] Yizhou[24] Shenhui][25]

Lao'an[27] ——————— Chen Chuzhang —— Baotang Li Liaofa
[= Chen Qige][28] [= Wuzhu][29]

Jue of Yangzhou[30]

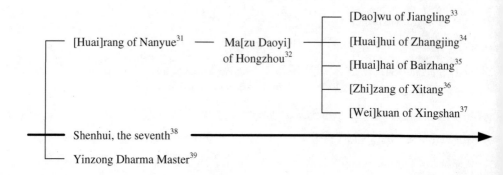

[Huai]rang of Nanyue[31] — Ma[zu Daoyi] of Hongzhou[32] —
- [Dao]wu of Jiangling[33]
- [Huai]hui of Zhangjing[34]
- [Huai]hai of Baizhang[35]
- [Zhi]zang of Xitang[36]
- [Wei]kuan of Xingshan[37]

Shenhui, the seventh[38]

Yinzong Dharma Master[39]

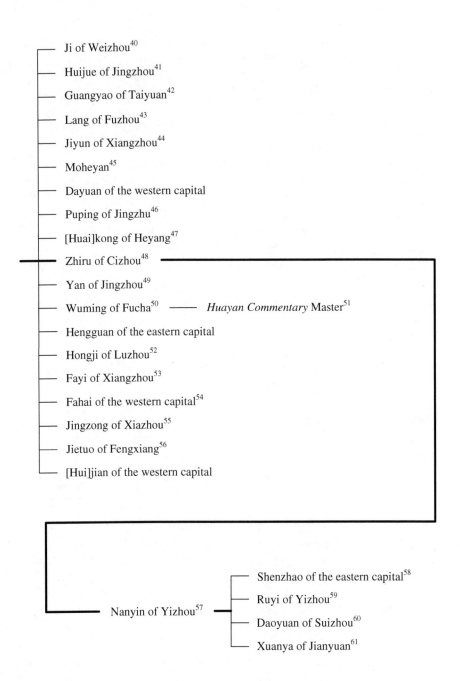

- Ji of Weizhou[40]
- Huijue of Jingzhou[41]
- Guangyao of Taiyuan[42]
- Lang of Fuzhou[43]
- Jiyun of Xiangzhou[44]
- Moheyan[45]
- Dayuan of the western capital
- Puping of Jingzhu[46]
- [Huai]kong of Heyang[47]
- Zhiru of Cizhou[48]
- Yan of Jingzhou[49]
- Wuming of Fucha[50] ——— *Huayan Commentary* Master[51]
- Hengguan of the eastern capital
- Hongji of Luzhou[52]
- Fayi of Xiangzhou[53]
- Fahai of the western capital[54]
- Jingzong of Xiazhou[55]
- Jietuo of Fengxiang[56]
- [Hui]jian of the western capital

Nanyin of Yizhou[57]
- Shenzhao of the eastern capital[58]
- Ruyi of Yizhou[59]
- Daoyuan of Suizhou[60]
- Xuanya of Jianyuan[61]

1. Two captions flank Bodhidharma: "Those written on the same level as [each of the seven] patriarchal masters [from Bodhidharma to Shenhui] are all co-students, older and younger brothers." And: "Those written on a line below the name [of a patriarch] are recognized as the collateral and central/orthodox followers of the transmission." Whereas in this edition of the chart there are seventy-five names, the *Pei Xiu shiyi wen* (Shinpuku-ji, 81–83) has only fifty-five. I provide some additional information, including alternate names and geographical references found in early Chan works. Modern geographical information mainly comes from the geographical encyclopedia Gu Zuyu, ed., *Dushi fangyu jiyao*, 6 vols. (Taipei: Hongshi chubanshe, 1981). The six names in bold font appear in the list of Hongren's ten major disciples in the *Lengjia renfa zhi/Lengjia shizi ji* (see Yanagida I, 273). I would like to thank William S. Jacobs for his kind assistance in drawing both this genealogical chart and the chart in section 54 of the *Chan Prolegomenon*.

2. After Dharani Nun there is a caption: "Gets the flesh. Cut off the depravities and obtain awakening."

3. After Huike, the second, there is a caption: "Get the marrow. From the outset there are no depravities, it is originally awakening."

4. After Daoyu there is a caption: "Gets the bone. Delusion is the depravities, and awakening is bodhi."

5. This is Daoxin of Dongshan (East Mountain) Monastery on Mt. Shuangfeng (west of Huangmei county, Qizhou, Hubei).

6. Huangmei is a mountain west of Huangmei county, Qizhou, Hubei. Three peaks in the area are associated with the East Mountain Dharma Gate of Daoxin and Hongren: Mt. Huangmei; Mt. Shuangfeng; and Mt. Fengmao. Originally the last was known as East Mountain.

7. Jingzhou is Jiangling county, Jingzhou superior prefecture, Hubei. This is the north bank of the Yangzi River in southern Hubei.

8. Shuzhou is Huaining county, Anqing superior prefecture, Anhui.

9. Hongren like his teacher Daoxin was of Dongshan (East Mountain) Monastery on Mt. Shuangfeng (west of Huangmei county, Qizhou, Hubei).

10. Here Zongmi is laying out the separate Niutou lineage. Huiyong is its first patriarch. Mt. Niutou is south of Jiangning county, Jiangning superior prefecture, Jiangsu.

11. *Chan Notes*, section 5, gives Preceptor Masu of Haolin Monastery in Runzhou (Zhenjiang county, Jiangsu) as a disciple of the fifth patriarch Zhiwei.

12. In *Chan Notes*, section 5, Daoqin of Mt. Jing (northwest of Yuhang county, Hangzhou superior prefecture, Zhejiang), is a disciple of Masu.

13. Luzhou is the eastern part of Changzhi county, Shanxi. Faru taught at Shaolin Monastery on Mt. Song near Luoyang.

14. Xiangzhou is the city Xiangyang in the northwest part of Hubei.

15. Shenxiu after his stay at East Mountain dwelled at Yuquan Monastery in Jing-zhou (Dangyang county, Hubei). Eventually Empress Wu invited him to the capital Luoyang.

16. Puji, after training under Shenxiu at Yuquan Monastery in Hubei, dwelled at Songyue Monastery on Mt. Song and at monasteries in Luoyang.

17. This was a monastery outside the Tonghua Gate of the east wall of the capital Chang'an.

18. Yuezhou is Shaoxing county, Zhejiang. During the Tang it was known as Kuaiji district.

19. Xuanshi is the fountainhead of the South Mountain Buddha-Recitation Chan Gate. Guozhou and Langzhou are Shunqing superior prefecture and Baoning superior prefecture, Sichuan. *Chan Notes*, section 6, lists Preceptor Wei of Guozhou, Yunyu of Langzhou, and Yisheng Nun of Xiangru county (Pengzhou, Sichuan) as those who spread the South Mountain Buddha-Recitation Gate Chan Lineage. South Mountain is in Nanbu county, which during the Tang belonged to Langzhou.

20. This is Huineng of Caoqi. Caoqi is Qujiang county, Shaozhou, Guangdong.

21. Yezhou is west of Zhijiang county, Hunan.

22. Zhishen was of Dechun Monastery in Zizhou, which is north of Zizhong county, Sichuan.

23. Chuji is also known as Preceptor Tang.

24. Kim was originally a Korean aristocrat of the family name Kim (=Chinese Jin), a blood relative of a Silla king. Yizhou is Chengdu superior prefecture, Sichuan (Jian-nan). He is also known as Musang (Korean reading of Wuxiang) of Jingzhong Monastery in Chengdu.

25. This is the Jingzhong lineage. Jingzhong Monastery was in Chengdu superior prefecture of Jiannan (Sichuan). *Chan Notes*, section 2, also lists as successors of Kim: Ma of Mt. Changsong (Jianzhou, Sichuan); Ji of Zhuzhou (=Suizhou, Sichuan); and Ji of Tongquan county (southeast of Shehong county, Sichuan).

26. This is Jiangning superior prefecture, Jiangsu, that is, the city Jinling/Nanjing.

27. Old An is Hui'an or Dao'an of Huishan Monastery on Mt. Song in Luozhou. Luozhou is north of Dengfeng county, Henan superior prefecture, Luozhou, Henan.

28. *Chan Notes*, section 3, adds as disciples of Lao'an: Teng Teng; Zizai; and Pozao Duo.

29. This is the Baotang lineage. Note that Zongmi considers Lao'an its fountain-head. Wuzhu was of Dali Baotang Monastery in Chengdu superior prefecture of Jiannan (Sichuan).

30. Yangzhou is Jiangdu county, Jiangsu, on the north bank of the Yangzi River.

31. Nanyue is Mt. Heng, which is northwest of Hengshan county, Hengzhou superior prefecture, Hunan.

32. This is the Hongzhou lineage. Hongzhou is Nanchang county, Jiangxi. The chart appears to make Huaihui the lineal successor of Hongzhou Ma and Daowu,

Huaihai, Zhizang, and Weikuan collateral successors, but it is possible that the arrangement of names has been jumbled in the course of textual transmission.

33. There is a note after Daowu's name: "Also received transmission from Jingshan [Daoqin of the Niutou lineage]." Jiangling is Jingzhou (Jiangling county, Jingzhou superior prefecture, Hubei; north bank of the Yangzi River in southern Hubei). This is Daowu of Tianhuang, that is, Tianhuang Monastery east of Jingzhou city.

34. Zhangjing Monastery was outside the Tonghua Gate of the east wall of the western capital Chang'an.

35. Mt. Baizhang is west of Fengxin county, Nanchang, Jiangxi.

36. Zhizang was of Qianzhou (Gan county, Jiangxi). Xitang (West Hall) refers to a new hall opened by Zhizang after Mazu Daoyi's death, presumably within the Kaiyuan Monastery in Hongzhou in Jiangxi.

37. Xingshan Monastery was in the western capital Chang'an.

38. This is Heze Shenhui. Heze Monastery was in the southwest corner of the eastern capital Luoyang.

39. After Yinzong Dharma Master there is a note: "Preceptor [Hui]neng [the sixth patriarch] heard the *Nirvana Sutra* beneath his seat." Yinzong was of Miaoxi Monastery on Mt. Kuaiji (southeast of Shaoxing county, Zhejiang).

40. Weizhou is Daming county, Hebei.

41. Jingzhou is Jiangling county, Jingzhou superior prefecture, Hubei (north bank of the Yangzi River in southern Hubei). He is also known as Xingjue of Guochang Monastery in Jingzhou and Xingjue of Jiangling.

42. Taiyuan is Yangqu county, Shanxi. He is also known as Guangyao of Baozhen Yuan in Yizhou (Linyi county, Shandong) and Guangyao of Yishui (northwest of Ju county, Shandong) and Mengshan (south of Mengyin county, Shandong).

43. Fuzhou is Fuling county, Sichuan.

44. Xiangzhou is the city Xiangyang in the northwest part of Hubei.

45. It is doubtful that this is the Chan monk known to the Tibetans as the Chinese interlocutor of the "Council of Tibet."

46. Jingzhu is presumably a monastery. Puping may be Jinping of Mt. Xiyin in the Huai'an district of Hebei.

47. Heyang is west of Meng county, Henan.

48. Zhiru was of Faguan Monastery in Cizhou (Ci county, Hebei). He is also known as Faru of Mt. Taihang (Boai county, Henan).

49. Jingzhou is Jiangling county, Jingzhou superior prefecture, Hubei. This is the north bank of the Yangzi River in southern Hubei.

50. He is also known as Wuming of the eastern capital Luoyang and Wuming of Mt. Wutai (northeast of Wutai county, Daizhou, Taiyuan superior prefecture, Shanxi).

51. This is the Huayan commentator Qingliang Chengguan, the teacher of Guifeng Zongmi in Huayan studies.

52. Luzhou is the eastern part of Changzhi county, Shanxi.

53. Xiangzhou is the city Xiangyang in the northwest part of Hubei.

54. This is not the Fahai of the *Platform Sutra*.

55. Xiazhou is Xia county, Henan.

56. Fengxiang is southeast of Qianyang county, Shaanxi.

57. Yizhou is Chengdu superior prefecture, Sichuan (Jiannan). He is also known as Weizhong of Jingnan (southern Jingzhou), Zhang of Jingnan, Preceptor Weizhong of Shengshou Monastery in Chengdu superior prefecture, and Nanyin of Yuanhe Shengshou Monastery in Chengdu superior prefecture.

58. He is known as Zhao Gong, the Chan Worthy and Great Master of Fengguo Monastery in the eastern capital.

59. Yizhou is Chengdu superior prefecture, Sichuan (Jiannan).

60. This is Zongmi's teacher. Daoyuan was at the Dayun Monastery in Suizhou on the southwest bank of the Fu River (west of Pengxi county, Sichuan). Zongmi, who sometimes refers to Daoyuan as Fushang, encountered Daoyuan in 804 and left home, receiving the master's seal in 807. Zongmi's abridged subcommentary *Yuanjuejing lueshu chao* (ZZ 1.15.2–3; CBETA *Wan Xuxangjing*, vol. 9, no. 248:863a22[2467]), which probably dates to around 823 or 824, explicitly identifies the Heze Shenhui tradition with the Shengshou Monastery, located in the southwestern part of Chengdu city, even though this monastery was technically within the Jingzhong tradition because Nanyin, installed as abbot in 807, was a disciple of Jingzhong Shenhui. Nanyin in his pre-Sichuan phase, however, had encountered either Heze Shenhui or (more likely) his disciple Zhiru and, as abbot of Shengshou Monastery, chose to identify with this tradition. Zongmi, writing in the early 820s in his abridged subcommmentary, states:

> Moreover, there are twenty-two people who transmitted dharma *in the line of the seventh patriarch*. Here I will relate *one branch aspect*. Preceptor Zhiru of Faguan Monastery in Cizhou was of the worldly family name Wang. Preceptor Weizhong of Shengshou Monastery in Chengdu superior prefecture, *who was in the Cizhou line*, was of the worldly family name Zhang and was also called Nanyin. Preceptor Daoyuan of Dayun Monastery in Suizhou, *who was in the Shengshou line*, was of the worldly family name Cheng. In Changqing 2 [822] the monks and lay people of Chengdu welcomed *his return to Sheng-shou Monastery to continue the succession of the former master [Nanyin]* and to make dharma transformation greatly flourish.

Thus, Daoyuan eventually followed in Nanyin's footsteps as abbot of Shengshou Monastery, and Zongmi, writing as Daoyuan's successor just after Daoyuan had assumed the abbotship of Shengshou, championed what we could call "Shengshou Chan," that is, the Sichuanese configuration of Heze Chan, in the metropolitan Chang'an region. There Zongmi held up the banner of Shengshou Chan against

Hongzhou Chan, which had representatives at the capital Chang'an, such as Huaihui and Weikuan (listed above under the Hongzhou lineage).

61. Jianyuan is perhaps the name of a monastery. He is also known as Ya of Donglin Monastery on Mt. Lu (northwest of Xingzi county, Nankang superior prefecture, Jiangxi).

The idea of the Northern lineage is that the innate awakening of all beings is covered by a patina of the depravities or thought of the unreal. By eliminating that patina, the awakening once again shines forth. Critique: This idea is mired in a polarity of impurity/purity.

10. The idea of the Northern lineage is: From the outset sentient beings have intrinsic awakening that is like the intrinsic brightness of a mirror. The depravities cover it, and so it cannot be seen, just as a mirror is obscured by dust. If one relies on the oral teachings[38] of the masters, one will extinguish thought of the unreal. When [such] thought is exhausted, then the mind nature awakens, and there is nothing it does not know. It is like rubbing off the dark dust [that is, the discoloration of an oxidized bronze mirror]. Once the dust has been removed, the mirror substance is bright and pure and reflects anything [placed before it]. Therefore, the Great Master Shenxiu, the ruler of this lineage, presented a verse to the fifth patriarch:

> The body is the tree of awakening.
> Mind is like a bright mirror stand.
> From time to time we must polish it.
> Do not let dust collect on it.[39]

Critique: This is just the dependently originated characteristics of impurity-purity.[40] It is a gate [that leads to] countering the [worldly] flow and turning against habit [energy inherited from past lives], but it is not aware that thought of the unreal from the outset is void and the mind nature from the outset pure. [Since this gate] has yet to penetrate to awakening, how can its practice be called true? (*In Jiannan [Sichuan] there is also the Jingzhong lineage, whose purport is much the same as this. There is also the Baotang lineage. Its understanding seems the same, but its practice is completely different. I cannot do an elaborate presentation. On another day I provided a discussion of them one by one.*)[41]

The idea of the Hongzhou lineage is that every single action is the functioning of the buddha nature. This idea finds canonical support in the *Lanka Descent Sutra*. According to Hongzhou, in practice you should not try to cut off the bad nor should you try to cultivate the good. "Just give free rein to mind" is practice.

11. The idea of the Hongzhou is: The raising of mind, the moving of thoughts, the snapping of the fingers, the shifting of the eyes, all doing and all acting, are the totalistic functioning of the buddha nature. There is no functioning separate [from the buddha nature]. Passion, hatred, stupidity, the creation of good and bad, the receiving of joy and suffering, these are in their totality the buddha nature. It is like preparing all sorts of foods and drinks out of flour. Every one of them [continues to be] flour. If one uses this [Hongzhou] idea to examine this physical body, [it becomes apparent that] the four elements [of earth, water, fire, and air], bones, flesh, throat, tongue, molars, teeth, eyes, ears, hands, and feet cannot by themselves speak, see, hear, move, or act. It is like the single moment of death, before any decomposition of the whole body. The mouth cannot speak, the eyes cannot see, the ears cannot hear, the feet cannot walk, and the hands cannot perform. Therefore, we know that the potentiality for speech and action must be the buddha nature. Moreover, if we examine the four elements and the bones and flesh carefully one by one, [it becomes apparent] that not one of them understands the depravities of passion and hatred. Therefore, we know that the depravities of passion and hatred are the buddha nature. The buddha nature is not in a substantialist sense all sorts of differentiations, and yet it has the potentiality to create all sorts of differentiations. "Is not in a substantialist sense all sorts of differentiations" means that this buddha nature is neither the noble one nor the common person, is neither cause nor effect, is neither good nor bad, has neither form nor characteristics, has neither sense organs nor [the vessel world wherein beings] dwell, up to and including, it has neither buddhas nor sentient beings. "Has the potentiality to create all sorts of differentiations" means that, because this [buddha] nature is functioning in a totalistic sense, it has the potentiality for both the noble one and the common person, for cause and sense organs, for good and bad, for manifesting forms and manifesting characteristics, for being buddhas and sentient beings, up to and including the potentiality for passion, hatred, etc. If you examine the [buddha] nature in its substantialist [aspect], then, in the end, it is invisible and cannot be proven [to exist]. This is like the eyes' not being able to see themselves, etc. If you [examine the buddha nature] in terms of its responsive functions, then all raising, moving, revolving, and acting are it [that is, the buddha nature]. There are no separate dharmas serving as the one who proves [it exists] and that which is proven. This idea accords with the *Lanka Descent Sutra* when it says: "The buddha-in-embryo [tathagatagarbha] is the cause of good and non-good, having the potentiality to create all the beings everywhere in the rebirth paths, the receptor of suffering and joy, synonymous with cause."[42] Further, [the *Lanka Descent Sutra* has a chapter entitled] "The Mind Behind the Words of the Buddhas"[43] wherein the sutra says: "A buddha land, a raising of the eyebrows, a shifting of the pupils of the eyes, a laugh, a cough, a bit of agitation, etc., are all buddha events."[44]

Once one has gained understanding awakening[45] into this principle, everything [partakes of] the spontaneity of the heavenly real. Therefore, the principle of practice should be in accordance with this, and you should not stir mind to cut off the bad, nor should you stir mind to cultivate the path. The path is mind. You should not use mind to cultivate [the path in] mind. The bad is also mind. You should not use mind to cut off [the bad in] mind. When you neither cut off [bad] nor create [karma], but just give free rein to luck and exist in freedom, then you are to be called a liberated person. There are no dharmas to get caught up in, no buddhas to become. It is like space that neither increases nor decreases. What could you possibly add to it? Why is this so? Outside the mind nature there is not even one dharma to be apprehended. Therefore, "just give free rein to mind" is practice.[46]

Critique: This and the previous [Northern] lineage are in diametric opposition. For the previous one, from dawn to dusk [in the midst of] discrimination and activity everything is unreal. For this one from dawn to dusk [in the midst of] discrimination and activity everything is real. I have received your question concerning their mutual slander and unwillingness to agree. With views so mutually opposed, how could they not slander one another? If [either of them were to] preserve the other, it would lose itself. How could they be willing to agree?

The idea of the Niutou lineage is that all dharmas are like a dream; mind and sense objects have always been void and calm. Awakening is the realization that "from the outset there is nothing to do," and practice is "forgetting feelings."

12. The idea of the Niutou lineage: All dharmas are like a dream; from the outset there is nothing to do; mind and sense objects from the outset are calmed; it is not that voidness [sunyata] has just begun. If you are deluded about this and hold [that entities] exist, then you will see such things as glory and decay, honor and meanness, etc. Because [in the sphere of] phenomenal traces there are both antagonisms and concurrences, feelings such as love and hate are engendered. When feelings are engendered, then you are bound by sufferings. Dream creation, dream perception, what is there to lose and what to be gained? The wisdom [prajna] capable of understanding this is also like a dreaming mind, up to and including, even if there were a dharma that transcended nirvana, it would still be like a dream or like illusion [maya].[47] Once you comprehend that from the outset there is nothing to do, then principle dictates that you should lose self and forget feelings. Forgetting feelings is cutting off the cause of suffering. You will then cross over all suffering and calamities [to the other shore of nirvana].[48] This [lineage] takes "forgetting feelings" as practice.[49]

Critique: The previous [Hongzhou lineage] takes "from moment to moment everything is real" as awakening and "giving free rein to mind" as practice. This [lineage] takes "from the outset there is nothing to do" as awakening and "forgetting feelings" as practice.

Northern, Hongzhou, and Niutou are drastically different in both their ideas and in their practices. I have done considerable research on each of them and have encountered a pronounced reluctance on their part to discuss such things. In fact, they are positively evasive when questioned. They are fearful of being entangled in the written word and in the acquisition of something.

13. The above three houses [show great] differences in their views: for the first [Northern] everything is unreal; for the second [Hongzhou] everything is real; and for the last [Niutou] everything is non-existent [that is, void]. If we discuss them in terms of their practices, the first subdues mind to extinguish the unreal; the second has confidence in and gives free rein to innate feelings; and the last has the mind take a rest [so that it] does not arise. *(I, Zongmi,)* have an innate disposition toward checking and verifying,[50] and so I visited [the Chan houses] one after the other and found each of their purports to be thus. If one were to question those [Chan] trainees about these encapsulations [of their views and practices,] none of them would have any part of it. If one asks about existence, they answer with voidness. [If one asks for] proof of voidness, they acknowledge existence. Or they say that both are to be negated. Or they say that nothing can be apprehended. It is the same in the matter of what they practice or do not practice, etc. In their ideas they are always fearful of being trapped in the written word, always afraid of stagnating in something to be apprehended. This is why they dismiss verbal formulations. In the case of a committed trainee, [these Chan houses] instruct him in some detail and then order him to devote much time to [the practice of] viewing-illumination. His practice and understanding are [thereby] ripened. However, beyond this each of these lineages has a plethora of teaching devices to ward off external criticism and guide followers. I cannot write about all of those. At the present I am just sifting out the purports of their ideas, raising only the headrope [of the net].

It is very difficult to describe Heze, but I must try. Its idea centers on the void and calm Knowing transmitted by Bodhidharma. This Knowing is no mindfulness. Heze practice is: "When a pulse of thought emerges, just be aware of it; being aware of it, it will slip into nothingness."

14. The Heze lineage is even more difficult to relate. It is the original idea behind Śākyamuni's coming out of the mountains [emaciated after years of the practice of austerities] and Bodhidharma's coming [to China] from afar. If you look at this [lineage] in terms of the former [lineages], this one is drastically different from the former. If you use this [lineage] to subsume the former, then the former are identical to this one. Therefore, [Heze] is difficult to talk about. I

will now force myself to talk about it. It says: All dharmas are like a dream. All the noble ones have said the same thing. Therefore, thought of the unreal from the outset is calmed, and sense objects from the outset are void. The mind of voidness and calm is a spiritual Knowing that never darkens.[51] This calm Knowing of voidness and calm is precisely the mind of voidness and calm that Bodhidharma formerly transmitted.[52] Whether you are deluded or awakened, mind from the outset is spontaneously Knowing. [Knowing] is not produced by conditions, nor does it arise in dependence on sense objects. Even during delusion the depravities are Knowing, but [Knowing] is not the depravities. Even during awakening the divine transformations are Knowing, but Knowing is not the divine transformations. Thus, the one word "Knowing" is the source of all excellence.[53] Because of delusion about this Knowing there arises the characteristic of a self. When one calculates self and mine, love and hatred spontaneously arise. According to the mind of love or hatred, one does good or bad, and, as retribution for this good or bad, is reborn in one of the six rebirth paths, life after life, birth after birth, cyclically, without end. If you find a good friend to show you [the path], you will all-at-once awaken to the Knowing of voidness and calm. Knowing is no mindfulness and no form. Who is characterized as self, and who is characterized as other? When you are aware that all characteristics are void, it is true mind, no mindfulness. If a thought arises, be aware of it; once you are aware of it, it will disappear.[54] The excellent gate of practice lies here alone. Therefore, even though you fully cultivate all the practices, just take no mindfulness as the axiom. If you just get the mind of no mindfulness, then love and hatred will spontaneously become pale and faint, compassion and wisdom [prajna] will spontaneously increase in brightness, sinful karma will spontaneously be eliminated, and you will spontaneously be zealous in meritorious practices. With respect to understanding, it is to see that all characteristics are non-characteristics. With respect to practice, it is called the practice of non-practice. When the depravities are exhausted, the rebirth process will cease; once arising and disappearing has extinguished, calmness and illumination will become manifest, and responsive functions will be without limit. It is called becoming a buddha.[55]

Knowing the two principles with respect to dharma (of the *Awakening of Faith*), the immutable and the conditioned, allows one to understand the thrust of the sutras and treatises. Knowing the two gates with respect to people, all-at-once awakening and step-by-step practice, allows one to understand the teaching devices of the former masters. These two provide us with a standard by which to evaluate the Chan lineages. I will now present this evaluation in terms of an extended simile.

15. Above, I have presented each of the lineages. Now I will make distinctions concerning levels of profundity. However, mind permeates the ten thousand

dharmas, and the flavors of the principles [of the teachings] are limitless. The teachings open outward, but the Chan lineages scoop up an abridgment. In the case of scooping up an abridgment, with respect to the dharma there are the two principles of immutable and conditioned,[56] and with respect to people there are two gates of all-at-once awakening and step-by-step practice. When the two principles are revealed, then one comes to know the purport of the sutras and treatises of the entire canon. When the two gates are opened, then one sees the tracks of all the worthies and noble ones. Bodhidharma's deep intention, in fact, lies here. The immutable and conditioned are principles outside of forms, and so, even if we discuss them directly, they are hard to confirm. Now I will utilize a simile as a scale or mirror [that is, a gauge] by which to ascertain the correct points and wrong points of the lineages. *(Dharma [explanations] accompany the simile and serve as a commentary on it. I hope that the dharma and the simile will illumine each other one by one and be easy to see. However, upon first reading, I just request that you read through the simile as a whole, and only after you have understood it from beginning to end, [read it] again with the commentary to gain an understanding of the principle.)*

The one mind is like the fabulous wishing jewel that yields its possessor all desires, and the mind's Knowing is like the jewel's brightness. The jewel can reflect any color (the conditioned principle), but it never changes (the immutable principle). When a black object is placed before it, it reflects black (ignorance). Fools will call it a black jewel. If you tell them it is actually a bright jewel, they will show resistance (the views of the Yogācāra and karmic cause-and-effect teachings). Even those who assent to the brightness of the jewel will say that it is hidden behind a veil of blackness, and they will try to wipe off the blackness (the view of the Northern lineage).

16. It is like the one jewel[57] *(the one spiritual mind)* that is just round, pure, and bright *(the Knowing of voidness and calm)*. It has no differentiations at all [in terms of] color characteristics. *(This Knowing from the outset is free of all discriminations and has neither noble one nor common person, neither good nor bad.)* Because its substance is brightness, when it is placed in front of an external object, it has the potentiality to reflect the complete variety of color characteristics. *(Because [the mind] substance is Knowing, when it is placed in front of objective supports, it has the potentiality to discriminate all rights and wrongs, likes and dislikes, up to and including managing and creating all mundane and supramundane events. This is the conditioned principle.)* The variety is inherent in the color characteristics themselves; the bright jewel never changes. *(The variety is inherent in the stupidity, wisdom, good, and bad themselves. The arising and disappearing is inherent in the sadness, joy, love, and hatred themselves. The mind with its potentiality for Knowing is never interrupted. This is the immutable principle.)* Though the jewel reflects hundreds of thousands of different colors,

let us now pick the color black, which is the opposite of the jewel's brightness, and employ it to illustrate spiritually bright Knowing-seeing and the blackness of ignorance. Though they are opposites, they are one substance. *(The dharma and simile have already been provided.)* It is like the times when the jewel reflects the color black; it is utterly black all the way through its substance. No brightness whatsoever is visible. *(When the mind of spiritual Knowing is in the common person, it is utterly delusion, stupidity, passion, and love. No Tathagata Knowing-seeing or great, perfect mirror knowledge[58] whatsoever is visible. Therefore, the sutra says: "Characteristics of body, mind, etc., are all ignorance."[59])* If an ignorant child or country bumpkin sees it, [he will say that it] is just a black jewel. *(The deluded person just sees fixed [entities]. He is a common person.)* Suppose someone tells [the child or country bumpkin]: "This is a bright jewel!" [The child or country bumpkin] will be obvious in his disbelief, resisting and scolding the previous [speaker], calling him a liar. Even if he were to explain the various principles [involved, the child or country bumpkin] would never listen or take a look. *(I, Zongmi, repeatedly encounter this type and say to them: "Your potentiality right now for Knowing-seeing is the buddha mind!" They are obvious in their disbelief and resist, saying: "These are words for leading old women and housewives astray." They are just unwilling to investigate [for themselves]. They just say: "I[60] am of dull faculties and cannot really absorb [such matters]." These are like the views of people who attach to characteristics in the dharma-characteristics and man-and-god teachings of the Mahayana and Hinayana.)* Even those with a willingness to believe in the jewel's brightness, taking the blackness that they see as an objective support, will assert that [the jewel] is wrapped in obscurity by the black color. They will try to wipe and wash to rid it of the blackness. Only when they have succeeded in making the brightness reemerge will they begin to say that they personally see the bright jewel. *(The view of the Northern lineage is like this.)*

Some people point out that the blackness *is* the jewel, that you will never see the inherent brightness of the jewel. Whatever color they see reflected on the jewel to them is the bright jewel. But upon seeing a jewel not facing any colors, they resist recognizing its brightness, fearing being limited to the singularity of the brightness. In other words, they are biased toward the principle of the conditioned. This is like the Hongzhou view.

17. There is also a type of person who points out: "This blackness *is* the bright jewel. The substance of the bright jewel is never to be seen. If you desire to come to know it, then [you must realize that] blackness *is* the bright jewel, up to and including, all the various [colors such as] blue and yellow *are* [the bright jewel]." The stupid ones are really made to believe in these words, to focus exclusively on the blackness characteristic, and to recognize the various [color]

characteristics as the bright jewel [itself]. When, on a different occasion, they see a black soapberry bead [used for making rosaries] or the vermilion instrument [used for chanting at dharma assemblies][61] or a blue jewel or a green jewel, up to and including a red jewel or a bead of amber or quartz, etc., in all cases they say: "This *is* the jewel!" When, on another occasion, they see a jewel that is not facing any colors whatsoever and that just possesses the characteristic of bright- ness and purity, they resist and do not recognize it. This is because they see none of the colors by which to recognize it. This is because they [fall into] doubt through fear of being limited to the one bright-jewel characteristic. *(The view of the Hongzhou is like this. "The stupid ones" refers to that lineage's junior trainees. "When, on a different occasion, they see a black soapberry," etc. refers to the fact that, when the mind passes through the world and discriminates sense objects, it experiences such thoughts as passion, hatred, love, and pride. "Amber or quartz" refers to thoughts such as friendliness, goodness, humility and rever- ence. "Not facing any colors" refers to having no [objective supports] to think on. "Just possesses brightness and purity" refers to clear, spontaneous Knowing, that is, no mindfulness. "Doubt [through fear of] being limited" refers to their bias to- ward recognizing only this [principle of the conditioned].)*

Some people say that the bright jewel is utterly void (*śūnya*) and no color can be ap- prehended. They are unaware that the site of the void colors is none other than the non-void jewel. This is like the Niutou view.

18. There is also a type of person who, when he hears it said [in the *Perfection of Wisdom Sutras*] that the various colors on the jewel are all unreal and com- pletely devoid of substance throughout, deduces that this one bright jewel is nothing but this voidness and says: "Nothing at all can be apprehended. That is truly to be a person of comprehension. If one recognizes the existence of [even] one dharma, it is [evidence of] an incomplete understanding." [Those of this view] are not awakened to the realization that the locus wherein the color char- acteristics are all void *is* precisely the non-void[62] jewel. *(The view of the Niutou is like this. "When he hears it said that it is void," etc., refers to the various sections of the [Perfection of] Wisdom [Sutras] that speak of voidness. "Deduces that this one jewel," etc., refers to the deduction that original awakening is also devoid of [self-]nature and has nothing to be recognized. "If one recognizes the existence of [even one dharma]," etc., refers to the fact that, when they hear it said [in other sutras] that the locus wherein all dharmas are void and calmed is, in the end, the potentiality for Knowing and is the true mind of original awakening, they resist, saying: "We do not understand and know nothing of the non-voidness of the mind substance." As to "non-voidness," the* Nirvana Sutra *says: "Expressions such as the jug is void mean that there is nothing in the jug [that is, no contents], and we call that the voidness of the jug. They do not mean that there is no jug."[63] "Inside the*

bright true mind"[64] means that inside mind there are no thoughts of discrimination such as passion and hatred, etc., and we call that the voidness of mind. It does not mean that there is no mind. "No mind"[65] is just discarding depravities inside mind. Therefore, we know that the Niutou just gets rid of what it is not but has yet to reveal what it is. From this point downward is all a metaphor for the idea of the Heze.)

The Heze idea is that the dazzling brightness (Knowing) is the jewel. Hongzhou and Niutou fail to reveal Knowing. As the parade of colors is reflected on the surface of the jewel, Heze sees only its brightness. In contrast, Hongzhou, Northern, and Niutou have yet to see the jewel.

19. What about saying directly: "Just the perfect brightness of jade-like purity is the jewel substance." *(Just the Knowing of voidness and calm. If one just speaks of voidness and calm without revealing Knowing, how does it differ from space? It is also like a round piece of porcelain of sparkling purity. Though perfectly pure, it lacks intrinsic brightness. How could you call that a jewel? Would it have the potentiality to give off reflections? Hongzhou and Niutou just say there is not one thing, but they do not reveal spiritual Knowing. This is like this [piece of porcelain].)* The black color, up to and including all the other colors, such as blue and yellow, etc., is unreal. *(Discrimination of good and bad, movement, and action are like the production of mind and movement of thoughts that Hongzhou recognizes [as the real]. They are the totality of characteristics, and these characteristics are all unreal. Therefore, the sutra says: "Whatever possesses characteristics is unreal."[66] It should be known that that lineage [Hongzhou] recognizes the unreal as the true nature.)* When one truly sees the color black, the black from the outset is not black. It is just the brightness. The blue from the outset is not blue. It is just the brightness, up to and including: all the [other colors], such as red, white, yellow, etc., are like this. They are just the brightness. If, at the locus of the color characteristics, one after the other you just see the perfect brightness of jade-like sparkling purity, then you are not confused about the jewel. *(Everything is void. Just mind is immutable. Even during delusion there is Knowing. Knowing from the outset is non-delusion. Even the arising of thoughts is Knowing, [but] Knowing from the outset is no mindfulness, up to and including: [at the locus wherein] pity, joy, happiness, hatred, love, and dislike [appear] one after the other they are all Knowing. Knowing from the outset is voidness and calm. It is void and calm and yet Knowing. Then you are not confused at all about the mind nature. The above all differs drastically from [the ideas of] the other lineages. Therefore, as I encapsulated it before [in section 14]: "If you look at this [Heze lineage] in terms of the former [lineages,] this one is drastically different from the former ones.")* If you are just free of confusion about the jewel, then black is non-black; black is the bright jewel, and so on with all colors. This is freedom

[from the two extremes of] existence and non-existence. The brightness and the blackness are in fusion. How could there be any further obstacle? *(This is identical to [the ideas of] those two lineages. "Black is non-blackness" is identical to [the idea of] the Niutou. The Niutou just says: "Everything is nonexistent [that is, void]." From "black is the [bright] jewel" downward is identical to [the idea of] the Hongzhou. Hongzhou says: "Everything is the buddha nature; the common person, the noble one, the good, and the bad are all unobstructed." Therefore, I just encapsulated it before [in section 14] as: "If you use this [lineage] to subsume the former, then the former are identical to this one." From here downward is the idea [behind] the metaphor. I will again take the basic lineage, the Heze, to connect the three lineages.)* If you do not[67] recognize that the bright jewel *is* the substance with the potentiality for reflecting [all the colors] and that it is eternally unchanging *(the Heze)*, then you will just say: "Black *is* the jewel" *(the Hongzhou lineage)*. Or you will try to get rid of the black and seek out the jewel *(the Northern lineage)*. Or you will say that the brightness and the blackness are both nonexistent [that is, void] *(the Niutou lineage)*. None [of these three lineages] has yet seen the jewel. *(They are all linked.)*

Pei Xiu asks why there is a need to speak of Knowing beyond the principles of the teachings found in the sutras and in Chan usage. Zongmi replies that these principles are merely negative expressions that do not reveal the mind substance, Knowing. Heze's teaching of the Knowing of voidness and calm subsumes all these negative expressions. By focusing exclusively on voidness and calm, etc., Niutou and Hongzhou miss the awakening aspect.

20. [Pei Xiu] asks: According to the Mahayana sutras and the Chan gates of all the lineages from the past to the present, up to and including what Heze says, the nature of principle is always the same. [They all] say: "There is neither arising nor disappearing; there is neither the conditioned nor characteristics; there is neither the noble one nor the common person; there is neither right nor wrong; [it is] not to be proven; [it is] not to be spoken of." If in the present we just rely on this, it will be correct. What need is there to speak of spiritual Knowing?

[Zongmi] answers: These are but negative expressions, which have yet openly to show the mind substance. If it is not pointed out that right now the complete and constant Knowing that never darkens *is* one's own mind, then what are we speaking of as "neither the conditioned nor characteristics," etc.? Thus, we know that the teachings just say that this Knowing neither arises nor disappears, etc. Therefore, the Heze, at the locus of voidness and the absence of characteristics, points out Knowing-seeing. This enables people to attain recognition, that is, awaken to their own mind, passing over the rebirth process and transcending the world, eternally without interruption, up to and including

becoming buddhas. Heze also takes care of various expressions such as "unconditioned," "non-abiding," up to and including "inexpressible," etc., just by speaking of "the Knowing of voidness and calm." Everything is subsumed. "Voidness" means to empty out all characteristics; it is still a negative term. Just
"calm" is the immutable principle of the real nature; it is not the same as voidness and nonexistence. Knowing is the principle of revealing the thing-in-
itself;[68] it is not the same as discrimination. Just this is the original substance of
the true mind. Therefore, from the first time one produces the thought [of
awakening] up to and including becoming a buddha [it is] just calm, just Knowing, immutable and uninterrupted. It is just that according to the stage [of prac-
tice] the terminology differs somewhat. That is to say, at the time of awakening
it is called the wisdom [prajna][69] of principle *(Principle is calm; wisdom is Knowing)*. At the time of production of the thought [of awakening] and practice it is
called stopping and viewing. *(Stopping is to bring to rest objective supports and
to coincide with calm; viewing is to illuminate nature and characteristics and to
mysteriously [fuse] with Knowing.)* As you perform and bring practice to completion, it is called concentration and wisdom. *(Because of stopping objective supports, the mind [enters] concentration; concentration is a calm immutability. Because of viewing-illuminating, wisdom is produced; wisdom is Knowing that is
non-discriminative.)* According to the time when the depravities are all exhausted,
meritorious practices are filled up, and one becomes a buddha, it is called bodhi or nirvana *("Bodhi" is a Sanskrit word. Its translation is "awakening" [jue]. It
is Knowing. "Nirvana" is a Sanskrit word. Its translation is "calmed" [jimie]. It is
calmness.)* You should know that, from the first time you produce the thought
[of awakening] up to and including the ultimate, [it is] just calm, just Knowing.
If the two lineages [of Niutou and Hongzhou] just speak of voidness and calm,
the unconditioned, etc., then they are lacking in the awakening aspect.

Pei Xiu counters that Hongzhou does, in fact, uses terms such as "spiritual awakening" and "mirror illumination" that seem to be indistinguishable from Knowing.
Zongmi answers that these Hongzhou terms do not apply to deluded beings, neutral
states of mind, etc., while Knowing pervades all sentient beings in all states of mind.
Hongzhou and Niutou hold up "sweeping away traces" as the pinnacle. In so doing
they have gotten the intention behind the negative teaching, true voidness, but are
still missing the intention behind the teaching that reveals, excellent existence. In
other words, they have gotten the substance but missed the functioning. Pei counters
that the Hongzhou teaching that the potentiality for action *is* the buddha nature, in
fact, does reveal the mind nature, and, hence, Hongzhou is not deficient with respect to
the functioning aspect. Zongmi replies that the true mind has two types of functioning,
intrinsic and conditioned. The Hongzhou teaching is just the responsive functioning
and misses the intrinsic. Also, revealing is of two types, by inference and by direct

perception. Hongzhou teaches that the potentiality for action allows us to infer the existence of the buddha nature, which cannot be directly perceived. Heze, on the other hand, reveals the mind substance by teaching that "Knowing *is* mind." This is the revealing by direct perception omitted by Hongzhou.

21. [Pei Xiu] asks: Hongzhou also speaks of "spiritual awakening"[70] and "mirror illumination," etc. How are these different from Knowing?

[Zongmi] answers: If one relies on many principles to reveal the one substance, then the ten thousand dharmas are one mind. How [can the Hongzhou lineage say that it is] just "spiritual awakening" or "mirror illumination," etc.? Now, in terms of pointing to the substance in itself,[71] in the stupid and the wise, in the good and the bad, up to and including in wild and domestic animals, the mind nature is always so. It is complete and constant Knowing that is different from trees and stones. These terms, "awakening," "wisdom," etc., do not have a universal application. That is to say, a deluded person is not awakened; a stupid one lacks wisdom. And when mind is neutral [that is, indifferent, neither good nor bad, and thus having no karmic effect], it is not called "mirror illumination," etc. How could ["mirror illumination"] be the same as the mind substance in spontaneous and constant Knowing, [which includes good, bad, and neutral]? Therefore, the *Huayan Commentary* Master [that is, Chengguan in his *Dharma Gate of the Mind Essence in*] *Answer to [Emperor] Shunzong* says: "The non-abiding mind substance is a spiritual Knowing that never darkens."[72] He also says: "Give free rein to luck in the Knowing of calm." He also says: "Dual illumination in the Knowing of calm." The *Huayan Sutra* also makes a distinction between Knowing and wisdom [prajna].[73] Moreover, even though Hongzhou speaks of "spiritual awakening," it just designates it as something possessed by sentient beings. Expressions such as "all have the buddha nature" are not a pointing out that hits the bull's-eye. In its pointing out [Hongzhou] just says: "The potentiality for speech [and action is the buddha nature]." If one questions them in detail, they say: "Everything is a provisional name; there are no really existent dharmas." Furthermore, speaking of the teachings of the buddhas in general, there are the two gates of negating and revealing. If we infer the real meanings [behind] these [two gates], there is true voidness and excellent existence. If we examine[74] original mind, [we see that it] is endowed with substance and function. At present the Hongzhou and Niutou take "sweeping away traces" as the ultimate. They have just apprehended the intention behind the negative teaching, the meaning of true voidness. This just completes the substance and misses the intention behind the teaching that reveals, the meaning of excellent existence. It omits the functioning.

[Pei Xiu] asks: Hungzhou takes [the idea that] "the potentiality for speech and action, etc., [is the buddha nature]" to reveal the mind nature. This corresponds to the teaching that reveals and is, in fact, the functioning. What is [Hongzhou] lacking?

[Zongmi] answers: The true mind's original substance has two types of functioning. The first is the intrinsic, original functioning; the second is the conditioned, responsive functioning. It is like a bronze mirror. The bronze material is the intrinsic substance. The brightness of the bronze is the intrinsic functioning. The reflections that the brightness gives off are the conditioned functioning. The reflections appear [when the mirror] is face to face with objective supports. They appear in a thousand varieties, but the brightness is an intrinsically constant brightness. The brightness is just one flavor. In terms of the metaphor, mind's constant calm is the intrinsic substance, and mind's constant Knowing is the intrinsic functioning. This [Hongzhou's] "potentiality for speech, potentiality for discrimination, action, etc.," is the conditioned, responsive functioning. At present Hongzhou points to the potentiality for speech, etc., but this is just the conditioned functioning, and [Hongzhou] is lacking in the intrinsic functioning. Furthermore, in the teaching that reveals there is revealing by inference and revealing by direct perception.[75] Hongzhou says: "The mind substance is not to be pointed to. It is just by means of the potentiality for speech, etc., that we can verify it and come to know of the existence of the buddha nature." This is revealing by inference. Heze directly says: "The mind substance is the potentiality for Knowing. Knowing *is* mind." Revealing mind in terms of Knowing is revealing by direct perception. Hongzhou is lacking in this.

All-at-once awakening is like an eminent official who dreams he is incarcerated in a prison. Someone comes along and wakes him up, and he suddenly sees that he has always been at home. Hongzhou's teaching that all action is the functioning of the buddha nature leads Hongzhou to refrain from any picking and choosing. Thus, they fail to distinguish between the functioning of delusion and awakening, between the functioning of perverted views and correct views. But we must distinguish the topsy-turvy from the correct. Even after all-at-once-understanding awakening, the habit energy from innumerable past lives is impossible to eliminate all at once, and so one must engage in a step-by-step practice grounded in intellectual-understanding awakening. Pei asks if engaging in such practice after awakening is not like the dreamer's continuing to try to escape from prison after waking from the dream. Zongmi replies that the dream simile applies only to all-at-once awakening and not to step-by-step practice. A simile for the latter is water (true mind) stirred by a wind (ignorance) to produce waves (depravities). The wetness of the water (Knowing) is immutable. The waves stop step-by-step. Hongzhou sees that wetness is undifferentiated but fails to realize that supporting a boat and capsizing it are two very different things, and, consequently, though close to all-at-once awakening, it is not quite there. Hongzhou is utterly deficient in step-by-step practice. Niutou has a partial understanding of all-at-once awakening and shows no deficiency concerning step-by-step practice. Northern is just step-by-step practice with no all-at-once awakening. Heze always champions putting all-at-once awakening at the beginning, followed by step-by-step practice. Each Chan lineage is directed to one type of disposition. Everything the Chan masters have said is the teaching of the buddhas.

22. Above I have related the two principles of immutable and conditioned. Now I will next clarify the two gates of all-at-once awakening and step-by-step practice. Thus, in the principle of thusness there are no buddhas or sentient beings. How much less could there be a transmission from master to disciple! But there has been a transmission from patriarch to patriarch since the Buddha, and we know that [this patriarchal transmission] accords with the gate whereby people practice, realize, and enter [awakening.] Speaking in terms of people, there is delusion and awakening, beginning [of practice] and end [of practice], and common person and noble one. Awakening from delusion is all-at-once. Turning over the common person and making him into a noble one is all-at-once awakening. All-at-once awakening means [the following]. Deluded from without beginning, you have recognized the four elements [of earth, water, fire, and air] as a body, thought of the unreal as mind, and the two together you have recognized as a self. If you encounter a good friend who explains in the manner above [the two principles of] immutable-conditioned, nature-characteristics and substance-function, you will suddenly awaken to the realization that spiritual Knowing-seeing is your own true mind; that mind from the outset is void and calm, limitless, and without characteristics; that it is the dharma body; that body and mind are non-dual; that it is the true self;[76] and that it is not the slightest bit different from all the buddhas. Therefore, we say: "All-at-once." *(From here down I will provide a simile, and then comment following the [simile] text. I will add the dharma to it [that is, the text of the simile].)* It is like a great official *(the buddha nature)* who dreams *(delusion)* that he is in prison *(the three realms [of desire, form, and non-form])* and that his body *(the root [storehouse] consciousness)* has been put into a wooden collar *(passion and love)*. He [undergoes] various sufferings *(the totality of karmic retribution)* and [devises] a hundred escape plans *(asks about the dharma and is diligent in practice)*. He encounters someone who summons him to arise *(a good friend)*, and suddenly he awakens *(by listening to the dharma his mind opens)*. He then sees that his own body *(the dharma body or true self)* has always been in his own home. *(The* Vimalakīrti Sutra *says: "The house of ultimate voidness and calm.")*[77] He is at ease and joyful *(the calmed is joyful)*,[78] rich and honored *(from the outset on the substance there are merits [as numberless as the grains of sand in] the Ganges)*. He is no different at all from the officials of the court. *(He is identical to the true nature of all the buddhas. The dharma added point by point like commentary should be understood.)*

If we rely on this dharma simile, point by point there will be clarity. It will be sufficient [to enable one] to discern that, even though the original source of body-mind in both the dream and wakeful states is one, in terms of its characteristics and functioning, an inverted [way of looking at things] and a correct [way of looking at things] are widely separated. One should not, having awakened, again do the things one did in the dream. By means of a simile [I will show that], even though the mind source is one, delusion and awakening are widely separated. To be a prime minister when dreaming *(to practice and attain the rank of the Great Brahma, king of the gods,*[79] *etc., when in a state of delusion)* is not as good as serving as a [mere prison] functionary when awake *(after awakening for the first time to enter the ten ranks of the [bodhisattva] faith).*[80] To obtain the seven treasures[81] in a dream *(to cultivate immeasurable merits when deluded)* is not as good as one hundred cash when awake *(to uphold the five precepts and ten good actions*[82] *when awake).* In all these cases one is unreal and the other real, and, therefore, they should not be considered similar *(All the teachings say: "To make a donation of three-thousand of the seven treasures is not as good as hearing one line of a verse."*[83] *This is the idea here).*[84] At the present time Hongzhou's just saying that every type of passion, hatred, precept [holding], or concentration [samadhi] is the functioning of the buddha nature fails to distinguish between the functioning of delusion and awakening, perverted [view] and correct [view]. Their idea lies in [the assumption that] the mind nature of thusness [tathata] is free of stupidity, and, therefore, they are not selective. [They hold that], in terms of the true nature, from the outset there is no verbalization, and so who [could possibly] say "different" or "same"? At present there has been a transmission from master to disciple, and thus we must distinguish the inverted from the correct. Next I will clarify step-by-step practice. Even though you all-at-once awaken to the realization that the true mind of the dharma body is identical to the buddhas, nevertheless, for many eons you have [engaged in] unreal grasping of the four elements as a self, and the habit energy has become your nature. Because finally this is difficult to eliminate all-at-once, you must [engage in] a step-by-step practice grounded in awakening. You destroy this [habit energy] and further destroy it, up to and including there being nothing left to destroy.[85] This is called becoming a buddha. It is not that outside of this mind there is a buddha you should become. Thus, even though you [engage in] step-by-step practice, because of the earlier awakening to the realization that the depravities from the outset are void and the mind nature from the outset pure, in the cutting off of bad there is no cutting off, in the cultivation of good no cultivating. This is true cultivating and cutting off.

[Pei Xiu] asks: As for one who [engages in] further practice after having awakened, in terms of the previous dream simile, is he not comparable to one who still tries to escape from the prison and throw off his wooden collar after having awakened [from the dream]?

[Zongmi] answers: The previous simile [applies] just to the principle of all-at-once awakening, not to the principle of step-by-step practice. Truly, in the dharma there are immeasurable principles. How could there be just one principle? Therefore, though the *Nirvana Sutra* just speaks of the buddha nature, each of its hundreds of similes has a referent. They should not be randomly interchanged. Now I will clarify a simile for step-by-step practice. It is like water that is being stirred by a wind. It becomes numerous waves, and there is the danger of bobbing up and down. If perhaps there is cold weather, it will coagulate into ice and obstruct the functioning of pouring and washing. Thus, the wetness of the water, even though its movement has quieted down and its flow has frozen, has [undergone] no change whatsoever. "Water" is a metaphor for the true mind. "Wind" refers to ignorance. "Waves" refers to the depravities. "Bobbing up and down" refers to [being reborn in] the six rebirth paths of wheel turning. "Cold weather" refers to the habit energies of ignorance, passion, and love. "Coagulate into ice" refers to rigidly grasping the four elements [until] they obstruct each other. In the case of "obstruct pouring and washing," "pouring" is a metaphor for the raining down of the great dharma rain, which nourishes all living things and makes the shoots of the path grow; "washing" is a metaphor for cleaning up the depravities. When one is deluded, neither of these can [be accomplished,] and, therefore, we say "obstruct." "Thus, the wetness of the water, even though its movement has quieted down and its flow has [undergone] no change whatsoever" is a metaphor [for the fact that], even when one is passionate and angry, there is Knowing. Even when one [feels] friendliness and [strives to] save [sentient beings,] there is Knowing. [Even during] sorrow, joy, pity, happiness, and all sorts of changes and movements there is never an absence of Knowing. Therefore, we say "immutable." If, in the present moment, you all-at-once awaken to original mind,[86] constant Knowing is like the unchanging wetness. Once the mind is without delusion and is not in ignorance, it is like the wind's all-at-once stopping. After awakening, objective supports spontaneously cease step-by-step. This is like the waves' coming to a halt step-by-step. By perfuming body and mind with concentration and wisdom step-by-step you come to exist in freedom, up to and including divine transformations[87] and no obstructions. You will bring benefit to all living things. This is like the spring sunshine's melting the ice. It pours down as a wash, enriching the ten thousand things. Hongzhou constantly says: "Passion, hatred, friendliness, and good are all the buddha nature. What distinctions exist?" This is like a person who just discerns that wetness from beginning to end is undifferentiated but does not realize that the merit of supporting a boat and the fault of overturning it are widely divergent. Therefore, even though that lineage is near to the gate of all-at-once awakening, it has yet to hit the bull's-eye. In the matter of the gate of step-by-step practice [Hongzhou] makes the mistake of completely deviating from it. Because Niutou comprehends voidness it half-understands the gate of all-at-once awakening. Because it "forgets feelings" it has no deficiency with respect to the gate of step-by-step practice. The Northern lineage is just step-by-step practice and is completely lacking in all-at-once awakening. Because it lacks all-at-once awakening even its practice is not true. For Heze, one must first all-at-once awaken and then [engage in] a practice grounded in that awakening. Therefore, the sutra says: "If all the bodhisattvas awaken to pure, perfect bodhi *(awakening)*, take a pure, awakened mind, take quietude as their practice, and rely on settling all thoughts, they will become aware of the movement of the depravities within consciousness, etc."[88] *(practice)*. This idea of all-at-once awakening and step-by-step practice is provided for in the whole canon of the Mahayana, and the *Awakening of Faith, Perfect Awakening,* and *Huayan* are its axiom. If each [Chan lineage], for the sake of one type of [trainee] disposition, [possesses] good skill in teaching devices, opens the door widely, attracts each and every [trainee] in, perfumes his habit-energy seeds birth after birth, and serves as a superior condition life after life, then whatever the [Chan] lineages say is always the teachings of the buddhas. All the sutras and all the treatises provide the texts [of these teachings].[89]

2 *Translation of the* Chan Prolegomenon

PROLEGOMENON TO THE COLLECTION OF EXPRESSIONS OF THE CHAN SOURCE FIRST ROLL

ALSO ENTITLED: COLLECTION OF EXPRESSIONS OF THE PRINCIPLE AND PRACTICE OF DHYANA[1]

By the Monk Zongmi of Caotang Monastery on Mt. Zhongnan[2]

Explanation of the title: The *Chan Canon* contains transcriptions of the sayings of the Chan houses on the principles of Chan.

1. The *Collection of Expressions of the Chan Source* transcribes the written words and lines of verse[3] that have been related by the [Chan] houses and that express the principles of the Chan-gate source. Collected into one basket, they will be a legacy for later generations. Therefore, I have used this terminology for the chief title. "Dhyana" is a Sanskrit term. The full form of the Chinese

transliteration is *"channa."* The Chinese translation is *"siweixiu* [thinking prac-
tice]" or *"jinglü* [quieting thoughts]." The two translations refer to both concentration [samadhi] and wisdom [prajna]. The source is the original awakening or
true nature of all sentient beings. It is also called the buddha nature or mind
ground. To awaken to it is called wisdom; to practice it is called concentration.
Concentration and wisdom together are referred to as "Chan." Because this
nature is the original source of Chan, I have also used the phrase "Chan
Source." I have used the phrase "Principle and Practice of Dhyana" [in my sub-
title]. This original source is the principle of Chan, and forgetting feelings and
coinciding with this is Chan practice. That is the reason for the phrase "Principle and Practice." However, the writings of the various houses herein collected speak mostly of the principle of Chan, while saying little of the practice
of Chan. This is the reason I have used the phrase "Chan Source" in my title.

Some mistaken Chan adepts unfortunately hold to the view that the true nature *is*
Chan, but the true nature is more than that. It is the source of all dharmas.

2. Today, there are those who just declare that the true nature *is* Chan.[4] They do
not comprehend the purport of principle and practice and misunderstand both
the Chinese and Sanskrit terms. It is not that a Chan entity exists separately
from the true nature. It is merely that, when a sentient being loses the real and
embraces sense objects, we say that it is a state of distraction, and, when there is
rejection of sense objects and fusion with the real, we say it is a state of dhyana
and concentration. If I were to speak directly of the original nature, [I would
have to say that] it is neither real nor unreal, that neither rejecting nor fusing
exists, that neither concentration nor distraction exists. [Were I to do this,] who
would then speak about Chan? This true nature is not merely the source of the
Chan gate, but the source of all dharmas as well, and thus it is called the
dharma nature. Because it is also the source of delusion and awakening in
sentient beings, we call it the buddha-in-embryo [tathagatagarbha] or storehouse consciousness *(from the* Lanka Descent Sutra). Because it is the source
of all the attributes of the buddhas, it is also called the buddha nature *(the*
Nirvana Sutra *and others)*. It is the source of all the practices of the bodhisattvas, and, for this reason, it is called the mind ground. *(In the "Chapter on the
Dharma Gate of the Mind Ground" of the* Brahma Net Sutra *it says: "This is
the original source of all the buddhas, the basis of the bodhisattva path, the basis of the great assembly of all the buddha sons.")*[5] The myriad practices are no
more that the six perfections [of giving, morality, forbearance, striving, dhyana,
and prajna], while the Chan gate is merely one of these six, namely, the fifth.
How can these people declare that the true nature is just the practice of
dhyana?

Dhyana is a necessity for all types of Buddhist practitioners.

3. Thus, the one practice of dhyana is most divine and excellent. It has the potential to produce from the nature wisdom that is without the outflows [of desire, existence, ignorance, and views]. All the excellent activities, practices, and attributes of a buddha, even to the superknowledges [such as the divine organ of sight, divine organ of hearing, etc.] and rays of light, derive from concentration. For this reason, those training in the three vehicles [of the hearer, private buddha, and bodhisattva] who wish to seek the path of the noble ones must practice dhyana. Apart from dhyana there is no gate, in the absence of dhyana no road. Even those who simply seek rebirth into a pure land through buddha-recitation cultivate the sixteen viewing dhyanas, the buddha-recitation concentration [samadhi], and the engendered concentration.[6]

There are five grades of dhyana, with Bodhidharma dhyana as the highest.

4. The true nature is neither stained nor pure, neither common nor noble. Within dhyana, however, there are different grades, ranging from the shallow to the deep. To hold deviant views and practice because one joyfully anticipates rebirth in a heaven and is weary of the present world is outsider dhyana.[7] Correctly to have confidence in karmic cause and effect and likewise practice because one joyfully anticipates rebirth into a heaven and is weary of the present world is common-person dhyana. To awaken to the incomplete truth of voidness of self and then practice is inferior-vehicle dhyana. To awaken to the true principle of the dual voidness of self and dharmas and then to practice is great-vehicle dhyana. (*All four of the above types show such distinctions as the four [dhyanas of the realm of] form and the four [concentrations of the] formless [realm].*) If one's practice is based on having all-at-once awakened to the realization that one's own mind is from the outset pure, that the depravities have never existed, that the nature of the wisdom without outflows is from the outset complete, that this mind is buddha, that they are ultimately without difference, then it is dhyana of the highest vehicle. This type is also known by such names as tathagata-purity dhyana, the one-practice concentration, and the thusness concentration. It is the basis of all concentrations. If one can practice it from moment to moment, one will naturally and gradually attain the myriad concentrations. This is precisely the dhyana that has been transmitted down from Bodhidharma. Before Bodhidharma arrived, all of the scholars from early times had understood only the four dhyanas [of the realm of form] and the eight concentrations [that is, those four plus the four formless concentrations of the formless realm]. Various illustrious monks had effectively practiced them, and they had all obtained results. Nanyue [Huisi] and Tiantai [Zhiyi] relied upon the principle of the three truths to practice the three tranquilizations and three

viewings.[8] Although the principles of their teachings are most perfect, their entrance gate is step-by-step. It also involves the type of dhyana mentioned above. It is only in the transmission from Bodhidharma that the practitioner all-at-once identifies with buddha substance. This is like no other gate.

Because in the later Bodhidharma tradition one master transmitted to more than one disciple by handing over some sort of sacred regalia as proof of transmission, there arose a bewildering plethora of torch illuminations. A degeneration in the quality of some Chan adepts ensued. This is why textual scholars grew very critical of Chan.

5. Therefore, those who practice in the [Bodhidharma] lineage find it difficult to apprehend its purport. If they do apprehend it, they become noble ones and quickly realize awakening. If they miss it, then they become common persons, slipping quickly into muddy water and raging fire. The early patriarchs [in the Bodhidharma lineage] reined in those who were still in the dark and excluded those who missed it, and so they transmitted to [just] one person. In later generations, there was something taken as a standard[9] [of proof for Chan transmission], and so this allowed thousands of [Chan] torches, thousands of [Chan] illuminations. Eventually the dharma was subject to malpractice, and mistaken people grew numerous. This is why there is widespread doubts and criticism [of Chan] on the part of sutra and treatise scholars.

At present scholars are extremist in stressing the step-by-step teaching, and Chan adepts are extremist in championing the all-at-once gate. I will prove that the words of the Chan masters tally with the intention of the Buddha found in the canonical texts.

6. Originally, the Buddha spoke both the all-at-once teaching and the step-by-step teaching, while Chan opens both the all-at-once gate and the step-by-step gate. The two teachings and the two gates fit together like the notches of a tally. At present, exegetes in a biased manner display the step-by-step principles, and Chan adepts in a biased manner encourage the all-at-once axiom. When a Chan adept and an exegete meet, the distance between them is that between a Central Asian barbarian and a barbarian from the South. I, Zongmi, do not know what they have done in past births to perfume their minds in this way. Having not yet liberated themselves, they desire to release the bonds of others. For the sake of the dharma, they disregard their own health. Pitying others, they cut off their own divine feelings. *(It is well known that the* Vimalakīrti *says:* "No one who is himself in bondage can release the bonds of others."[10] *Thus, if they desire to stop what they are doing but cannot do so, it must be because habit [energy] from past lives is difficult to change.)* I always lament discrepancies between people and the dharma, when the dharma becomes a disease for people. Therefore, I have selected passages from the sutras, the rules of discipline

[vinaya], the treatises, and the commentaries, and have opened widely the gate of precepts, concentration, and wisdom. I will show that all-at-once awakening is enriched by step-by-step practice and will prove that what the [Chan] masters say tallies with the intention of the Buddha. Even though that intention is manifest throughout [the entire canon], the texts are extensive and difficult to examine. Though careless scholars are numerous, determined ones are rare. Passing through terms and characteristics, who can distinguish gold from brass? Followers weary of the labor before they find that to which their disposition is receptive. Even though the Buddha said that increasing compassion is practice, I worried that my progress was being blocked by desiring views and discarded the multitude to enter the mountains. There I practiced making concentration equal to wisdom. My earlier and later sojourns of practicing the quieting of thoughts total a decade.[11] *(By earlier and later sojourns I refer to the fact that, during [my stay in the mountains], I was summoned by imperial edict to the court and lived within the city for two years. I then requested permission to return to the mountains.)* The rising and falling of subtle, fine habit-energy feelings are shown in dhyana and wisdom. Lines of different principles of the teachings appear in the void mind. When a ray of the sun streams through a crack, it shows the disturbance of the dust. At the bottom of a serene body of water images are reflected clearly. How can I reconcile stupid Chan adepts who in voidness cling to quietism and crazy devotees of wisdom who just wallow in the texts? Because I have come to an understanding of my own mind and have a grasp of the teachings, I have cordial feelings for the [Chan] mind axiom. On the other hand, because I have a grasp of the teachings and have come to understand cultivation of mind, I am prudent about sincerity towards the principles of the teachings.

The sutras are prolix and oriented to all types of beings. Chan texts are an abridgement oriented to the Chinese temperament. Chan goes right to the heart of the matter and is readily accessible.

7. The teachings are the sutras and treatises left behind by the buddhas and bodhisattvas. Chan is the lines of verse related by the various good friends [on the path]. The buddha sutras open outward, catching the thousands of the beings of the eight classes,[12] while Chan verses scoop up an abridgment, being oriented to one type of disposition found in this land [of China].[13] [The teachings,] which catch [the thousands of] beings [of the eight classes], are broad and vast, and hence it is difficult to rely upon them. [Chan,] which is oriented to dispositions, points to the bull's-eye and hence is easy to use. Herein rests my intention in making the present compilation.

Question: You stated that Chan texts are a succinct abridgement. Nevertheless, they must be comprehensive. Sutras have a standard, comprehensive vocabulary: dharma and principles; cause and effect; faith and understanding; practice and realization. But the texts in your *Chan Canon* are mostly question upon question in which some questions stand and others are negated, there being no discernible order to it. How can you call that a succinct statement of Buddhist teachings?

Answer: Since the sutras are a foundation for generations, they, of course, must be comprehensive. But Chan instruction is geared to bringing people to liberation right now, and this liberation involves forgetting words. The answers given by Chan masters that you find in Chan dialogues are simply responses to the dispositions of particular students at the time in question.

8. Question: You said [that Chan verses] scoop up an abridgment. Even if the [Chan] texts are simple and concise, the principles [therein] must be comprehensive and complete. It is axiomatic that [Chan] texts should scoop up many principles within a small amount of text. The sutras of buddha word all include [such terms as] "dharma" *(dharma substance)*, "principles" *(doctrinal principles)*, "causes" *(the three worthies, ten stages, thirty-seven parts of the path, and ten perfections)*,[14] "effects" *(the qualities and functions of a buddha)*, "faith" *(faith in the dharma)*, "understanding" *(understanding principles)*, "practice" *(passage through the stages cultivating causes)*, and "realization" *(realizing effect)*. Even though the locations and modes of discourse are different [for each of these sutras], in the teachings that they set up they all possess this [terminology]. Thus, in every assembly and every stage of the *Huayan* the worlds of the ten directions are spoken of in this vocabulary.[15] [But] as I now browse through the collected Chan writings of the various houses, [I find that] most of them are [cast in the form of] an unrelenting succession of questions [asked of the preceptor by a disciple, which are either] abruptly affirmed or abruptly repudiated [by the preceptor].[16] There is no order to it. I see no beginning and end. How can you call that a scooped-up abridgment of the buddha teachings?

Answer: A buddha's appearing in the world and setting up the teachings [that is, the sutras] and the [Chan] masters' crossing people over [to nirvana] according to the place differ in the manner of substance and phenomena. The Buddha teachings are a support for ten thousand generations, and it is axiomatic that they must be comprehensive. The instructions of the [Chan] masters lie in liberation in the here and now. The intention [of the Chan masters] is to enable people to realize dark understanding, and dark understanding necessarily entails forgetting words.[17] Therefore, if all at once [the Chan trainee] does not retain any traces, the traces are cut off at his mind ground, and principle appears at his mind source, then faith, understanding, practice, and realization are not acted upon, and yet they are spontaneously achieved. The sutras, rules of discipline [vinaya], treatises, and commentaries are not rehearsed, and yet they are spontaneously understood in a mysterious way. Thus, if someone asks about cultivating the path, [Chan preceptors] respond: "No cultivation." If someone asks about seeking liberation, they answer with the question: "Who is bound?" If someone asks about the road to becoming a buddha, they say: "From the outset no common person." If someone asks about quieting mind on the verge of death, they reply: "From the outset nothing to do." Some even say: "This is the unreal. This is the real. Exert yourself in this manner. Stop karma in this manner." Essentially speaking, [these Chan dialogues] are just things in accordance with the present time, a response to the dispositions [of sentient beings] of the present time. How could there be a real dharma called unexcelled, perfect awakening? How could there be a real practice called great wisdom? Just to attain [the state wherein] feelings have nothing to think about, ideation has nothing to do, mind has nothing that arises, and wisdom has no place to abide, is real faith, real understanding, real practice, and real realization. If a seeker of the buddha path merely grasps at the terms in the teachings without understanding his own mind, then he will come to know the written words and [be able to] read the sutras, but never realize awakening. He will wear down the texts in explaining their principles, but kindle only passion, hatred, and false views. [The Buddha's disciple] Ānanda heard everything the Buddha said and held it in his memory but grew old without ascending to the fruit of a noble one.[18] If you stop objective supports and return to illumination, after a short time, you will realize non-arising. Then you will know that there is a reason behind each of the bequeathed teachings and each of the approaches to crossing people over [to nirvana]. You should not place the blame on the written words.

The *Chan Canon* serves two audiences. Those currently in training can use it in their own practice, and those aspiring to become teaching masters can use it to increase their repertoire of teaching devices for dialogues with trainees. The *Chan Canon* is geared not only to the Chan enterprise of forgetting words; it contains the canonical teachings as well.

9. Question: Since the important thing is to get the idea and not to value specialization in the texts, what is the need for you to compile all these [Chan] lines of verses?

Answer: This compilation serves two purposes: First, there are those who have not fully awakened, in spite of the fact that they have been studying under a master, and, also, those who are conducting an earnest search, but have not yet met a good friend. By enabling them to browse through this compilation, they will have before them the ideas behind the words of the masters, and they will use these to penetrate their own minds and cut off any remaining thoughts. Second, there are those who are already awakened, but who desire to go on and become masters. [This compilation] will enable them to broaden their learning and increase their good skill in teaching devices in order to embrace sentient beings and answer questions during instruction.[19] Above [in section 7] I said that [the teachings], which catch the thousand worlds, are broad and hence difficult to rely upon, while [Chan], which is oriented to one place [China], points to the bull's-eye and is easy to use. This [is my answer to your question]. However, [this compilation is not meant] solely as an aid to the [Chan] gate of forgetting words. [It is intended to present] concurrently the benefits of Chan and the bequeathed teachings. [It will] not only make the intentions [of the Chan patriarchs] tally with the Buddha [mind]; I also want to make the [Chan] texts coincide with the [Buddha] sutras. Since the [Chan] texts seem to contradict each other, it is impossible to consider all of them the real teaching. I must classify the entire canon into Hinayana and Mahayana, those of provisional principle and those of the real principle, those of complete meaning and those of incomplete meaning. Once this is done, I can critically evaluate the Chan gates of the various lineages. Each of them has a purport; none of them is in conflict with the intention of the Buddha.[20] I mean by this that the sutras and treatises of the entire canon in all are of just three types, and the oral teachings of the Chan gate also in all are of just three axioms. *(Each is explained separately in the following text.)* [When the three types and three axioms] are matched up like a tally, they become the perfect view.

There are ten reasons why the Chan sayings in the *Chan Canon* are connected to the Mahayana sutras and treatises.

10. Question: How are the Chan explanations in the present[21] collection [=the *Chan Canon*] connected to the sutras and treatises?

Answer: There are ten grounds for [the connection]. You must [first] know which sutras and treatises are provisional and which real, and only then will you understand the rights and wrongs of the Chan [axioms]. Furthermore, you must first know about the nature and characteristics among the Chan minds, and then you will understand principle and phenomena within the sutras and treatises.

1. There are [two sorts of] masters, the root [the Buddha] and the branches [the bodhisattvas]; we rely on the root to seal the branches.
2. Chan has various lineages which conflict with one another.
3. The sutras are like a [carpenter's] inked marking string, serving as a model by which to establish the false and the correct.
4. Some sutras express the provisional and some the real; we must rely upon the complete meaning [that is, the real].
5. There are three sources of knowledge, and they must coincide.
6. There are various sorts of doubts, and they must all be resolved.

7. Dharma and the principles [of the teachings] are not the same, and one must be good at distinguishing [what is dharma and what is a principle.]

8. [The term] "mind" penetrates both the nature and characteristics; [the term] "mind" is always the same, but its meaning varies.

9. The various sayings having to do with all-at-once and step-by-step awakening and practice seem to be contradictory.

10. Masters instruct through teaching devices, and they must know the medicine [for each and every] disease.

Śākyamuni Buddha is the first patriarch of all the Chan lineages. There is no contradiction between buddha word (the sutras) and the intention of the buddhas/buddha mind (Chan). Bodhidharma saw that in China Buddhist followers were bogged down in scholasticism and an exclusive focus on phenomenal characteristics, so he propagated his slogan about a mind transmission uninvolved with the written word. The purpose of his slogan was to destroy grasping; it does not posit that inexpressibility itself is liberation. In the present climate there are many who harbor erroneous assumptions about this slogan.

11. No. 1: To say that there are [two sorts of] masters, the root and the branches, means that the first patriarch of all the [Chan] lineages is Śākyamuni. The sutras are buddha word, while Chan is the intention of the buddhas. The mouth and mind of the buddhas cannot possibly be contradictory. The lines of descent of all the [Chan] patriarchs go directly back to the disciples of the Buddha. [These] bodhisattvas composed treatises, and, in all cases, they were just propagating the Buddha sutras. Certainly, in the [Chan] transmission from Mahākāśyapa through Upagupta all were equally versed in all three baskets [of rules of discipline, sutra, and scholasticism].[22] However, after Dhrtaka disputes arose among the monks, and henceforth the rules of discipline and the teachings [that is, sutras and scholasticism] were practiced separately.[23] Further, because of the trouble with the Kashmir king, the sutras and treatises [that is, scholasticism] began to be propagated separately.[24] In the meantime [between Dhrtaka and Simha] Asvaghosa and Nagarjuna were both patriarchal masters.[25] They compiled treatises and commentaries on the sutras in ten thousands of verses. Viewing and transformation of beings [that is, dhyana practice and teaching] did not have definite [or separate] rules. Exegetes did not yet deprecate Chan, nor did Chan adepts deprecate exegesis. Bodhidharma received dharma in India and personally brought it to China. He saw that most of the scholars of this land had not yet obtained dharma, that their understanding was based merely on [scholastic] nomenclature and numerical [lists,] and that their [dhyana] practice was concerned only with phenomenal characteristics. Because his

desire was to inform them that the moon does not lie in the finger [pointing at the moon] and that dharma *is* our mind, he just [raised the slogan] "a mind-to-mind transmission; no involvement with the written word."[26] To reveal his [mind] axiom and eradicate grasping he had this saying. It is not that he was preaching a liberation [consisting] of freedom from the written word. This explains why those who gave instruction in getting [Bodhidharma's] idea incessantly praised the *Thunderbolt-Cutter* and the *Lanka Descent*, declaring that these two sutras are the essence of our mind.[27] At present, disciples everywhere entertain mistaken notions about the origin [of Bodhidharma's saying]. Those who cultivate mind consider the sutras and treatises as a separate axiom, while those who explain [texts] view the Chan gate as a separate dharma. [These days,] when people hear someone speak of cause and effect or practice and realization, they immediately conclude [that the speaker] is a sutra or treatise scholar, without realizing that it is precisely practice and realization that are the basic events of the Chan gate. If they hear someone say "mind is buddha," they immediately conclude [that the speaker] is a subjective Chan adept, without realizing that it is precisely mind and buddha that are the basic ideas of the sutras and treatises. *(There are some people who make the following objection: "How can a Chan master explain [the sutras and treatises]?" I have now answered this.)* If at the present juncture we do not correlate the provisional and the real among the sutras and treatises with the relative gradations of Chan axioms, how can we illuminate our minds with the teachings or understand the teachings with our minds?

Polemics are rife among the ten houses of Chan, but none of them is heterodox. Below I will distill their ideas into three axioms and juxtapose these three axioms to the three canonical teachings. This approach will unify them into one substitute, skillful teaching device.

12. No. 2: Chan has various lineages that conflict with one another. In fact, the writings collected herein are like the one hundred [contending] schools [of China's classical age]. [However,] differences in the principles of their axioms involve only ten houses. They are: [Hongzhou of] Jiangxi; Heze; the Northern [Shen]xiu; [Zhi]shen in the South [=Jingzhong]; Niutou [Oxhead]; Shitou; Baotang; Xuanshi [=the South Mountain Buddha–Recitation Gate Chan Lineage]; as well as [Hui]chou-[Gu]na[bhadra], Tiantai, etc.[28] Although there is no disagreement among them over comprehension, in setting up axioms and transmitting dharma, they conflict with one another. Some base themselves on voidness [Niutou], while others take Knowing as the source [Heze]. Some say that calm and silence are the real, while others say that [all ordinary activity such as] standing, sitting, etc., is the real [Hongzhou]. Some say that right now from dawn to dusk [in the midst of] discrimination and action everything is unreal

[Northern], while others say [in the midst of] discrimination and action everything is real [Hongzhou]. Some carry out all the practices [perhaps Jingzhong
and Xuanshi], while others disregard even the Buddha [Baotang]. Some let
loose their will and give it free rein [Hongzhou], while others restrain their
minds [perhaps Jingzhong and Xuanshi]. Some take the sutras and rules of discipline as a support [Jingzhong], while others consider the sutras and rules of
discipline an obstruction to the path [Baotang]. This is not just vague talk. It is
concrete talk, for [each house] concretely spreads its axiom and concretely at-
tacks the other types. Junior trainees cling to these sayings and miss the intention. With their emotional viewpoints they obstinately dispute one another and
fail to come together.

Question: [Why can you not simply] select what is right [from these Chan
houses] and disregard what is wrong? What is the need for these crooked [Chan
houses] to come together?

Answer: Some discuss voidness, while others discuss existence; some discuss
the nature, while others discuss characteristics. But none of them is heterodox.
The problem is merely that each considers itself to be a coterie in possession of
right and criticizes the others as wrong. Each of them is firm in its certainty.
This is the reason why they must be brought together.

Question: Since none of them is heterodox and each is firmly certain, what
is the need to bring them together?

Answer: The true path leads back to oneness. The subtle principle is non-
duality. There should be no duality. The true path is not an extreme. The
[teachings of] complete meaning do not lean to a side. No one should grasp a
single biased viewpoint. For this reason, I must bring them into oneness and
make them all perfect.

Question: If one mixes ice with fire, both of them cannot remain intact.
Likewise, if one strikes a shield with a sword, both of them cannot be victorious.
Whenever the collected writings of the various lineages contradict each other,
one is right and one is wrong. How can you bring them [into oneness] and make
them all perfect?

Answer: In all cases, I will preserve their dharma and get rid of their diseases. All of them will then be excellent. In other words, to take dharma to go to
people is difficult, but to take people to go to dharma is easy. Most people follow feelings into mutual grasping; grasping entails mutual conflict. Indeed, this
is difficult in the same sense that a mix of ice and fire or a clash of sword and
shield is difficult. Dharma from the outset proclaims principle and is mutual
penetration; penetration entails mutual accord. This is easy in the same sense
that frozen and running water are both water, or all gold rings gold. Essentially
speaking, if one considers [the Chan houses] individually, then they are all
wrong. If one brings them together, then they are all right. I will use buddha

word to illustrate the intention behind each of them, to select the strong points of each of them, to unify them into three axioms, and to juxtapose these to the three canonical teachings. [Without this approach,] how could they be brought together into one substitute skillful [teaching device], and how could they all become the essential dharma gate? If each [of these Chan houses] would forget its feelings, they would all flow back into the sea of wisdom. (*What the buddhas have said shows variations and yet is sameness, and so, if you condense the Buddha sutras, you bring the three [canonical teachings] into oneness.*)

A skilled carpenter uses an inked string as a measuring standard. The string is not the skill itself. A Chan adept likewise uses the sutras and treatises as a measuring standard. The sutras and treatises are not Chan itself.

13. No. 3: The sutras are like an inked marking string, serving as a model by which to establish the false and the correct. The inked marking string is not the skill itself; a skillful craftsman must use the string as a standard. The sutras and treatises are not Chan; one who transmits Chan must use the sutras and treatises as a norm. Those of medium and inferior faculties must rely on a master. The master sizes up [each student's] ability and instructs him accordingly. Those of high ability must be of perfect penetration[29] in their awakening, but, if they have not yet fully probed Buddha word, how can they be equal to the Buddha view?

Question: [Up until now,] all that has existed [in the way of texts] are the Buddha sutras. It has been left to the students to turn [the scrolls] and read them, checking and verifying.[30] Now you have collected the essentials of Chan, so what further need exists to understand the sutras?

Answer: This point comes up later and will be answered at that time.

The *Chan Canon* includes twenty-plus sheets of sutra passages so that the reader will gain an overall view of the intention of the Buddha. Having seen the intention of the Buddha, the reader will be able to classify every phrase of the sutras.

14. No. 4: Some sutras express the provisional and some the real; we must rely upon the complete meaning [that is, the real]. This means that, among the various sutras in which the Buddha speaks, in some cases he is speaking in accordance with his own mind, and, in other cases, he is speaking in accordance with the minds of others. Some [of the sutras] proclaim ultimate principle, while some are geared to the dispositions [of sentient beings] of the present time. Some speak in terms of the nature and some in terms of characteristics. Some are all-at-once and some step-by-step, some Mahayana and some Hinayana, some of complete meaning and some of incomplete meaning. But,

even though the texts sometimes contradict each other, the principles must always be of unobstructed perfect penetration. The dragon treasury [that is, the three baskets of the canon] is vast. How can one see where it is guiding to? Therefore, I have made a comprehensive selection from this [treasury] in twenty-plus sheets[31] in order to enable [the reader] suddenly to have a perfect view of the intention of the Buddha.[32] Once he has seen the intention of the Buddha, when he reads through the entire canonical treasury, he will come to know the axiom of every phrase.

Indian masters always held to the three sources of knowledge. Of the three, most Chan lineages have direct perception and inference. They must seal them with the third source, the sutras.

15. No. 5: There are three sources of knowledge, and they must *coincide*.[33] In their understanding of the principles of dharma, the worthies and nobles ones of the western lands always considered the three sources of knowledge to be definitive: (1) inference, (2) direct perception, and (3) buddha word. "Sources of knowledge" means to weigh something in the scales to determine its exact weight. "Inference" means to infer from causal analogy. For instance, when one sees smoke in the distance, one knows for certain that there is a fire. Even though one does not see the fire, it is not unreal. "Direct perception" means that one sees [something] before one's own eyes, without relying on inference; it is spontaneously definitive. "Buddha word" means that the sutras are definitive. [When I say that] they must coincide, [I mean that,] if one just takes buddha word as a standard and does not infer for himself, then his realization will be a thing of empty belief, bringing no benefit to him. If one just takes direct perception, that is, seeing it for oneself, to be definitive and does not inquire into Buddha word, then how will he know [the difference between] false and correct? The followers of outside paths [that is, the six heretical teachers at the time of the Buddha] also directly perceived the principles to which they held, and, practicing them, obtained results. They called themselves correct. How would we know that they were false [without Buddha word]? If one were to rely only on inference without the teachings of the noble ones and seeing it for one-self, then what would he infer about? What dharma would he infer about? Thus, the three sources of knowledge must coincide to be definitive. The Chan lineages already for the most part have the two sources of knowledge of direct perception and inference. Once they have gone on to seal them with [the third,] the sutras and treatises, the three sources of knowledge will be complete.

Both scholars and Chan adepts harbor a multitude of doubts. By classifying the canon into the three types of teachings, I will at one stroke put all these doubts to rest.

16. No. 6: There are various sorts of doubts, and they must all be resolved. During the last several decades there have been a number of great worthies of the sutras and treatises[34] who have asked me the following question: The four dhyanas and eight concentrations [samadhis] are all in the upper realms [of form and non-form]. There is no dhyana in this realm [of desire where humans reside]. Whoever practices dhyana must rely on the sutras and treatises. He practices in this realm in order to be drawn up into the dhyanas and concentrations of the upper realms. Anyone whose practice has reached completion is in [one of] those dhyanas [and concentrations of the upper realms]. The teachings are clear on this point. There are no exceptions to this. How can anyone speak of a Chan gate that is separate from this? Since [such a separate Chan gate] is not grounded in the sutras and treatises, it is a false path.

Another question is: The sutras speak of step-by-step practice, that after limitless eons one realizes awakening. Chan proclaims all-at-once awakening, that in a moment one achieves perfect awakening. The sutras are Buddha word, while Chan is the word of monks. I am skeptical about contravening Buddha [word] in order to honor [the word of] monks.

Another question is: The essential purport of the Chan gate is neither affirmation nor negation, neither enmity nor affection, neither anger nor happiness. [If this is so,] what is the reason for the hatred between the Southern [lineage of the sixth patriarch Hui]neng and the Northern [lineage of Shen]xiu, which are like fire and water, and for the hostility between the Heze and Hongzhou [houses], which are like the *shen* star [in the west] and the *shang* star [in the east, that is, like brothers who do not get along]?

Another question is: For six generations [from Bodhidharma to Huineng] the Chan dharma was transmitted from master to disciple. [In each successive generation masters] said [to their disciples]: "Within, I confer upon you the secret oral transmission [*miyu*]; without, I hand to you [Bodhidharma's] robe of faith." The·robe and the dharma were complementary, serving as a tally seal. Since Caoqi [Huineng], no one has heard of this procedure.[35] I am skeptical. In present Chan procedure, are secret oral transmissions spoken in transforming people or not? If they are not spoken, then what is transmitted is not Bodhidharma's dharma. If they are, then [those disciples] who hear them should all obtain the robe.

Also, there are Chan worthies who ask: Bodhidharma's transmission of mind was uninvolved with the written word.[36] Why do you go against the former patriarch by explaining the treatises and transmitting the sutras?

Lately, there has been this question: Vimalakīrti shouted his disapproval of quiet sitting.[37] Shenhui always attacked [the practice of] freezing mind.[38] When Caoqi [Huineng] saw someone in cross-legged posture, he took his staff and hit him until he got up.[39] Now let me ask you: You [Zongmi] always rely on the injunctions of the teachings to encourage cross-legged Chan sitting. [Due to your exhortations] lines of Chan huts fill the cliffs and ravines. This perverts the [Chan] axiom and goes against the [Chan] patriarchs, and hence I am doubtful about it.

Although on a number of occasions I have responded to each of these questions, those with doubts still number in the thousands. It is a pity that they have not yet listened. Those who raise these objections are all led by their feelings into biased grasping. The things that they grasp are in each case different. They conflict with each other, and thus, in resolving these doubts, I may well increase the disease [from which they have been suffering]. For this reason, I must unveil the principles of the three gates and classify the entire canon [within these three gates]. This will answer all these doubts with one stroke, and every one [of the above questioners] will understand thoroughly. *(Below, I will add notes in answer to these questions after the appropriate passage. You must consult these notes to see my answers.)*

The *Awakening of Faith* makes a distinction between dharma and principles. Most Chan adepts neglect the latter and go about shouting "mind is Chan!" Most scholars have not come to know dharma and so get bogged down in detailed discussions of doctrinal principles. To clear up this situation I will classify the sutras and treatises into three types of teachings.

17. No. 7: Dharma and the principles [of the teachings][40] are not the same, and one must be good at distinguishing [what is dharma and what is a principle]. Whoever wishes to clearly understand the nature and characteristics of all dharmas must first be able to differentiate between dharma and principles. If we rely on dharma to understand principles, then the principles will be clear. If we discuss dharma in terms of principles, then dharma will be revealed. Let me make this clear now with a worldly analogy. Real gold is conditioned by artisans into rings, bracelets, bowls, cups, and other utensils, but the nature of the gold never changes into brass or iron. Gold is dharma, while immutable and conditioned are principles. Should someone ask what is immutable and what is conditioned, I would merely reply in both cases: gold. By analogy, the principles of the sutras and treatises of the entire canon are talking only about mind. Mind is dharma; all [of the sutras and treatises] are principles. Therefore, the sutra says: "Immeasurable principles arise from the one dharma."[41] However, the incalculable principles fall into only two types. The first is the immutable and the second the conditioned. Various sutras just say that this mind follows conditions of delusion or awakening, becoming stained or pure, common person or noble one, depravities or awakening, with outflows or without outflows, etc. They also just say that, while this mind is stained or pure, it is from the outset immutable, constantly calmed, reality and thusness, etc. Should someone ask what dharma

is immutable and what dharma is conditioned, I would merely reply in both cases: mind. Immutable is the nature, while conditioned is characteristics. You must know that the nature and characteristics are both principles on the one mind.[42] The fact that at present [those of] the two axioms, nature and characteristics,[43] criticize each is because they do not know the true mind. Whenever they hear the word "mind," they think that it signifies only the eight consciousnesses,[44] not realizing that the eight consciousnesses are merely conditioned principles on the true mind. Thus, Asvaghosa Bodhisattva[45] considered the one mind to be dharma and the two gates, thusness and arising-disappearing, to be principles. The treatise says: "Grounded in this mind, the Mahayana principles are revealed."[46] The true thusness of mind is the substance; the arising-disappearing of mind is the characteristics and functions. Because this mind is not unreal, we say it is true; because it is immutable, we say it is thusness. Thus, the treatise speaks repeatedly of the thusness of mind and the arising-disappearing of mind.[47] Today, most Chan adepts, unaware of principles, merely shout "mind is Chan," and most exegetes, not knowing dharma, merely use nomenclature to speak of principles. By following these nomenclatures they give rise to grasping, and it becomes difficult for them to be able to harmonize [the seemingly contradictory ideas found in the various teachings]. When they hear [the word] "mind," they say it is shallow. When they hear [the word] "nature," they say it is profound. Some of them even take "nature" to be dharma and "mind" to be a principle. In order to illuminate things, I must classify the sutras and treatises according to three axioms. Once dharma and the principles are revealed, there will be only reversion to one mind. Spontaneously, there will be no more contention.

There are four types of mind: the fleshly mind; the pondering-of-objective-supports mind (the eight consciousnesses); the mind that accumulates karmic seeds and produces the seven active consciousnesses (the eighth consciousness or *ālaya-vijñāna* ["storehouse consciousness"]); and the true mind. This true mind, when unawakened, has the two principles of mixed with thought of the unreal (the storehouse consciousness) and unmixed (thusness). The nature (the fourth type of mind) and characteristics (the first three types of mind) together are one mind. Pedantic scholars and subjective Chan adepts miss this.

18. No. 8: [The term] "mind" penetrates both the nature and characteristics; [the term] "mind" is always the same but its meaning varies. Some of the sutras criticize mind as a thief and [say that we should exert] control to cut off [its activities]. Some praise mind as a buddha and encourage us to subject it to practice. Some speak of the good mind and the bad mind, the pure mind and the stained mind, the covetous mind and the angry mind, the mind of friendliness

and the mind of compassion. Some say that mind arises in dependence on sense objects. Some say that mind gives rise to sense objects. Some say that calm is mind. Some say that pondering of objective supports is mind. These various [formulations] contradict one another. If the [three] axioms [that is, the three types of teachings of section 21] are not juxtaposed and laid before the sutra reader, how can [the reader] differentiate these [definitions of "mind"]? Are there many sorts of mind or merely one kind of mind? Let me now explain in brief the terms and substance [of this matter]. Generally speaking, mind can be reduced to four types. The Sanskrit is different in each case, and hence the [Chinese] translations [and transliterations] also differ.

The first is *helituoye*. This means the mind that is a lump of flesh. This is the mind in each of the five viscera in the body. *(The full details are given in the discussion on the five viscera in the* Yellow Court Classic *[Huangting jing].)*[48]

The second is the pondering-of-objective-supports[49] mind. This is the eight consciousnesses [*vijñāna*], because all [eight] are capable of pondering as objective supports their own sense objects. *(Forms are the sense objects of the eye consciousness, up to and including the organ body, the [karmic] seeds, and the vessel world are the sense objects of the storehouse consciousness.*[50] *Because each [consciousness] takes as its objective support only one particular [type of sense object], we say: "Its own [sense objects]."*) Each of these eight [consciousnesses] has mentals [*caitta*]. Within these, some are just neutral, while others are distinguished as either good or impure. Some sutras declare mind to be a collective term for all these mentals. They speak of the good mind, the bad mind, etc.

The third is *zhiduoye* [*citta*]. This means the mind that accumulates and produces, because only the eighth consciousness accumulates [karmic] seeds and produces the [seven] active [consciousnesses]. *(The discussion on the five viscera in the* Yellow Court Classic *declares this type of mind to be a spirit. Followers of outside paths in the western countries consider it to be an [eternal] atman [Self].)*

The fourth is *ganlituoye*. This means real mind or true mind. This is *the true mind.* However, it is not an entity separate from the eighth consciousness. It is just that this true mind, when unawakened, has [two] principles: in concord with and not in concord with unreal thought.[51] In its principle of being in concord [with unreal thought], it can contain impurity and purity, and we view it as the storehouse consciousness. In its [principle] of not being in concord [with unreal thought], its substance is constant and immutable, and we view it as thusness. [The storehouse consciousness and thusness] taken together are the buddha-in-embryo [tathagatagarbha]. Therefore, the *Lanka Descent* says: "The calmed is called one mind. One mind is the buddha-in-embryo."[52] The buddha-in-embryo is also the dharma body in bondage, as the *Śrīmālā Sutra* says.[53]

Thus, we know that the four types of mind are from the outset one substance. Therefore, the *Secret Array Sutra* says: "The Buddha said that the buddha-in-embryo *(the name of the dharma body in bondage)* is to be taken as identical to the *ālaya (storehouse consciousness)*. The uninformed are incapable of realizing that the [tathagata]garbha is the *ālaya* consciousness. *(There are those who hold to [the mistaken view] that thusness and the* ālaya *are different in substance. They are uninformed.)* The pure buddha-in-embryo and the worldly *ālaya* are like gold and a gold ring, absolutely without difference."[54] *(The ring is like the* ālaya, *while the gold is like thusness. Together they are called the buddha-in-embryo.)* However, even though they are identical in substance, as real and unreal principles [of the true mind] they differ, just as beginning and end differ. The first three [types of mind] are characteristics; the last one is the nature. Grounded in the nature, characteristics are originated through causation. Bringing characteristics back to the nature is not impossible. The nature and characteristics are without obstruction; together they are the one mind. If you lose your way here, any direction you go you will face a wall. If you are awakened to this, then the ten thousand dharmas [will appear as if] in a mirror. If one vainly searches through the phraseology of the texts [as some exegetes do] or [just] puts one's confidence in one's subjective feeling[55] [as some Chan adepts do], how can he understand the nature and characteristics of this one mind?

The canonical texts and the Chan gates propound all sorts of variations on all-at-once and step-by-step in both awakening and practice. Though all-at-once and step-by-step seem mutually exclusive, they are, in fact, complementary.

19. No. 9: The all-at-once and step-by-step of awakening and practice seem to be contradictory but [in reality] fit together like a tally. Of the various sutras and treatises and the various Chan gates, some say that one first relies on the merit accumulated through step-by-step practice and then suddenly all-at-once awakens. Some say that one first relies on all-at-once awakening and then can engage in step-by-step practice. Some say that relying on all-at-once practice, one step-by-step awakens. Some say that awakening and practice are both step-by-step. Some say that they are both all-at-once. Some say that the dharma has neither all-at-once nor step-by-step, that all-at-once and step-by-step are in the dispositions [of trainees]. Each of the above theories is significant. "Seem to be contradictory" means that, having awakened, one becomes a buddha: from the outset no depravities. We call this all-at-once. Thus, there is no need to practice cutting off [the depravities], so how can anyone speak further of step-by-step practice? Step-by-step practice implies that the depravities have not yet been fully exhausted, that the practice of causes is not yet perfect, that the virtues of effect are not yet full, so how can it be called all-at-once? All-at-once is not step-by-step. Step-by-step is not all-at-once. Thus, they are said to be contradictory.[56]

If in the following I bring them together to face each other, then [it will be clear that] all-at-once and step-by-step are not just not contradictory, but are complementary.

All instructional devices aim first to bring the trainee to awakening to the nature and subsequently to a practice grounded in this nature. Grasping of characteristics is the usual obstacle to awakening, and masters must here employ teaching devices of the negative sort, "neither x nor y," "the path is like a dream or illusion," and so forth. Unfortunately, novices show a tendency to take this type of saying as ultimate truth. In the case of the practice following awakening, masters are given to exhortations about diligence, regulation of the body and breath, and so forth. Unfortunately, novices, upon hearing these exhortations, have a tendency to lose sight of original awakening and fall into the grasping of characteristics. Only the best students get the meaning of both awakening and practice. Shallow students quit after getting only one. The latter then become teaching masters in their own right and in a biased fashion champion either all-at-once or step-by-step. A potential teaching master must see that the three Chan axioms do not conflict, so that he feels free to draw from the vast repertoire of teaching devices found in all the Chan houses.

20. No. 10: In a master-student transmission, [the master] must know the medicine [for each and every] disease. This means that all instructional teaching devices inherited from the past first show the original nature and then require reliance on this nature to practice dhyana. In most cases, when the nature is not easily awakened to, it is due to the grasping of characteristics. Thus, if [a master] wants to reveal this nature, he must first eradicate grasping [on the part of the student]. In [the master's] teaching devices for eradicating this grasping, he must [employ a type of rhetoric in which] common person and noble one are both cut off, merits and faults are both gotten rid of, in the precepts there is neither violation nor observance, in dhyana there is neither concentration nor distraction, the thirty-two marks[57] are all like flowers in the sky, and the thirty-seven parts of the path[58] are all a dream or illusion. The idea is that, if [the master] enables [the student] to have a mind free of attachment, then [the student] can practice dhyana. [But] junior trainees and those of shallow knowledge just grasp these [Chan] phrases as the ultimate path. Furthermore, as to the gate of practice, because most people are self-indulgent and indolent, [masters] further speak a great deal of taking joy [in the path] and wearying [of this world]. They criticize passion and anger and commend diligence, regulation of the body and regulation of breath, and the sequence of coarse and subtle [characteristics].[59] When novices hear this, they become deluded about the function of original awakening[60] and single-mindedly grasp characteristics. Only those [trainees] of great ability and fixed will serve their masters for the full course [of training]. They then attain the purport of [both] awakening and practice.

[Trainees] of a light, shallow nature, upon hearing only one idea, [i.e., either the original nature or gradual practice], say that they already have had enough. Still depending upon their small intelligence, they become masters of others. Having not yet investigated from beginning to end, they produce a lot of biased grasping. Thus, [some stand] under the all-at-once gate and [some] stand under the step-by-step, glaring at each other like enemies. The Northern and Southern lineages are mutual enemies in the manner of [the warring kingdoms of] Chu and Han.[61] The practice of washing the feet and the analogy of [the blind men] feeling the elephant are relevant here.[62] Why do I desire to bring together these [Chan] writings by making them into a separate compilation? [My reasoning is best explained by] reference to the three round marks of the [triangular] letter *i*.[63] Three marks standing apart would not constitute an *i*. If the three [Chan] axioms ran counter to each other, how could they make buddhas? Thus, we realize that, if one wants to know the medicine [for each and every] disease in [the course of] instructing [trainees], he must see that the three [Chan] axioms do not conflict. If he wants to see that the three [Chan] axioms do not conflict, he must understand the three types of Buddha teachings. (*As mentioned previously [in section 16], there are some people who make the following objection: "Why do you, a Chan master, explain [the sutras and treatises]?" I have now answered this fully through ten ideas. This is why I remarked earlier [in section 11] that the [Chan] patriarchs of the western regions all propagated the sutras and treatises.*)

The teachings authenticate the Chan gate. Each of the three teachings is *identical* to its counterpart among the three Chan axioms.

21. The above ten ideas have been made clear through examples. Once the three axioms of Chan and the three types of teachings have been paired off with each other, it will be like weighing each of them, sufficient to determine which are shallow and which deep. I will first discuss the Chan gate and later use the teachings to authenticate it. The three axioms of Chan are:

1. [Realizing] the axiom of stopping [thought of] the unreal and cultivating mind [only]
2. [Realizing] the axiom of cutting off and not leaning on anything
3. [Realizing] the axiom of directly revealing the mind nature

The three types of teachings are:

1. The teaching of cryptic meaning[64] that relies on [dharma] nature to speak of characteristics

2. The teaching of cryptic meaning that eradicates characteristics to reveal [dharma] nature

3. The teaching that openly [with no cryptic or hidden meaning] shows
that the true mind is [dharma] nature

Each of these three teachings is identical to its counterpart among the previous
three axioms. Once I have juxtaposed [the three Chan axioms and three types
of teachings] and authenticated [the axioms] one by one, I will fashion a comprehensive fusion into the one taste [of dharma].

The first Chan axiom involves withdrawal from sense objects and the extinguishing
of thought of the unreal. It employs such teaching devices as seclusion, cross-legged
sitting, breath counting, etc. Jingzhong, Northern, Baotang, and the South Mountain
Buddha–Recitation Gate Chan Lineage belong to this axiom. Niutou and three non-
Bodhidharma Chan lineages employ preliminary teaching devices similar to those of
this axiom, but their theoretical framework is different.

22. At this time I will start with a discussion of the Chan axioms. The first is the
axiom of stopping [thought of] the unreal and cultivating mind [only].[65] It says
that, even though from the outset sentient beings possess the buddha nature,
beginningless ignorance has always covered it so that it could not be seen. Because of this, the wheel [of rebirth] turns. Because the buddhas have cut off
thought of the unreal, they see the nature in its entirety, escape the rebirth process, [come into possession of] the superknowledges, and exist in freedom.
[This Chan axiom says:] You must realize that the common person and the
noble one are not the same in their achievements, that external sense objects
and internal mind are separated. Thus, you must, relying on the oral teachings
of the [Chan] masters,[66] turn away from sense objects and view mind,[67] extinguishing thought of the unreal. When these thoughts are exhausted, you will
awaken. There will be nothing you will not know. It is like a mirror beclouded
by dust.[68] You must vigorously wipe it, for, once the dust is removed, the brightness will reappear, and [the mirror] will reflect anything placed before it. Further, you must clearly understand the teaching devices leading into the realm of
Chan: Divorce yourself from confusion and noise; seclude yourself in a quiet
place; regulate the body and regulate the breath; sit silently in cross-legged sitting posture; press the tongue against the roof of the mouth [in order to inhibit
salivation]; and have the mind concentrate on one sense object. The disciples of
[Zhi]shen in the South, the Northern [Shen]xiu, Baotang, [the South Mountain Buddha–Recitation Gate Chan Lineage of] Xuanshi, and others are all of
this type. The preliminary teaching devices of Niutou, Tiantai, Huichou, Gunabhadra, and others are much the same [as this type], but their understanding is
different.[69]

The second Chan axiom holds that from the outset there is only voidness and calm. It often employs negative sayings in the mode of "neither *x* nor *y*." The Shitou and Niutou houses belong to this axiom. Frivolous Daoists, Confucians, and Buddhists get a touch of this Chan principle and become infatuated with its negative sayings, claiming they are ultimate truth. Heze and Hongzhou, as well as one non-Bodhidharma lineage, touch on this principle, but it is not their axiom.

23. The second is the axiom of cutting off and not leaning on anything.[70] It says that the dharmas of both the common person and the noble one are like a dream or illusion;[71] none of them has any [real] existence. From the outset [there is only] voidness and calm. It is not a case of coming to non-existence for the first time now. Thus, even the wisdom that comprehends this non-existence cannot be apprehended. In the dharma sphere of sameness there is neither buddha nor sentient being.[72] Even "dharma sphere" is a provisional name. Since mind is not [really] existent, who [could possibly exist to] say "dharma sphere"? There is neither practice nor non-practice, neither buddha nor non-buddha. Suppose there were a dharma that excelled nirvana. I say that even it would be like a dream or illusion.[73] There is no dharma to adhere to and no buddha to become. Whatever is created is unreal.[74] If one comprehends in this way that from the outset there is nothing to do[75] and mind has nothing to rely upon, then he will escape inverted [views] and for the first time be called liberated. [The lineage of] Shitou and [the lineage running] from Niutou to Jingshan both evince this principle.[76] They make their mind sphere bonded with this and do not allow feelings to stagnate on [any] dharma. When, after many days, achievement arrives and habit [energy directed toward] sense objects disappears, they [no longer] have anything to do with enemies, friends, suffering, or joy. But there exists a type of Daoist master[77] or Confucian scholar or idle Buddhist monk who, having only lightly trained in this Chan principle, says that these sayings ["neither buddha nor sentient beings," etc.] are the ultimate. [Such foolish people] do not understand that [those realizing] this [Chan] axiom do not just take these sayings as dharma [but practice so that they do not allow feelings to stagnate on anything]. The disciples of Heze, [Hongzhou of] Jiangxi, Tiantai, and others also speak of this principle, but it is not what they take as their axiom.[78]

The third axiom holds that all dharmas *are* the true nature, reality. Two houses, Hongzhou and Heze, belong to this axiom. Hongzhou exalts giving free rein to luck and existing in freedom. Heze says that your true nature is the Knowing of voidness and calm. Despite differences among all the Chan houses of the three axioms, each of them is appropriate for a particular type of being.

24. The third is the axiom of directly revealing the mind nature.[79] It says that all dharmas, even though they are both existent and void, are just the true nature.

The true nature is unconditioned; it is not anything substantial. This is what is meant [by such phrases as] "neither common nor noble," "neither cause nor effect," "neither good nor bad," etc. However, in its functional aspect it has the potentiality to create all sorts of [dharmas]. This is what is meant [by such phrases as] "can be the common person and can be the noble one," "manifests form and manifests characteristics," etc.

Within [this axiom] there are two types [of Chan houses] that point to and show the mind nature. The first, [the Hongzhou house],[80] says: "Your potentiality right now to talk, act, [experience] passion, anger, friendliness, patience, create good or bad and receive suffering or joy, etc., is your buddha nature. By virtue of this you have been a buddha from the outset. There is no other buddha than this. Once you understand this spontaneity of the heavenly real,[81] you should not stir your mind to cultivate the path. The path is mind. You should not use mind to cultivate [the path in] mind. The bad is also mind. You should not use mind to cut off [the bad in] mind. When you neither cut off [bad] nor cultivate [good], but just give free rein to luck and exist in freedom, then you are to be called liberated. The nature is like space; it neither increases nor decreases. What could you possibly add to it? Whatever time it is, wherever you are, just stop karma and nourish the spirit.[82] Your noble embryo[83] will grow and become manifest, spontaneously divine and excellent. This is true awakening, true practice, and true realization."

The second, [the Heze house],[84] says: "All dharmas are like a dream. All the noble ones have said the same thing. Thus, thought of the unreal from the outset is calm. Sense objects are from the outset void. The mind of voidness and calm is a spiritual Knowing that never darkens.[85] It is precisely this Knowing of voidness and calm that is your true nature. No matter whether you are deluded or awakened, mind from the outset is spontaneously Knowing. [Knowing] is not produced by conditions, nor does it arise in dependence on any sense object. The one word "Knowing" is the gate of all excellence.[86] Because of beginningless delusion about it, you have falsely grasped body and mind as a self and produced such thoughts as passion and anger. If you find a good friend to open up and show [the path], then you will all-at-once awaken to the Knowing of voidness and calm. Knowing is no mindfulness and no form. Who is it that is characterized as a self, and who is it that is characterized as the other? When you awaken to the voidness of all characteristics, mind is naturally no mindfulness. If a thought arises, be aware of it; once you are aware of it, it will disappear.[87] The excellent gate of practice lies here alone. Thus, even though you fully cultivate all the practices, just take no mindfulness as the axiom. If you just attain the Knowing-seeing of no mindfulness, then love and hatred will spontaneously decrease, compassion and wisdom will spontaneously increase, sinful karma will spontaneously be eliminated, and meritorious practices will spontaneously increase. Once you have understood that all characteristics are non-characteristics, you will practice in a spontaneous manner, but it will be a non-practice. When the depravities are exhausted, the rebirth process will cease; once arising-disappearing is extinguished, calm and illumination will become manifest, and you will respond to everything. This is called becoming a buddha." Thus, both these houses, [the Hongzhou and the Heze], gather characteristics back to the nature and are, therefore, of the same single axiom.[88]

Nevertheless, within the above three [Chan] axioms, there are [Chan houses] that honor the teachings and those that disparage them, those that follow characteristics and those that destroy characteristics. There are a great many differences [among the Chan houses in terms of] doors to refuting the arguments of outsiders, good skillful [teaching devices] for receiving outsiders, and rules for teaching disciples, but all of them are the practice gate of dual benefit [of self and other]. Each is suitable for a particular type of person, and hence, none of them misses [the mark]. It is just that the principles that they take as their axioms should not involve duality. Thus, I must bring them together in accordance with the Buddha.

The first of the three teachings is the teaching of cryptic meaning that relies on the nature to speak of characteristics. It has three subdivisions: the karmic cause-and-effect teaching that enables one to be reborn as a human or god (worldly cause and effect = the first two of the four noble truths); the teaching that cuts off the depravities and extinguishes suffering (the cause and effect of transcending the world = the four noble truths = the negation of self found the Hinayana sutras and treatises); and the teaching that takes consciousness to eradicate sense objects (the teaching of unreal consciousness transformation found in the Yogācāra sutras and treatises)

25. I will now divide the whole of the Buddha's teachings into three types. The first is the teaching of cryptic meaning that relies on the [dharma] nature to speak of characteristics. *(The Buddha saw that the three realms [of desire, form, and non-form] and six rebirth paths [of hell beings, hungry ghosts, animals, asuras, humans, and gods] are all characteristics of the true nature. They arise merely because sentient beings are deluded about the nature. They have no substance of their own separate [from the nature]. Therefore, we say: "Rely on the nature." Nevertheless, for those whose faculties are dull, it is unexpectedly difficult to open up awakening. For this reason, the dharma is spoken to them in terms of the characteristics of the sense objects that they see, and step-by-step they cross over [to nirvana]. Therefore, we say: "Speaks of characteristics." Its speaking does not go so far as to reveal [the nature] and, therefore, we say: "Cryptic meaning.")* Within this first teaching there are three subdivisions.

The first is the karmic cause-and-effect teaching [that allows rebirth as a] human or a god. It speaks of good and bad karmic retribution. It makes beings know that there is no discrepancy between cause and effect, makes them fear suffering in one of the three [bad] rebirth paths [of hell beings, hungry ghosts, and animals], makes them seek the joy of [being reborn as] a man or a god, makes them carry out all such good practices as giving, precepts, and dhyana, enabling them to be reborn into the path of humans or the path of the gods up through the realms of form and non-form. Therefore, we say: "Humans-and-gods teaching."

The second is the teaching of the cutting off of the depravities and the extinguishing of suffering.[89] It says that there is no peace in the three realms [of desire, form, and non-form], that [rebirth within any of the three realms] is like suffering in a burning house.[90] It enables beings to cut off their accumulation of karma and the depravities, to cultivate the path, and to realize extinction. In order to accord with the [varying] dispositions [of sentient beings] its methods of teaching dharma[91] [show a focus on] intense differentiation, picking out false and correct, discriminating between common person and noble one, dividing up weariness and joy, and clarifying cause and effect. [This second subdivision] says that sentient beings, [composed of] the five aggregates [of form, feelings, thoughts, karmic formations, and consciousness], all lack a self and are just bodily form and cognitive mind. From without beginning, because of the power of causes and conditions, arising and disappearing from moment to moment, the personal continuity series[92] is without end, like water bubbles or the flame of a lamp. Body and mind temporarily unite, but seem to be a permanent whole. The ignorant, those not yet awakened, grasp this as a self. To protect this self, they produce the three poisons, passion *(covet fame and profit in order to glorify the self)*, anger *(are angry when things go against their feelings and fear harm to the self)*, and stupidity *(any direction they go they misunderstand, calculating in an irrational way)*. The three poisons attack consciousness and produce bodily movement and speech, creating all karma. Once karma is brought into being, it is impossible to escape it. *(A shadow follows a form; an echo responds to a sound.)* Therefore, one is reborn into a suffering or joyful body in one of the five rebirth paths *(this is in response to individual karma)*[93] and into a superior or inferior place in the three realms *(this is the place in response to common karma)*[94]. Once again [the ignorant] grasp the body that they have received as a self, once again producing passion, etc., creating [more] karma and receiving retribution. The body [passes through] birth, old age, sickness, and death. Once dead, it is reborn. The realms come into being, stabilize, disintegrate, and [reenter] the void. From the void they come into being again. Kalpa after kalpa, birth after birth, the wheel turns ceaselessly, without end and without beginning, just as a well wheel draws [water]. All this is because they do not understand that this body has never been a self. *(Up to this point everything is the worldly cause and effect in the previous humans-and-gods teaching. The previous [humans-and-gods teaching] merely makes people weary of the present world and joyfully anticipate rebirth in a heaven. It does not yet say that the three realms are all a calamity to become weary of. Also, it does not eradicate the self. If I were now to summarize it, it is the two truths of suffering and the accumulation [of suffering]. Below [this point] eradicates the grasping of self, enabling beings to cultivate the two [further] truths of extinction and the path.[95] It clarifies the cause and effect of transcending the world, and, for this reason, we call it the teaching of the four truths.)* "Is not a self" means that this body from the outset takes the concord of form and mind as a characteristic. When we now investigate and analyze, [we find that] there are four types of form (earth, water, fire, and wind) and four types of mind: feelings *(taking in agreeable and disagreeable events)* thoughts *(apprehending images)*, karmic formations *(karmic fashioning of everything)*, and consciousness *(perceiving one thing after another)*. *(These four [types of mind] plus form are called the five aggregates.)* If each and every one of these [types of form and mind] were a self, then there would be eight selves. Furthermore, within the form [of the body] there are three-hundred-and-sixty bones, each one different from the other, and skin, hair, muscles, flesh, liver, heart, spleen, and kidney, no one of them identical to another. *(Skin is not hair, etc.)* The various mentals[96] are also different from each other. Seeing is not hearing; happiness is not anger. Since there are this many components, we do not know what definitively to take as a self. If all of them are selves, then there are a hundred thousand of them, many subjects in confusion within one body. There are no other dharmas beyond these, but, upon analysis, a self cannot be apprehended in any of them. Thus, one awakens to the realization that these [types of] body and mind are merely conditions, with the characteristic of seeming concord, but were never one substance. They are characterized as an apparent self and others, but there never existed a self and others. Who is passionate and angry? Who kills and steals? Who practices giving and the precepts? Who is reborn as a human or a god? *(This is knowledge of the accumulation of suffering.)* One then does not let the mind sink into the good and bad of having outflows in the three realms *(the truth of the cutting off of the accumulation [of suffering])*. One just cultivates the discerning wisdom of non-self *(the truth of the path)* in order to cut off passion, etc., stop all karma, and realize the thusness of voidness of self. He obtains the fruit of stream enterer, [the fruit of once-returner to this world, and the fruit of non-returner to this world,] up to and including extinguishing all evil bonds and obtaining the fruit of arhat *(the truth of extinction)*. Having burned up body and extinguished knowledge, he is eternally free of all suffering. Sutras in six-hundred-and-eighteen fascicles, the *Āgamas*,[97] etc., and treatises numbering six-hundred-and-ninety-eight fascicles, the *Explanations*,[98] and *[Abhidharma-]kośa*,[99] etc., discuss only this Hinayana and the previous karmic cause-and-effect [teaching that allows rebirth] as a human or a god. Although the sections and cases [of these canonical texts] are voluminous, their principle does not go beyond this.

The third is the teaching that takes consciousness to eradicate sense objects.[100] *(It says that sense-object characteristics, which the previous [subdivision] speaks of as arising and disappearing [from moment to moment], are not just lacking a self, but are not even dharmas in the sense in which the previous [subdivision uses that term], that they are just unreal transformations of consciousness. Therefore, we say: "Takes consciousness to eradicate sense objects.")* [This subdivision] says that the above arising-disappearing dharmas are unconnected to thusness [tathata].[101] It is just that in each of these sentient beings eight types of consciousness have existed spontaneously from without beginning. Within these the eighth, the storehouse consciousness [*ālaya-vijñāna*], is the basis. All-at-once transforming into the organ body, the vessel world, and the [karmic] seeds, its turnings produce the seven [active] consciousnesses, each of which has the potentiality to manifest its own objective supports [*ālambana*].[102] *(The eye [consciousness] takes forms as its objective supports [and so on], up to the seventh [consciousness], which takes as its objective support the seeing [part] of the eighth [consciousness].[103] The eighth takes as its objective supports the organ [body], the [karmic] seeds, and the vessel world.)* There are no real dharmas whatsoever outside these eight consciousnesses.

Question: How does this [consciousness] transformation work?

Answer: Because of the power of fumigating habit [energy; *vāsanā*] that discriminates a self and dharmas, when the various consciousnesses arise, they transform into a seeming self and dharmas.[104] Because two consciousnesses, the sixth and seventh, are covered by ignorance [*avidyā*], they take this [apparent self and dharmas] as objective supports, grasping them as a real self and real dharmas. It is like one who is ill *(when one is seriously sick, the mind is beclouded and sees people and things in strange colors)* or one who is dreaming *(things seen in the dream state can be remembered)*. Because of the power of the illness or the dream, in the mind the characteristics of various external sense objects seem to arise. Even though when dreaming one grasps them as really existent external things, when awakening comes, one knows that they are just dream transformations. This body characteristic and external world of ours are also like this, just consciousness transformations. Because of delusion, one grasps [the mistaken notion] that a self and sense objects exist. Having awakened to the realization that there has never been a self and dharmas, that only mind [*citta-mātra*] has existed, one then relies on this wisdom of dual voidness [of self and dharmas] to cultivate such practices as the [five-tiered] consciousness-only viewing,[105] the six perfections, and the four articles of attraction.[106] Step-by-step one extinguishes the two hindrances of the depravities and objects of knowledge[107] and realizes the thusness revealed by dual voidness.[108] The ten [bodhisattva] stages fill up completely, turning over the eight consciousnesses to become the awakening of the four knowledges.[109] Once the hindrances to thusness have been exhausted, the body of the dharma nature and great nirvana actualize.[110] The principle spoken of in several tens of sutras such as the *Unraveling the Deep Secret*[111] and several hundreds of fascicles of treatises [such as] the *Yoga*[112] and the *[Cheng] weishi [lun]*[113] do not go beyond this.[114] The three subdivisions above are all the first teaching of cryptic meaning that relies on the nature to speak of characteristics.

The teaching that takes consciousness to negate sense objects (the Yogācāra sutras and treatises) is *identical* to the Chan axiom of stopping the unreal and cultivating mind. Thus, the teaching devices of the Chan houses belonging to this axiom, such as cross-legged sitting, breath control, etc., find canonical support in the Yogācāra sutras. How can anyone possibly condemn such praxes? Whether or not to encourage a trainee to do cross-legged sitting depends upon a considered assessment of the trainee's disposition. Even Bodhidharma himself and the East Mountain patriarchs practiced cross-legged sitting!

26. However, only the third [subdivision of the first teaching], the teaching that takes consciousness to eradicate sense objects, comes together like a tally with the Chan gate's axiom of stopping [thought of] the unreal and cultivating mind [only]. Knowing that all external objects are void, [this Chan axiom] does not cultivate the phenomenal characteristics of external sense objects, but just stops [thought of] the unreal and cultivates mind [only]. "Stopping [thought of] the unreal" means to stop the unreality of self and dharmas; "cultivating mind [only]" means to cultivate the mind of consciousness only.[115] Thus, [this Chan axiom] is *identical* to the consciousness-only teaching. Since it is identical to buddha [word as recorded in such sutras as the *Unraveling the Deep Secret*], how can anyone condemn its step-by-step gate of stopping [thought of the] unreal and gazing at purity,[116] sweeping away [dust] from time to time,[117] freezing mind and abiding in mind,[118] concentrating completely on one object, doing cross-legged sitting, regulating the body and regulating the breath, etc.? These sorts of teaching devices were all encouraged and praised by the Buddha. The *Vimalakīrti* says: "It is not necessary that one sit."[119] It does not say: "It is necessary that one not sit." To do sitting or not to do sitting depends upon what is a suitable response to the disposition [of the trainee in question]. Whether to freeze mind or to make mind attentive [to ritual acts depends] in each case [on

a master's] estimate of the [trainee's] habit-energy nature. During the interval from the great Emperor Gaozong [r. 650–683] to the court of Xuanzong [r. 713–755] the basic axiom of the perfect and all-at-once [that is, the Southern lineage of Huineng] was not yet practiced in the North. [In the North during that time] there was only Chan Master Shenxiu. He spread widely the step-by-step teaching and became the Dharma Ruler of the Two Capitals [Chang'an and Luoyang] and Master of the Gate to Three Emperors [Empress Wu, Ruizong, and Zhongzong].[120] Everyone called it the Bodhidharma lineage, and yet it did not reveal the purport of "[mind] is buddha." Caoqi [Huineng] and Heze [Shenhui] feared that the perfect axiom would die off, and so they scolded and condemned such things as abiding in mind, breath control, etc. This was just a case of getting rid of disease and was not a case of getting rid of dharma.[121] These teaching devices were precisely those that the Great Master, the fifth patriarch [Hongren], used in instruction. Each [of his ten major disciples] was sanctioned as the master of one direction.[122] Bodhidharma used the practice of wall viewing to teach people how to quiet mind.[123] He said: "Externally, stop all objective supports. Internally, make the mind free of panting [*nei xin wu chuan*]. When the mind is like a wall, one can enter the path with it."[124] Certainly this is a dharma of cross-legged Chan sitting! Furthermore, the *Damochanjing* in two fascicles, which was translated by [Hui]yuan Gong of Mt. Lu and the two Indian monks Buddha and Yaśas,[125] clarifies in detail the gate of cross-legged Chan sitting and step-by-step teaching devices. The idea is no different from that of the Tiantai [lineage] and the [Jingzhong and Northern] schools of [Zhi]shen and [Shen]xiu [respectively]. The fourth [Chan] patriarch [Daoxin] for a period of several decades did not touch his ribs to a mat.[126] Thus, we know whether a [Chan] axiom is explicit or implicit by whether its understanding is deep or shallow. We do not take its practice or lack of practice of breath control, etc., to ascertain whether the principles of its dharma are biased or perfect. One merely applies antidotes in accordance with the disease. One must not praise this and condemn that. *(Earlier [in section 16] I mentioned that there was a person who criticized me, saying: "Why do you encourage cross-legged Chan sitting?" This is now my answer.)*

The second teaching, the teaching of cryptic meaning that eradicates characteristics to reveal the dharma nature, on the surface negates everything, but its hidden meaning is more positive, to reveal reality or the true nature. This teaching critiques the third subdivision of the first teaching, stating that *both* mind and sense objects are mutually dependent and hence void. The canonical texts of this second teaching include the *Perfection of Wisdom Sutras* and the treatises of the Madhyamaka school.

27. The second is the teaching of cryptic meaning that eradicates characteristics to reveal the [dharma] nature. *(According to the real, complete meaning, grasping*

of the unreal has always been void and need not be further eradicated. The dhar-
mas without outflows have always been the true nature. The excellent functioning
of the conditioned has never ceased. It should not be eradicated. It is just for the sake
of a type of sentient being who grasps unreal characteristics, obstructs the per-
fected nature, and [finds it] difficult to obtain profound awakening, that the Bud-
dha [in such sutras as the Perfection of Wisdom] *does not sort out good and bad,*
stained and pure, nature and characteristics, but eradicates everything. Even
though the true nature and excellent functioning are not nonexistent, [the Bud-
dha in the Perfection of Wisdom Sutras] *says that they are nonexistent. This is*
the reason we say [this second teaching] is of "cryptic meaning." Even though its
[hidden] meaning lies in revealing the nature, its words are an eradication of char-
acteristics, and, hence, the [hidden] meaning is not manifest in the words. Hence
it is "cryptic.") This teaching states [the following critique]: Since in the previous [consciousness-only] teaching, the sense objects, which are transformations
[of consciousness], are all unreal, how could the consciousnesses with the potentiality to transform alone be real? This is because mind and sense objects are
mutually supportive; they are void but seem to exist. In other words, mind does
not arise alone. It is arises in dependence on sense objects. Sense objects do not
arise by themselves. They are manifested from mind. If mind is void, then sense
objects fade. If sense objects are extinguished, then mind is void. There has
never been mind without sense objects, nor have there ever been sense objects
without mind. It is like seeing things in a dream, where there seems to be a difference between the seer and the seen [that is, the sense objects]. In fact, they are
equally unreal, neither of them having any existence whatsoever. The consciousnesses and the sense objects are also like this. This is because they both are dependent upon [causes and] conditions [*hetu pratyaya*] and have no self nature [*asvabhāva*]. There has never been a dharma that did not arise from causes and
conditions; therefore, among all dharmas, there are none that are not void
[*śūnya*].[127] Whatever has characteristics is unreal.[128] Therefore, in voidness [*śūn-
yatā*] there are no eyes, ears, nose, tongue, body, mind; no eighteen [psycho-
physical] elements [of the personality], twelve [members of the chain of] causation, four truths; no knowledge and also no attainment.[129] There is no karma and
no retribution, no practice and no realization. Samsara and nirvana are equal, like
an illusion. Just take not being fixed in anything, no grasping, and no attaching, as
practice of the path. The thousand-plus fascicles of the [*Perfection of*] *Wisdom*
Sutras[130] in various sections and the three treatises, the *Zhong[lun]*,[131] the
Bai[lun],[132] and the *[Shi'er] men*,[133] as well as the *Guang bai[lun]*,[134] etc., all discuss
this [teaching]. *(The [Da] zhidu lun*[135] *in one hundred fascicles also speaks of this*
principle, but, since this treatise emphasizes the comprehension of non-grasping, it
includes dharma characteristics of both the Mahayana and Hinayana and is co-
vertly identical to the later true-nature axiom [that is, the third teaching].)[136]

The second teaching and the second Chan axiom are *identical.* Chan gradualists such as the Northern lineage and dharma-characteristics exegetes are critical of voidness formulations, holding that they fall into the extreme of negating cause and effect. But Nagarjuna's voidness and Asanga's existence form a perfect whole, and this is also the case with the later Indian masters Bhavaviveka of the Madhyamaka school and Dharmapala of the Yogācāra school. According to the teachings of the Huayan master Fazang, existence and voidness in contradiction annihilate each other and, at the same time, in agreement fuse into oneness: The extreme of contradiction *is* the extreme of agreement. In the case of the Indians negation equaled confirmation, but, lamentably, in China negation has led to jealousy. Some Chinese have not taken the Indian medicine.

28. This [second] teaching and the Chan gate's axiom of cutting off and not leaning on anything are *identical.* Since they are identical to what the World-honored-one has said [in the voidness sutras] and what the bodhisattvas have propagated [in the Madhyamaka treatises], why is it that whenever Chan adepts of the step-by-step gate [such as Northern lineage] and [some] followers of exegesis [such as those of the dharma-characteristics axiom] hear these [negative] expressions [used by Chan adepts of the all-at-once gate and exegetes of the eradication-of-characteristics axiom], they are critical? They say: "It abolishes cause and effect." But the Buddha himself said: "There is neither karma nor retribution." How could this be a false view? [These Chan adepts and exegetes] might say: "When the Buddha spoke these words, they had a deeper [that is, cryptic or hidden] meaning." [But then I would in turn ask]: "Why is it that when [some under] the Chan gate employ these expressions, there is no such deeper meaning?" They might say: "I have investigated the awakening [of such-and-such Chan adepts], and there is no deeper meaning." [I would reply:] "You have met those who have misunderstood. You should abhor only the people involved. How can you reject the dharma?" The above two teachings [that is, the third subdivision of the first teaching, the teaching that takes consciousness to eradicate sense objects, and the second teaching, the teaching of cryptic meaning that eradicates characteristics to reveal the dharma nature] are in accordance with the Buddha's basic intention. Even though they do not conflict, in what junior trainees transmitted there was a great deal of grasping the written word and missing the purport. Either each grasped one view [that is, taking consciousness to eradicate sense objects or eradicating characteristics to reveal the nature] and denied the other, or both of them were of floating faith and too dull in terms of ability to understand. Therefore, the bodhisattvas Nagarjuna and [his disciple] Aryadeva relied on the teaching that eradicates characteristics and spoke widely of the principle of voidness.[137] They eradicated this grasping of existence [on the part of junior trainees] and enabled them to come to a

penetrating understanding of true voidness. True voidness is a voidness that does not go against existence. The bodhisattvas Asaṅga and Vasubandhu relied on the consciousness-only teaching and engaged in extensive discussions of terms and characteristics. They analyzed the nature and characteristics as different, impurity and purity as different, and eradicated this grasping of voidness [on the part of junior trainees], enabling them to come to a clear understanding of excellent existence. Excellent existence is an existence that does not go against voidness. Although each writes of one principle, [true voidness or excellent existence, they form a] perfect whole. That is why they do not go against each other.

Question: If so, why later were there treatise masters such as Bhavaviveka and Dharmapāla who eradicated each other's [teaching]?[138]

Answer: This [voidness of the Mādhyamika Bhavaviveka and existence of the Yogācārin Dharmapāla] confirm each other; they do not eradicate each other. Why? The reason is that the faculties of scholars during the final phase [of the dharma][139] are gradualistic and dull, and they grasp either voidness or existence. Bhavaviveka and others eradicated really existent characteristics, enabling [those who grasped existence] to plumb the ultimate depth of true voidness. This confirmed the excellent existence of origination by dependence of the other [that is, Dharmapāla]. Dharmapāla and others eradicated a biased voidness of the annihilationist [view that denies cause and effect]. Their intention lay in excellent existence. Because excellent existence is preserved, it is identical to the no-self-nature [*asvabhāva*] and true voidness of the other [Bhavaviveka]. The texts negate each other, but the intentions confirm each other. *(With this the previously mentioned doubt [in section 16] about the clash between the Southern and Northern Chan gates has been resolved.)* This is because there are two principles to excellent existence and true voidness.[140] The first is the principle of mutual contradiction in the extreme. This means that they clash and are completely snatched up and eternally exhausted. The second is the principle of mutual agreement in the extreme. This means that they mysteriously fuse into one characteristic, and the whole substance is completely taken in. If they did not snatch each other up and completely exhaust each other, there would be no way for the whole substance to be completely drawn in. Thus, contradiction in the extreme *is* agreement in the extreme. Because Nāgarjuna and Asaṅga, etc., accorded with the gate of agreement in the extreme, they confirmed each other. Because Bhavaviveka and Dharmapāla, etc., are based on the gate of contradiction in the extreme, they eradicated each other. Contradiction and agreement exist in freedom; confirmation and eradication are unobstructed. Thus, within all dharmas there are none that are not brought together. Alas! In this land [of China], junior students of the sutras and treatises of these two axioms [that is, dharma-characteristics and eradication-of-characteristics] denied and criticized each other as if they were mutual enemies. When will they be capable of realizing the patience [that comes from recognizing that] dharmas are non-arising [and non-disappearing]? Today's all-at-once and step-by-step Chan adepts are the same way. Exert effort to penetrate the [mind] mirror. Do not be biased.

Question: Since for the former worthies of the western regions mutual eradication was identical to mutual confirmation, how can it be that in this land mutual negation becomes mutual jealousy?

Answer: It is like a person's drinking water. He himself knows whether it is cold or warm.[141] Everyone [must] view mind. Everyone [must] investigate thoughts. [The former worthies of the western regions] left behind medicine to prevent disease, [but some in this land] have not become healthy. [The western worthies] set up a dharma to prevent error, [but some Chinese] have not become worthies.

The third teaching, the teaching that openly shows that the true mind *is* dharma nature/true nature, does not discuss characteristics, does not negate characteristics, does not employ teaching devices, and is without any cryptic meaning. It just teaches that mind=the true nature=Knowing. This teaching is found in sutras such as the *Huayan*, *Perfect Awakening*, and *Buddha Top-knot* (=*Heroic Progress Samadhi*) and in treatises like the *Awakening of Faith*. It is *identical* to the third Chan axiom.

29. The third is the teaching that openly shows that the true mind *is* the [dharma] nature. *(It points directly to the realization that one's own mind [svacitta] is the true nature [tattva].[142] It does not show in terms of phenomenal characteristics, nor does it show by eradicating characteristics. Therefore, we say: "Is the nature." It does not involve teaching devices or a hidden, cryptic meaning, and, therefore, we say: "Openly shows.")* This teaching says that all sentient beings possess the true mind of voidness and calm that is intrinsically pure from without beginning. *(It is not a case of becoming pure by cutting off the depravities and, therefore, we say: "Intrinsically pure." The* Ratnagotra-śāstra *says: "There are two kinds of purity. The first is intrinsic purity, and the second is the purity [that results from] the removal of stain."[143] The* Śrīmālā *says: "The intrinsically pure mind is difficult to understand. This mind made impure by the depravities is also difficult to understand."[144] Comment: This mind transcends the principles of the two previous axioms of voidness and existence, and that is why it is difficult to understand.)* Bright and never darkening, it is a clear and constant Knowing. *(From here down I quote buddha word.)* Exhausting the limit of the future, always abiding and never extinguishing, we call it the buddha nature. It is also called the buddha-in-embryo or mind ground. *(Bodhidharma's transmission was this mind.)* From beginningless time thought of the unreal [abhūta-vikalpa] forms a screen over it, so that, never self-realized, it sinks into the rebirth process.

The one of great awakening, feeling sadness at this, appears in the world in order to say that all the dharmas of samsara are void and to openly show that this mind is identical to all of the buddhas. It is as the "Chapter on the Appearance [of the Tathagatas]" of the *Huayan Sutra* says: "Buddha sons, there is not one sentient being who does not possess the wisdom of the Tathagata. It is just that sentient beings do not realize [they possess it] because of thought of the unreal and grasping. If thought of the unreal is removed, then complete wisdom, spontaneous wisdom, unobstructed wisdom, can appear. It is like a great sutra roll *(analogous to the Buddha's wisdom)*. In size it is three-thousand great thousand of worlds. *(The wisdom substance is without limit; it circulates throughout the dharma sphere.)* It narrates the events in the three thousand great thousand of worlds, exhausting all of them. *(It is like merits and excellent functions as numberless as the grains of sand of the Ganges from the outset existing on the substance.)* In spite of the fact that this great sutra roll is a great thousand of worlds in size, it exists in its entirety within one speck of dust. *(It is like the Buddha wisdom existing in its entirety within the body of [every] sentient being, perfect and complete.)* [I have made] an example of one speck of dust *(raised the example of one sentient being)*, but all specks of dust are like this. Once there was a person whose wisdom was clear and comprehensive *(like the World-honored-one)*. Having brought to perfection the pure, divine eye, he saw the sutra roll within the speck of dust. *(The divine eye cuts through hindrances to see forms, just as the buddha eye cuts through the depravities to see the buddha wisdom.)* [Hidden within the speck of dust, the sutra roll] was not of the least benefit to sentient beings. *(When [sentient beings] are deluded, none of them attains this function; there are none that are not separated from it, etc.)* [The good friend on the path then] produces teaching devices with which to break open that speck of dust *(just as [the Buddha] speaks dharma in order to destroy hindrances)*. He brings out this great sutra which enables all sentient beings to obtain abundant benefit *(etc.)*. The wisdom of the Tathagata is also like this. Immeasurable, unobstructed, it can benefit all sentient beings everywhere. *(This is like the [sutra's] narration of events in the three thousand worlds.)* [Yet it exists] perfect and complete within the body of every sentient being. *(This is like the [sutra roll] within [each and every] speck of dust.)* It is just that the ordinary, ignorant ones engage in thought of the unreal and grasping. Unaware, not awakened, they do not obtain benefit. It is then that the Tathagata, gazing upon all sentient beings in the dharma sphere with his unobstructed, pure wisdom eye, speaks these words: 'Strange! Strange! Why is it that, [even though] all these sentient beings possess the wisdom of the Tathagata, [they continue in] stupidity, delusion, and the depravities, not Knowing and not seeing? I will teach them by means of the path of the noble ones that will free them forever from thought of the unreal and grasping, enabling them to come to see the great wisdom of the

Tathagata within their own bodies, no different from that of a buddha. He then teaches those sentient beings how to practice the path of the noble ones *(the six perfections and the thirty-seven parts of the path)* that will free them from thought of the unreal. Once free of thought of the unreal, they will realize the immeasurable wisdom of the Tathagata, which benefits and brings peace to all sentient beings.'"[145]

Question: Above you have spoken of the "complete and constant Knowing that is intrinsically [pure from without beginning]." Why would it be necessary for the buddhas to open it up and show it?

Answer: This Knowing is not the knowing of realization. My intention was to explain that the true nature is not identical to the sky or a tree or a stone, and, therefore, I said "Knowing."[146] [Knowing] is not like the consciousnesses that take sense objects as objective supports and discriminate. It is not like the wisdom that illuminates substance and comprehends. It is just that the nature of thusness is spontaneously constant Knowing.

Therefore, Asvaghosa Bodhisattva says: "Thusness is the self substance and the Knowing of reality."[147] The "Chapter on Dedications" of the *Huayan* also says: "Thusness takes illumination as its nature."[148] Also, according to the "Chapter on Questions on Enlightenment" [of the *Huayan,* which is quoted below,] there is a difference between wisdom [prajna] and Knowing. Wisdom is limited to the noble ones; it does not pervade common persons. Knowing is possessed by both common persons and noble ones; it pervades both principle and wisdom.

[The "Chapter on Questions on Enlightenment" says:] "Therefore, nine bodhisattvas, including Awakened Head, asked Mañjuśrī: 'What is the wisdom of the buddha realm *(the wisdom of realization awakening)?* What is the Knowing of the buddha realm *(the true mind that exists from the outset)?*'

Mañjuśrī answered about wisdom: 'The wisdom of all the buddhas exists in freedom, unobstructed in the three times.'

(It comprehends all events in the past, future, and present, and so it exists in freedom and is unobstructed.)

In answering about Knowing, he said: 'It is not something that consciousness can be conscious of.'

(One cannot by means of consciousness be conscious of it because consciousness belongs to discrimination, and discrimination is not true Knowing. True Knowing is only seen in no mindfulness.)[149]

'It is not an object of mind.'

(One cannot by means of wisdom [have] Knowing. This means that if one could realize it by means of wisdom, then it would be an object that had been realized. Because true Knowing is not an object, one cannot realize it by means of wisdom. If one even for a split second produces an illuminated mind, then it

is not true Knowing. Therefore, the sutra says: "If one's own mind seizes one's own mind, then what is not an illusion becomes an illusionary dharma."[150] *The treatise says: "Mind does not see mind."*[151] *The Great Master Heze [Shenhui] said: "Deliberate and you are [already] in error."*[152] *This is why the Northern lineage's gazing at mind misses the true purport. If mind could be gazed at, then it would be an object. Therefore, this [Mañjuśrī] says: "It is not an object of mind.")*

'This nature from the outset is pure.'

(It does not become pure after the removal of stain and extinction of the depravities. It does not become pure after cutting off the hindrances and congealing turbulence. This is why we say: "From the outset pure." The Ratnagotra-śāstra *calls the purity that does not [require] the removal of stain that "intrinsic purity." Therefore, we say: "This nature from the outset is pure.")*

'[Knowing] is opened up and shown to all sentient beings.'"[153]

(It has already been said that it is from the outset pure, that it does not require the cutting off of hindrances, and thus we know that all beings from the outset have possessed it. It is just that, because of a screen of the depravities, they are not spontaneously Knowing. Therefore, the Buddha opens it up and shows them and enables them all to gain entrance to awakening. In the Lotus *[it speaks of] opening up and showing [sentient beings how to] awaken to buddha Knowing-seeing.*[154] *As it says in this passage, the Buddha originally appeared in the world just for the sake of this task. It says: "to have them attain purity." That is the purity [that results from] the removal of stain in the* Ratnagotra. *Although this mind is intrinsically pure, one must always be awakened to it and cultivating it. Only then will one attain perfect purity of nature and characteristics. Therefore, a number of sutras and treatises speak of the two types of purity and the two types of liberation. Among present-day people whose learning is shallow, some know just the purity [that results from] the removal of stain and the liberation [that results from] the removal of hindrances, and so they criticize the Chan gate's "mind is buddha." Others, knowing just intrinsic purity and the liberation [coming from awakening to] intrinsic purity, make light of teaching characteristics [that is, doctrinal formulations] and reject such practices as holding to the disciplinary rules, cross-legged Chan sitting, [breath] control, etc. They do not know that one must all-at-once awaken to intrinsic purity [to attain] intrinsic liberation and [engage in] step-by-step practice so as to attain the purity [that results from] the removal of stain and the liberation [resulting from] the removal of hindrances, becoming perfectly pure and in ultimate liberation. Free from obstruction in both mind and body, one is then identical to Śākyamuni Buddha.)*

The *Baozanglun* says: "If you know existence, you will be destroyed by existence. If you know non-existence, you will be ruined by non-existence. *(These are both the wisdom that is capable of knowing existence or non-existence.)* The

Knowing of this Knowing does not make any distinction between existence and non-existence."[155] *(Making no distinction between existence and non-existence, it is the Knowing that is intrinsic non-discrimination.)* Thus, [this third teaching] opens up and shows the mind of spiritual Knowing that is the true nature, no different from a buddha. Thus, this is called the teaching that openly shows that the true mind *is* the [dharma] nature.

More than forty sections of such sutras as the *Huayan*,[156] *Secret Array*,[157] *Perfect Awakening*,[158] *Buddha Top-knot* [=*Heroic Progress Samadhi*],[159] *Śrīmālā*,[160] *Buddha-in-Embryo*,[161] *Lotus*,[162] and *Nirvana*,[163] and fifteen sections of such treatises as the *Ratnagotra*,[164] *Buddha Nature*,[165] *Awakening of Faith*,[166] *Ten Stages*,[167] *Dharma Sphere*,[168] and *Nirvana*[169] base themselves on the revealed dharma substance and [hence] all belong to this teaching, though there are some differences concerning all-at-once versus step-by-step. [This teaching] is *identical* to the Chan gate's third axiom of directly revealing the mind nature.

Mādhyamikas speak only of the calmed and neglect Knowing; Yogācārins hold that the ordinary person differs from those advanced on the path, neglecting the Chan slogan "mind is buddha." The schema of three teachings is for these people. Bodhidharma never transmitted the word "Knowing." He simply waited for trainees to experience the real on their own. This is why his teaching was called "silent transmission of the mind seal." The word "silent" implies that he was silent about Knowing, not that he did not speak at all. This was the pattern for the next six generations. Shenhui wanted to continue this pattern, but the conditions were inopportune. He worried that Bodhidharma's teaching was in peril, and, consequently, he spoke the line: "The one word 'Knowing' is the gate of all excellence." This open style of transmission was easily comprehensible.

30. Since Asvaghosa designates mind as the original source[170] and Mañjuśrī selects Knowing as the true substance,[171] why does the party that negates characteristics [that is, eradication-of-charactersitics/Madhyamaka] just speak of calm and not allow true Knowing? Why does the party that discusses characteristics [that is, dharma-characteristics/Yogācāra] grasp [the view that] the common person is different from the noble one and not allow [the Chan gate's "mind] is buddha"? [My] present [schema for] classifying the teachings of the Buddha is for precisely these people. Therefore I said earlier [in section 11] that many of those [Chan patriarchs] in the western regions who transmitted mind were equally versed in the sutras and treatises, [following] the road of non-duality. It was just because this land [of China] was deluded about mind and grasped the written word, took the name for the substance, that Bodhidharma's good skill [in teaching devices] was to select the phrase "transmission of mind." He raised this term *("mind" is a term)*, but was silent about its substance *("Knowing" is its*

substance). As a metaphor he took wall viewing[172] (*mentioned above [in section 26]*) to effect the cutting off of all objective supports.

Question: When one has cut off all objective supports, is that not [the extreme view of] annihilationism?[173]

Answer: Although one cuts off all thoughts, it is not annihilationism.

Question: How do you verify the statement that it is not annihilationism?

Answer: Complete and spontaneous Knowing, words cannot reach it. The master [Bodhidharma], when sealing [a disciple], said: "Just this is the intrinsically pure mind. Have no further doubts."

If the answers did not coincide, just in order to cut off all errors, he had [the disciple] engage in further reflection. To the very end, [Bodhidharma] did not give others the previously mentioned word "Knowing." He simply waited for them to awaken of their own accord and then, for the first time, said: "That is how it really is!" Only when they had personally realized the substance did he seal them, cutting off remaining doubts. This is why [his teaching] was called "silent transmission of the mind seal." The word "silent" means only that he was silent about the word "Knowing," not that he did not say anything. For six generations of transmission, it was always like this. But, by the time of Heze [Shenhui], other lineages were spreading competing teachings. [Shenhui] wanted to seek a silent coinciding, but he did not encounter a karmic nexus. Further, meditating on Bodhidharma's prediction about the hanging thread (*Bodhidharma had said: "After the sixth generation the fate of my dharma will be like a hanging thread"*), he feared that the purport of the [Bodhidharma mind] axiom would be extinguished.[174] Consequently, he spoke [the line]: "The one word 'Knowing' is the gate of all excellence."[175] He trusted that trainees would awaken to this in a deep or shallow manner. In other words, his plan was to ensure that the [Bodhidharma mind] axiom would not be cut off. Also, the fortunes of the great dharma in this country had reached the point where a type of worldly person [who talks about] the path was being heard everywhere. This is the reason [Shenhui] responded in this way. This silent transmission [of Bodhidharma] was unknown to others, and so [Shenhui] took the robe as [a seal of] faith. This open transmission [of Shenhui] was easily comprehensible to trainees. He just dispelled doubts through the spoken word. Since it has already been put into words, is it necessary to quote the sutras and treatises as proof? (*An objection previously mentioned [in section 16]: "Do those who at present transmit the dharma speak secret oral transmissions [miyu] or not?" I have now answered this question. The dharma is Bodhidharma's dharma. Therefore, those who hear it, however deep or shallow, are all benefited. It is just that in the past it was secret, whereas now it is open. Therefore, it is not called a secret oral transmission. Just because the name is different [from what it was in Bodhidharma's time] does not imply that the dharma is also different.*)

Question: Having awakened to the true mind of the third teaching, how does one practice it? Does one employ the cross-legged Chan sitting of the first teaching?

Answer: The person who is prone to turbulent, uncontrollable emotions does make use of the teaching devices of the first teaching, but the person of weak depravities and strong intellect relies on the one-practice concentration (samadhi) of Southern Chan and the third teaching. The one-practice concentration is movement and is carried out in the midst of all activities.

31. Question: Once one has awakened to this [intrinsically pure] mind, how does one practice it? Does one still rely on the command to practice cross-legged Chan sitting within the first teaching, the one that speaks of characteristics?[176]

Answer: There are two ideas here. When one is prone to strong emotions that are difficult to control, such as heavy depression and extreme excitability, passion and anger, etc., then one makes use of all sorts of teaching devices within the previous teaching, regulating according to the disease. If one's depravities are quite weak and one's intellect is sharp, then one relies on the one-practice concentration of the basic axiom [the third Chan axiom/Southern Chan] and the basic teaching [the third teaching that openly shows that the true mind *is* dharma nature].[177] As the *Awakening of Faith* says: "If you practice tranquilization, dwell in a quiet place, straighten the body, and rectify the mind. Rely on neither breath nor bodily form, until you reach mind only, without external sense objects."[178] The *Jingang sanmei [jing]* says: "Chan is movement. No movement, no Chan. This is non-arising Chan."[179] The *Fajujing* says: "If one trains in the various concentrations, it is movement, not cross-legged Chan sitting. The mind following along in the flow of sense objects, how could that be called concentration?"[180] The *Vimalakīrti* says: "To manifest all the deportments *(walking, standing, sitting, and lying)* without arising from the extinction concentration, to manifest neither body nor mind in the three realms [of desire, form, and non-form], this is quiet sitting."[181] [This is a concentration that] the Buddha sanctioned. According to this, once one has comprehended that the three realms [of desire, form, and non-form] are like a flower in the sky, that the four forms of birth [from an embryo, from an egg, from wetness, and from itself] are like a bed of dreams, then, grounded in substance, one produces practice; one practices and yet it is a non-practice. Dwelling in neither buddha nor mind, who is it that discusses higher realms and lower realms? *(A previous objection [in section 16] was that, according to the teachings, one must [practice in this realm of desire in order to] be drawn up into the [dhyanas and] concentrations of the upper realms [of form and non-form], thereby stealing a peak into the heavens.[182] [The person who presented this objection] has grasped the words of just one axiom. Having seen this principle of the complete teaching, he should feel shame and withdraw.)*

The true mind of the third teaching can be completely selected out from all dharmas or can be completely inclusive of all dharmas. Direct realization that Knowing *is* the true mind constitutes the former; the latter means that without exception every single dharma *is* true mind. The gate of completely selecting out envelops the second teaching; the gate of completely including envelops the first teaching. The third teaching, which directly reveals true mind and within that encompasses both completely selecting out and completely including, subsumes the first two.

32. Within this [third] teaching the one true mind nature faces all dharmas, both impure and pure, and [can be] completely selected out or [can] completely include [all dharmas]. Completely selecting out means, as discussed above [in section 29], just *the thing-in-itself*:[183] directly pointing out that spiritual Knowing *is* the mind nature, and all else in unreal. This is why [Mañjuśrī] said that Knowing is not something that consciousness is conscious of,[184] that is not an object of mind, up to and including that it is neither nature nor characteristics, that it is neither buddha nor sentient beings, that it is divorced from the four alternatives [of is, is not, both is and is not, and neither is nor is not] and cuts off the hundred negations. "Completely including" means that, of all dharmas, both impure and pure, there are none that are not mind. When mind is deluded, it falsely produces depravities and karma, [which lead] to the four forms of birth, the six rebirth paths, and the worlds of miscellaneous filth; when mind is awakened, from substance it produces functions [such as] the four immeasurables, the six perfections, up to and including the four [unobstructed] understandings, the ten powers, and the pure lands of excellent bodies.[185] All of these are its manifestations. Because this mind manifests all dharmas, every single dharma is true mind. It is like the fact that all of the events that occur in a dream happen to the dreamer. When gold is made into utensils, each and every utensil is still the gold. With reflections in a mirror, every reflection is still the mirror. (*Dreaming is like thought of the unreal and karmic retribution; utensils are like practice; reflections are like responsive transformations.*) Therefore, the *Huayan* says: "Know that all dharmas are the mind self-nature and bring to perfection the wisdom body. Do not rely on others for awakening."[186] The *Awakening of Faith* says: "The three realms are unreal, created by mind only. When one is free of mind, then the six sense objects do not exist. . . . All discrimination discriminates one's own mind. Mind cannot see mind; there are no characteristics that can be apprehended. Therefore, all dharmas are like images in a mirror."[187] The *Lanka Descent Sutra* says: "The calmed is called one mind. One mind is called buddha-in-embryo [tathagatagarbha]. It has the potentiality to create all the beings in the rebirth paths, to create good and to create bad, to receive suffering and joy, to be the cause of everything."[188] Therefore, we know that there is nothing that is not mind. The gate of completely selecting out takes

in the previous second teaching, the one that eradicates characteristics. The gate of completely including takes in the previous first teaching, the one that discusses characteristics. If we take [those two] previous [teachings] to view this [third teaching], this one is very different from the previous [two]. If we use this [teaching] to take in the previous [two teachings], then the previous [two teachings] are identical to this [teaching]. Depth always includes shallowness, but shallowness does not reach to depth. Depth means directly to reveal the substance of true mind and within that to select out everything and include everything. If, in this way, inclusion and selection exist in freedom, and nature and characteristics are unobstructed, then one is capable of having no place to abide within all dharmas. Just this is called the complete meaning [of the teachings]. There are still the differences between "mind" and "nature," the conflict between all-at-once and step-by-step, and the ranked oral teachings of the various houses. I will deal with all these topics in sequence in the second roll.

COLLECTION OF EXPRESSIONS OF THE CHAN SOURCE[189] FIRST ROLL

PROLEGOMENON TO THE COLLECTION OF EXPRESSIONS OF THE CHAN SOURCE SECOND ROLL

By the Monk Zongmi of Caotang Monastery on Mt. Zhongnan

The three teachings can be referred to as three principles or axioms (here not referring specifically to the three Chan axioms). The first and second principles can be understood as the polarity between existence and voidness, the third and first principles as the polarity between nature and characteristics. Everyone agrees on this. However, the second and third principles show the polarity between eradicating characteristics and revealing the nature, and there is widespread misunderstanding about this opposition. Both scholars and Chan people hold that these two are one teaching, one axiom. In other words, they hold that eradicating characteristics is, ipso facto, the true nature. To clarify this situation below I will lay out ten differences between the voidness principle and the nature principle.

33. The above three teachings take in all of the sutras spoken by the Tathagata in the course of his lifetime and all of the treatises composed by the bodhisattvas. A close examination of dharma and principles will reveal that the three principles [that is, the three teachings] are completely different, while the one dharma is without difference. Of the three principles the first and second are

opposed as existence is to voidness,[190] and the third and the first are opposed as nature is to characteristics.[191] Both of these [oppositions] are easily seen, even from a distance. Just the second and third are opposed as eradicating characteristics is [in contrast] to revealing the nature. Exegetes and Chan adepts are equally deluded [about this opposition].[192] They both say that [the second and third teachings] are one axiom or one teaching. They both hold that eradicating characteristics *is* the true nature. Therefore, I will now broadly explain the ten differences between the voidness axiom and the nature axiom:

1. difference between them concerning dharma and principles, real and worldly
2. difference between them concerning the two terms "mind" and "nature"
3. difference between them concerning the two substances of the word "nature"
4. difference between them concerning true wisdom and true Knowing
5. difference between them concerning the existence or non-existence of a self-dharma
6. difference between them concerning negativistic explanation and expressive [that is, positivistic or affirmative] explanation
7. difference between them concerning what is recognized as name and what is recognized as substance
8. difference between them concerning the two truths and the three truths
9. difference between them concerning the voidness or existence of the three natures
10. difference between them concerning the voidness or existence of the buddha qualities[193]

The voidness axiom takes characteristics as dharmas, that is, worldly truth, and takes negative statements such as "no arising and no disappearing" as principles, that is, the real truth. The nature axiom takes the true nature as dharma and voidness, existence, etc., as principles.

34. No. 1: The difference between them concerning dharma and principles, real and worldly. The voidness axiom, because it does not yet reveal the true spiritual nature, merely considers all differentiated characteristics to be dharmas; dharmas are the worldly truth. It considers "unconditioned," "no characteristics," "no arising–no disappearing," "no increasing–no decreasing," etc., which illuminate all dharmas, as principles. Principles are the real truth. Therefore, the *Zhilun* considers the worldly truth to be dharma-unobstructed wisdom

and the real truth to be principle-unobstructed wisdom.[194] The nature axiom considers the one true nature to be dharma and the various differentiations, such as voidness and existence, to be principles. Therefore, the sutra says: "Immeasurable principles arise from the one dharma."[195] Also, the "[Chapter on the] Ten Stages" of the *Huayan* says: "Dharma is knowing self-nature. Principles are knowing arising-disappearing. Dharma is knowing the real truth. Principles are knowing the worldly truth. Dharma is knowing the one vehicle. Principles are knowing the various vehicles."[196] [This sutra] in this way explains ten [differences in] meaning between the two non-obstructions of dharma and principles.

The voidness axiom views the source of all dharmas as their lack of an inherent nature, their voidness, while the nature axiom views the source of all dharmas as true mind or Knowing.

35. No. 2: The difference between them concerning the two terms "mind" and "nature." The voidness axiom with its unidirectional eye regards the original source of all dharmas as the [lack of self-] "nature" [or voidness of self-nature], while the nature axiom with its multiple eyes regards the original source of all dharmas as "mind." As to regarding it as the [lack of self-] "nature," there are many identical [passages] in the treatises, and it is not necessary to quote them here. As to regarding it as "mind," the *Śrīmālā* says: "The intrinsically pure mind."[197] The *Awakening of Faith* says: "All dharmas from the outset are divorced from such characteristics as speech, names, objective supports of mind, etc. . . . They are just the one mind."[198] The *Lanka Descent* says: "The real mind."[199] Indeed, the original nature spoken of in this axiom is not just voidness and calm, but is spontaneous, constant Knowing, and, for this reason, we should regard it as "mind."

For the voidness axiom no-self-nature is the nature; for the nature axiom the non-void substance, in other words, Knowing, is the nature.

36. No. 3: The difference between them concerning the two substances of the word "nature." The voidness axiom regards the naturelessness [*wuxing=asvabhāva*] of all dharmas to be the "nature" [*xing*], while the nature axiom regards the bright, constantly abiding, non-void substance as the "nature."[200] Therefore, although [they use] the same word for "nature," they differ about its substance.

For the voidness axiom, wisdom is non-discrimination, and Knowing is discrimination. For the nature axiom, wisdom is limited to the noble ones, but Knowing, that is, the true nature, pervades both common persons and noble ones.

37. No. 4: The difference between them concerning true wisdom and true Knowing. The voidness axiom holds that discrimination is Knowing and

non-discrimination is wisdom, wisdom being deep and Knowing shallow. The nature axiom holds that the excellent wisdom with the potential to realize the principle of the noble ones is wisdom and the true nature, which encompasses [both] principle and wisdom, pervading [both] the common person and the noble one, is Knowng. Knowing is pervasive, but wisdom is limited.[201] The "Chapter on Questions on Enlightenment" [of the *Huayan Sutra*] quoted above [in section 29] has already made this distinction. Furthermore, the "Chapter on the Ten Dedications" [of the *Huayan*,] in speaking of thusness, says: "Illumination is its nature."[202] The *Awakening of Faith* says that "the self-substance of thusness is real Knowing."[203]

Whereas the voidness axiom holds that self is unreal and non-self is real, the nature axiom reverses them.

38. No. 5: The difference between them concerning the existence or non-existence of a self-dharma. The voidness axiom takes self [atman] as unreal and non-self [anatman] as real. The nature axiom takes non-self as unreal and self as real. Therefore, the *Nirvana Sutra* says: "Non-self is called samsara. Self is called Tathagata."[204] [This sutra] also says: "To consider self as non-self is a topsy-turvy dharma."[205] [The sutra goes on,] up to and including a broad refutation of the impermanence and non-self views of the two vehicles [of the hearers and private buddhas, saying they are] "like stones in a spring pond mistaken for treasures."[206] [It gives] broad praise to permanence, joy, self, and purity as the ultimate, up to and including: "Within the nonself dharmas, there is the true self."[207] (*Indeed, sentient beings, being deluded about their own true self, falsely grasp the five aggregates as a self. Therefore, the Buddha, in the Mahayana and Hinayana dharma-characteristics and eradication-of-characteristics teachings [that is, in the second and third subdivisions of the first teaching and in the second teaching] negates it [the self], saying: "It does not exist." Now in the nature axiom [the Buddha] directly illumines the real substance, revealing it by saying: "It exists."*)

The voidness axiom is just negativistic explanation, saying what the nature is not. This is incomplete. The nature axiom is both negativistic and expressive explanation, leading to a personal realization in the here and now that Knowing *is* the mind nature.

39. No. 6: The difference between them concerning negativistic explanation and expressive [that is, positivistic or affirmative] explanation.[208] "Negativistic" means getting rid of what it is not; "expressive" means revealing what it is. In other words, "negativistic" is rejection of all that is superfluous; and "expressive" is directly showing the thing-in-itself.[209] [The thing-in-itself] is the true, excel-

lent principle nature as spoken of in various sutras. Every one [of those sutras] says it "neither arises nor disappears," "is neither stained nor pure," "has neither cause nor effect," "is without characteristics and unconditioned," "is neither common person nor noble one," "is neither nature nor characteristics," etc. [Such phrases] are all negativistic explanation. *(Sutras and treatises often negate all dharmas with the word "it-is-not [fei zi]." Sometimes there are thirty to fifty instances of the word "it-is-not." The words "not [bu zi]" and "no [wu zi]" are also [used in] this manner. This is why we speak of "the cutting off of the hundred negations.")* If [a text] speaks of "Knowing-seeing and awakened illumination," "the brightness of the spiritual mirror," "radiancy and luminosity," "awakened calm," etc., it is always a case of expressive explanation. If there were no substance such as Knowing-seeing, what dharma could be revealed as the nature, and what dharma could be spoken of as "neither arising nor disappearing," etc.? You must recognize right now, completely, that Knowing *is* the mind nature, and only then say that this Knowing "neither arises nor disappears," etc. It is like talk about salt. To say that it does not have a weak taste is negativistic, while to say that it is salty is expressive. In speaking of water, to say that it is not dry is negativistic, while to say that it is wet is expressive. The cutting off of the hundred negations that is always spoken of in the teachings is all negativistic phraseology. To directly reveal the one reality expressive language is used. The words of the voidness axiom are [just] negativistic explanation, while the words of the nature axiom have [both] the negativistic and the expressive. [Language that is] just negativistic is not yet the [teaching of] complete [meaning]. Combined with the expressive it then hits the bull's-eye. Today everyone says that negativistic words are deep and expressive words are shallow, and, for this reason, they value only such phrases as "neither mind nor buddha," "unconditioned and without characteristics," up to and including "nothing can be apprehended."[210] Indeed, it is like this because they just take negativistic phraseology to be excellent and do not want a personal realization of the dharma substance.

The voidness axiom and the characteristics axiom are afraid that inexperienced students and people of shallow dispositions will become attached to the words of the texts and produce grasping. This is why the former negates names and the latter engages in lengthy expositions of aspects and functions. The nature axiom, on the other hand, gears itself to experienced students and those of superior faculties. This axiom forgets the words and recognizes substance, that is, points to Knowing.

40. No. 7: The difference between them concerning what is recognized as name and what is recognized as substance. This means that there are [many] names and [one] substance to both the buddha dharma and mundane dharmas. According to mundane expression, the great elements are no more than four. As

the *Zhilun* says: "Earth, water, fire, and air are the names of the four things. Solidity, wetness, heat, and movement are the substance of the four things."[211] Now, let us discuss water.

Suppose someone asked: I am always hearing that when one settles it, it is clear; that when one stirs it up, it is cloudy; that when one dams it up, it stops; that when one releases it, it flows; that it has the potentiality to irrigate all living things and wash away all filth. What is this thing? *(The question is phrased in terms of its [latent] power aspect.)*[212]

Answer: It is water. *(The answer is in terms of its name.)*

The stupid, upon recognizing this name, immediately say that they have understood, but the wise will further ask: What is water? *([They aim at] understanding its substance.)*

Answer: Wetness is water. *(This is pointing to the thing-in-itself.*[213] *This single word ["wetness"] is immediately definitive; no other word could be substituted for it. If one were to say that waves or ice or clear water or turbid water is water, how would that differ from the phraseology of his question?)*

The buddha dharma is also like this. Suppose someone asked: I am always hearing the sutras say that delusion about it is stain; that awakening to it is purity; that letting it go is worldliness; that practicing it is noble; that it has the potentiality to produce all mundane and supramundane dharmas. What is this thing? *(The question is phrased in terms of its [latent] power aspect.)*

Answer: It is mind. *(The answer is in terms of its name.)*

The stupid, upon recognizing this name, will immediately say that they have understood, but those of wisdom will further ask: What is mind? *([They aim at] understanding its substance.)*

Answer: Knowing is mind.[214] *(This is pointing to its substance. This word ["Knowing"] hits the bull's-eye; no other word is as appropriate. If one were to say that "neither nature nor characteristics" or "the potentiality for speech and movement," etc., is mind, how would that differ from the phraseology of his question?)*[215]

By this we know that there is just one word for the name of water and just one for its substance and that all others [denote] its functions. Likewise, [there is just one word for the] name of mind and [just one for its] substance. The one word "wetness" penetrates to the inside of the myriad functions and aspects such as clear water, turbid water, etc. The one word "Knowing"[216] penetrates to the locus of the myriad functions and aspects such as passion, anger, friendliness, patience, good, bad, suffering, joy, etc. Today many of the people who train in Chan are skeptical, saying: "Bodhidharma just discussed *mind*. Why did Heze [Shenhui] speak of *Knowing*?" This sort of doubt is like saying: "Recently I have only heard that there is water in the well. Why today am I suddenly aware of wetness in the well?" You must be able to awaken to the realization that "water" is a name, that it is not wet, that being wet *is* water, not a name. You will then understand all the aspects such as clear water, turbid water, waves, and ice. By analogy "mind" is a name, not mind [the thing-in-itself]; "Knowing" *is* mind, not a name. You will then understand all the aspects such as real, unreal, stained, pure, good, and bad. The voidness axiom and the characteristics axiom are afraid that novice trainees and those of shallow dispositions will conform to the words [of the texts] to produce grasping, and so, [to counter this tendency, the voidness axiom] just designates names and then negates them, and [the characteristics axiom] just extensively engages in drawing out the meanings of aspects and functions. The nature axiom gears itself to trainees with long experience and those of superior faculties. Because [this axiom] has them forget words and recognize substance, it shows directly with the one word ["Knowing"]. *(Bodhidharma said: "I point to one word to show directly."*[217] *Later people did not understand his meaning and wondered what word is the one word. If some [such as Hongzhou people] say "the mind is buddha [jixin shi fo]" is the one word, this is four words. What name is the one word?)* Once one has been able to recognize substance, he will in illumination examine the aspects and functions on top of substance, and, therefore, understand all of them.

The voidness axiom holds that all dharmas are included within the two truths, the worldly (origination by dependence) and the real (voidness). The nature axiom has three truths: nature (voidness); characteristics (origination by dependence); and self substance (true mind). The self substance is neither voidness nor form, etc.; it is the potentiality to be both. This corresponds to a mirror's specific images, the voidness of those images, and the brightness or reflectivity of the mirror itself.

41. No. 8: The difference between them concerning the two truths and the three truths. All scholars know that the voidness axiom says that all dharmas, both mundane and supramundane, do not go beyond the two truths. There is no need for quotations to elucidate this.[218] The nature axiom, however, gathers up nature, characteristics, and the self substance [*xing xiang ji ziti*] and considers them together as the three truths.[219] It takes all·dharmas that originate by dependence, such as forms, etc., as the worldly truth and takes [the truth that] conditions lack a self nature and [hence] all dharmas are void as the real truth. *(This much is no different in terms of principle from the two truths of the voidness axiom and the characteristics axiom.)* That the one true mind substance is neither voidness nor form [but] has the potentiality to be void and the potentiality to be form is the truth of the highest meaning of the middle path. This is like a bright mirror that also has three aspects. One must not call a green image in the mirror yellow. A beautiful [image] and an ugly one are different from each other. This is like the worldly truth. Because the images lack a self nature, every

one of them is completely void. This is like the real truth. The substance [of the mirror], its constant brightness, is neither void nor green nor yellow [but] has the potentiality to be void and the potentiality to be green or yellow. This is like the truth of the highest meaning. This is just as the *Yingluo*,[220] *Dapin*,[221] *Benye*,[222] and other sutras say. Therefore, the Tiantai lineage relies on these three truths and cultivates the three tranquilizations and three viewings,[223] bringing to perfection the three virtues.[224]

Concerning the three natures, the voidness axiom holds that the completely imagined and the dependent-on-something-else are existence and that the completely perfected is voidness. All three are devoid of self nature or void. However, for the nature axiom, following the Huayan master Fazang, each of the three natures possesses a void aspect and an existent aspect.

42. No. 9: The difference between them concerning the voidness or existence of the three natures. The three are: the completely imagined nature[225] *(feelings of the unreal everywhere calculate a self and all dharmas and grasp them one after the other as really existent; it is like a foolish child's seeing the images of the faces of people in a mirror and grasping them as being alive, solid, with flesh and bones, etc.)*; the arising-through-dependence-on-something-else nature[226] *(these grasped dharmas are in dependence upon a host of other conditions; they arise serving as a cause for each other, and, lacking a self nature, they are just unreal characteristics, like images in a mirror)*; and the completely perfected nature[227] *(the true mind of original awakening manifests itself at initial awakening, completely perfected, real, and constantly abiding, like the brightness of a mirror).* The voidness axiom says: "Whenever the sutras discuss existence, it is according to the completely imagined and dependent-on-something else. Whenever they discuss voidness, it is the completely perfected nature. The three dharmas [=three natures] all lack [self-]nature." For the nature axiom each of the three dharmas possesses a void aspect and an existent aspect.[228] This means that the completely imagined exists in feelings, but not in principle; the dependent-on-something-else exists in characteristics, but not in the nature; and the completely perfected does not exist in feelings, but does in principle; does not exist in characteristics, but does in the nature.

The voidness axiom takes voidness as the buddha quality. The nature axiom holds that the self substance of the buddhas has real qualities, such as permanence, joy, self, purity, rays of light, etc.

43. No. 10: The difference between them concerning the voidness or existence of the buddha qualities. The voidness axiom, in speaking of the Buddha, takes voidness as his quality,[229] [saying that] no dharma whatsoever exists that can be

called awakening,[230] that to see [the Buddha in terms of] form or seek him as sound is to walk a false path.[231] The *Zhonglun* says: "[The Tathagata] is not the aggregates and is not apart from the aggregates. This [the Tathagata] and that [the aggregates] do not exist in each other. If the Tathagata does not have aggregates, where is the Tathagata?"[232] Divorcing from all characteristics is called "all the buddhas."[233] For the nature axiom the self-substance of all the buddhas has permanence, joy, self, and purity,[234] real qualities [such as] the ten bodies and the ten knowledges,[235] and the [thirty-two] marks and the [eighty minor] signs[236] that are like limitless shafts of light one after the other. The nature has existed from the outset; it does not await a karmic nexus.

Once the practitioner has accorded with the three teachings in order to realize the three Chan minds, then every thought will be a buddha thought, every poetic line a Chan line. One will sense that all strains of Chan are valid, that all coincide.

44. By specifying these ten differences, the two gates [of the voidness axiom and the nature axiom] are clarified. Although I have made divisions on characteristics of the teachings, do not[237] stagnate on feelings. The three teachings and the three [Chan] axioms are the dharma of one taste. Therefore, one must first, according to the three types of buddha teachings, realize the Chan minds of the three [Chan] axioms, and only after that will both Chan and the teachings be forgotten, both mind and buddha calmed. When both are calmed, then thought after thought all is the buddha; there will not be a single thought that is not buddha mind. When both are forgotten, then line after line all is Chan; there will not be a single line that is not Chan teaching. When one is like this, upon happening to hear talk of [the Chan axiom of] cutting off and not leaning on anything, one knows that it eradicates grasping feelings of self. Upon hearing the words of [the Chan axiom of] stopping [thought of] the unreal and cultivating mind [only], one knows that it cuts off the habit energy of self. If grasping feelings are eradicated and the true nature revealed, then cutting off [and not leaning on anything] is an axiom that reveals the nature. If habit energy is exhausted and the buddha path completed, then [stopping thought of the unreal] and cultivating mind [only] is a practice to become a buddha. As to the voidness or existence of all-at-once and step-by-step, since there is no error anywhere, how could Hong[zhou], He[ze Shenhui], [Hui]neng, and [Shen]xiu not coincide? If you are capable of attaining this sort of comprehension, everything you say to others will be excellent devices, while everything you hear from others will be excellent medicine. Medicine is to disease just as comprehension is to grasping. This is why a former worthy said: "When you are grasping, word after word [in the texts] is a boil or a wart. When you comprehend, text after text is excellent medicine."[238] The one who comprehends understands that the three [Chan] axioms do not conflict with one another.

The step-by-step teaching is all three subdivisions of the first teaching (humans-and-gods, Hinayana, and dharma characteristics) and the second teaching (eradication of characteristics). The Buddha delivered these teachings for those of medium and inferior faculties. After their faculties had matured, he spoke for them the explicit teaching of the *Lotus Sutra* and the *Nirvana Sutra*. The all-at-once teaching is divided into two types: the all-at-once of the Buddha's responding throughout his teaching career to beings of the highest disposition and the all-at-once of the Buddha's rite of transforming beings at the site of his enlightenment. Whenever during his long career the Buddha encountered a being of superior faculties he spoke the former, and the being in question all-at-once awakened on the spot. However, these superior persons at the outset still engaged in the type of step-by-step practice found in the first two teachings to rid themselves gradually of the habit energy inherited from past births. This type of all-at-once is found in "one part" of the *Huayan Sutra* and in the buddha-in-embryo sutras; it is identical to the third Chan axiom. Immediately after the awakening beneath the tree, for the sake of those of superior faculties, he spoke the all-at-once of the rite of transforming beings. This all-at-once is "one sutra" of the *Huayan* collection and the *Treatise on the Ten Stages*. The explicit teaching of the *Lotus* and *Nirvana* plus the all-at-once teaching of responding to beings of the highest disposition constitute the third teaching of my schema.

45. Question: You said earlier [in section 6]: "The Buddha spoke both the all-at-once teaching and the step-by-step teaching, while Chan opens both the all-at-once gate and the step-by-step gate." I have not yet determined which within the three types of teaching are all-at-once and which step-by-step.

Answer: The principles of the dharma [run] from deep to shallow. I have already dealt fully with their three types. It is just that the teaching styles of the World-honored-one varied, and so there were all-at-once sermons conforming to principle and step-by-step sermons in accordance with the dispositions [of the audience]. Therefore, we use the additional terms "all-at-once teaching" and "step-by-step teaching." It is not the case that there are separate all-at-once and step-by-step [teachings] outside the three teachings. "Step-by-step" means that, for the sake of those of medium and inferior faculties, those who at the time in question were not yet able to believe in and awaken to the excellent principle of perfect awakening, [the Buddha] spoke the previous humans-and-gods [teaching], the Hinayana, and up through the dharma characteristics *(all the above being the first teaching)* and the eradication of characteristics *(the second teaching)*. He waited for their faculties to ripen and then spoke for them the complete meaning, that is, the *Lotus*, the *Nirvana Sutra*, etc. *(This and the all-at-once teaching of responding to [beings of the highest] disposition, [which is explained] below, join together to constitute the third teaching. The all-at-once of the rite of transforming [beings explained below] totally subsumes the three* kinds.[239] *The classifications of the teachings set up by the worthies of the western regions and this land from ancient times until today, such as the three periods and the five periods,*[240] *are just one kind of the step-by-step teaching. They do not take in the* Huayan *and other sutras.)*

There are also two [types of] all-at-once. The first is the all-at-once of responding to [beings of the highest] disposition, and the second is the rite of transforming [beings].[241] The all-at-once of responding to [beings of the highest] disposition [refers to those situations in which the Buddha,] having met a common person of superior faculties and sharp intellect, directly showed him the true dharma. As soon as he heard [the Buddha speak this type of all-at-once] he all-at-once awakened and gained the identical fruit of a buddha. As in the *Huayan*: "When one first raises the thought [of awakening], one attains unexcelled, perfect awakening."[242] In the *Perfect Awakening*: "Practice is completion of the buddha path."[243] After that[244] [these common persons of superior faculties use] the same practice gates [found] in the previous two teachings in order step-by-step to get rid of the habit [energy] of the common person and step-by-step reveal the qualities of the noble one.[245] It is like a wind blowing over the great ocean so that it can no longer reflect images. If the wind all-at-once stops, the waves step-by-step cease, and the reflections reappear. *(Wind is like feelings of delusion, ocean like the mind nature, waves like the depravities, and reflections like functions. These are arranged one after the other in the* Awakening of Faith.*)*[246] [This all-at-once of responding to beings of the highest disposition] is one part of the *Huayan*[247] and such sutras as the *Perfect Awakening*, the *Buddha Top-knot* [=*Heroic Progress Samadhi*], the *Secret Array*, the *Śrīmālā*, and the *Buddha-in-Embryo*,[248] over twenty sections in all. Whenever [the Buddha] encountered this disposition, he spoke this; it is not restricted to either the first or the last [part of his teaching career]. It is utterly identical to the Chan gate's third axiom of directly revealing the mind nature.

The second, the all-at-once of the rite of transforming [beings], refers to [the occasion when] the Buddha first completed the path. For the sake of those who possessed superior faculties as a result of the conditions of past lives, he on one occasion [immediately after awakening] spoke all-at-once of nature and characteristics, phenomena and principle, the myriad depravities of sentient beings, the myriad practices of the bodhisattvas, the stages of the worthies and noble ones, and the myriad qualities of the buddhas. Causes suffuse the sea of effects; when one first [raises] the thought [of awakening], one attains awakening; and effects penetrate to the source of causes.[249] Even when the stages are filled, one is still called a bodhisattva. [This second type of all-at-once] is only one sutra of the *Huayan* [collection][250] and the *Treatise on the Ten Stages* [*Sutra*][251] and is called the perfect all-at-once teaching. None of the other [sutras or treatises] contains it. *(A previously mentioned objection [in section 16] was that all-at-once awakening to become a buddha contravenes the sutras. Here I have now cleared this up.)* The "all dharmas" spoken of by this [second type of all-at-once] is an "all dharmas" that fulfills the one mind, and the one mind is a one mind that fulfills "all dharmas," nature and characteristics being perfectly fused and the one and the many existing in freedom. Therefore, buddhas and sentient beings penetrate each other; pure lands and filthy lands are completely fused; every single dharma includes within itself every other dharma; every single speck of dust includes the worlds, mutually penetrating and mutually identical; there is fusion without obstruction in the gates of the ten profundities, again and again without limit.[252] This is called the unobstructed dharma sphere.[253]

Now I will discuss all-at-once and step-by-step in terms of the varying dispositions of beings for awakening and practice. Among the Chan houses there are numerous variants for all-at-once and step-by-step. In these sometimes awakening refers to direct realization, sometimes to intellectual understanding of doctrine. It should be noted that these variants are working only from the perspective of the present life; from a rebirth perspective there is only step-by-step. Recently many have objected that all-at-once awakening followed by step-by-step practice is a contradiction. Actually, it is the most essential formulation.

46. Up until now all-at-once and step-by-step have both been spoken of according to the Buddha and in conformity with the teachings. The meanings [of all-at-once and step-by-step] are something quite different if we speak of them according to the dispositions [of beings] and in conformity with awakening and practice.[254]

Among the [Chan] houses listed previously [in section 12], some say: "One first relies on step-by-step practice [to accumulate] merit and then deeply all-at-once awakens." *(This is like chopping down a tree; slice after slice is step-by-step chopped away, until at a certain point it all-at-once falls. It is also like pointing towards a city far off in the distance; step-by-step one approaches, until, on a certain day, one all-at-once arrives.)* Some say: "One relies on all-at-once practice to step-by-step awaken." *(This is like a person training in archery. "All-at-once" is that, [while releasing] arrows, he concentrates his attention right on the bull's-eye. "Step-by-step" is that a long time elapses before [the arrows] first begin step-by-step to approach and finally hit the bull's-eye. This is talking about girding mind for all-at-once cultivation; it does not imply that one is all-at-once finished with effortful practice.)*

Some say: "One step-by-step practices and step-by-step awakens." *(This is like ascending a nine-storied platform. Step-by-step one ascends, and step-by-step one can see further and further into the distance. And so there is a poem that goes:*

Wanting to investigate with the eye of a thousand li,
I went up one more story.)[255]

In all [three of these variants awakening] means [direct] realization awakening.[256]

Some say: "One must first all-at-once awaken and then should step-by-step practice." This is in conformity with [intellectual] understanding awakening.[257] *(If we speak in conformity with the cutting off of hindrances, this is like the sun's rising all-at-once but the frost's melting step-by-step. If we speak in conformity with the perfecting of attributes, this is like the fact that, upon birth, a child all-at-once possesses four limbs and six senses and as it matures step-by-step perfects its will and functions.)* Therefore, the *Huayan* says: "When one first raises the thought [of awakening], one attains perfect awakening."[258] Only after this are the three worthies and the ten [stages of] the noble one step-by-step cultivated and realized.[259] If one practices without having awakened, it is not true practice. *(Indeed, if it is not a practice that is in the true stream, there is no way to conform to truth. How could there be a practice to cultivate truth that does not itself arise from truth? Therefore, the sutra says that, without having heard this dharma, one will never realize truth, even if one practices the six perfections and the myriad practices for many eons.)*[260]

Some say: "One all-at-once awakens and all-at-once practices." This refers to those whose extra-high intellectual faculties *(because their abilities are superior, they awaken)* and joyful desire *(because their desire is superior, they practice)* are both superior. They hear once and have a thousand awakenings; they obtain the great dharani.[261] In one moment [there is] non-arising, the limit between before and after being cut off. *([In terms of] cutting off hindrances, this is like cutting a piece of silk; a myriad silk threads are all-at-once severed. [In terms of] cultivating attributes, this is like dyeing a piece of silk; a myriad of silk threads all-at-once takes on the color. Heze [Shenhui] said: "Having seen the substance of no mindfulness, one does not pursue the arising of things."[262] He also said: "If for a single moment one is in conjunction with the original nature, eighty thousand perfection practices will at one time come into effect.")*[263] The triple karma [of body, speech, and mind] of this person [of extra-high intellectual faculties] shines alone as something other people cannot reach. *(The* Jingang sanmei [jing] *says: "The mind of voidness is immobile and endowed with the perfections."[264] The Lotus says: "The eyes and ears [given to you] at birth by your father and mother see through the three thousand worlds, etc.")*[265] If we talk about this [variant] according to phenomenal manifestations [in the world], it is like the type [of Chan] of the Great Master Nuitou Yong.[266] In this gate [of all-at-once awakening and all-at-once practice] there are two meanings [to awakening]. If one relies on awakening to practice, it is [intellectual] understanding awakening, but, if one relies on practice to awaken, it is [direct] realization awakening.

However, all of the above [variants] are propounded only from the perspective of the present life. If one infers from a distance about past lives, then it is just step-by-step with no all-at-once. What we see today as all-at-once has arisen through the step-by-step perfuming of many past lives.

Some say: "In the dharma there is neither all-at-once nor step-by-step; all-at-once and step-by-step lie in the dispositions [of beings]."[267] Truly, this is correct. There is no concreteness to the words ["all-at-once" and "step-by-step"]; they have always just referred to dispositions. Who ever said that they are dharma substance? There are this many gates to the meanings of all-at-once and step-by-step, and every gate has meaning. This is not a case of forcing strained interpretations.[268] How much more so for the *Lanka Descent's* four step-by-step [similes] and four all-at-once [similes]![269] (*The principles [of that sutra] are of the step-by-step practice and all-at-once awakening type.*)

I still have not dared to speak of the complexities involved here. Recently I have come into frequent contact with discussants who just use the words "all-at-once" and "step-by step" without making any distinctions: that according to the teachings, there is the all-at-once and step-by-step of the rite of transforming [beings] and the all-at-once and step-by-step of responding to [beings of the highest] disposition; and that, according to people, there is the all-at-once and step-by-step of instructional devices, the all-at-once and step-by-step of ability for awakening, and the all-at-once and step-by-step of willpower for practice. These discussants just say: "To first all-at-once awaken and afterwards step-by-step practice seems to be contradictory." But how can those who desire to remove doubt not see that the sun rises all-at-once, but the frost melts step-by-step; that a child is born all-at-once (*possessing four limbs and six senses*), but its will is established step-by-step (*muscles, character,*[270] *and the art of conduct are all perfected step-by-step*); that when a fierce wind all-at-once ceases, the waves stop step-by-step; and that intellectual brightness comes into being all-at-once, whereas ritual and music are learned step-by-step. (*It is like a highborn son or grandson who, when young, falls into dissipation and becomes a servant. In future lives he is unaware of his aristocratic lineage, but, at some point, he is able to visit*[271] *his noble father and mother. On that day he is completely an aristocrat, but the traces of his actions and his course of conduct cannot be all-at-once changed, and so he must step-by-step train.*) This [all-at-once intellectual understanding awakening followed by step-by-step practice followed by direct realization awakening] we know to be the most essential of the aspects of all-at-once and step-by-step.

I originally envisioned a work (the *Chan Prolegomenon*) that would merely lay out the three teachings and three Chan axioms, the ten connections between Chan and the sutras, etc., but, in view of the variety and breadth of the available Chan literature, I decided to assemble the Chan writings and relevant sutra passages into a new basket (the *Chan Canon*). Such a basket will serve as a gate to all aspects of the path.

47. Although my original intention with this work was just to present the Chan explanations [that is, the three teachings and three corresponding Chan axioms, ten reasons why Chan is connected to the sutras and treatises, ten differences between the voidness axiom and the nature axiom, the chart, etc.], in view of the fact that Bodhidharma's one [mind] axiom[272] is the pervasive substance of the buddha dharma and the [lines of verses] related by the [Chan] houses are so different from each other, I have now collected [all these Chan writings and relevant sutra passages] into one basket.[273] Gathered together [these materials] will bring completeness to principle and phenomena and fulfill from beginning to end the gates to awakening, understanding, practice, and realization. Therefore, in presenting them [that is, the Chan explanations] it is necessary to give an exhaustive account of the ideas [behind them] and to make the bloodlines continuous, the roots and branches in the [correct] order. If one wishes to see the sequence of root and branches, one must first investigate thoroughly the above three types of all-at-once and step-by step sermons.[274]

From what root does the dharma discussed in the teachings come forth? Where is it now? Also, one must look up to view the various sermons of the Buddha [and ask] what event lies behind the original intention of this teaching. Then the entire great storehouse of sutras, from beginning to end, from root to branches, will at one time all of a sudden become clear. Moreover, as to the thorough investigation of where the dharma of the teachings comes from, originally it emanates from the substance of the one true mind of the World-honored-one, revolving until it reaches the ears of the people of this time, the eyes of the people of the present time. The principles [of the teachings] it speaks of also just emanate following conditions [from] the substance of the one true mind that both common persons and noble ones are grounded in,[275] revolving to penetrate everywhere, penetrating to the center of the bodies of the minds of all sentient beings. If each just in his own mind quiets thoughts and does thinking practice [dhyana] according to principle, then just so [will this true mind] be revealed. (*The* Huayan *says:* "*If just so you do thinking practice, just so it will be revealed.*")[276]

The intention of the Buddha was to show Knowing-seeing to all beings and have them awaken. The *Huayan Sutra*, delivered at the site of the enlightenment, proclaims the dharma sphere (the third teaching in my schema). Then, for beings of lesser faculties, sutras concerning the four truths, twelvefold origination by dependence, and the six perfections were delivered (the first teaching). Subsequently the Buddha spoke the *Perfection of Wisdom Sutras* (the second teaching). The *Lotus* and

Nirvana, as the pinnacle of the step-by-step teaching, are no different in depth from the all-at-once *Huayan*.

48. Next, view the original intention of the Buddha's sermons in the sutras. The World-honored-one himself [in the *Lotus Sutra*] says: "As to my original intention, I appeared in the world only for the sake of the one great task. The one great task is my desire to enable sentient beings to open buddha Knowing-seeing . . . entering on the path of buddha Knowing-seeing. Therefore, everything I do is always for the sake of the one task. I just show buddha Knowing-seeing to all sentient beings and make them awaken. . . . There is no second or third vehicle [of hearers and private buddhas]. The dharmas of all the buddhas of the ten directions and the three times are like this. Even though [the buddhas] have employed immeasurable and innumerable teaching devices and all sorts of metaphorical language in order to speak dharma to sentient beings, every one of these dharmas has been the one buddha vehicle."[277]

[In the *Huayan Sutra* he says:] "Therefore, under the tree of awakening I first attained perfect awakening and everywhere saw all sentient beings attaining perfect awakening, up to and including everywhere I saw all sentient beings in complete nirvana."[278] *(The "Chapter on the Arrangement [of the World Protectors]" of the* Huayan *says: "The Buddha was at the awakening site in the state of Magadha when he first attained perfect awakening. The ground was hard, as if made of diamond. The tree of awakening was tall and broad, inspiring in its majesty."[279] The "Chapter on the Arising [of the Tathagatas]" says: "When the Tathagata attained perfect awakening, everywhere he saw sentient beings, etc."[280] This is an exact quotation for the passage [above].)*

[In the *Buddha-in-Embryo Sutra* he says:] "Everywhere I saw that all sentient beings, within the depravities of passion, hatred, and stupidity, possessed the wisdom of the Tathagata's body, eternally free of impurities and endowed with all qualities and characteristics"[281] *(text of the* Buddha-in-Embryo Sutra*).*

[In the *Huayan Sutra* he says:] "There is not one sentient being who does not possess the wisdom of the Tathagata. It is just because of thought of the unreal and grasping that they cannot achieve realization of it. I desire to teach them the path of the noble ones, which will make them eternally free of thought of the unreal. Within their own bodies they will come to see the broad, great wisdom of the Tathagata, which is no different from me."[282] *(The text of the* Huayan's *"Chapter on the Arising [of the Tathagatas]." I have merely changed the word "should [dang]" to the word "desire [yu]" in order to make the passage smoother. Also, the Lotus says: "My original vow was to enable all sentient beings to be no different from me.")*[283]

Thus, for the sake of these sentient beings, at the awakening site, in accordance with *(falling tone)* the *Great Expanded Dharma Sphere* [=*Huayan Sutra*], he announced the causation flower of the myriad practices by which the origi-

nal nature is adorned, bringing to perfection the buddha fruit of myriad qualities: "Some, having planted good roots in past eons just as I have done, found
me in the sea of eons. They were drawn to me by the four articles of attraction"[284]
(also the text of the "Chapter on the Arrangement").

When they first saw my body *(the body of Vairocana in the [lion's] sport concen-*
tration) and heard my sermon *(the above* Huayan *sermon),* then they all believed,
received, and entered into the wisdom of the Tathagata. . . . at the Jeta Grove [in
Śrāvastī] I entered the lion's sport concentration, and the great multitude all real-
ized the dharma sphere, except those who had earlier practiced and trained in the
Hinayana[285] *(The Buddha, at the* Lotus *assembly, said that in the past, at the*
Huayan *assembly, five-hundred arhats [had acted] as if they were deaf and blind.*[286]
They had neither seen the buddha realm nor heard the dharma of perfect fusion.
[Those who had earlier practiced and trained in the Hinayana are] these [arhats].
Next, he said: "I will now enable them to hear this sutra and enter into buddha
wisdom."[287] *[Those who had earlier practiced and trained in the Hinayana] are*
those who, exactly forty years later, in the Lotus *assembly, all received a prediction.)*[288]
and those who had sunk into the waters of passion and love. *(Also, the "Chapter on*
the Arising [of the Tathagatas]" says: "There are only two places where the wisdom
of the Tathagata cannot create and extend benefit. These are [the followers] of the
two vehicles [of hearers and private buddhas] who have fallen into the broad, deep
pit of the unconditioned and those sentient beings who have destroyed their good
roots and lack ability. They have sunk into the great sea of false views, passion, and
desire. Nevertheless, [the Buddha] never deserted even these."[289] *Comment: Those*
who are spoken of in the Huayan *as having trained in the Hinayana, nevertheless,*
in the Lotus *assembly received a prediction [of future buddhahood]. Even though*
*they were not present at this [*Lotus*] assembly, [the Buddha] remembered them and*
gave them the prediction. This is what is meant by "never deserted.")

[In the *Lotus Sutra* he says:] "The karmic roots of such sentient beings are dark
and dull; they are attached to pleasure and blinded by stupidity, and it is difficult
for them to cross to liberation. For three weeks I pondered this state of affairs: If I
just praise the buddha vehicle to them, they will sink into suffering and be critical
and unbelieving. For this they will speedily enter bad rebirth paths. If I teach the
Hinayana to even one person, I will fall into being close-fisted and greedy. This is
an impossible situation. It is impossible to put into effect an advance or a retreat.
Thinking on the power of the teaching devices practiced by past buddhas, I remembered that all past buddhas had used the Hinayana to entice and only later
enabled them to enter the ultimate one vehicle. Therefore, concerning the path I
have now apprehended, I also should speak of three vehicles. While I was in such
a state of pondering, the buddhas of the ten directions appeared, and the voice of
[the god] Brahma consoled me: 'Wonderful, Śākyamuni! You are the supreme
teacher of the path. You have apprehended this unexcelled dharma, and, following

all the buddhas, you will use the power of teaching devices.' Having heard this consoling voice, in accordance with the intention of all the buddhas, I therefore began my way to Benares, where I turned the dharma wheel of the four truths, crossing over [to nirvana] five persons, including Kaundinya."[290]

[In the *Lotus Sutra* he says:] "I step-by-step [went on to speak of the four truths] at up to a myriad places *(like a sheep cart)*. Also, I spoke of the twelvefold origination by dependence to those who sought to become private buddhas *(like a deer cart)*. I spoke of the six perfections to those who sought the Mahayana."[291] *(Like an ox cart. All these above correspond to the first teaching of cryptic meaning that relies on the nature to speak of characteristics. All of the above three carts stand outside the gate pointing into the house. They are one by one like the three vehicles of the provisional teaching, etc.)* "Meanwhile I spoke the exceedingly deep perfection of wisdom. It rinsed clean the above arhats, advancing them to the status of small bodhisattvas. *(This corresponds to the second teaching of cryptic meaning that eradicates characteristics to reveal the nature.)* Step-by-step I saw their faculties ripen, and, subsequently, at Vulture Peak, [the site of the *Lotus Sutra*], I showed them the Knowing-seeing of the Tathagata and gave every one of them predictions of unexcelled, perfect awakening. *(The ultimate one vehicle that is like a white ox-cart in the middle of a crossroads.*[292] *As to the differences between the ox-cart Mahayana of the provisional teaching and the white ox-cart one vehicle of the real teaching, more that thirty sutras and treatises [of the third teaching] all have illuminating passages.)* I openly showed the sameness of the dharma body of the three vehicles and entrance into the path of the one vehicle. . . ."

[The *Nirvana Sutra* says:] "As I was about to extinguish and cross over [to nirvana] between the pair of śāla trees outside the town of Kuśinagara [the site of the *Nirvana Sutra*,] giving out a great lion's roar, I revealed the eternally abiding dharma and spoke explicitly: 'All sentient beings possess the buddha nature. Whatever has mind will certainly become a buddha. Nirvana is ultimately permanence, joy, self, and purity. All are enabled to dwell peacefully in the secret storehouse.'"[293] *(The* Lotus *gathers in the three vehicles, until the* Nirvana Sutra *gathers in all [sentient beings] in the six [rebirth] paths. This is because bringing the provisional into the real must be step-by step.)*

[These two sutras] are no different from the lion's sport [concentration] of the ocean assembly of the *Huayan* with the great assembly all-at-once [attaining] realization. *(The* Lotus *and the* Nirvana *are the pinnacle within the step-by-step teaching and are no different in depth from the all-at-once teaching of the* Huayan *and others. They are all the third teaching that openly shows that the true mind is the nature.)*

[The *Fo yijiao jing* says:] "Those whom I was to cross over [to nirvana] have already been crossed over. Those who have not yet attained crossing over have already created the karmic conditions for attaining crossing over."[294]

Therefore, between the pair of *śāla* trees, I entered the great concentration of calm and returned to the root, to the source. Together with all the buddhas of the ten directions and three times, I eternally abide in the dharma sphere, which is forever calm and forever luminous.

I ask only that the reader match up the above sutra quotations with the three teachings and three Chan axioms. My basic assumption is that the teachings serve as legitimizing precedents for the Chan axioms.

49. Critique: The above three sheets [of the previous section] consist entirely of the Buddha's own words as recorded in the sutras. I just jotted down [the appropriate passages,] and so I could not avoid adding or subtracting or changing two or three words at the points where [the passages] connect. *(The one and a half lines that describe the* Huayan *site[295] are the only ones that reveal the Buddha's intention in terms of the sutra's theme and are not the original words of the Buddha.)* I request that [the reader] take these [passages] in which the Buddha himself relates his original intention to make distinctions among the previous three types of teachings and [Chan] axioms. How can anyone say that the provisional and the real are one and the same type? How can anyone say that the beginning and the end [that is, the *Huayan Sutra* at the beginning of the Buddha's teaching career and the *Nirvana Sutra* at the end] are two dharmas? The Chan axioms are modeled on the teachings.[296] Who would say this is not so? Indeed, my desire to bring [Chan and the teachings] together is grounded in this. Who has heard these words and still not rid himself of doubts? If [anyone] still clings to delusion, I cannot repeat myself.

The apparent contradiction between the *Huayan*'s proclamation that all beings are perfectly awakened and the *Lotus*'s talk about beings of dull faculties blinded by stupidity is conveniently explained in the *Awakening of Faith*. That text shows that the luminous dharma-sphere mind follows conditions of delusion to become beings undergoing rebirth and follows conditions of awakening to become buddhas. Even so, this one mind remains unchanging and indestructible. The one mind has two aspects, real and unreal, while those two aspects each have two further aspects. The real is subdivided into the immutable and the conditioned, the unreal into the void and the phenomenal. Because the real is immutable, the unreal is void (the gate of thusness). Because the real is conditioned, the unreal transmutes into phenomena (the gate of arising-disappearing). The two gates are identical.

50. Thus, in the quotations above [in section 48] the Buddha himself says: "I saw sentient beings attaining perfect awakening," and he also says: "Their karmic roots are dull, and they are blinded by stupidity."[297] I would like to explain the apparent contradiction between these two passages. I fear that, with further quotations from buddha word [that is, the sutras], the texts will become inter-

twined [and hence too complicated]. From here onward I will begin to rely exclusively on [the *Awakening of Faith* of] the ancient patriarch Asvaghosa Bodhisattva.[298] Clarifying both the delusion and the awakening of sentient-being mind, the root and branches, the beginning and end, he made everything reveal itself. He spontaneously showed that sentient beings who are identical to buddhas [dwell] miserably in rebirth process; that buddhas who are identical to sentient beings [dwell] calmly in nirvana; that habit energy that is identical to all-at-once awakening from moment to moment seizes objective supports; that all-at-once awakening that is identical to habit energy from thought to thought shines in the midst of awakening. Thus, we see that the contradictions in buddha word are not contradictions at all. In other words, the common persons of the six rebirth paths and the worthies and noble ones of the three vehicles are all rooted in the luminous, pure, one dharma-sphere mind, intrinsically awakened and shining like a treasure; everything is perfect and full and is never called either buddha or sentient being. It is just because this mind is luminous, excellent, free, and possesses no nature of its own that, following conditions of delusion and awakening, it creates karma, receives suffering, and consequently is called sentient being; and that it cultivates the path, realizes the real, and consequently is called a buddha. Also, even though it follows conditions, because it never loses its own nature, it is never unreal, never changes, is indestructible, is just the one mind, and consequently is called thusness. Therefore, this one mind always possesses two gates, but no gap between them has ever existed. Within only the conditioned gate, common person and noble one are not really existent. In other words, because from the outset there has been no awakening, we say that the depravities are beginningless. If one practices and realizes, the depravities will be cut off, and so we say that they have an end. However, in reality, there exists neither a separate initial awakening nor nonawakening. They are, ultimately, the same. Therefore, this one mind, by its very nature, has two principles, real and unreal, while these two principles each have two further principles. Therefore, [the one mind] always possesses the two gates of thusness and arising-disappearing. As to the two [further] principles of each of these, the real has the two principles of immutable and conditioned, while the unreal has the two principles of devoid of substance and phenomenal. This means that, because the real is immutable, the unreal from the outset is devoid of substance. This is the gate of thusness. Because the real is conditioned, unreal consciousness becomes phenomena. This is the gate of arising-disappearing. Because arising-disappearing is identical to thusness, the sutras employ such phrases as "neither buddha nor sentient beings," "from the outset nirvana," "characterized by constant calm." Also, because thusness is identical to arising-disappearing, a sutra says: "The flow of the dharma body through the five rebirth paths is called sentient beings."[299]

The storehouse consciousness found in common persons has two aspects, awakening and non-awakening. The latter is the root of beings caught up in the rebirth process. There are ten stages to this process of non-awakening. Below each stage I will append a running dream analogy in which a wealthy aristocrat falls asleep in his home and forgets who he is.

51. We have come to know that delusion, the common person, and awakening, the noble one, lie within the arising-disappearing gate. Within this gate, let me now clarify the two characteristics, the common person and the noble one. When the real and the unreal are in concord, neither one nor different, it is called the storehouse consciousness.[300] This consciousness, present in common persons, from the outset has always possessed two principles, awakening and non-awakening. Awakening is the root of the worthies and noble ones of the three vehicles, while non-awakening is the root of the common persons in the six rebirth paths. I will now show that there are altogether ten levels to the process of being a common person. *(I will now provide a dream analogy beneath each stage so that they can be read together.)*

1. All sentient beings possess the true mind of original awakening. *(A wealthy nobleman, endowed with both virtue and wisdom, is inside his own house.)*

2. Having not yet met a good friend who opens up and shows [the path], inevitably from the outset there is non-awakening. *(The nobleman falls asleep in his own house and forgets who he is. The treatise says: "Grounded in original awakening there is non-awakening.")*[301]

3. Thoughts arise as a natural consequence of non-awakening. *(There is dreaming as a natural consequence of sleep. The treatise says: "Grounded in non-awakening, three types of characteristics are produced."*[302] *This is the first.)*

4. Because thoughts have arisen, there is the characteristic of a seer [that is, a subject] *(thought in a dream).*

5. Because there is a seer, an organ body and world falsely appear. *(In his dream [the nobleman] sees himself in another place in [a condition of] poverty and suffering, and he sees all sorts of likable and dislikable phenomenal sense objects.)*

6. Unaware that these [that is, the organ body and world] have arisen from his own thoughts, he grasps them as real existents. This is called dharma grasping. *(While in the dream he inevitably grasps the things that he sees in the dream as real things.)*

7. Because he has grasped dharmas as really [existent entities], just at that very moment he sees a distinction between himself and others. This is

called self-grasping. *(While dreaming he inevitably believes that the person who is in another place in [a condition of] poverty and suffering is his own person.)*

8. Because he clings to [the notion that] these four elements [of earth, water, fire, and air] constitute his own body, naturally [he falls into] desiring and loving sense objects that accord with his feelings, wanting to adorn the self, while [he falls into] hating and despising those sense objects that are contrary to his feelings, fearing that they will harm and vex his self. Stupid feelings make all sorts of calculations and comparisons. *(This is the three poisons [of passion; hatred; and stupidity]. In his dream he also desires agreeable events in the other place and hates disagreeable events.)*

9. From this [emergence of the three poisons comes] the creation of good and bad karma. *(In his dream he either steals and murders or practices kindness and spreads virtue.)*

10. Once karma comes into existence, it is impossible to escape. It is like the shadow trailing the form or the echo trailing the voice. Therefore, he receives a form of karma-bondage suffering in [one of] the six rebirth paths. *(If in his dream he steals and murders, then he is apprehended, put into a wooden collar, and sent to prison. On the other hand, if he practices kindness and obtains rewards, he is recommended for office and takes up his position.)*

The above ten levels rise step-by-step. The bloodline is continuous, its mode of operation very clear. If [the reader] will merely view mind in compliance with principle and study it, the sequence will be clearly visible.

There are also ten levels to the practice and direct realization-awakening that follow intellectual understanding-awakening. The ten levels of the awakening sequence begin at the end of the delusion sequence and work backwards, overturning the ten levels of delusion. However, the first level of awakening corresponds to both the first and second of delusion, while the tenth of awakening corresponds to the first of delusion. Of the remaining eight of awakening, each in reverse order successively flips over one of the eight of delusion, that is, delusion's level ten to level three. At level one causes subsume effects; at level ten effects penetrate to the source of causes.

52. I will next explain the practice and realization that come after awakening. This too has ten levels. Overturn the unreal, and it is the real.[303] This is because they are not separate dharmas. However, the principles of delusion and awakening are separate. The flow and counterflow sequences [that is, the delusion stages and the awakening stages] are different. The former is to be deluded about the real and pursue the unreal. It arises in sequence from the fine and

subtle [characteristics of root ignorance], revolving toward the coarse [characteristics of branch ignorance].[304] This [awakening sequence] is to awaken to the unreal and return to the real. Proceeding from the coarse and heavy, in opposite sequence it cuts off [each successive level of delusion], revolving toward the subtle. The wisdom necessary to overturn [each successive stage of delusion] proceeds from shallow to deep. The coarse hindrances are easily eliminated because shallow wisdom can overturn them. The subtle depravities are more difficult to get rid of, because only deep wisdom can cut them off. Therefore, these ten [of the awakening sequence] begin at the end [of the delusion sequence] and work backward, overturning and eradicating the former ten. It is just that there is a small discrepancy involving the first level of this [awakening sequence] and the first two levels of the former [sequence of delusion]. Below I will show this. The ten levels [of awakening] are:

1. It is said there is a sentient being who meets a good friend. [The good friend] opens up and shows the true mind of original awakening spoken of above. He has heard of it in a past life, and thus, in the present life, is capable of awakening and understanding that *(Had he not heard of it in a past birth, upon hearing of it in the present, he would certainly be unbelieving or would believe without understanding. Even though everyone has the buddha nature, some in their present [life] are unbelieving, and some are unawakened. This [refers to] this type.)* the four elements are non-self; that the five aggregates are all void.[305] He [comes to] believe in his own thusness and the qualities of the three jewels [of buddha, dharma, and monastic community]. *(Because he believes one's own mind has never been unreal, has never changed, we speak of thusness. Therefore, the treatise says: "When the self believes in its own nature, one knows that mind movement is unreal and that the [external] sense objects [spoken of] previously do not exist."[306] It also says: "The faith mind is of four types. The first is faith in the root, joyfully being mindful of thusness. The second is faith that the buddhas have immeasurable qualities, constantly being mindful of approaching to worship them. The third is faith that the dharma has great benefit, constantly being mindful of practicing it. The fourth is faith that the community can cultivate the correct practices that are of benefit to self and others, constantly taking joy in approaching [the community]."[307] Awakening to the first stage of the former [that is, the first stage of delusion, the true mind of original awakening,] and overturning the second stage of the former [that is, non-awakening] constitutes the first stage.)*

2. He produces compassion, wisdom, and the vow, resolving to realize awakening. *(To produce a mind of compassion is to desire to cross over*

sentient beings [to nirvana]. To produce a mind of wisdom is to desire to attain complete understanding. To produce a mind of the vow is to desire to cultivate the ten thousand practices as a complement to compassion and wisdom.)

3. To the best of his ability he practices the gates of giving, precepts, forbearance, striving, and stopping-viewing, which makes the roots of faith grow. *(The treatise says: "There are five practices that can perfect this faith."*[308] *Because stopping and viewing have been combined into one practice, the six perfections become just five.)*

4. The great thought of awakening arises from here. *(At this point the three minds [mentioned] above open up. The treatise says: "The minds that are produced by the perfection of faith are of three types. The first is straight mind, because it is correctly mindful of the dharma of thusness. The second is deep mind, because it takes joy in cultivating all good practices. The third is the mind of great compassion, because it desires to pluck all sentient beings out of suffering.")*[309]

5. He realizes that in the dharma nature there is no mind of stinginess, etc.[310] *("Etc." refers to passion, hatred, lethargy, distraction, and stupidity.)*

6. Flowing along, he practices the six perfections. By the power of concentration and wisdom *(initial practice is called stopping and viewing; completed, it is called concentration and wisdom)*, self and dharmas are both done away with. *(When one first raises the thought [of awakening], one has already, according to the principle of the teaching, discerned that the two graspings [that is, grasped and grasper] are void. Now, because of the power of concentration and wisdom, one views that one's own awakening is void.)* There is neither self nor other. *(Realization that self is void is the fifth [stage].)* It is eternally void and eternally like an illusion. *(Realization that dharmas are void is the sixth [stage]. Form is not different from voidness; voidness is not different from form.*[311] *Therefore, it is eternally void and eternally like an illusion.)*

7. There is mastery over forms, and everything is in fusion. *(When deluded, one does not realize that [forms] evolve from one's own mind, and therefore there is no mastery. Now, due to the knowledge of dual voidness [of self and dharmas], one comprehends this, and therefore there is fusion.)*

8. There is mastery over mind,[312] and there is nothing that is not illuminated. *(Earlier he had ceased to see sense objects existing separately outside mind. Sense objects are mind only. Therefore, there is mastery.)*

9. Full of teaching devices, in a moment he is in conjunction.[313] Aware of the first arising of mind, mind has nothing to be characterized as *first*, and one is divorced from subtle thoughts. Mind is then eternally abiding, awakened to the origin of delusion. It is called ultimate awakening.

(From first raising the thought [of awakening], he cultivates no mindful-
ness. Arriving at this point he attains perfection. Because of perfection, he
enters the buddha position.)

10. The mind having no mindfulness, there is no separate original awakening.[314] From the outset it is sameness, a single awakening, and so it is
mysteriously in the basic, true, pure mind source. Its responsive functions are [limitless like] grains of sand [of the Ganges]. It exhausts the
limit of the future; it is the constantly abiding dharma sphere. Touch
anywhere and you have penetrated it. We call it the honored one of
great awakening. No buddha is different from another buddha. They are
the original buddha and do not arise anew each time. Therefore, they
see everywhere all sentient beings equally attaining perfect awakening.

Therefore, delusion and awakening each have ten levels, flow and counterflow overturning each other. Its mode of operation is very apparent. The first
level of this [awakening sequence] corresponds to the first and second levels of
the former [sequence of delusion], while the tenth level of this corresponds to
the first level of the former. Of the remaining eight levels [of the awakening
sequence], each in reverse order [successively] overturns and eradicates [one
of] the eight levels of the former [that run from level ten down to level three].
In the first level one awakens to the original awakening of the first level of the
former, overturning the non-awakening of the second level of the former. Previously, non-awakening perverted original awakening, real and unreal contra-
dicted each other, and so they opened into two levels. Now, having awakened,
they mysteriously tally.[315] Mysteriously tallying, they are in accord with one
another, and because there is no separate initial awakening, they are combined
into one. Also, if we were to adhere [strictly] to the flow and counterflow sequences, the first level of this would correspond to and overturn the tenth level
of the former. At present within the gate of all-at-once awakening, by principle
one must directly recognize the original substance, overturning the original
delusion of the former, and so [the first level of awakening] corresponds to levels one and two of the former. *(This is the discrepancy I mentioned earlier.)* In
the second level because of fear of suffering in the rebirth process one produces the three minds [that is, mind of compassion, mind of wisdom, and
mind of the vow] to cross oneself and others over [to nirvana]. Therefore, it corresponds to the tenth level of the former, which is rebirth in the six paths. The
third level, the cultivation of the five practices, overturns the ninth level of the
former, the creation of karma. In the fourth level the three minds open up,
overturning the eighth level of the former, the three poisons [of passion, hatred, and stupidity]. *(The mind of compassion overturns hatred; the mind of wis-*
dom overturns stupidity; and the mind of the vow overturns passion.)[316] The fifth

level, realization that self is void, overturns the seventh level of the former, self-grasping. The sixth level, realization that dharmas are void, overturns the sixth level of the former, dharma-grasping. The seventh level, mastery over forms, overturns the fifth level of the former, sense objects. The eighth level, mastery over mind, overturns the fourth level of the former, a seer [or subject]. The ninth level, divorcing from thoughts, overturns the third level of the former, the arising of thoughts. Therefore, at the tenth level, becoming a buddha, "buddha" is not a separate substance; it is merely initial awakening, overturning the second level of the former, non-awakening, and combining with the first level of the former, original awakening. Initial and original are non-dual. They are just manifestations of thusness and are called dharma body and great awakening. Therefore, [level ten, becoming a buddha,] and initial awakening are not two substances. The discrepancy between the flow and counterflow sequences is right here. At [level] one, causes suffuse the sea of effects; at [level] ten, effects penetrate to the source of causes.[317] The *Nirvana Sutra* says: "The two, raising the thought [of awakening] and the ultimate, are not separate."[318] The *Huayan Sutra* says: "When one first raises the thought [of awakening], one attains unexcelled, perfect awakening."[319] [These sutras are speaking of] precisely this idea.

In order to aid the reader I have supplied a chart based upon the *Awakening of Faith*. At the top the chart reads "Sentient-Being Mind." From there it separates into two paths, with red script indicating pure dharmas and black script impure dharmas.

53. The flow and counterflow [sequences] correspond to each other. The former and latter illuminate each other, and the principles of dharma are clear. Nevertheless, I am still beset by the fear that my text will not be immediately intelligible; that the intention will not be clear all-at-once; that the head and the tail will be cut off from each other; and that [the reader] will not get an overall view. I will now provide a chart that sketches out these things in order to make the common-person and noble-one sequences and the axioms of the great storehouse of sutras appear at a single time in the mind mirror [of the reader]. At the top-center position of this chart there are three words: "Sentient-Being Mind." Reading downward from these three words, [the chart] separates into two paths. Red writing indicates pure, excellent dharmas; black writing indicates stained, impure dharmas. Investigate each item of the bloodline in detail. Red is for the labels[320] that represent the ten-staged sequence of pure dharmas. Black is for the labels that represent the ten-staged sequence of impure dharmas. These labels are from the text of the root treatise [the *Awakening of Faith*], while the [captions under the labels in] small script is discussion of principles[321] in the text of the [root] treatise.

The chart of Sentient-Being Mind:

54.   FIGURE 2.1

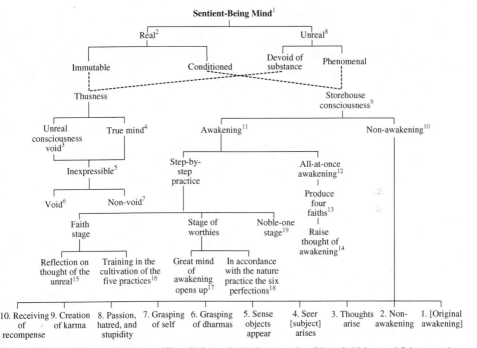

Sentient-Being Mind[1]

Real[2] — Unreal[8]

Immutable — Conditioned — Devoid of substance — Phenomenal

Thusness — Storehouse consciousness[9]

Unreal consciousness void[3] — True mind[4] — Awakening[11] — Non-awakening[10]

Inexpressible[5] — Step-by-step practice — All-at-once awakening[12]

Void[6] — Non-void[7] — Produce four faiths[13]

Faith stage — Stage of worthies — Noble-one stage[19] — Raise thought of awakening[14]

Reflection on thought of the unreal[15] — Training in the cultivation of the five practices[16] — Great mind of awakening opens up[17] — In accordance with the nature practice the six perfections[18]

10. Receiving of recompense — 9. Creation of karma — 8. Passion, hatred, and stupidity — 7. Grasping of self — 6. Grasping of dharmas — 5. Sense objects appear — 4. Seer [subject] arises — 3. Thoughts arise — 2. Non-awakening — 1. [Original awakening]

These eight stages [no. 3 to no. 10] are the locus wherein the two armies of the real and the unreal fight as enemies.

Buddha

Function — Characteristics — Substance

Magical-creation body[20] — Enjoyment body[21] — Dharma body[22]

Examine yourself closely in light of the chart. The ten levels of non-awakening are like the progression of a disease. The ten levels of awakening are like a course of therapy directed by a medical doctor.

55. Examine in detail what has been related above and carefully view this chart. Compare self and others and think upon the noble ones and worthies. Are you the same as they or different? Are you in the unreal or the real? What gate am I in? What stage is a buddha in? Am I of a different substance [from a buddha]? Do we have a common source? Then spontaneously forego attachment to [yourself as] a common person, but do not pretend to [occupy] the stage of the noble ones; do not sink into the love view; do not be modest about the buddha mind.

NOTES TO FIGURE 2.1

1. I would like to thank William S. Jacobs for his kind assistance in drawing this chart. Zongmi has provided captions below certain labels in this chart. I have placed my translations of the captions in the following notes. Caption for "Sentient-Being Mind": "The sutra says: The *one real object* means *sentient-being mind*. . . . Mind is of two types. One is true mind, and one is mind of the unreal." The treatise says: "The term 'dharma' means 'sentient-being mind.' This mind includes all mundane and supramundane dharmas. Grounded in this mind, the Mahayana principles are revealed." The sutra quotation is from the apocryphal sutra *Zhancha shan'e yebao jing*, T 17:907a4–b15. In this apocryphal sutra Earth Womb Bodhisattva for the sake of sentient beings during the end time of the dharma relieves them of the calamities of karmic obstacles and proclaims the deep meaning of the buddha dharma. He teaches the dharma of divining karmic recompense through using the form of a wooden wheel, a heterodox idea, and next teaches two types of viewing. The second fascicle shows similarities to the themes of the *Dasheng qixin lun* (Daizōkyō, 246–47). The treatise quotation here is *Dasheng qixin lun*, T 32:575c21–23; all treatise quotations in the chart are from this treatise.

2. Caption: "The treatise says: 'This mind from the outset is intrinsically pure' [T 32:577c2–3]. It is in a free and easy manner void and calm, complete Knowing awareness. It is like a virtuous, wise, and stern nobleman lying asleep in a hall of his own house. It is also like a tree stump in an empty field [that may seem like a ghost but is in reality void]."

3. Caption: "All dharmas are differentiated only on the basis of thought of the unreal. If one is free of thoughts, then no sense object has any characteristic" [T 32:576a9–10].

4. Caption: "The thusness of mind is the one dharma sphere, the totality of characteristics, the substance of the dharma gate. The *mind nature* neither arises nor disappears [T 32:576a8–9]. Also: "The *mind nature* is constantly in no mindfulness and so is called immutable" [T 32:577c5].

5. Caption: "Therefore, all dharmas from the outset are free of the characteristics of speech, free of the characteristics of the written word, free of the characteristics of objective supports of mind, ultimately sameness, without change, and indestructible. Because it is just one mind, we call it thusness" [T 32:576a10–13].

6. Caption: "From the outset one is not in conjunction with impure dharmas. This means that, free of all differentiated characteristics, there will be no thought of the unreal, and therefore one will not be in conjunction with discrimination of the unreal" [T 32:576a27–b4].

7. Caption: "[It is non-void] because there is the self substance endowed with the qualities of the nature free of the outflows [T 32:576a26]. Also: 'Because the revealed dharma substance is void and without the unreal, it is the one mind. It is

constantly abiding and immutable, perfectly endowed with purity and excellence'"
[T 32:576b5–6].

8. Caption: "The treatise says: 'Because of lack of comprehension of the one
dharma sphere, suddenly thoughts arise. This is called ignorance' [T 32:577c5–7].
Made impure by ignorance, there is this impure mind. Certainly, the organ body and
sense objects in confusion [entail] discrimination and the pondering of objective supports. It is like a person who is lying asleep. In his dream he sees himself as poor and
mean and in all sort of strange circumstances, and [he undergoes] all sorts of sorrows
and joys. Also, it is like a delusive tree stump that is taken for the ghost of a person.
These are not the same as a person that is not sleeping and a stump that is not
delusive."

9. Caption: "The markings above this point demonstrate the ranks of the chart.
'Sentient-Being Mind' is the buddha nature in bondage; the root treatise [*Dasheng
qixin lun*] and the sutras view this as the buddha-in-embryo. And it is the gate of the
principles. The [two sets of] two principles below, real and unreal, are the fundamental principles of the gate of thusness and the storehouse consciousness. The two path-
ways within the ['Sentient-Being] Mind' label are the nature *(thusness)* and characteristics *(ālaya)*, the impure *(all dharmas within the non-awakening rank)* and the pure
(all dharmas within awakening), that is, the dharma substance. Even at the time of
delusion the pure, excellent functions without the outflows are merely hidden and not
extinguished. Therefore, thusness and original awakening exist within the consciousnesses with the outflows. *(The fact that all sentient beings possess the buddha nature is
this principle.)* At the time of awakening the contents of the consciousnesses with
outflows most certainly do not exist. Therefore, the consciousness characteristics,
thought of the unreal, karmic fruits, etc., of ignorance do not exist in the gate of thusness. Only the pure, excellent functions alone exist within the mind of thusness. It is
called the buddha."

10. In the stages of non-awakening below, the Hongzhi 6 (1493) Korean edition,
which is identical to the 1576 Korean edition used by Kamata, has only stage no. 2 to
stage no. 9. See Yanagida Seizan, ed., *Kōrai-bon*, Zengaku sōsho 2 (Kyoto: Chūbun
shuppansha, 1974), 145. Kamata slightly revises this, making *jue* (Awakening) into
stage no. 1 (probably influenced by Ui, 140, and T 48:410a, both of which make stage
no. 1 *benjue* [*Original awakening*], thus creating ten steps rather than the nine of the
Korean editions. I have made the first stage "[1. Original awakening]." Adding a no. 1
stage coincides with the text in section 52, which states: "Awakening to the first stage
of the former [that is, the first stage of delusion, the true mind of original awakening] and
overturning the second stage of the former [that is, non-awakening] constitutes the
first stage." Each of the nine stages from no. 2 to no. 10 has a caption:

2. Non-awakening: "Delusion about the real. Not knowing the dharma
of thusness as it really is."

3. Thoughts arise: "Because of non-awakening, thoughts naturally arise."

4. Seer [subject] arises: "Because of thoughts, there is the characteristic of a seer."

5. Sense objects appear: "Because of a seer, an organ body and world falsely appear."

6. Grasping of dharmas: "Because one does not know that sense objects arise from one's own mind, one grasps them as really existent."

7. Grasping of self: "Because one grasps dharmas as definitely [existent], one sees a difference between 'my own' and 'other' and calculates that 'my own' is a self."

8. Passion, hatred, and stupidity: "Because of grasping of a self, one is greedy for sense objects that accord with one's feelings, hostile toward sense objects that go against one's feelings, and out of stupidity one makes calculations."

9. Creation of karma: "Because of bondage by the three poisons [of passion, hatred, and stupidity], there is the creation of good and bad karma."

10. Receiving recompense: "Karma having come into being, it is impossible to escape, and so one receives the suffering of karmic bondage in one of the six rebirth paths. Because the body that one has received is not something that can be severed, there is no antidote stage."

11. Caption: "Having attained realization, in reality, [original awakening] is no different from initial awakening. This is because arising-disappearing from the outset is sameness, and there is but one identical awakening. As to cutting off lack of comprehension of the one dharma sphere aspect, from the first raising of the thought one trains in cutting off until arrival at the tathagata stage, where one ultimately divorces from the stage of divorcing from thoughts. In a moment of conjunction, one is aware of the first arising of mind, but mind has no characteristic *first*. One is divorced from subtle thoughts, and mind obtains an eternal abidingness" [T 32:576c2–4 and 576b24–26].

12. Caption: "Due to the perfuming [laid down by] hearing [dharma] in past lives one in the present encounters a good friend who shows that the mind of awakening from the outset is pure and awareness of the unreal from the outset void."

13. Caption: "(1) Have faith in the root and joyfully be mindful of thusness; (2) have faith in the qualities of the buddhas and constantly be mindful of worshipping them; (3) have faith in the benefits of the dharma and constantly be mindful of practicing it; and (4) have faith in the correct practice of the community and constantly be mindful of approaching [the community]."

14. Caption: "Produce compassion, wisdom, and the vow, resolving to seize awakening." In this and the previous caption Zongmi succinctly clarifies just what constitutes sudden awakening in his sudden awakening-gradual practice formula. Sudden

awakening (*dunwu*) is a combination of faith (*xin* = *śraddhā*) and the mental attitude that aspires to buddhahood or bodhisattvahood (*putixin* = *bodhicitta*). Thus, Zongmi glosses a Chan term with classical Buddhist terminology.

15. Caption: "Dwell in quietude and correct thought and stop all sense objects; be correctly mindful of mind only and reflect [*guancha*] that there is nothing in the world for which one should be joyful. Be aware that prior thoughts have produced bad things; be capable of stopping later thoughts to make sure that they do not arise."

16. Caption: "(1) Giving according to one's lot; (2) precepts against the ten evils; if one has left home, then the practice of austerities; (3) forbearance concerning the depravities of others; (4) zeal without laziness; and (5) stopping and viewing."

17. Caption: "The previous three minds of compassion, wisdom, and the vow now open up. The straight mind is correctly mindful of thusness; the deep mind takes joy in practicing good actions; and the mind of compassion desires to pluck out the sufferings of others" [T 32:580c6–9]. The Hongzhi 6 (1493) Korean edition (Yanagida, *Kōrai-bon*, 145) has "straight mind [*zhixin*]," which Kamata has transcribed as "true mind [*zhenxin*]."

18. This is the *nature* of the nature axiom (*xingzong*) or dharma-nature axiom (*faxing zong*). Caption: "In the principle of thusness profound understanding manifests itself, and one practices divorcing from characteristics. Because one knows that the nature substance is without stinginess, without impurity, free of hatred, free of laziness, and constantly bright, one accordingly practices giving, precepts, forbearance, striving, dhyana, and wisdom." Zongmi's gradual practice (*jianxiu*) is a combination of reflection, that is, thorough consideration or contemplation (*guancha*), plus the five practices of the *Awakening of Faith* and the six paramitas.

19. Caption: "At the stage of mind freedom one does not see really existent external sense objects, and therefore in the midst of everything one is free. There is nothing that is not illuminated. At the stage of freedom in forms one has already realized that sense objects are the manifestations of one's own mind, and therefore within all forms one is in the fusion of freedom. Utilizing the power of concentration and wisdom, self and dharmas are both lost. (*Because dharmas have no [self] nature, they are constantly void and constantly [like] an illusion. Because one is free of self grasping, there is neither self nor other.*)"

20. Caption: "As to the functioning of thusness, the buddhas from the outset dwell in the stage of [karmic] causes. They practice the six perfections, transform sentient beings, and through great teaching devices and wisdom, eliminate ignorance. They see the original dharma body and spontaneously possess inconceivable karmic functions, penetrating everywhere. Sentient beings obtain benefit according to what they have seen and heard. Because it is grounded in what the minds of ordinary people and [the followers of] the two vehicles [hearers and private buddhas] see, it is called the magical-creation body. Because they do not know that [the magical-creation body is] a manifestation of the active consciousnesses, they see it [as if it is] coming from

without and seize on the regularity of its forms. This is because they are not [yet] capable of exhaustive Knowing" [T 32:579b9–23].

21. Caption: "Relying on the bodhisattvas, from [the point at which] one first produces the thought [of awakening] up to and including what the mind of the tenth stage sees is called the enjoyment body. This body has immeasurable forms; its forms have immeasurable characteristics; and its characteristics have immeasurable good [marks]. The ground where one abides [due to karmic] recompense also has an immeasurable variety of ornamentation. There is no limit to what is revealed. It is inexhaustible. Because it is in all cases brought to perfection by the perfuming of actions free of the outflows and the perfuming of original awakening, and because it is endowed with immeasurable joyful characteristics, it is called the enjoyment body" [T 32:579b23-c1].

22. Caption: "Because the characteristics of the self substance of thusness have such aspects as the ray of light of great wisdom, the pervasive illumination of the dharma sphere, true Knowing, and permanency, joy, self, and purity, it is endowed. with such inconceivable buddha dharmas that surpass the [number of] grains of sand in the Ganges. It is perfectly endowed and lacks for nothing and is called the dharma body of the Tathagata" [T 32:579a12–20].

Thus, the first ten levels [the non-awakening sequence] are: the dharma body medically treated by the sutras *(the first level)*; an explanation of how the disease of the depravities arises *(the next three levels)*; a step-by-step increase *(dharma grasping and self grasping)*, up to and including arrival at the coarse [forms of ignorance] *(the three poisons and the creation of karma)*; and the extinction of wisdom *(receiving of retribution)*.

The second ten levels [the awakening sequence] are: taking the medicine of belief in the dharma body *(the first three levels)*; curing the disease *(the opening up of the thought of awakening)*; taking principle to correct dharmas *(the six perfections)*; a step-by-step decrease *(six through nine)*, up to and including arrival at full recovery *(becoming a buddha)*.

It is like a person *(the dharma body in bondage)* who possesses all his faculties *(qualities as numberless as the grains of sand of the Ganges)* and is strong *(constantly abiding, immutable, incapable of being rendered impure by the unreal)*. [He possesses] many talents *(excellent functions as numberless as the grains of sand of the Ganges)*. Suddenly he contracts a disease *(beginningless ignorance)* that step-by-step increases *(the next seven levels)*, up to and including expiration *(the tenth level)*. Only his heart is warm *(the no-outflows seeds of wisdom in the storehouse consciousness)*.[322]

Suddenly along comes a good doctor *(the great, good friend)*, who knows that there is still life in him *(sees that in the common person "mind is buddha")*. [The doctor] has him swallow a divine prescription. *(When they first hear [the dharma, people] are unbelieving, but after hearing it a few more times, they are not indifferent.)* Suddenly he revives *([intellectual] understanding awakening)*. At first, he cannot yet speak *(when people are newly awakened, their answers to the questions and objections of others do not yet hit the bull's-eye)* up to and including the step-by-step [return of his] speech *(explaining and expounding the dharma)*. Step-by-step he becomes capable of traveling *(the ten stages and the ten perfections)*.[323] He arrives directly at a full recovery *(becoming a buddha)*. He can once again practice all the skills he has mastered *(the superknowledges, the rays of light, omniscience)*.

Compare the dharma one by one. How can there be any doubts that are not removed? Then you will know that the reason why sentient beings are incapable of functioning with the superknowledges is just that they are afflicted by the disease of karmic consciousness and the depravities. It is not that they do not yet possess the excellent qualities in the dharma body.

Recently, a stupid person objected: Once you have all-at-once awakened, you are a buddha. Why do you not give off rays of light?

[Answer:] How does this differ from commanding a sick man who is not yet fully recovered to resume his normal employment? Thus, the methodology of a worldly doctor is always first to feel the pulse. If he does not ascertain the severity of the disease, how can he know which prescription is correct? If he does not gauge the depth of the healing process, how can he talk about taking principle and applying it to a specific case? Dharma doctors are also like this.

Practitioners who have all-at-once awakened must to the very end engage in step-by-step practice. These days some people toss around Chan sayings about "no mind" in order to make light of learning, but they do not look into themselves to see if, in fact, they have attained this "no mind." Many of them have not.

56. Therefore, I have now related in detail the delusion sequence of ten levels and the awakening sequence of ten levels. I have taken the sutras and treatises to bring together the three types [of teachings running from] shallow to deep. [With the chart and the canonical texts plus the threefold schema] facing each other, everything will be illuminated. It will be like laying your finger on your palm.[324] Those who encourage trainees are themselves good at quieting mind. Practice is entrusted to the one gate of according with [the varying dispositions of beings]. Understanding must be comprehension of the unobstructed. And one must not consider the biased and limited, for then there will be confusion with nothing to serve as a guide. You must[325] clearly investigate the stream and its source and make a distinction between beans and barley.[326] You have to see differences in sameness and sameness in differences. Though a thousand

variegated images are in a mirror, do not grasp some as beautiful and others as ugly. Though the mirror is uniformly bright, do not shun [the many colors of the images, such as] green and yellow. Even though a thousand utensils [are made out of] one piece of gold without a break between them, the thousand reflections [on the surface of] one pearl are from the outset unmixed. Establishing will and girding mind are equal [in their limitless scope] to the realm of space, but warding off of what is wrong and investigating thoughts lie within the smallest increment. When one sees a color or hears a sound, one must ponder whether or not it is like a reflection or an echo. With bodily movements and incipient thoughts, one must consider whether or not they are for the sake of the buddha dharma. With delicious food and coarse food, one must think over whether or not one is free of likes and dislikes. When it is hot or cool or freezing or warm, one must gaze into oneself concerning whether or not one is foregoing both avoidance and seeking out. [This pondering should proceed] up to and including profit, weakness, slander, glory, praise, criticism, suffering, and joy.[327] Do a reverse illumination on yourself concerning these matters one by one. In fact, have you gotten the idea or not? If, when you consider, [it is apparent that] you have not yet gotten it in this way, then forms do not yet seem to be shadows, and sounds do not yet seem to be echoes. Suppose [someone] in fact all-at-once awakens; to the end he must step-by-step practice.[328] Do not be like the poor man who, till the end of his days, counted the treasures of others, while he himself did not have a halfpenny. The Great Teacher, the sixth patriarch [Huineng] said: "The Buddha spoke of all dharmas in order to cross over all minds [to nirvana]; I lack *all mind*, so what need have I of *all dharmas*?"[329] At the present time people just utilize such sayings to belittle learning [*qing yu tingxue*]. None of them ever gazes at whether or not he himself in fact has no mind. *No mind* means that the eight winds cannot move [mind]. Suppose habit energy is not yet exhausted and a thought of anger happens to arise; at that moment have no mind to strike or abuse the other. If a thought of greed happens to arise, at that moment have no mind that prays for acquiring [the coveted object]. Should one see another prosper and become famous, at that moment, have no mind that envies him or seeks to outdo him. At all times in oneself have no mind that is sorrowful or hungry or cold; have no mind that fears being despised by others, up to and including all these sorts of things. We can even call it "lacking all mind." This is called cultivating the path. If you have obtained [the state wherein] toward agreeable and disagreeable sense objects you have no passion or hatred or desire or dislike at all, this is called obtaining the path. Do a reverse illumination on each of these. If you have a disease, apply an antidote. If you have no disease, there is no [need for] a prescription.

Question: Passion, hatred, etc., are void, and if we call it "lacking all mind," what is the need for applying an antidote?

Answer: If you were now suddenly to contract a severe disease with pain and suffering, the fact that pain and suffering are void [could] be called "no dis- ease," and what need would you have for an antidote, the prescription? You must come to know that passion and hatred are permanently void, but they have the potentiality to produce karma. Karma is also void, but it has the potentiality to bring on suffering. Suffering is also void—[it is] just[330] that it is difficult to bear. Therefore, in the previous chart [I divided the unreal into] devoid of sub- stance and phenomenal. *(It is like the fact that [at night] the tree stump [misper- ceived] as a ghost is completely void—[it is] just that it can startle people, [causing them to] run and fall to the ground, cracking open their foreheads.)* You may hold that karma is void—[it is] just that in voidness karma is produced. You must come to know that the pain of burning in a hell is also void—[it is] just that in voidness there is pain. You might say: "Bear the pain!" But supposing right now someone burned you with fire and slit you with a knife. Why would you be un- able to bear it? In viewing trainees on the path these days, [I must say that,] upon hearing even a word that contradicts their feelings, they cannot bear it. Would they consent to bear up under burning or slitting? *(Nine out of ten of them are like this.)*

Question: The *Chan Prolegomenon* alone is a sufficient guide for Chan practice. Why should it be necessary for anyone to go on and read the Chan literature collected in the *Chan Canon*?

Answer: Since the karmic diseases of beings are virtually infinite in number and vari- ety, the *Chan Canon* is a useful repository of teaching devices to treat these diseases. The *Chan Prolegomenon* is like the headrope by which a fishing net, the *Chan Canon*, is hauled up from the sea with its catch. Those training alone do not need to study the whole of the latter; only those intending to become teaching masters must do so.

57. Question: Above you have presented the three types of teachings and the three axioms of Chan, the ten reasons why [Chan is connected to the sutras and the treatises], the ten differences [between the voidness axiom and the nature axiom], and the ten stages each of wheel turning and practice-realization. Of both principle and phenomena, there are none you have not exhausted. For in- vestigating and testing the taste, [your *Chan Prolegomenon*] is sufficient to [en- able one to pursue] mind cultivation. What need is there to go further and read the canonical sutras and Chan verses [that you have collected in the volumi- nous *Chan Canon*]?[331]

Answer: The depravity diseases of sentient beings are each different and are equal in number to the grains of sand of the Ganges. How could there be only eighty thousand?[332] The teaching devices of the noble ones have innumerable gates. The nature and characteristics of the one mind have innumerable aspects. What is related above is just a holding up of the headrope [of a fishing net, that is, something that raises the essential points of a matter or a rule that ties every-thing together]. Even though in making this summary I have not gone beyond the things presented, if you use it, [you will experience] a thousand changes and ten thousand powers. The former wise ones and later eminent ones each have their strong points. The ancient noble ones and present-day worthies each have their beneficial [points]. Therefore, I have collected the good points of all the [Chan] houses and recorded the followers of their lineages.[333] There are those that [make me] uneasy, but even those have not been altered.[334] Only in those [passages] where there was a hiatus in meaning have I added a note to perfect it. Only in those where the phrasing was cumbersome have I added a note to eluci-date it. Furthermore, at the head [of the section] on each [Chan] house I have added as a note a critique of its overall idea.[335] The intention behind raising the headrope [of a fishing net] lies in spreading out the net. One should not discard the net and save the headrope. *(The* Huayan *says: "Spread out the great teaching net, strain out the men and gods [as if they were] fish, and place them on the [other] shore of nirvana.")*[336] The intention behind holding up the garment collar lies in putting on the garment. You should not throw down the garment and keep the collar. If I had just made a [Chan] collection [that is, a *Chan Canon*] without presenting [the three types of teachings, three axioms of Chan, ten rea-sons why Chan is connected to the sutras and treatises, etc., that is, without pre-senting a *Chan Prolegomenon* as a preface], it would have been like a net without a headrope. If I had just made a presentation [that is, just presented the *Chan Prolegomenon* as a preface] without the collection [of the *Chan Canon*], it would have been like a headrope without a net. Ponder the whole of it, but do not trouble yourself if there should be difficulties. Thus, those who conquer self and perfect themselves independently do not need to examine [the *Chan Canon*] from beginning to end. [But] if you wish to become a teacher of men, then you simply must comprehend the whole [of the *Chan Canon*]. When scholars who love learning open this [*Chan Canon*] and read it, they will certainly have to examine it in detail point by point. [They will have to ask themselves:] Which [Chan] axiom and which teaching [does such and such] principle [belong to]? If one uses [this *Chan Canon*] without mistakes, the whole thing will become ex-cellent medicine. If one uses it in the wrong fashion, everything will become a return to the hateful. *(The reading [of the word for "hateful"] is* "wu.")

I experienced some difficulty in deciding how to order the *Chan Canon*. Eventually I settled on the following order: the one axiom of Bodhidharma, the mind axiom; the literary productions of all the Chan houses; and, finally, excerpts from the sutras and treatises that "seal" the Chan axioms. The canonical excerpts total a little over ten rolls (out of the one hundred or so of the *Chan Canon*). May students and the patriarchs find my efforts in this work acceptable. If they do so, then I vow to hasten to meet the assembly of the buddhas.

58. Nevertheless, it was not easy to decide in what order I should arrange the collection [the *Chan Canon*]. According to *Teaching Devices for Entering the Path,*[337] I should have first opened up original mind; next, penetrated both principle and phenomena; next, praised the surpassing excellence of the dharma and castigated worldly faults; next, encouraged practice; and, finally, illustrated the step-by-step gate of teaching devices to be used as antidotes. I wanted to arrange it according to this [schema], but then I realized that the *zhao* and *mu* temples[338] of the [Chan] masters and their disciples would be upside down. As a companion [a *Chan Canon* arranged in this fashion] would not be a convenience. I refer to the fact that, after the sixth generation [of Huineng], most [masters of Chan] related the one reality, while the [first-generation] Great Teacher Bodhidharma, on the contrary, taught the four practices.[339] It is not permissible to put the grandsons in the head section and the grandfather [Bodhidharma] in the final chapter. For several days I pondered this matter. I had wanted to place those outside the branches of the Bodhidharma lineage at the head [of the *Chan Canon*], but, in the case of the Chan that those houses taught and the principles they related, there have been no sanctioned masters for generations. They are not the constant path that pervades every region.

Some [of these Chan masters outside of the Bodhidharma fold] proceeded from the merit of cultivation and refinement to realization and then took that to show people. (*Gunabhadra, Huichou,*[340] *and Wolun*[341] *were of this type.*) Some relied on listening to readings of the teachings of the sutras to produce understanding [that is, gave lectures on the sutras] and took that to embrace the multitude. (*Chan Master Huiwen*[342] *was of this type.*) Some corrected natures by sending down their traces, by the hour chastising the multitude for its delusions. (*Zhi Gong,*[343] *Great Master Fu,*[344] *and Wang Fanzhi*[345] *were of this type.*) Some protected the dharma by their high moral conduct, becoming model monks for the entire country. (*Yuan Gong*[346] *of Mt. Lu was of this type.*) As to the literary productions of these [non-Bodhidharma Chan masters], some are odes to the great path; some are laments for the deluded common person; some just explain principles [of the teachings]; and some just exhort practice. Some catch all the teachings, but, in the end, do not point south [that is, are not useful as a guide]. Some praise one gate in a biased manner and do not penetrate all phenomena. Although all of them are shadows and echoes of the Chan gate, reeds in the wind instrument [*sheng huang*][347] of the buddha dharma, if one were to rely exclusively on [any one of] them as the dharma of Śākyamuni, it would not do. *(The teaching of Tiantai [Zhiyi]*[348] *is broad and great. Even though it constitutes a comprehensive treatment, it also is not contained in this [Chan Canon] collection.)*

Only the Bodhidharma lineage transmits by mind. Mind is the dharma source. What dharma is not included [in mind]? The Chan practice cultivated [in the Bodhidharma lineage] seems to be limited to one gate [of the five gates of the *Awakening of Faith*],[349] but the mind axiom transmitted [in the Bodhidharma lineage in fact] penetrates the three instructions [of precepts, concentration, and wisdom]. Examine once again its first [patriarchs]. *(The first were Kāśyapa and Ānanda.)*[350] They personally received [the mind transmission] from Śākyamuni. This was continued generation after generation, each [generation] passing it on in a face-to-face [encounter]. After thirty-seven generations, *(It is said: "The western countries have had twenty-eight patriarchs." They are enumerated in order in the preface to the* Sixth Patriarch Transmission*)*[351] the patriarchate fell to me. *(I sometimes think how fortunate I am to be a thirty-eighth generation successor of Śākyamuni.)*

Therefore, as to the order of the present [*Chan Canon*] collection: First, I record Bodhidharma's one axiom;[352] next come the miscellaneous writings of the [Chan] houses; and, lastly, I have copied out the noble teachings that seal the [Chan] axioms.[353] As for the placement of the noble teachings last, it is like a worldly lawsuit document in which the clerk's judgment comes first and the esteemed official's judgment last.[354] *(Since I have copied out only those passages [of the sutras and treatises] that strike the bull's-eye, [they amount to little] more than ten rolls.)*[355] Because within the various [Chan] lineages I have taken the chronological sequence of those of high and low status, the *zhao* and *mu* [ancestral temples],[356] as my order, all-at-once and step-by-step within those will be mixed up. Principle and practice will intermingle, and, working in tandem, will loosen bonds. Spontaneously, mind will have no place to abide. *(The* Vimalakīrti *says: "To covet the taste of dhyana is the bondage of the bodhisattva. To be born through [skill in] teaching devices is the release of the bodhisattva."*[357] *Further, the* Yoga *says that, when compassion and wisdom increase, together they release bonds.)*[358] Having completed the path of awakening and cultivation, the activities of release are thereupon of perfect penetration.

Next, as a bystander inspect all of the [Chan] houses in order to broaden your knowledge. Lastly, hold up and read the noble teachings in order to seal the whole of it. Relying on this, how could the true dharma not abide for a long time? Though in my ambition I have sought nothing, for my thought of protecting the dharma, may divine principle not bend me down. For my efforts in continuing the [Chan] succession, may the former patriarchs not cast me aside. For my kindness in dharma giving, may junior trainees not be ungrateful to me. If they are not ungrateful, and I am neither bent down nor cast aside, then I vow to hasten, together with those of the same karmic conditions, to meet the assembly of all the buddhas.

PROLEGOMENON TO THE COLLECTION
OF EXPRESSIONS OF THE CHAN SOURCE
SECOND ROLL ENDS

3 *Translation of the* Chan Notes

FROM *EXTRACTS FROM THE GREAT COMMENTARY ON THE PERFECT AWAKENING SUTRA*[1]

Of the seven houses Northern is the first. Its idea is "sweep away dust"; its practice is "teaching devices pervade the sutras." The teaching devices are five in number, and each is grounded in a sutra or treatise.

1. "Sweep away dust; gaze at purity; teaching devices pervade the sutras"[2] [is the first house]. . . . In brief I will present seven houses. Now the first: It is descended from the fifth patriarch [Hongren]. The Great Master [Shen]xiu[3] is the source of this lineage. His disciple Puji and others widely spread it. "Sweep away dust [sense objects]" is their root verse: "From time to time we must polish [the mirror]; do not let dust collect on it."[4] The idea is: From the outset sentient beings have the nature of awakening that is like the brightness of a mirror. The depravities cover it, like the dust on a mirror. One extinguishes thought of the unreal. When thoughts are exhausted, then the original nature is perfectly bright. It is like rubbing off the dust until the mirror is bright; then all things reach an extreme.

This is just the dependently originated characteristics of impurity-purity,[5] having not yet seen that thought of the unreal from the outset is non-existent and the one nature from the outset pure. Since it has yet to have gotten to the bottom of awakening, how can its practice be called true? Since its practice cannot be called true, [even] over numerous eons how could it reach realization? In "teaching devices pervade the sutras," teaching devices refers to the five teaching devices.[6] The first totally displays the buddha substance and relies on the *Awakening of Faith*. . . . The second opens the gate of wisdom and relies on the *Lotus Sutra*. . . . The third reveals inconceivable liberation and relies on the *Vimalakīrti Sutra*. . . . The fourth clarifies the true nature of all dharmas and relies on the *Thinking of Benefit [Brahma] Sutra*. . . . The fifth realizes the liberation of nondifference, spontaneity, and non-obstruction and relies on the *Huayan Sutra*. . . .

The second house is the Jingzhong, located in the superior prefecture of Chengdu in Sichuan. Its idea is "exertion in the three topics." The three topics are: "No remembering, no mindfulness, and do not forget." Its practice is "precepts, concentration, and wisdom." The former three correspond respectively to the latter three. This house holds large nighttime assemblies lasting a matter of weeks, with both monastics and lay people in attendance. In its instructional style it is similar to the Vinaya lineage.

2. "Exertion in [focusing concentrated attention on] the three topics is precepts, concentration, and wisdom"[7] is the second house. At its origin it is an offshoot down from the fifth patriarch [Hongren] through one named Zhishen.[8] He was one of the ten disciples [of Hongren]. He was originally a man of Zizhou [in Sichuan], and, after [his stay on East Mountain in Hubei under Hongren], he returned to Dechun Monastery in his native prefecture to begin teaching. His disciple Chuji, family name Tang, received [the succession]. Later Tang produced four sons, the preeminent of which was Preceptor Kim [Korean reading of Jin] of Jingzhong Monastery in the superior prefecture Chengdu, dharma name Musang [Korean reading of Wuxiang]. He greatly spread this teaching. *(As to Kim's disciples, Zhao of that [Jingzhong] Monastery [Zhao=Yizhou Shi=Jingzhong Shenhui], Ma of Mt. Changsong, Ji of Zhuzhou, and Ji of Tongquan county all succeeded him.)*[9] The "three topics" are: "no remembering, no mindfulness, and do not forget."[10] The idea is as follows. Do not recall past sense objects. Do not anticipate glorious events in the future. Constantly be yoked to this wisdom, never darkening, never erring; this is called do not forget. Sometimes [the three topics are]: no remembering external sense objects; no thinking of internal mind, dried up with nothing to rely upon *(do not forget as above)*. "Precepts, concentration, and wisdom" correspond respectively to the three topics. Even though [Jingzhong's] teaching devices in opening its axiom to discussion are numerous, its axiom purport is distilled into these three topics. Their instructional rituals are a little like the method of receiving the full precepts on a government-sponsored ordination platform at the present time in this country. That is, in the first and second months they first pick a date and post notices, summoning monks, nuns, and laypeople.[11] They arrange a mahayana

practice site, worship [the three treasures], and confess [transgressions]. Sometimes it is three to five weeks long. Only after this do they hand over dharma. All of this is at night. Their idea is to cut off external [sense objects] and reject confusion. The dharma having been handed over, immediately beneath the words [of the master] they are made to stop thoughts and do cross-legged Chan sitting. Even those who come from distant parts, sometimes nuns and lay types, must not tarry for long. Directly they must do one or two weeks of cross-legged Chan sitting. Only afterward do they disperse according to their conditions. It is even like the method of mounting the ordination platform [to receive the precepts] in the Vinaya lineage. It is obligatory to have a group. Since they use a tablet with an official statement [that is, an official license] on it, it is called "opening conditions." Sometimes once in a year, sometimes once in two or three years, it is irregular in its opening.

The third house is the Baotang of Wuzhu, centered at the Baotang Monastery in Chengdu in Sichuan. Wuzhu had contact with Jingzhong and came to recognize Preceptor Kim as his master, even though earlier he had attained an awakening under a lay master named Chen. The Baotang idea is quite similar to that of Jingzhong, but the two have utterly different instructional styles. The Baotang idea is "not caught up in the teachings/practices," and its practice is "extinguishing consciousness." Baotang ignores virtually all Buddhist practices. After cutting off their hair, they put away their Buddhist robes—there is no precept taking, obeisance, confession, reading the sutras, iconography, teaching, begging, chanting, etc. They do not even stand up when someone enters one of their halls. They *just give free rein to other.* Baotang transmits a slightly different form of the "three topics," and says that Preceptor Kim's followers at the Jingzhong Monastery are transmitting a distorted form.

3. "Not caught up in the teachings/practices and extinguishing consciousness"[12] is the third house. At its first it is also an offshoot down from the fifth patriarch [Hongren], through Preceptor Old Mother An.[13] At sixty years of age he left home and received the precepts. When he expired sixty summers later, he was one hundred twenty years old. Therefore, at the time he was styled "Old An." An was his given name. He was honored as a master by the Noble Empress [Wu] Zetian. His virtue on the path was profound, his determination and integrity singular. None of the famous worthies could compare to him. He had four disciples, all of whom were high in the path and famous. Among them there was a lay disciple Chen Chuzhang *(the other three were Teng Teng, Zizai, and Pozao Duo),*[14] at that time styled Chen Qige. There was a monk named Wuzhu.[15] He met Chen, who showed him and guided him to awakening. [Wuzhu] was also singular in his determination. Later he traveled within Shu [Sichuan] and encountered Preceptor Kim's opening up of Chan, even attending his assembly. [Wuzhu] just asked further questions, and, seeing that it was not a matter of changing his previous awak-

ening, wanted to transmit it to those who had not yet heard it. Fearing in his mind that it was improper to have received the succession from a layman [such as Chen Qige], he subsequently recognized Preceptor Kim as his master. Even though the dharma idea that [Wuzhu] pointed to was just about the same [as that of Kim], his [that is, Wuzhu's] instructional rituals were completely different from those of Kim's school. The difference lies in the fact that [Wuzhu's Baotang house] practices none of the phenomenal characteristics of the Śākya gate.[16] Having shaved off their hair, they immediately hang up the seven-piece [robe on a hook], without taking the prohibitory precepts. When it comes to doing obeisance and confession, turning and reading [the sutras], making paintings of buddhas, and copying out sutras, they revile all such things as thought of the unreal. In the halls where they dwell they set up no buddha artifacts. Therefore, I say [their idea is] "not caught up in the teachings/practices." "Extinguishing consciousness" is the path practiced, meaning that all wheel turning in the rebirth process is the production of mind. The production of mind is the unreal. No matter whether good or bad, not producing [mind] is the real. [Their practice] shows no resemblance whatsoever to [ordinary Buddhist] practices in terms of phenomenal characteristics. They take discrimination as the enemy and non-discrimination as the excellent path. They do transmit Preceptor Kim's spoken teaching on the "three topics," but they just change the word for "forget" to the word for "unreal."[17] They say: "Co-students [of Master Wuzhu, that is, Preceptor Kim's disciples at the Jingzhong Monastery in Chengdu] are making a mistake in the spoken teaching of the former master [Preceptor Kim] entrusted to them."[18] The idea is: No remembering and no mindfulness are the real. Remembering thoughts is the unreal, [so] remembering thoughts is not allowed. Therefore, they say "do not [allow the] unreal" [rather than "do not forget"]. Moreover, their idea in reviling all characteristics of the teachings lies in extinguishing discrimination and [manifesting] the completely real. Therefore, in their dwellings they do not discuss clothing and food, but give free rein to people's sending of offerings. If sent, then they have warm clothing and enough to eat. If not sent, then they give free rein to hunger and give free rein to cold. Also, they do not seek to transform [beings], nor do they beg for food. If someone enters their halls, regardless of whether he is of high status or low status, in no case do they go out to welcome him, not even rising [when he enters].[19] As to singing hymns and praises, doing worship, reprimanding abuses, in all things they give free rein to other. Indeed, because their axiom purport speaks of non-discrimination, their practice gate has neither right nor wrong. They just value "no mind" as the excellent ultimate. Therefore, I say [their practice is] "extinguishing consciousness." The above three houses are all at their roots [descended from] co-students of the sixth patriarch [Huineng]. It is just the difference between collateral and central/orthodox [with the above three all being collateral].

The fourth house is the Hongzhou. Its idea is "everything is the Dao." This means that every single action—a thought, a snapping of the fingers, a tinkling of chimes, a spreading of a fan, depravities, good actions, bad actions, suffering, joy, etc.—is the functioning of the buddha nature, the real. Hongzhou practice is "give free rein to mind." This means the practitioner does not try to engage in any kind of practice whatsoever, but *just gives free rein to luck and exists in freedom*. Its founder Mazu Daoyi was originally a student of Preceptor Kim of the Jingzhong lineage in Sichuan. Later he encountered the mountain recluse Huairang, a disciple of the sixth patriarch, and put himself under Huairang's tutelage. Eventually Daoyi propagated Huairang's teaching in Jiangxi.

4. "Everything is the Dao and give free rein to mind"[20] is the fourth house. Its first is an offshoot down from the sixth patriarch [Huineng], that is, Preceptor [Huai]rang of Avalokiteśvara Terrace in Nanyue [Mt. Heng in Hunan], who was a disciple of the sixth patriarch.[21] Never opening a dharma [that is, teaching], he just dwelled in the mountains practicing the path. In this connection there was a monk from Jiannan [Sichuan] Daoyi. His worldly family name was Ma. He was a disciple of Preceptor Kim [of the Jingzhong house in Chengdu, Sichuan].[22] He was of a lofty determination in the path. Wherever he was, he did cross-legged Chan sitting. He dwelled for a long time on Mt. Mingyue in Jingnan [that is, southern Jingzhou in Hubei]. Later, when he was on a pilgrimage to [sites of] the traces of noble ones, he arrived at Preceptor [Huai]rang's place. They had a dialogue concerning the logic of the axiom and contended about the extreme principle. [Daoyi's] principle did not measure up to that of [Huai]rang. Also, [Daoyi] realized that Caoqi [Huineng] was the legitimate successor who had transmitted the robe and handed over the dharma. He immediately relied on this to practice. He dwelled in Ganzhou [in Sichuan], Hongzhou [in Jiangxi], and Huzhou [that is, Chuzhou in Zhejiang]. In both the mountains and towns he broadly opened up worship and guided followers of the path. He widely spread this dharma.

The raising of mind, the moving of thoughts, the snapping of the fingers, a tinkling of musical chimes, a spreading of a fan, all doing and all acting are the totalistic functioning of the buddha nature. There is no second controller. It is like preparing many types of drinks and foods out of flour. Every one of them [continues to be] flour. The buddha nature is also that way. Passion, hatred, stupidity, the creation of good and bad, the receiving of suffering and joy, in their totality every one of them is the [buddha] nature. If one uses [this Hongzhou] idea to examine [this physical body, it becomes apparent that] the four elements, bones, flesh, tongue, teeth, eyes, ears, hands, and feet cannot by themselves speak, see, hear, move, or act. It is like the moment of death, before any decomposition of the whole body. At that time the mouth cannot speak, the eyes cannot see, the ears cannot hear, the feet cannot walk, and the hands cannot perform. Therefore, we know that speech and action must be the buddha nature. If we examine the four elements and the bones and flesh carefully one by one, [it becomes apparent that] not a one of them understands passion and hatred. Therefore, the depravities of passion and hatred are the buddha nature. The buddha nature is not [in a substantialist sense] all sorts of differentiations, and yet it has the potentiality to create all sorts of differentiations. The [Hongzhou] idea accords with the *Lanka Descent Sutra* when it says: "The buddha-in-embryo [tathagatagarbha] is the cause of good and non-good, having the potentiality to create all the beings everywhere in the rebirth paths, the receptor of suffering and joy, synonymous with cause."[23] Also, [the chapter entitled] "The Mind Behind the Words of the Buddhas"[24] [of that sutra] also says: "A buddha land, a raising of the eyebrows, a movement of the eyeballs, a laugh, a yawn, [a ringing of a Buddhist] bell, a cough, or a swaying, etc., are all buddha events."[25] Therefore, I say "everything is the Dao" [is Hongzhou's idea]. "Give free rein to mind" is their practice gate of "stopping karma and nourishing the spirit" *(sometimes it is "stopping spirit and nourishing the path")*. This means that you do not stir your mind to cut off bad or cultivate good. You do not even cultivate the path. The path is mind. You should not use mind to cultivate [the path in] mind. The bad is also mind. You should not use mind to cut off [the bad in] mind. When you neither cut off nor create, but *just give free rein to luck and exist in freedom*, then you are to be called a liberated person. You are also to be called a person who surpasses the measure. There are no dharmas to be caught up in, no buddhas to become. Why? Outside the mind nature there is not one dharma to be apprehended. Therefore, I say "just giving free rein to mind." That is their practice.[26]

This and the third house [Baotang] contradict each other like opposing enemies, that is, for the previous one *everything is unreal*, and for this one *everything is real*.

The fifth house is Niutou, a collateral offshoot from the fourth patriarch Daoxin. Its idea is "from the outset nothing to do." This means that mind and sense objects have always been void and calmed. Delusion about this leads to the production of feelings and consequent suffering. Thus, there is nothing to do. Its practice is "forgetting feelings"; it has the mind take a rest or pause.

5. "From the outset nothing to do and forgetting feelings"[27] is the fifth house. It is an offshoot down from the fourth patriarch [Daoxin]. Its first is the Great Master Niutou Huiyong [or Huirong].[28] He was a co-student of the fifth patriarch, the Great Master [Hong]ren. Just after the fourth patriarch entrusted the succession to the Great Master [Hong]ren, he and [Hui]yong met. [Hui]yong's nature of comprehension was lofty, his divine wisdom spiritually sharp. He was long

skilled at the wisdom-voidness [prajna-sunyata] axiom. He was already without calculation or grasping toward dharmas. Later he encountered the fourth patriarch. Because he dwelt in the substance of voidness and no-characteristics [and yet] openly produced the absolute original awakening of the spiritual mind, without the need of lengthy training his awakening-understanding was clear. The fourth patriarch told him: "This dharma from ancient times has been entrusted to only one person at each generation. I already have a successor [that is, Hongren]. You may set yourself up [separately]." Subsequently at Mt. Niutou [in Jiangsu] he stopped objective supports, forgot feelings, and practiced the principle of no-characteristics. He served as first patriarch [of Niutou]. Zhiyan was the second; Huifang the third; Fachi the fourth; Zhiwei the fifth; and Huizhong the sixth. Zhiwei's disciple was Preceptor Masu of Haolin Monastery in Runzhou [in Jiangsu]. [Ma]su's disciple Preceptor Daoqin of Mt. Jing [in Zhejiang] inherited. They transmitted this axiom purport.

"From the outset nothing to do" is the principle awakened to. This means that mind and sense objects from the outset are void; it is not a case of coming to be calmed for the first time now. Because you are deluded about this and hold that things exist, you produce such feelings as hatred, love, etc. When feelings are engendered, then you are bound by various sufferings. Created in a dream, perceived in a dream, therefore, [Niutou] comprehends from the outset that there is nothing to do. Then they must *lose self and forget feelings.* Feelings forgotten, they cross over suffering and calamities.[29] Therefore, [Niutou] takes "forgetting feelings" as practice.[30]

For one house back [Hongzhou], "everything is the Dao" is awakening and "giving free rein to mind" is practice. This [house] takes "from the outset nothing to do" as awakening and "forgetting feelings" as practice. This and the previous two houses [that is, Baotang and Hongzhou] are completely different. That is, speaking in terms of the principle awakened to, for the third house [Baotang] *everything is unreal;* for the fourth [Hongzhou] *everything is real;* and [for this one] *everything is non-existent [void/śūnya].* Speaking in terms of practice, the third *subdues mind to extinguish the unreal;*[31] the fourth *indulges the mind nature;*[32] and this one has the *mind take a rest [so that it] does not arise.*[33] Also, the third *extinguishes the disease;* the fourth *gives free rein to the disease;* and the fifth *stops the disease.*

The sixth house is the South Mountain Buddha-Recitation Gate Chan Lineage in Sichuan. Its idea is "transmission of the incense," a ceremony conducted in an assembly much like the Jingzhong assemblies of Preceptor Kim. The master passes the incense to the disciple, who hands it back. The master hands it to him again. The incense is a seal of faith. South Mountain Buddha–Recitation Gate's practice is "maintaining the buddha-recitation consisting of the one syllable for '*buddha.*'" This is a musical buddha-recitation in which the practitioners sing the single syllable for "*buddha*" in a gradually lowering pitch, until their voices die out. Eventually they reach no thought. I know little of the genealogy of this house.

6. "Relying on the transmission of the incense and maintaining [the buddha-recitation consisting of the single syllable] '*fhut*' (-'*buddha*')"[34] is the sixth house, that is, the South Mountain Buddha–Recitation Gate Chan Lineage. Its first is also an offshoot down from the fifth patriarch [Hongren], through one with the dharma name Xuanshi.[35] Wei Preceptor of Guozhou [in Sichuan], Yunyu of Langzhou [in Sichuan], and the Yisheng Nun of Xiangru county [in Sichuan] all spread it. I do not clearly know the *zhao* and *mu* [ancestral temples][36] of the masters and disciples of this succession [that is, I lack knowledge of its genealogy]. As to "transmission of the incense," when they first gather the community and [conduct such] rituals as obeisance and confession, etc., it is like Preceptor Kim's [Jingzhong] line.[37] When they are about to hand over dharma, they take transmission of the incense as [a seal of] faith between disciple and master.[38] The preceptor transfers [the incense] by hand. The disciple hands it back to the preceptor. The preceptor hands it back to the disciple. Thus [it is handed between them] three times. It is the same for every person [attending the ceremony]. As to "maintaining the '*fhut*,'" just as they hand over dharma, [the preceptor] first speaks on the principles of their dharma gate and the significance of practice. Only afterwards does he enjoin the one-syllable buddha-recitation. At the beginning they chant this buddha-recitation as a gentle [or slow] song.[39] Later they gradually lower the sound to a finer and finer sound, up to and including no sound. They are dispatching the "*fhut*" to [the seventh consciousness,] the manas,[40] but in the manas the buddha-recitation is still coarse. They go on to dispatch [the "*fhut*"] to [the eighth consciousness,] the *citta* [that is, the storehouse consciousness], maintaining thought recitation after recitation. They have the "*fhut*" constantly inside the *citta*, up to and including the no-thought concentration.[41] [By such a practice] how could they not attain the path?

The seventh house is the Heze coming down from the seventh patriarch Shenhui. Its idea is "Knowing points to the substance." "Knowing" is the equivalent of awakening or nirvana. Heze practice is "no mindfulness is the axiom." This means that, having attained all-at-once understanding awakening into the truth that the original source is Knowing, one must exert oneself in not stirring up thought of the unreal.

7. "The Knowing of calm points to the substance and no mindfulness is the axiom"[42] is the seventh house. It was transmitted by the Great Master Heze [Shenhui], the seventh patriarch of the Southern lineage.[43] It says that since the ten thousand dharmas are void, the mind substance from the outset is calmed.

Calm is the dharma body, calm and yet Knowing. Knowing is true knowing. It is also called awakening or nirvana. . . . This is the mind of purity that is the original source of all sentient beings. It is dharma that has spontaneously existed from the outset. As to "no mindfulness is the axiom," having awakened to the realization that this dharma from the outset is calm and from the outset is Knowing, by principle one must praise original exertion [that is, having concentrated attention]. One should not subsequently produce thought of the unreal. "Just no mindfulness of the unreal" is practice.[44] Therefore, this is the one [Chan] gate that finds its axiom in "no mindfulness."

Appendix 1

EDITIONS USED IN THE TRANSLATIONS

Chan Letter

My translation of the *Chan Letter* is based on the *Zhonghua chuanxindi chan-men shizi chengxi tu* (*Chart of the Master-Disciple Succession of the Chan Gate that Transmits the Mind Ground in China*) in Kamata. Kamata used ZZ 2.15.5 (CBETA *Wan Xuzangjing* vol. 63, no. 1225). This text was discovered in 1910 at the Nichiren school's Dai-honzan Myōken-ji in Kyoto and inserted into the *Manji zokuzō* (ZZ), which was being published at the time. In addition, I have consulted Ui, which also uses ZZ 2.15.5. In 1981 a Kamakura-period manuscript of the text stored in a Shingon temple in Nagoya, Shinpuku-ji, was published. It is entitled *Pei Xiu shiyi wen* (*Imperial Redactor Pei Xiu's Inquiry*) and is dated Ninji 2 (1241). I have found the *Pei Xiu shiyi wen* to be quite useful and have occasionally followed its readings. Neither Kamata nor Ui provides a modern Japanese translation of the Myōken-ji text, but for a modern Japanese translation of the Shinpuku-ji text, see Ishii Shudō, trans., *Zen goroku*, Daijō butten Chūgoku Nihon hen 12 (Tokyo: Chūōkōronsha, 1992). In section 22 of the *Chan Letter*, Kamata follows Chinul's *Pŏpchip pyŏrhaeng nok chŏryo pyŏngip sagi* (*Excerpts from the Separately Circulated Record of the Dharma Collection with Inserted*

Personal Notes) for a missing portion. My translation, however, in section 22 follows the *Pei Xiu shiyi wen* found in the article Shinpuku-ji (this is indicated in the notes; see notes 84 and 86). In section 22, Shinpuku-ji's *Pei Xiu shiyi wen* includes nineteen characters not found in Kamata, Ui, or Chinul's *Excerpts*.

Chan Prolegomenon

My translation of the *Chan Prolegomenon* is based on the Wanli 4 (1576) Korean edition of the *Chanyuan zhuquanji duxu* (*Prolegomenon to the Collection of Expressions of the Chan Source*) in Kamata. Kamata used the copy stored in the Tōyō Bunko in Tokyo. This Korean edition, one of many produced in Korea, has the standard preface by Pei Xiu (translation in appendix 2) and two colophons: a reproduction of the undated Song dynasty colophon (translation in appendix 3) followed by a colophon added at the time of this printing in Korea (Kamata, 262). The Korean colophon states at the end: "Printed at Kwanŭm Monastery of Sokri Mountain [Ch'ungch'ŏng-do] in the summer of Wanli 4 [1576]." Sokri Mountain is in the south-central portion of the peninsula. Two other editions have been useful, and I have occasionally followed their readings: Ui uses the *Ming Canon* edition of 1601 (the first time the *Chan Prolegomenon* was printed in a canon) as found in ZZ 2.8.4 (also T 48, no. 2015); Ishii (1–10) uses the Gozan edition of Enbun 3 (1358) stored in the British Museum. For this Gozan edition, see Ishii Shudō, "Daiei toshokan shozō no Gozanban *Zengen shosenshū tojo* ni tsuite," *Indogaku Bukkyōgaku kenkyū* 44, no. 2 (March 1996): 117–24. Neither Kamata nor Ui provides a modern Japanese translation of the *Chan Prolegomenon*, and so Ishii (1–10) is the first to do so. Urs App, ed., *Concordance to the "Preface" by Zongmi*, Hanazono Concordance Series vol. 11 (Kyoto: International Research Institute for Zen Buddhism Hanazono University, 1996), which uses T no. 2015 as newly punctuated by Xiaohong Liang, has been extremely helpful in translating a text as long and intricate as the *Chan Prolegomenon*. I have also consulted the edition of the Five Dynasties (952) Dunhuang manuscript fragment (Taipei no. 133) found in Tanaka Ryōshō, *Tonkō Zenshū bunken no kenkyū* (Tokyo: Daitō shuppansha, 1983), 413–42. A reproduction of that fragment appears in Lin Shitian and others, eds., *Dunhuang Chanzong wenxian jicheng* (Beijing: Quanguo tushuguan wenxian suowei fuzhi zhongxin, 1998), 1:479–89.

Chan Notes

My translation of the *Chan Notes*, a lengthy passage on the Chan houses embedded in Zongmi's *Yuanjuejing dashu chao* (*Extracts from the Great*

Commentary on the Perfect Awakening Sutra), is based on the edition in ZZ 1.14.3.277c-279d (CBETA *Wan Xuzangjing* vol. 9, no. 245:532c18[00]–535a08[03]). There are many misprints in the ZZ text, and these have been corrected, to some extent, by consulting parallel passages in the *Chan Letter* and *Chan Prolegomenon*.

Appendix 2

PEI XIU'S PREFACE TO THE
CHAN PROLEGOMENON IN THE WANLI 4 (1576)
KOREAN EDITION (KAMATA, 3–4)
PREFACE TO THE PROLEGOMENON
TO THE COLLECTION OF EXPRESSIONS OF
THE CHAN SOURCE

*By Hongzhou Prefect Concurrently Vice-President of
the Tribunal of Censors Pei Xiu*[1]

Chan Master Guifeng collected the *Expressions of the Chan Source* as a Chan basket [a new *basket* in addition to the traditional three of vinaya, sutra, and *abhidharma*] and made a prolegomenon to it. Hedong Pei Xiu says: "There has never been such a thing!"[2] Since the Tathagata appeared in the world to establish the teachings according to the dispositions [of beings], the bodhisattvas in the interim arose to point to medicines appropriate for the diseases. Therefore, all the teachings [spoken by the Tathagata] during his whole lifetime opened three gates of varying depth [dharma characteristics, voidness, and dharma nature]. As to the one true, pure mind, he elaborated separate dharmas of the nature and characteristics. Though the two scholars Asvaghosa and Nagarjuna both spread the sutras of the charioteer of humans,[3] they were of different axioms—voidness and [dharma] nature. Though the two [Chan] masters [Hui]neng and [Shen]xiu both transmitted the mind of Bodhidharma, they were of different transmissions—all-at-once and step-by-step. Tiantai specializes in reliance upon the three tranquilizations.[4] For Niutou there is not one dharma. For Jiangxi [Hongzhou] everything in its entirety is real. Heze points directly to Knowing-seeing. In addition, voidness and existence eradicate each other; real and unreal take each other in; opposites snatch each other up and are in accord; [there is] secret pointing and open preaching. In the Western Regions and in China the lineages have, in fact, been manifold. Truly, disease has a thousand sources, and so in medicine there [must] be many items. To respond to dispositions and conform to capacities, there cannot be just a uniform sameness. Although in all cases it is the gate of realization awakening, it [must] always be the correct and true path [of unexcelled, perfect awakening]. Therefore, while among the followers of all the [Chan] lineages there have been awakened people, nevertheless, each [lineage] rests in its own practices, [and so] the flexible are few and the limited numerous. For several decades the teachings of the [Chan] masters has increasingly declined. They have taken their transmissions as doors-and-windows[5] [separate sects], each opening outward in its own way. They take the sutras and treatises as weaponry and attack each other. The feelings of body-armor [makers] and arrow [makers] are different. *(The* Zhou Rites *says: "Body-armor [pronunciation 'han'] makers make carapaces."[6] The* Mencius *says: "How are arrow makers more inhumane than body-armor makers? Body-armor makers only fear harm to people. Arrow makers only fear a lack of harm to people. This is because the arts they practice make it so."[7] Trainees of the present time just follow [their own] lineages and vainly negate each other over this and that.)* Chasing after self and others brings on highness and lowness in dharmas. Right and wrong are seized upon in the midst of disorder, and no one can discriminate among them. Thus, in the past the World-honored-one, the bodhisattvas, and the teachings and [Chan] lineages of the various regions have unexpectedly been sufficient to produce conflict among junior people, increasing the disease of the depravities. What benefit could there be in this? The Great Master of Guishan [Zongmi] sighed over this for a long time, saying: "At this juncture I can no longer remain silent." Thereupon [he composed his *Chan Prolegomenon* that] took the three types of teachings principles of the Tathagata [the three teachings] to seal the three types of dharma gates of the Chan axioms [the three axioms]. [In his *Chan Prolegomenon* he] melted down sheet metal, platters, hairpins, and bracelets into one metal; he stirred butter, butter fat, and cream into one taste. He raised up the headrope [of the *Chan Canon* net in order to hoist it from the sea] and the collar [of the *Chan Canon* garment in order to put the garment on], and everything fell into accord. *(The* Xunzi *says: "It is like lifting up the collar of a hide coat. You bend your five fingers and arrange it. Those who can accord with this are uncountable.")[8]* Rely on the main point and those who come will be of an identical tenor. *(The* Brief Examples from the Zhou Changes *says: "If you rely on the main point in order to discern what comes, then even assembling from heaven and earth and the four directions, they will not [be called] 'many.'"[9] The* Prolegomenon *relies on the perfect teaching [as its main point] in order to seal the [Chan] lineages. Even though [the Chan lineages are of] a hundred [contending] schools [much like the contending schools of thought in late Zhou dynasty times], there are none that are not subsumed.)* Still [Chan Master Guifeng] feared that for trainees it would be difficult to understand this. And so he once again directly showed the root and the branches of the axiom source [in section 11], the fusion of real and unreal [in sections 50–51], the concealed voidness [teaching] and the revealed nature [teaching from section 33 onward], the difference between dharma and principle [in sections 17 and 34], the difference and sameness of all-at-once and step-by-step [in section 19], the mutuality of negativistic [explanation] and expressive [explanation in section 39], the varying depth of the provisional and real [teachings in section 14], and the rightness and wrongness of the flexible and the limited. *(From this point onward [Chan Master Guifeng in his* Chan Prolegomenon] *sighs over whether the narration is clear and [serves up] a warning, desiring to make people awaken.)* There is no case in which he does not raise the ears [of his readers] and inform them, point to his palm to show them,[10] deliver the lion's roar for them, love the weak [among them, and offer] enticement. *(From this point onward [in the* Chan Prolegomenon] *he sighs out of compassion and anxious thoughts, like one caring for a newborn baby.)* [As if] suckling [an infant or applying] a medicine, he worries about the early death of their buddha seeds. *(Cutting off good [karmic] roots and creating an* icchantika[11] *is early death.)* [As if] holding them to his belly, he thinks of their floating adrift on the waters or being burned by fire. *([Placing on the] belly is embracing.[12] Three years after birth the child is free of the father and mother's worries. They no longer have thoughts of water and fire. The person of the present has grown up a little and sinks into the five desires—that is water and fire.)* He lifts them up and leads them, afraid of[13] the trap of delusions false and small. *(When they already have good [karmic] roots and are also free of the five desires, he has the further fear that they will not enter into the Mahayana.)* He disperses [their delusions], out of compassion for their prison of fighting and quarreling. *(Having already entered into the dharma of the Mahayana, they once again [engage in] mutual negation and assertion, and so he disperses [such contentions]. That is the axiom of the* Prolegomenon.) The great brightness cannot eradicate the darkness of the long night; a compassionate mother cannot protect her child after its death. *(From this point onward [in the* Chan Prolegomenon] *he exclaims that compassion and wisdom are identical to the buddhas. Even though the buddha sun is flourishing, after having gotten my teacher, that radiance shined out in every nook and corner; even though the buddha compassion is universal, after having gotten my teacher, that broad benefit [increased] more and more.)* As to what my teacher is like, he lifts up the buddha sun that illumines every nook and corner, and the cloudiness of doubt is dissipated. In accordance with buddha mind, he diffuses great compassion in every direction, throughout eons bringing benefit. Thus, the World-honored-one is the master of explaining the teachings, and my teacher is the person who harmonizes the [seemingly contradictory ideas found in the various] teachings. The root [the World-honored-one] and the branches [my teacher] fit into each other like a tally, the distant and the near il-lumining each other. You could say that [my teacher] completes the capabili-ties[14] of all the teachings [spoken by the Tathagata] during his whole lifetime. *(From the World-honored-one's developing the teachings until today, [Chan Mas-ter Guifeng] harmonizes [the seemingly contradictory ideas found in the various teachings so that for the first time][15] their capabilities are completed.)*

Someone says: "[Even though] the Tathagata never did a great gist[16] [like the *Chan Prolegomenon*] that harmonizes [the seemingly contradictory ideas found in the various teachings,] now one morning [Chan Master Guifeng] contra-venes the axiom, failing to maintain it. If [Guifeng] abandons the monastery and does not rely on it, is it not perverting the [Chan] way of cryptic coinciding [found in] the secret treasury?"

Answer: "Even though the Tathagata at the beginning preached separately the three vehicles, later he harmonized [the seemingly contradictory ideas found in the various teachings] into one path [as Guifeng shows in section 48]." *(Thirty years earlier he sometimes had preached the Hinayana, sometimes had preached the voidness teaching, and sometimes had preached the characteristics teaching. Those who listened according to their dispositions came to a realization awaken-ing, but they did not come to a knowledge that harmonized [the seemingly contra-dictory ideas found in all of them]. Forty years later sitting at Vulture Peak [where he delivered the* Lotus Sutra*] he made the three vehicles converge. He went to Ku-śinagara [where he delivered the* Nirvana Sutra *and died] and revealed the one nature. This is the [underlying] norm for these earlier and later [teachings].)* There-fore, in the *Nirvana Sutra* the bodhisattva Kāśyapa says: "The buddhas some-times speak with a secret [intention] but they do not have a secret storehouse."[17] The World-honored-one praises him, saying: "The words of the Tathagata are open and revealed dew, pure without concealment. The stupid ones do not un-derstand and call it a secret storehouse. Since the wise ones comprehend, they do not call it a storehouse." This is proof. Therefore, when the kingly way pros-pers, doors are not shut [for security], and there is protection against barbarians. When the buddha way is provided, it is the dharani of all the teachings and a defense against the Evil One from without. *(The perfect teaching of the* Nirvana *brings together all the teachings. It only excludes theories of the Evil One and the false axioms of the outsider [non-Buddhist] paths.)* You should not once again [in a state of] grasping feelings roll up your sleeves[18] [to make an exhaustive effort] in the midst of this. Ah! Junior trainees should take their faith from the Buddha and not take their faith from people. They should take their proof[19] from the root dharma and not take their proof from branch practices. *(The* Prolegome-non *takes buddha word to seal the [Chan] axioms and takes the root dharma to illumine slanted theories. Therefore, it repeatedly exhorts deep faith.)* If you can be like this, then you will not be ungrateful for the trouble to which the Great Master Guishan has put himself. (*My poor father and mother in giving me life went to great trouble,*[20] *but my teacher's virtue surpasses this. Later people who look at his dharma [that is, the* Chan Prolegomenon] *and do not produce a sense of compassion*[21] *are no different from trees or stones.*)

Appendix 3

SONG DYNASTY COLOPHON TO THE *CHAN PROLEGOMENON* AS REPRODUCED IN THE WANLI 4 (1576) KOREAN EDITION (KAMATA, 260)

Colophon[1] [*houji*]: In Dazhong 11 *dingchou* year of the Tang [857] Minister Pei personally copied out a manuscript [*qin bi xieben*]. He handed it over to [*fu yu*] the Old Monk [*lao su*][2] of Taiyi Yanchang Monastery on Mt. Wudang in Jinzhou [in Shaanxi]. [The Old Monk] kept it in his possession for fifty years. In the *renshen* year of the Great Liang [912] the Old Monk transmitted it to [*shou yu*] Chan Master Weijing,[3] who took it back to Hunan [*gui Hunan*]. And then, twenty-three years later in the *jiawu* year [934], the Chan Master transmitted it to Qixuan,[4] who took it back to Min [Fujian; *chanshi shou yu Qixuan gui Min*]. And then, after twenty-two years, in the *jiayin* and *yimao* years [954–955], in possession of it he entered Wu [southern Jiangsu and northern Zhejiang] and Yue [eastern Zhejiang]. [There he] copied and disseminated it [*shuxie shixing yi*]. Recorded by the Fuzhou [Fujian] Sramana Qixuan. Public Affairs Officer [*goudang*] Yan Kai,[5] the son of Yan Ming of Qiantang [Hangzhou in Zhejiang] of the Great Song, [was in charge of] the carving [of the woodblocks] and printing [*diaokai ban*].[6]

NOTES

INTRODUCTION

1. For the demon simile, see "Genpō Rōshi no meigen sono ichi, monku kei," http://www.marino.ne.jp/%7Erendaico/kuromakuron/genpo.htm. For a biography of Genpō, see Obigane Mitsutoshi, *Sairai: Yamamoto Genpō den* (Tokyo: Daihōrin kaku, 2002).

2. Zengaku daijiten hensansho, ed., *Zengaku daijiten* (Tokyo: Taishūkan shoten, 1978), 2:1100. The slogan is "*furyū monji kyōge betsuden.*"

3. The term "Knowing" (*zhi*), a translation equivalent of the Sanskrit term *jñāna* (Hirakawa, 885), is the core of Zongmi's Chan. In both Buddhist and non-Buddhist Indian contexts *jñāna* ("sacred knowledge" or "abstract knowledge") is contrasted with *vi-jñāna* ("practical knowledge" or "applied knowledge"). Zongmi (*Chan Prolegomenon*, section 24) says of this Knowing: "The mind of voidness and calm is a spiritual Knowing that never darkens. It is precisely this Knowing of voidness and calm that is your true nature. No matter whether you are deluded or awakened, mind from the outset is spontaneously Knowing. [Knowing] is not produced by conditions, nor does it arise in dependence on any sense object. The one word 'Knowing' is the gate of all excellence." I would like to thank F. Stanley Jones for suggesting the term "prolegomenon."

4. The following biography, including the division into phases, is based on Peter N. Gregory, *Tsung-mi and the Sinification of Buddhism* (Princeton, N.J.: Princeton

University Press, 1991), 27–90. See Gregory for details and information on sources. I have at nodal points quoted Pei Xiu's funerary inscription for Zongmi, the *Guifeng chanshi beiming bing xu*.

5. Pei Xiu's inscription for Zongmi, the *Guifeng chanshi beiming bing xu*, begins: "Chan Master Guifeng, name Zongmi, of the He family [*xing Heshi*], was a man of Xichong county in Guo prefecture [*Guozhou Xichong xian ren*]. . . . The Great Master was originally of a wealthy and powerful family [*haojia*]" (Shūmitsu, 49–50; QTW 16:743.9730b18 and 9731a16–17). Zongmi's given name is not recorded. His birthplace is just east of present-day Nanchong county in Sichuan province, about 110 miles east of Chengdu, the provincial capital.

6. Such schools, which ran on public or private money, were established in local areas. The Righteousness Learning Academy (*Yixueyuan*) was in Suizhou on the west bank of the Fu River (*Fujiang*), not far from Zongmi's home in Guozhou.

7. Pei's *Guifeng chanshi beiming bing xu* reports: "When young he was conversant with Confucian books, and he wanted to make a life in the world, but by chance he called on [*ou ye*] Suizhou [Daoyuan]. Before Suizhou had said anything, [Zongmi] retired to become one of his followers. . . . In Yuanhe 2 [807] he received the sealed mind from [*yinxin yu*] Preceptor [Dao]yuan" (Shūmitsu, 50–51; QTW 16:743.9731a17–18 and 9732b6–7).

8. Pei's *Guifeng chanshi beiming bing xu* reports that Zongmi first encountered this sutra at a vegetarian banquet in Sichuan: "At the beginning in Sichuan, at the time of a vegetarian banquet [*yin zhai ci*], he received sutras and got the *Perfect Awakening* in thirteen chapters. He had a deep comprehension of its principles and subsequently transmitted the *Perfect Awakening*" (Shūmitsu, 50; QTW 16:743.9731b3–4). T no. 842, the *Da fangguang yuanjue xiuduoluo liaoyi jing*, purports to be a translation by Buddhatara/Buddhatrata done in 693, but it is thought to be a Chinese apocryphon based on the *Heroic Progress Samadhi Sutra* (T no. 945) and the *Awakening of Faith* (T no. 1666) (Daizōkyō, 247–248). Yanagida Seizan, ed. and trans., *Chūgoku senjutsu kyōten* 1 *Engakukyō*, Bukkyō kyōten-sen 13 (Tokyo: Chikuma shobō, 1987) has Chinese text, modern Japanese translation, and notes. For an English translation, see Charles Muller, "The Sutra of Perfect Enlightenment (Yuanjuejing)," http://www.acmuller .net/bud-canon/sutra_of_perfect_enlightenment.html. Muller's description (2–3) is useful: "The *Sutra of Perfect Enlightenment* is arranged in twelve chapters, plus the short convocation. The convocation section describes the scene of the sermon and lists the major participants. The location is a state of deep meditative concentration (*samā-dhi*) and the participants are the Buddha and one hundred thousand great bodhisattvas, among whom twelve eminent bodhisattvas act as spokesmen. Each one of the twelve gets up one by one and asks the Buddha a set of questions about doctrine, practice, and enlightenment. *The structure of the sutra is such that the most 'essential' and suddenistic discussions occur in the earlier chapters and the more 'functional' and gradualistic dialogues occur later*. . . . In the first two chapters (the chapters of Mañjuśrī and

Samantabhadra), the Buddha holds very strictly to the sudden position, denying the possibility of enlightenment through gradual practice. In the third chapter [the chapter of Universal Vision/Puyan Bodhisattva] he begins to allow for a bit of a gradual view, and the next several chapters become mixtures of the two. The final few chapters offer a fully gradualistic perspective" (italics mine). In the second chapter (T 17:913c23–914a4) Samantabhadra asks how one can use illusion to come back to practice cultivation in the midst of illusion (*yi huan huan xiu yu huan*). After remarking that if sentient beings never practice, then in the midst of the rebirth process they will always find themselves in illusion transformation (*changju huanhua*), Samantabhadra asks what teaching device for gradual practice (*jianci xiuxi*) will allow sentient beings in the end period of the dharma eternally to escape illusion. Given this theme, it is little wonder this sutra remained the main object of Zongmi's commentarial energies throughout his career. An autobiographical comment contained in one of Zongmi's numerous commentaries on this sutra, the *Da fangguang yuanjue xiuduoluo liaoyi jing lueshu zhu* (T 39:524b20–23), is revealing: "When a child with hair hanging down and tied I specialized in the 'commandments of Lu' [that is, the Confucian classics]. At the age of putting on a cap [twenty] I inquired into the Indian mounds [of Buddhist texts]. In both cases I drowned in the fish net, stealing a glance downward and getting only the flavor of husks and dregs. Fortunately, at the Fu [River I met Daoyuan, and my disposition] responded to him like a needle [attracted by a magnet] or a particle [attracted by amber]. In Chan I encountered the Southern lineage. In the teachings I had a rendezvous with this [*Perfect Awakening*] classic. At one word [from Daoyuan] my mind ground opened all the way up. In the midst of one scroll [containing this sutra] the principles [of the teachings] became clear and bright like the heavens."

9. Gregory, *Tsung-mi*, 48. Gregory has solved the vexing problem of Zongmi's Chan filiation.

10. Zongmi's first letter to Chengguan of October 4, 811, is contained in his *Da fangguang yuanjue xiuduoluo liaoyi jing lueshu zhu* (T 39:576c1–577c8). Zongmi begins by describing himself as "originally a low-status scholar from Sichuan." He relates his meeting with Reverend Daoyuan and Heze Chan, his encountering Chengguan's commentaries on the *Huayan Sutra* in Xiangyang, his trip to the eastern capital Luoyang to bow at the stupa of the patriarchal master Shenhui (*li zushi ta*), and the story of the monk Taihong who cut off his arm. He closes with a request for instruction: "In prostration I beg for your compassion. If you would specially grant your assistance, my good fortune would be extreme. Your unprepared apprentice Zongmi is terrified and does a hundred obeisances." Chengguan's answer of November 1 (577c9–24) says that he accepts Zongmi and will certainly transmit the teaching to him. Zongmi's second letter of November 12 is also included (577c26–578a6). In it Zongmi says he will rush to get to Chengguan in order to serve him.

11. Pei Xiu's inscription for Chengguan, the *Qingliang guoshi shi miaojue ta ji*, states: "Of disciples who left home [under Chengguan] and became teachers of

men there were thirty-eight. Haian Xuji was at the head. Students who had received [Chengguan's] teaching reached the number of one thousand, but just Sengrui of the eastern capital and Guifeng Zongmi alone attained its inner recesses" (Kamata Shigeo, *Chūgoku Kegon shisō-shi no kenkyū* [Tokyo: Tokyo daigaku shuppankai, 1965], 158). This makes its sound as if Zongmi was not a member of the inner circle of disciples but merely one of the very best of a large number of students who came to Chengguan. Pei's inscription for Zongmi, the *Guifeng chanshi beiming bing xu*, reports Chengguan's assessment of Zongmi: "Guan said: 'It is you who can accompany me roaming in the flower womb of Vairocana!'" (Shūmitsu, 50; QTW 16:743.9731b3).

12. The chart in Zongmi's *Chan Letter* (Kamata, 290; section 7) lists Chengguan (called the *Huayan Commentary* Master) as a disciple of Fucha Wuming (=Wuming of the eastern capital Luoyang=Wuming of Mt. Wutai in Shanxi province). Wuming was a collateral disciple of Heze Shenhui. Pei Xiu's inscription for Chengguan (Kamata, *Chūgoku Kegon*, 157) states that he "also trained under the Great Master Wuming." The *Song gaoseng zhuan* (T 50:737a18–20) adds to this Heze experience contact with Niutou and Northern Chan: "He also had audiences with Master [Hui]zhong of Mt. Niutou, Master [Fa]qin of Mt. Jing, and Master Wuming of Luoyang, in which he surveyed the dharma of the Chan of the Southern lineage. He also saw Chan Master Huiyun and understood the profound principle of the Northern lineage." In his *Da fangguang fohuayan jing suishu yanyi chao* (T 36:62b1–4), Chengguan places Chan in the fourth of the five teachings of Huayan, the all-at-once teaching (*dunjiao*): "[As to saying that the all-at-once teaching] accords with the Chan axiom, Bodhidharma's taking mind to transmit mind is precisely this teaching. If [Chan] did not point to one word and thereby directly preach *mind is buddha* [*ruo bu zhi yi yan yi zhi shuo jixin shi fo*], how could [Chan] be transmitted? Therefore, relying on wordlessness [referring to Vimalakīrti's silence in the *Vimalakīrti Sutra*, T 14:551c22: "At that time Vimalakīrti was silent and wordless (*moran wuyan*)"] and taking that as the word, [Chan] directly expresses the principle of cutting off words. The [all-at-once] teaching is also [thereby] clarified. Therefore, the Chan of the Southern and Northern lineages does not go beyond the all-at-once teaching." This is subcommentary on a passage in a commentary on the *Huayan*, the *Da fangguang fohuayan jing shu* (T 35:512c4–5). Thus, both Southern and Northern Chan rank below Huayan, the fifth or perfect teaching (*yuanjiao*). Later in the *Yanyi chao* (T 36:224a21–23), he remarks: "[As to saying that] the exhaustion of feelings and manifestation of principle is called making a buddha, this accords with the Chan axiom. It is the gate of the non-obstruction of phenomena and principle [*shili wuai men*]. According to the Samantabhadra gate, truly Huayan is the gate of the non-obstruction of phenomenon and phenomenon [*shishi wuai men*]." Hence, in the schema of the four dharma spheres, Chan ranks as the third, the non-obstruction of phenomena and principle, and Huayan as the highest, the fourth dharma sphere of the non-obstruction of phenomenon and phenomenon. See Yoshizu

Yoshihide, *Kegon Zen no shisō-shi teki kenkyū* (Tokyo: Daitō shuppansha, 1985), 224 and 237–38. Chengguan makes Chan as a whole *subordinate* to Huayan.

13. The titles are: (1) *Qixinlun shu*; (2) *Jingang banruo jing shulun zuanyao*; (3) *Yuanjuejing lueshu*; (4) *Yuanjuejing lueshu chao*; (5) *Yuanjuejing daochang xiuzheng yi*; (6) *Yuanjuejing dashu*; (7) *Yuanjuejing dashu chao*; (8) *Huayan lunguan* (not extant); (9) *Sifenlü shu* (not extant); (10) *Yuanjuejing zuanyao* (not extant); and (11) *Weishisong shu* (not extant) and *Weishisong shu chao* (not extant). The *Nirvana Sutra* commentary below is *Niepanjing shu* (not extant). For information on these works, see the reconstruction of Zongmi's oeuvre in Gregory, *Tsung-mi*, 315–25.

14. Gregory, *Tsung-mi*, 315–25, shows thirty-one titles, though some works are listed twice under different titles. The Dunhuang manuscript fragment of the *Chan Prolegomenon*, which is dated 952, closes with a catalogue of twenty-five Zongmi works. At the end of this early list, compiled 111 years after Zongmi's death, is the line: "Altogether two-hundred and fifty rolls [plus] charts." This list shows Zongmi's affinity for charts, since we find:

- *Chart of the Three Teachings*
- *Chart of the* Awakening of Faith *in One Roll*
- *Chart of Eighteen Commentaries on the* Thunderbolt-Cutter Sutra
- *Chart of the* Perfect Awakening Complete Meaning Sutra
- *Chart of the Genealogy of the Patriarchal Masters from Generation to Generation* (*Leidai zushi xuemai tu* = *Chan Letter*)

To these we could add the *Chan Prolegomenon* itself, which includes a chart (section 54). For a reproduction of this Dunhuang list, see Lin Shitian and others, eds., *Dunhuang Chanzong wenxian jicheng* (Beijing: Quanguo tushuguan wenxian suowei fuzhi zhongxin, 1998), 1:488–89; for an edition and discussion, see Tanaka Ryōshō, *Tonkō Zenshū bunken no kenkyū* (Tokyo: Daitō shuppansha, 1983), 437–42.

15. For all information on Pei Xiu and the other literati around Zongmi, see Gregory, *Tsung-mi*, 73–85. The funerary inscription, the *Guifeng chanshi beiming bing xu*, ends with Pei's description of their relationship: "As for me and the Great Master, in the dharma we were older brother and younger brother; in righteousness we were intimate friends; in my deepest thoughts he was my guide [*shan zhishi*]; and for the teachings we were internal and external protectors [*neiwai hu*]. Therefore, I am able to present him in detail. As to other people [I could] not [present them] in [such] detail" (Shūmitsu, 51; QTW 16:743.9733a5–6). For a thorough treatment of Pei's biography, see Yoshikawa Tadao, "Hai Kyū den: Tōdai no ichi shidaifu to Bukkyō," *Tōhō gakuhō* 64 (March 1992): 115–277.

16. CBETA *Wan Xuzangjing* vol. 58, no. 1010:485c9[04]–[05].

17. Liu Xu and others, comps., *Jiu Tangshu* (Beijing: Zhonghua shuju, 1975), 7:177.4594. This high assessment of Pei's abilities in the literary arts is noteworthy, but

it is the praise of his calligraphy (*zicheng bifa*) that stands out. For an example of Pei's calligraphy in regular style, see the reproduction of a rubbing of his funerary inscription for Zongmi in Pei Xiu, *Tang Pei Xiu shu Guifeng chanshi bei* (Taipei: Xinshi chubanshe, 1981). To this day his calligraphy is emulated in Japan. He is one of twenty-eight calligraphers used as exemplars for the Tang period in the calligraphy dictionary entitled *Character Types in Five Styles*: Takada Takeyama, ed., *Gotai jirui*, 3rd ed. (Tokyo: Nigashi-higashi shobō, 2002). Many of the Pei Xiu entries are in running style.

18. On the morning of December 14 it was announced at court that sweet dew (*ganlu*), an auspicious omen, had fallen on a palace courtyard, where armed men lay in wait for the chief eunuchs. The eunuchs were ordered to investigate and report back. Something went afoul, and the eunuchs became aware of what was afoot. Eunuch forces then counterattacked, carrying out systematic executions of high officials and their clans. The biography of Li Xun, a key plotter, in the *Old Tang History* (Liu, *Jiu Tangshu*, 7:169.4398) says: "On that day Xun clenched his fists and fell to the ground. Knowing that the matter [of the coup] had not been accomplished, he then raced on horseback alone into Mt. Zhongnan [southwest of the capital Chang'an]. He flung himself before the monastery monk Zongmi. Xun's [relationship] with Zongmi heretofore had been good. [Zongmi] wanted to shave his hair and hide him away, but his followers would not permit it, and so [Xun] hastened to Fengxiang [northwest of the capital], desiring to rely on Zheng Zhu. [Xun] came out of the mountains and was apprehended by Zhou Zhi and Commander of the Garrison Zong Chu. [Xun] was sent bound into the capital. They arrived at Kunming Pond, and Xun, fearing that he would enter the army camp and undergo special torture, said to the soldiers: 'You soldiers right here! Having apprehended me you will get riches and honor, but it will not be as good as going in holding up my head. [That way] you will avoid having me snatched away from you.' They then beheaded Xun and went in carrying the head. Xun's younger brother Zhongjing and his cousin Auxiliary Secretary of the Bureau of Finances Yuangao both suffered the extreme penalty. Because Zongmi had taken in Li Xun, [the eunuch] Chou Shiliang had him sent bound into the Left Army camp. He charged [Zongmi] with the crime of withholding information [*bugao zhi zui*] and was going to execute him. Zongmi said with composure [*yiran*]: 'I have known Xun for many years, and I even knew he was in rebellion. However, according to the teachings of my root master, I must alleviate any suffering I encounter. I am not in love with my own life, and I will assuredly die with a sweet heart [*ganxin*].' [This was perhaps a dangerous pun on "*ganlu*"/"sweet dew."] Chief of the Army Yu Hongzhi admired this and sent up a memorial releasing him from the crime." The *New Tang History* account is substantially the same. See Ouyang Xiu and others, comps., *Xin Tangshu* (Beijing: Zhonghua shuju, 1975), 17:179.5313–14. Zongmi's entry in the *Song gaoseng zhuan* (T 50:742a–b), gives the story of Zongmi's arrest. Zongmi's words in the face of imminent execution evoke the man of courage spoken of in the *Mencius*, 6.1: "The man of will never forgets that [he might end up thrown away] in a ditch; the courageous man never forgets he

might lose his head." There is also a bit of the loyal official (*zhongchen*), loyal to Emperor Wenzong, in his stance. After the abortive coup, Emperor Wenzong expressed his sense of isolation in a quatrain entitled "Theme in the Palace" that is found in *Complete Tang Poems* (*Quan Tangshi* [Beijing: Zhonghua shuju, 1979] 1:4.48):

> On the road of the imperial carriage spring vegetation is sprouting.
> In the Shanglin Park it is the time when flowers open up.
> Looking off into the distance, how could there be limits to my thoughts?
> But there are no longer officials at my side to know them.

19. Pei's inscription, the *Guifeng chanshi beiming bing xu*, reports: "On the sixth day of the first month of Huichang 1 [February 1, 841] in sitting posture he expired at the Xingfu [Monastery's] Stupa Compound [*Xingfu tayuan*]. He was majestic as if alive, his countenance all the more pleased. After seven days they shifted the body to a coffin. His realization power could be known. On the twenty-second day of that month [February 17] monks and laypeople presented the corpse at Guifeng. On the thirteen day of the second month [March 9] he was cremated, and they initially got ten grains of relics [*śarīra*]" (Shūmitsu, 51; QTW 16:743.9732b8–11). According to the *Liang jing xinji* (*New Record of the Two Capitals*, fascicle 3) Xingfu Monastery was in the northwest corner of the Xiude Lane (*Xiude fang xibei yu Xingfu si*), just west of the imperial palace (*gongcheng*) in the northern part of the city (Hiraoka Takeo, *Chōan to Rakuyō: Shiryō*, Tōdai kenkyū no shiori [T'ang Civilization Reference Series] 6 [Kyoto: Kyoto daigaku jinbun kagaku kenkyūjo, 1956], 182).

20. Pei's inscription, the *Guifeng chanshi beiming bing xu*, reports: "The present emperor [Xuanzong] further expounded the true axiom, bestowing the posthumous title 'Samadhi-Prajna Chan Master' [*Dinghui chanshi*] and the 'Stupa of the Blue Lotus' [*Qinglian zhi ta*]" (Shūmitsu, 51; QTW 16:743.9732b17–18).

21. The Chan sacred history *Lengjia shizi ji*, which dates to about 719 or 720, says (T 85:1289b11–14 and 1290a28–b2; Yanagida I, 268 and 298): "The sixth [patriarch], the Great Master, named Hongren, of Yuju Monastery on Mt. Shuangfeng in Qizhou of the Tang dynasty, received the succession from Chan Master [Dao]xin. The dharma that Hongren transmitted was a wonderful dharma. People honored it and at the time called it the 'East Mountain Purity Gate [*Dongshan jingmen*].' Also, the monks and laypeople of the capital and [Luo]yang extolled it, sighing: 'East Mountain in Qizhou has many people who have obtained the fruit.' This is why they called it 'East Mountain Dharma Gate [*Dongshan famen*].' . . . In Dazu 1 [701] [Shenxiu] was invited to enter the eastern capital. He followed the [imperial] carriage back and forth [between the two capitals]. In the two capitals he gave instruction in the teachings and personally served as Imperial Teacher. The Great Sagely Empress Zetian questioned Chan Master Shenxiu: 'In your transmitted dharma, of what house is the axiom purport?' He answered: 'I have received the East Mountain Dharma Gate of Qizhou.'"

22. The *Chan Notes* refers to the theory, the doctrinal aspect, with the following terminology: *idea (yi)*; *axiom purport (zongzhi)*; *dharma idea (fayi)*; and *principle awakened to (suowu li)*. It calls the practical aspect: *practice* or *cultivation (xiuxing/ xing/xiu)*; *the path practiced (suoxiu zhi dao)*; and *practice gate (xingmen)*.

23. The Tibetans call the view part "*lta ba'i cha*" and the praxis part "*spyod pa'i cha.*" See Alex Wayman, "Nāgārjuna: Moralist Reformer of Buddhism," in *Untying the Knots in Buddhism: Selected Essays*, Buddhist Tradition Series 28 (Delhi: Motilal Banarsidass, 1997), 75–76; and Ferdinand D. Lessing and Alex Wayman, eds. and trans., *Mkhas grub rje's Fundamentals of the Buddhist Tantras* (The Hague: Mouton, 1968), 81–99. Mainstream (Hinayana) Buddhism is the first wheel. For the second wheel, the view is the treatises of Nagarjuna and the second half of Aryadeva's *Four Hundred Verses*, and practice is the first half of Aryadeva's treatise. For the third, the *Adornment of Mahayana Sutras* equally expounds view and practice; the "Chapter on Reality" of Asanga's *Bodhisattva Stages* expounds only view; and the remaining chapters of that treatise are concerned with practice.

24. In selecting "*renxin*" ("give free rein to mind") to describe Hongzhou practice, I think Zongmi probably was thinking of a passage in the "Discussion on the Art of Writing" (Zongshu) chapter of the *Wenxin diaolong*. In the translation of Vincent Yu-chung Shih: "Therefore, when one plies this art as the rein with which he guides his composition, he may be likened to a good chess player who knows his moves and the inevitable results of them. But the one who *abandons the art for the whims of his own mind [qishu renxin]* is like a gambler whose success is a matter of luck" (Vincent Yu-chung Shih, trans., *The Literary Mind and the Carving of Dragons: A Study of Thought and Pattern in Chinese Literature* [New York: Columbia University Press, 1959], 231). The first element ("*chulei*") of this Hongzhou slogan is one of a set of idioms. See Iriya Yoshitaka and Koga Hidehiko, *Zengo jiten* (Kyoto: Shibunkaku shuppan, 1991), 275–76; and Jiang Lansheng and Cao Guangshun, eds., *Tang Wudai yuyan cidian* (Shanghai: Shanghai jiaoyu chubanshe, 1997), 66.

25. Titles of the *Chan Letter* include:

• *Chart of the Genealogy of the Patriarchal Masters from Generation to Generation (Leidai zushi xuemai tu)*.
Listed in a catalogue of Zongmi works at the end of a Dunhuang manuscript dated 952. Lin, *Dunhuang Chanzong wenxian jicheng*, 1:489; Tanaka, *Tonkō Zenshū bunken no kenkyū*, 438.
• *Guifeng Answers Minister Pei's Letter on the Purports of the [Chan] Lineages (Guifeng da Pei Xiangguo zongqu zhuang)*
Cited in the 1107 *Linjianlu* (ZZ 2B.21.4.296d; CBETA *Wan Xuzangjing* vol. 87, no. 1624:248c15[06]–16[06]).
• *Imperial Redactor Pei Xiu's Inquiry (Hai Kyū shūi mon; Pei Xiu shiyi wen)*.

The existence of a 1241 manuscript under this title at the Shingon temple Shinpu-ku-ji in Nagoya was mentioned in a 1936 catalogue of the temple's holdings, but its introduction to the scholarly world was not until the publication of Ishii's article "Shinpuku-ji bunko shozō no *Hai Kyū shūi mon* no honkoku" in 1981. The edition in Shinpuku-ji includes at the end three additional sections: Zongmi's comments on views presented to him by Xiao Xianggong; Zongmi's answers to ten questions of Shi Shanren; and Zongmi's answers to questions of Wen Shangshu of Shannan). For a modern Japanese translation, see Ishii Shudō, trans., *Zen goroku*, Daijō butten Chūgoku Nihon hen 12 (Tokyo: Chuōkōronsha, 1992), 41–90.

• *Guishan Answers Pei Xiu's Letter of Inquiry* (*Keizan to Hai Kyū monsho*; *Guishan da Pei Xiu wenshu*).
Cited in the 1255 *Zenshū kōmoku* of Shōjō (1194–?). Kamata Shigeo and Tanaka Hisao, eds., *Kamakura kyū Bukkyō*, Nihon shisō taikei 15 (Tokyo: Iwanami shoten, 1971), 185.
• *Chart of the Master-Disciple Succession of the Chan Gate that Transmits the Mind Ground in China* (*Chūka denshinji zenmon shiji shōshū zu*; *Zhonghua chuan-xindi chanmen shizi chengxi tu*).
Undated text discovered in 1910 at the Nichiren Dai-honzan Myōken-ji in Kyoto and subsequently included in the *Manji zoku-zōkyō* (ZZ 2.15.5; CBETA *Wan Xu-jangjing* vol. 63, no. 1225).

Titles for a posthumous collection include:

• *Collection of [Zongmi's] Responses to [Questions from] Monks and Laypeople* (*Daosu chouda wenji*).
Listed in a catalogue of Zongmi's works at the end of a Dunhuang manuscript dated 952. It is described as in ten rolls. Lin, *Dunhuang Chanzong wenxian jicheng*, 1:489; Tanaka, *Tonkō Zenshū bunken no kenkyū*, 438. See Jan Yün-hua, "Tsung-mi chu *Tao-su ch'ou-ta wen-chi* te yen-chiu," *Hwakang Buddhist Journal* 4 (1980): 132–66.
• *Posthumous Collection of Guifeng* (*Guifeng houji*).
Cited in a letter by the Tiantai monk Zhili (960–1028) found in the 1202 *Teachings and Practice Record of the Honorable One of Siming* (*Siming zunzhe jiaoxinglu*; T 46:894c29–895a6): "But you are unaware that this comes from the *Posthumous Collection of Guifeng*. . . . A printed edition of this *Posthumous Collection* is extant [*yin-ben jianzun*]. It is transmitted in both the South and the North; its circulation has been uninterrupted [*liuxing bu jue*]." Since this letter dates to sometime between 1010 and Zhili/Siming's death in 1028 (judging from the fact that Siming identifies himself as the head priest of Yanqing Yuan at the beginning of his letter [T 46:894c18], and the

name Baoen Yuan was changed by imperial order to Yanqing Yuan in 1010 [T 46:857c10–12]), we know that a woodblock-printed edition of a posthumous Zongmi collection containing the *Chan Letter* was in circulation in various regions of China around 1010 through 1030.

• *Essentials of Chan Master Caotang's Letters (Caotang chanshi jianyao).*

Quoted in the 1107 *Linjianlu* (ZZ 2B.21.4.296d–297a; CBETA *Wan Xuzangjing* vol. 87, no. 1624:248c18[00]–249a02[02]).

It is unclear whether or not we are dealing with one collection or several, and the last may even be another title for the *Chan Letter* standing alone rather than a collection containing it.

26. Ui Hakuju, *Zenshū-shi kenkyū* (1935; repr., Tokyo: Iwanami shoten, 1966), 3:48.

27. The *Chan Letter* uses not just the *idea* and *purport* of the earlier work, but *understanding* (*suojie/jie*) and *view* (*suojian/jianjie*) as well.

28. The sutra says: "Good sons! It is like the pure treasure jewel that reflects the five colors, manifesting [different colors] according to what is facing it. The foolish ones see that jewel as really having the five colors" (T 17:914c; Yanagida, *Engakukyō*, 56; Muller, "The Sutra of Perfect Enlightenment [Yuanjuejing]," 10).

29. For these two Hongzhou figures, see Mario Poceski, *Ordinary Mind as the Way: The Hongzhou School and the Growth of Chan Buddhism* (New York: Oxford University Press, 2007), 63–67. Poceski says: "Among them [disciples of Mazu], Huaihui and Weikuan had the greatest impact on the Hongzhou school's fortunes in Chang'an and beyond. . . . Dayi, Weikuan, and Huaihui were the best-known monks associated with the Hongzhou school to teach in Chang'an, but not the only ones. Other disciples of Mazu active in Chang'an were Huayan Zhizang, Haozhi (who, like Weikuan, resided at Anguo monastery), Caotang, and Xingping." For biographical information, see Poceski's note 143.

30. *Chan Prolegomenon*, section 24, has a parallel passage that clarifies the abbreviated form of Pei's question: "Your potentiality right now to talk, act, [experience] passion, anger, friendliness, patience, create good or bad and receive suffering or joy, etc., is your buddha nature [*ji ru foxing*]. By virtue of this you have been a buddha from the outset. There is no other buddha than this."

31. For an example of these books (*gongguo zhuang*), see Ouyang, *Xin Tangshu*, 4:46.1190–91.

32. This accords with Poceski, *Ordinary Mind as the Way*, 11: "Once we move beyond this sort of 'evidence' [iconoclastic stories in Song texts] and look instead at extant Tang sources, the unabashed iconoclasm habitually associated with the Hongzhou school gives way to a more complex and nuanced historical reality. The historical image of Mazu and his disciples we are confronted with is not simply that of a radical re-

ligious movement bent on subverting established norms and traditions. Instead, as we will see, the Hongzhou school comes across as being much closer to the mainstream of Buddhism—and to early Chan—than Zen apologetics would have us believe."

33. Bai Juyi, *Bai Juyi ji* (Beijing: Zhonghua shuju, 1979), 3:41.912; and *Jingde chuan-deng lu*, T 51:255a29–b2. See Poceski, *Ordinary Mind as the Way*, 65n. 130.

34. Yanagida Seizan was the first to suggest that Zongmi's criticism of Hongzhou was taken over intact by the Song neo-Confucians as the basis of their criticism of Buddhism. See Iriya Yoshitaka, ed. and trans., *Denshin hōyō Enryōroku*, Zen no goroku 8 (Tokyo: Chikuma shobō, 1969), 162.

35. Gregory, *Tsung-mi*, 301.

36. Gregory, *Tsung-mi*, 311.

37. Pei Xiu's preface to his record of Xiyun, which is dated October 22–29, 857, provides a detailed account of the genesis of the text: "In Huichang 2 [842] I was stationed as Commissioner of Inspection in Zhongling, and I welcomed [the Master Xiyun] from [Huangbo] Mountain [in Gao'an county, Jiangxi] to [Hong]zhou [northwest of Zhongling] to take repose [that is, become abbot] at Longxing Monastery. Day and night I inquired of him about the path. In Dazhong 2 [848] when I was stationed as Commissioner of Inspection at Wanling [in Jiangxi] I again went to do obeisance in welcoming him to the administrative department and had him dwell peacefully at the Kaiyuan Monastery, day and night receiving his dharma. I withdrew to record it [his talks], but out of ten I got but one or two. I wore it at my waist as a mind-seal pendant, not daring to publish it. But now I have come to fear that its divine, pure meaning may not be heard in the future. At last I took it out and handed it over to his monk disciples Taizhou and Fajian. They took it back to Guangtang Monastery on the old mountain [that is, Xiyun's original Mt. Huangbo in coastal Fuzhou] and asked the venerables and dharma assembly how it differed from what they had personally heard constantly in the past" (T 48:379c5–12; Iriya, *Denshin hōyō*, 3). On the colloquial nature of this Xiyun record, Iriya (foreword, 4) remarks: "The question-and-answer portion of the text, as a whole, is an account in spoken-language format. The spoken language of the day is freely used. A modern Japanese translation of it is all the easier, but the *kundoku* method of reading it used up until now [that is, the traditional Japanese system for reading literary Chinese], in short, the method of directly reading it as literary language on purpose, makes no sense in the first place." This aspect of the *Chuanxin fayao-Wanlinglu* led Henri Maspero to include it as one of the five texts used in his pioneering study of "ancient spoken Chinese" published in 1914: Henri Maspero, "Sur Quelques Textes Anciens de Chinois Parlé," *Bulletin de l'École Française d'Estrème-Orient* 14, no. 4 (1914): 1–36. This article was translated into English in an unpublished paper: Yoshitaka Iriya, Ruth F. Sasaki, and Burton F. Watson, "On Some Texts of Ancient Spoken Chinese with Comments and Emendations" (photocopy, Kyoto, 1954).

38. I have adopted this term from the modern Chinese-Japanese dictionary: Aichi daigaku Chū-Nichi daijiten hensansho, ed., *Chū-Nichi daijiten*, 2nd ed. (Tokyo: Taishū-

kan shoten, 1999), 10. Ping Chen, *Modern Chinese: History and Sociolinguistics* (Cambridge: Cambridge University Press, 1999), 68–69, provides a good description, referring to it as *traditional baihua*: "By the end of the Tang dynasty, as an increasing number of words and grammatical constructions from the vernacular found their way into writing, a new type of written language, *baihua* 'vernacular literary language' (literally 'unadorned speech'), emerged and matured. *Baihua* differed from *wenyan* in that it was much closer to the contemporary vernacular. While *wenyan* remained supreme as the standard written language, *baihua* served all low-culture functions such as transcriptions of Buddhist admonitions, and scripts for folk stories and plays. . . . *Baihua* gained in currency from the end of the Tang dynasty, providing the medium for many representative literary works of the later periods. . . . For a long period, there co-existed two types of written Chinese, *wenyan* and *baihua*. Due to the conservatism prevalent among the ruling class and the literati, *wenyan* was considered refined and elegant, thus ideal for high-culture functions, while *baihua* was despised as coarse and vulgar, suitable only for low-culture functions. . . . The language used in such writings [vernacular verse, stories, and novels] known later as traditional *baihua* in contrast to the modern *baihua* as used in the twentieth century, was quite well established as a written language for informal purposes such as keeping diaries and writing casual essays, and on specific occasions which required a text that approximated as far as possible what was actually being said, as in the recording of court proceedings, official negotiations, etc."

39. These include: the miscellany of abstract statements and sayings loosely called the *Bodhidharma Anthology* (*Damo lun*); sacred histories tracing the transmission of Bodhidharma Chan by a sequence of biographies of its patriarchs, such as the *Annals of the Transmission of the Dharma Treasure* (*Chuan fabao ji*), *Record of the Lanka Masters and Disciples* (*Lengjia shizi ji*), and *Record of the Dharma Treasure Through the Generations* (*Lidai fabao ji*); treatises on Chan method and teachings, often in question-and-answer format, such as the *Essentials of Mind Cultivation* (*Xiuxin yaolun*), *On Cutting Off Examining* (*Jueguanlun*), and *Essential Judgments on All-at-Once Awakening to the True Axiom* (*Dunwu zhenzong yaojue*); Heze Shenhui's lectures and discourses, such as his *Platform Talks* (*Tanyu*); and apocryphal sutras closely associated with the growing Chan movement, such as the *Chan Gate Sutra* (*Chanmenjing*). The best introduction to this corpus is Shinohara Hisao and Tanaka Ryōshō, eds., *Tonkō butten to Zen*, Tonkō kōza 8 (Tokyo: Daitō shuppansha, 1980).

40. A good place to begin to get a sense of the *baihua* overlap between transformation texts, tales, traditions of strange matters, poetry, etc., and Chan texts is this dictionary of Tang–Five Dynasties language: Jiang and Cao eds., *Tang Wudai yuyan cidian*.

41. For a history of the text (T no. 1988), see Urs App, "The Making of a Chan Record," *Zen bunka kenkyūjo kiyō* 17 (1991): 1–90.

42. There is a link between the *suyu* (the meaning runs from colloquial set phrases through popular language, slang, and vernacular) of the southeast coastal area of Zhejiang and Fujian (Wu, Yue, and Min) and the language of Chan texts in the post-

Tang period. Zhejiang/Fujian speech rhythms, modal particle usage, interjections, onomatopoetic words, idioms, and perhaps even profanities surely found their way into Chan texts. And thus what is often thought of as (enigmatic) "Chan language" may, to some extent at least, be Zhejiang/Fujian *suyu*. This area was the center of gravity of Chan (and the production of Chan texts) in the post-Tang period. One cannot help but thinking that in texts like the *Extensive Record of Yunmen* we are hearing something of the voices of the common people of the farms, towns, shops, and markets of Wu, Yue, and Min. Zongmi's speech, on the other hand, was surely the elite vernacular of the metropolitan Chang'an area in the faraway northwest.

43. The figures on its size in China, Japan, and Korea vary quite a bit:

• The earliest reference is in the catalogue of Zongmi works at the end of the Dunhuang manuscript fragment of the *Chan Prolegomenon*, dated 952, where it· is described as "*Collected Essentials of the Discourses on the Chan Source [Ji chanyuan zhulun guanyao]* in 130 Rolls" (Lin, *Dunhuang Chanzong wenxian jicheng*, 1:489; Tanaka, *Tonkō Zenshū bunken no kenkyū*, 438).

• The *New Tang History* lists it as "Zongmi's *Collection of Expressions of the Chan Source [Chanyuan zhuquanji]* in 101 Rolls" (Ouyang, *Xin Tangshu*, 5:59.1530).

• The Enbun 3 (1358) Gozan edition of the *Chan Prolegomenon* in a question (section 57) not found in other editions mentions that the *Chan Canon* "in number surpasses one-hundred rolls (one-hundred sixty rolls)" (Ishii [10], 70).

• A late-eighteenth-century Korean commentary on the *Chan Prolegomenon*, the *Sŏnwŏn jejŏnjip tosŏ kwamok pyŏngip sagi* by Yŏndam Yuil, remarks (Shūmitsu, 270) that "the *Collection of Expressions of the Chan Source* in one-hundred rolls at present is not transmitted in Korea."

44. Pei makes this point in both his preface to the *Chan Prolegomenon* (T 48:398b7–8; Kamata, 3; translation in appendix 2) and in his inscription for Zongmi (Shūmitsu, 50; QTW 16:743.9731b7). The former opens with: "Chan Master Guifeng collected the *Expressions of the Chan Source* as a Chan basket [*chanzang*] and did a prolegomenon to it. Hedong Pei Xiu says: 'There has never been such a thing!'" For a modern Japanese translation of Pei's preface with annotations, see Ishii (2), 39–51.

45. Kamata, 358. Kamata feels that Zongmi planned to compile the *Chan Canon* but probably never got around to writing out a copy.

46. This short work, found at the beginning of the *Bodhidharma Anthology*, appears to be the ur-text of Chan literature. The "two entrances" are entrance by principle (*liru*) and entrance by practice (*xingru*). Of the former it is said: "Entrance by principle means that one by means of the teachings awakens to the axiom [*ji jiao wu zong*] and deeply believes that all beings, common and noble, are identical to the true nature [*tongyi zhenxing*]; that it is merely because of the unreal covering of adventitious dust that [the true nature] is not revealed." The four practices are: the

practice of requiting injury (*baoyuan xing*); the practice of following conditions (*suiyuan xing*); the practice of nothing to be sought (*wusuoqiu xing*); and the practice of according with dharma (*chengfa xing*). See Yanagida Seizan, ed. and trans., *Daruma no goroku*, Zen no goroku 1 (Tokyo: Chikuma shobō, 1969), 31–32.

47. Yanshou has biographical entries at *Song gaoseng zhuan*, T 50:887a29–b16, and *Jingde chuandeng lu*, T 51:421c8–422a20. The *Zongjinglu* is T no. 2016. The traditional date for its completion is Jianlong 2 (961) of the Song. According to prefaces (T 48:415a1 and b13) it was also called the *Zongjianlu* (*Record of the Axiom Mirror*) and *Xinjinglu* (*Record of the Mind Mirror*). Therefore, *zong* ("axiom")=*xin* ("mind"). Perhaps Yanshou derived the title for his great compendium from a passage in Zongmi's *Chan Prolegomenon*. Yanshou's own preface to his work explains his title as follows (T 48:417a19–22): "Now, to clearly understand the great ideas of the [Chan] patriarchs and the buddhas and the correct axiom of the sutras and treatises, I will pare down the complicated texts, seek out just their essential purports, set up imaginary questions and answers, and widely quote proofs and clarifications. I will *raise the one mind as the axiom* [*ju yixin wei zong*] and illuminate *the ten thousand dharmas as if in a mirror* [*zhao wanfa ru jing*]. I will arrange the profound meanings of the ancient [literary] productions and scoop up an abridgement of the perfect explanations of the treasure storehouse. Displaying all of this in common, I will call it a *record* and divide it into one-hundred rolls." I think this takes off from *Chan Prolegomenon*, section 18: "The nature and characteristics are without obstruction; together *they are one mind* [*yixin*]. If you lose your way here, any direction you go you will face a wall. If you are awake to this, then *the ten-thousand dharmas* [*will appear as if*] *in a mirror* [*wanfa lin jing*]." (See also *Chan Prolegomenon*, section 53: "I will now provide a chart that sketches out these things in order to make the common-person and noble-once sequences and the axioms of the great storehouse of sutras appear at a single time in the *mind mirror* [*xinjing*].") Yün-hua Jan, "Two Problems Concerning Tsung-mi's Compilation of Ch'an-tsang," *Transactions of the International Conference of Orientalists in Japan* 19 (1974): 46, remarks that Sekiguchi Shindai first suggested in a conversation that Zongmi's *Chan Canon* had been absorbed into Yanshou's *Zongjinglu*. Fascicles 94 to 100 may contain quotations from the *Chan Canon*. At the beginning of that section Yanshou states (T 48:924a14–16): "Now, I will for the sake of those whose faith power is not yet deep and whose minute doubts are not yet severed further quote one hundred twenty Mahayana sutras, *one hundred twenty books of the sayings of the* [Chan] *patriarchs* [*zhuzuyu yibai ershi ben*], and sixty collections of the worthies and noble ones, altogether the subtle words of three hundred books." Fascicles 97 and 98 (T 48:937c1–947b6) consist of a large block of Chan sayings: a verse from each of the twenty-eight Indian patriarchs; a quotation from Bodhidharmatara's (Putida-moduoluo) *Dharma Gate of Quieting Mind* (*Anxin famen*); sayings for the second through sixth patriarchs of China (the Sixth Patriarch being the Great Master Hui-neng); sayings for the Great Master [Huai]rang and the Great Master [Hongzhou]

Ma; and finally a very long set of Chan sayings, the order of which appears to be somewhat jumbled, coming from various periods and lineages in early Chan. Perhaps at least some of these sayings derive ultimately from Zongmi's collecting efforts about a century earlier in the north.

48. Yi-Hsun Huang, *Integrating Chinese Buddhism: A Study of Yongming Yanshou's* Guanxin Xuanshu, Series of the Chung-Hwa Institute of Buddhist Studies 43 (Taipei: Dharma Drum Publishing Corporation, 2005), 47 and 56–57. A SAT Daizōkyō Text Database (http://2ldzk.l.u<>tokyo.ac.jp/SAT/) search for the term *"fayan"* ("dharma eye") in the *Zongjinglu* gives twenty-five hits, always in the traditional Buddhist sense of "obtain the dharma eye," "incapable of fathoming the dharma eye," "open the dharma eye," and so forth. It never denotes the Chan house of that name.

49. A thorough search via the SAT Daizōkyō Text Database or CBETA will be necessary, but the following lists just a few quotations and paraphrases of the *Chan Prolegomenon* found in the *Zongjinglu*:

Chan Prolegomenon (sections)	Zongjinglu (T 48:)
4	586b
11	418b; 660a7–8
21, 29 and 33–44	614a–617a
28	456a onward
39	quoted 616b; paraphrased 560a–b; terminology appears 449a, 610a, 621a, and 820a
45–46	627a–b
47	627b; also see 580b, 641a, and 657c
50–51	442c–443a

50. The *Chan Prolegomenon* (section 58) speaks of the tripartite structure of the *Chan Canon*: "Therefore, as to the order of the present [*Chan Canon*] collection: First, I record Bodhidharma's one axiom [*Damo yi zong*=mind/one mind]; next come the miscellaneous writings of the [Chan] houses [*zhujia zashu*]; and, lastly, I have copied out the noble teachings [=sutras and treatises] that seal the [Chan] axioms [*yin zong shengjiao*]." The tripartite structure of the *Zongjinglu* is: first the Designating-the-Axiom Section [*biaozong zhang*=the first half of fascicle 1]; next the Questions-and-Answers Section [*wenda zhang*=from midpoint in fascicle 1 through fascicle 93]; and lastly the *Quotations-to-Authenticate Section* [*yinzheng zhang*=from fascicle 94 through fascicle 100]. Though not a perfect fit, there is some congruency.

51. See note 43.

52. *Zhuangzi*, Waiwu: "The reason for the fish trap lies in the fish; you get the fish and forget the trap. The reason for the rabbit net lies in the rabbit; you get the rabbit and forget the net."

53. T 48:417b3–15.

54. We can definitely trace the *Chan Prolegomenon* from Zongmi in the Chang'an area to the Hangzhou area, where Yanshou spent his entire career, through the undated Song-dynasty colophon reproduced in the Wanli 4 (1576) Korean edition (Kamata, 260). For a translation, see appendix 3. According to this colophon, an 857 copy of the *Chan Prolegomenon* in Pei Xiu's hand just over a century later wound up in the hands of a layman in the Hangzhou area, who arranged for a woodblock printing. The Weijing mentioned in this colophon as part of the transmission to the Hangzhou printing is Nanyue Weijing, a disciple of Xuefeng Yizun (822–908). In the early 930s Yanshou took ordination under another disciple of Yizun. All of the monasteries that Yanshou was associated with throughout his career were in the Hangzhou area. In short, Yanshou was in the right place at the right time with the right connections to come across a copy not only of the *Chan Prolegomenon* but perhaps the *Chan Canon* (or at least some fragments of it) as well.

55. For an example of esoteric Buddhist *fu* drawings, see the (possibly apocryphal) *Huiji jingang jin baibianfa jing* (T no. 1129), a sutra representative of the cult of the *vidyārāja* ("King of Magical Knowledge") Ucchusma, who has the power to transform filth into purity by means of fire. It contains a number of strange *fu* drawings with instructions beneath. These drawings were in red and are similar to those in the *Baopuzi* of Ge Hong of the Jin period.

56. The eight tally pairs are:

san zhong jiao	san zong
dunjiao	dunmen
jianjiao	jianmen
shishuo	foyi
[zu]yi	fo[xin]
[chan]wen	[fo]jing
dunwu	jianxiu
benjue/zhen	bujue/wang

57. 1. *miyi yixing shuoxiang jiao*; 2. *miyi poxiang xianxing jiao*; and 3. *xianshi zhenxin jixing jiao*.

58. For information on these sutras and treatises as well as those of c., see the notes to section 25.

59. a. *rentian yinguo jiao*; b. *duanhuo mieku jiao*; and c. *jiangshi pojing jiao*.

60. For information on these sutras and treatises, see the notes to section 27.

61. Zongmi always refers to this sutra as the *Foding jing* (Buddha Top-knot Sutra), but it is commonly known as the *Shoulengyan jing* (Heroic Progress [Samadhi] Sutra). The full title is *Da foding rulai miyin xiuzheng liaoyi zhupusa wanxing shoulengyan jing*.

62. For information on these sutras and treatises (a few are Chinese apocrypha), see the notes to section 29.

63. "*mingming bumei liaoliao changzhi*."

64. In the *Chan Notes yi* (*idea*)=*zongzhi* (*axiom purport*). See note 22.

65. The first meaning issues from *tongzu* ("having a common ancestor"), found in standard dictionaries such as *Hanyu dacidian, Cihai*, etc. Here it is a synonym of *jia* ("house/family"), as in the seven Chan houses of the *Chan Notes*. The second meaning, *zong* as a translation equivalent for *siddhānta* (Hirakawa, 375), is working from the extended meaning of *zong* as *benzhi* ("basic purport") or *zhuzhi* ("main purport") found in *Hanyu dacidian, Wang Li gu Hanyu zidian, Ciyuan*, and so forth.

66. T 16:499b27–c6; *zongtong ji shuotong=siddhānta-naya deśanā*=Tibetan *grub pa'i mtha' dang bstan pa* ("established conclusion and teachings").

67. Zhang Yisun and others, eds., *Bod-Rgya tshig mdzod chen mo* (1993; repr., Beijing: Minzu chubanshe, 2000), 1:403, gives for "*grub mtha*'": "‹*siddhānta*› *phyi nang gi chos lugs so so'i lta ba 'dzin tshul te*" ("The diverse *views* upheld by the Buddhist and non-Buddhist doctrinal traditions"). The four Buddhist philosophical systems are referred to as *grub mtha' smra ba bzhi* and given (404) as: (1) *bye brag smra ba*; (2) *mdo sde pa*; (3) *sems tsam pa*; and (4) *dbu ma pa*.

68. The *Chan Prolegomenon* (section 33) mentions the opposition between existence and voidness: "The above three teachings take in all of the sutras spoken by the Tathagata in the course of his lifetime and all of the treatises composed by the bodhisattvas. A close examination of dharma and principles will reveal that the three principles [*san yi*=three teachings=three axioms] are completely different, while the one dharma is without difference. *Of the three principles the first and second are opposed as existence is to voidness* [*kong you xiangdui*], and the third and the first are opposed as nature is to characteristics. Both of these [oppositions] *are easily seen*, even from a distance." An early discussion of this opposition between existence and voidness is in Fazang's *Dasheng qixin lun yiji* (T 44:242a29–b27). Fazang relates that he got his information on this topic from questioning the Central Indian master Divakara, who worked in Chang'an and Luoyang from 680 to 688. Divakara informed Fazang that at India's Nālandā (Nalantuo) Monastery in the recent period there were simultaneously two great treatise masters, the Yogācārin Silabhadra (Jiexian) and the Mādhyamika Jnanaprabha (Zhiguang). Fazang lays out the three-tiered schemas of these Indian pandits.

69. 1. *xin jing ju you*; 2. *jing kong xin you*; and 3. *xin jing ju kong*.

70. 1. *xiwang xiuxin zong*; 2. *minjue wuji zong*; and 3. *zhixian xinxing zong*.

71. For information on these Chan houses and those below (with the exception of Shitou), see the notes to *Chan Notes*.

72. "*yiti qi xing xiu er wu xiu*." Zongmi quotes the apocryphal *Jingang sanmei jing* (*Vajrasamadhi Sutra*) about the one-practice samadhi (*yixing sanmei*): "Chan is movement. No movement, no Chan. This is non-arising Chan [*chan jishi dong bu dong bu chan shi wusheng chan*]." See *Chan Prolegomenon*, n. 179.

73. Heze "*dan de wunian zhi xin*" and Hongzhou "*dan renxin*." On the pejorative aspect of the term "*renxin*," see note 24.

74. "*zhuji dun*" and "*huayi dun*." This terminological pair is adapted from Fazang's *Huayan yisheng jiaoyi fenji zhang* (T 45:482b18–c8). See the translation of the *Chan Prolegomenon*, n. 241.

75. For information on these two texts, see *Chan Prolegomenon*, nn. 250 and 167.

76. T 10:89a1–2.

77. For information on all these sutras, see *Chan Prolegomenon*, nn. 157–61. Also see note 248. Note that this list of sutras for one type of the all-at-once teaching is the same as the list of sutras for the nature axiom (=third teaching) with two differences: the nature axiom has the whole of the *Huayan Sutra* rather than one part; and the nature axiom includes the *Lotus Sutra* and *Nirvana Sutra*, which are missing here.

78. Zongmi surely studied this classic during his early student years. The full passage from the *Book of Rites*, Music Record, runs: "Music is the unchangeableness of the feelings. Ritual is the immutability of principle. Music gathers in sameness, and ritual distinguishes difference. The teachings of ritual and music discipline human feelings [*guan hu renqing yi*]." Zongmi's "Confucian" side was not so much a matter of abstract thought patterns as an affinity for the discipline of ritual.

79. For references, see *Chan Prolegomenon*, nn. 249 and 318–19.

80. Yanagida Seizan, ed., *Sodōshū*, Zengaku sōsho 4 (Kyoto: Chūbun shuppansha, 1974), 114a: "For Zongmi we have seen no activities record [*wei du xinglu*] and so cannot provide a complete narrative."

81. T 51:305c11–308b27.

82. T 48:944b24–26. See the "Glossary of Chinese Characters" under *fu Digang*.

83. Daizōkyō, 601.

84. Komazawa daigaku toshokan, ed., *Shinsan Zenseki mokuroku* (Tokyo: Komazawa daigaku toshokan, 1962), 224, lists five ancillary works for the *Zongjinglu* dating to the Song period.

85. See note 52. Yanshou is saying that his treatise does use fish traps and rabbit snares (the sutras and treatises) to catch the fish and rabbits (liberation) but teaches that once the goal is realized, the means or expedients are to be forgotten, with no attachment to the words themselves. This is consistent with Zongmi's *Chan Prolegomenon*.

86. Zongmi never uses the term *Huayan* in this context—he uses "nature axiom" (*xingzong*; *Chan Prolegomenon*, section 33) to refer to the third teaching (*jiao*) or third principle (*yi*).

87. T 48:417b15–20; 417c11–13; 418b4–6; 426b27–29; 440a24–26; 499a20–22; 614a14–17; 653b19–20; and c20–21.

88. Albert Welter, "The Problem with Orthodoxy in Zen Buddhism: Yongming Yanshou's Notion of *Zong* in the *Zongjinglu* (Records of the Source Mirror)," *Studies in Religion/Sciences Religieuses* 31, no. 1 (2002): 5–9. Note that in the above quotation

from the *Zongjinglu* (417b18), Yanshou uses the pair *zong-shuo* (axiom and theory/ teachings), which comes from the *Lanka Descent Sutra* (see note 66), as a substitute for *zong-jiao*.

89. An exception is: Wang Tsui-ling, "Yōmei Enju no Zenshū-kan ni tsuite," *Indogaku Bukkyōgaku kenkyū* 47, no. 1 (December 1998): 201–4. Wang states (204): "Yongming Yanshou's views fundamentally follow the theories of Guifeng Zongmi, but at the same time differences between two are visible—Zongmi keeps coming back to exerting himself in doing various classifications of the factions of *zong* [Chan] and *jiao* [the teachings]. . . . Against these various theories of Zongmi, Yanshou simply adopts as his basis the theory of the *Chan Prolegomenon*. In essence, an obvious difference is visible between Yanshou's attitude toward Chan and Zongmi's attitude of striving to prove that the Heze lineage is the mainline of [the sixth patriarch] Caoqi. Did not Yanshou take the position that the whole of Chan is one school? And so he did not do a detailed classification of Chan and make distinctions such as 'collateral' and 'orthodox' in the manner of Zongmi's *Chan Notes* and *Chan Letter*. In a word, Yanshou stresses 'bringing together' [*hehui*] and Zongmi stresses 'checking and verifying' [*kanhui*]." Actually, it is more accurate to say that Zongmi stresses "bringing together" in the *Chan Prolegomenon* and "checking and verifyng" in the *Chan Letter* and *Chan Notes*.

90. On the *Perfect Awakening*'s sudden awakening–gradual practice structure, see note 8. The *Heroic Progress Samadhi Sutra* (T no. 945; considered an apocrypal in part) is found in the tantric (Mikkyō) section of the *Taishō Canon*. Its structure is somewhat similar to that of the *Perfect Awakening*. In a concise statement of the sudden awakening–gradual practice model, the *Heroic Progress Samadhi* says (T 19:155a8–9): "As to principle, one all-at-once awakens; riding this awakening, [false thoughts] are merged into annulment [*li ze dunwu chengwu bingxiao*]. But phenomena are not all-at-once removed; [only] by a graduated sequence are they exhausted [*shi fei dunchu yin cidi jin*]." In fascicles 5 and 6, the *Heroic Progress Samadhi* expounds perfect penetration (*yuantong*). Twenty-five bodhisattvas and arhats speak (T 29:124b7–132c26), and the culmination is Avalokiteśvara Bodhisattva's attainment of perfect penetration via the gate of the wonderful ear (*miaoer men*). Nakamura Hajime and others, eds., *Iwanami Bukkyō jiten*, 2nd ed. (Tokyo: Iwanami shoten, 2002), 490, says of the *Heroic Progress Samadhi Sutra*: "However, it accompanied the development of the Zen school and, from the Song period onward, together with the *Perfect Awakening Sutra* (also an apocryphon), saw wide circulation. Especially in the Ming period it was emphasized as a sutra that provided the basis for the sudden awakening-gradual practice that was the fundamental position of the Zen school of the time." Reflections of the prominence of these two sutras during the Song are found in Zhu Xi's *Classified Conversations of Master Zhu (Zhuzi yulei)* and in Kigen Dōgen's *Hōkyōki*. In the *Zhuzi yulei* (fascicle 124), Zhu Xi in passing talks of these two sutras and one Chan case topic (*huatou*) as if they were utterly representative of the Chan of his day: "It is like

Chan sayings such as *cylinder-of-dried-shit*. On top of [the saying] there is no further meaning, nor can you think of any logic to it. When you check and stabilize this thought completely, after a long time there will suddenly be a lucid and lively locus, and that is called *getting it*. . . . Zhuzhang said to me: 'Old [Dahui Zong]gao's Chan learning really has good points.' I asked him: 'Vice President! Have you really seen any good points?' But he said: 'I have not.' At present Jinxi's [Lu Xiangshan's] learning is truly Chan. Qinfu and Bogong have not read Buddhist books, and that is why they have not seen through them. I am the only one who knows them. For instance, if you give books like the *Heroic Progress Samadhi* and the *Perfect Awakening* a single perusal, you should be able to estimate their overall meaning. With Buddhist learning, for the most part, if you see right through it, you will cope with a thousand evils—there is no end to it" (Li Jingde, ed., *Zhuzi yulei*, vol. 8 [Beijing: Zhonghua shuju, 1986], 2973). Dōgen's *Hōkyōki*, which dates to 1225 through 1227 of the Southern Song when Dōgen was in China, has the following in answer to a question about these two sutras: "From of old there have been doubts about the *Heroic Progress Samadhi Sutra*, that is, was this sutra fabricated by later people? The patriarchal masters of former generations never saw this sutra. *In recent times stupid and dim people read it and love it.* This is also the case with the *Perfect Awakening Sutra*. The structure of composition [of these two sutras] is somewhat similar" (Ōkubo Dōchū, ed., *Dōgen zenji zenshū* [1970; repr., Kyoto: Rinsen shoten, 1989], 2:375).

91. See *Chan Prolegomenon*, nn. 158–59 and 248. For references for the numerous quotations from these two sutras in the *Zongjinglu*, see Daizōkyō gakujutsu yōgo kenkyūkai, ed., *Taishō shinshū daizōkyō sakuin shoshūbu* 3, vol. 27 (Tokyo: Daizōkyō gakujutsu yōgo kenkyūkai, 1983), 34 and 173. A SAT Daizōkyō Text Database search shows 21 *Perfect Awakening* quotations and 50 *Heroic Progress Samadhi* quotations.

92. *Yunmen Kuangzhen chanshi guanglu*, T 47:545c24–25, 548b2–3, 550b15, 550b27–29, and 550c27–28. See note 41. The record of Yunmen Wenyan (864–949) and the *Zhenzhou Linji Huizhao chanshi yulu* (T no. 1985), the record of Linji Yixuan (d. 866), are two of the core texts of Song rhetorical Chan. Both come to us from the editorial hands of the southern editor Yuanjue Zongyan (1074–1146), who was in the Yunmen line. The *Taishō Canon* Yunmen record in the colophons to each fascicle says: "Collated and edited by Yuanjue Zongyan of Mt. Gu in Fuzhou." Zongyan's 1120 "reprint" of the Linji record, which was actually a reworking, has been the standard text of that record down to today (see Iriya Yoshitaka, ed. and trans., *Rinzairoku* [Tokyo: Iwanami shoten, 1989], 227). These two records share certain characteristics in language style:

1. Heavy use of old *baihua*

2. Scatological and iconoclastic rhetoric: The Yunmen record uses the word "shit" (*shi*) twenty-seven times and "cylinder of dried shit" (*ganshijue*) six (one in the quotation here); the Linji record uses the former four times and the latter once (the famous

"the true man of no rank is a cylinder of dried shit!" [T 47:496c13]). For references, see Urs App, ed., *Concordance to the Record of Yunmen*, Hanazono Concordance Series vol. 15 (Kyoto: International Research Institute for Zen Buddhism Hanazono University, 1996), 183; and Urs App, ed., *Concordance to the Record of Linji (Rinzai)* (Kyoto: International Research Institute for Zen Buddhism Hanazono University, 1993), 119. The Linji record also has: "arhats and private buddhas are like privy waste [*cehui*]" (497c10–11); "the three vehicles and twelve divisions of the teachings are old toilet paper that wipes away filth [*shi bujing guzhi*]" (499c20); and "do not take the Buddha as the ultimate—I see him as like a privy hole [*cekong*]" (502c5–6).

3. Use of the slogan "*separate transmission outside the teachings*" (*jiaowai biechuan*), which occurs in the Yunmen material quoted here and in the memorial inscription at the end of the Linji record (T 47:506c11; Iriya, *Rinzairoku*, 213): Albert Welter, "The Formation of the *Linji lu*: An Examination of the *Guangdeng lu/Sijia yulu* and *Linji Huizhao Chanshi yulu* Versions of the *Linji lu* in Historical Context," www.skb.or.kr/2006/down/papers/063.pdf, says: "Ultimately, 'a separate practice outside the teaching' [*jiaowai biexing*] became a catchphrase of the Song Linji faction, and a crowning definition of Linji Chan identity. . . . There is no verifiable usage of the term *jiaowai biechuan* until well after the end of the Tang dynasty, and it did not achieve common status until the Song. It clearly represents a retrospective attribution by Song Linji faction proponents on to their alleged founding patriarch, used as a device to affirm contemporary factional identity." For more on the record of Linji in this sort of light, see Albert Welter, *The* Linji Lu *and the Creation of Chan Orthodoxy: The Development of Chan's Records of Sayings Literature* (Oxford: Oxford University Press, 2008). For a heavily annotated English translation of the *Linjilu* originally done in Japan by an international team of scholars including Iriya Yoshitaka, Yanagida Seizan, Philip Yampolsky, and Burton Watson, see Thomas Yuho Kirchner, ed., *The Record of Linji* (Honolulu: University of Hawai'i Press, 2008).

None of the above three characteristics shows up in the *Chan Prolegomenon* or the *Zongjinglu*, the core texts of Song moderate Chan.

93. The *Record of Linji* proclaims: "And the three vehicles and twelve divisions of the teachings are old toilet paper that wipes away filth [*shi bujing guzhi*]. The Buddha is an illusionary transformation body, and the patriarchs are old monks. You were born from women, were you not? If you seek buddhas, then you will be gathered in by buddha-Evil Ones. If you seek the patriarchs, then you will be bound by patriarch-Evil Ones. If you have any seeking at all, then everything will be suffering. It's better to have nothing to do" (T 47:499c20–23; Iriya, *Rinzairoku*, 83). The passage on the Linji's encounter with a lecture specialist occurs near the beginning of the *Record of Linji*: "There was a Director of Lecturing [*zuozhu*] who asked: 'The three vehicles and twelve divisions of the teachings certainly enlighten concerning the buddha nature.' The Master [Linji] said: 'The wild grass [of ignorance/*avidyā*] has never been

cut.' The Director said: 'How could the Buddha deceive people?' The Master said: 'Where is the Buddha?' The Director was silent. The Master said: 'Are you about to hide the truth from me [*niman laoseng*] right in front of the Constant Attendant? Get back! Get back! You are blocking the others from asking questions.' . . . 'Because your faith is insufficient [there is] today's kudzu [*jinri geteng*]. I fear you are causing trouble for the Constant Attendant and his officials, darkening their buddha nature. It's better that I withdraw.' He gave a shout, saying: 'For those of shallow roots of faith, there will never be a day when it is settled. [I appreciate your] standing for so long. Take good care of yourselves'" (T 47:496b20–c3; Iriya, *Rinzairoku*, 17–19).

94. Welter, "The Problem with Orthodoxy," 7.

95. *Song gaoseng zhuan*, T 50:887b12–14.

96. For references, see the index of Robert E. Buswell Jr., *The Korean Approach to Zen: The Collected Works of Chinul* (Honolulu: University of Hawaii Press, 1983), 465.

97. See K 1499 in Lewis R. Lancaster and others, eds., *The Korean Buddhist Canon: A Descriptive Catalogue* (Berkeley: University of California Press, 1979), 477.

98. Mangen Shiban's 1702 *Honchō kōsōden* (*Biographies of Eminent Monks of Our Country*; fascicle 19) says: "Shōkō of Chinzei came to attend Nōnin's assembly and asked about essential passages of the *Sugyōroku* [=*Zongjinglu*]" (Suzuki gakujutsu zaidan, ed., *Dai Nihon Bukkyō zensho* [Tokyo: Suzuki gakujutsu zaidan, 1972], 63:121). Also see Bernard Faure, "The Daruma-shū, Dōgen, and Sōtō Zen," *Monumenta Nipponica* 42, no. 1 (Spring 1987): 28. For a synoptic treatment of parallels in the *Zongjinglu* and the *Jōtōshōgakuron*, see Ishii Shudō, *Dōgen Zen no seiritsu-shi teki kenkyū* (Tokyo: Daizō shuppan, 1991), 649–64. Nōnin's reliance on the *Zongjinglu*, which advocates the sudden awakening–gradual practice model of Guifeng Chan, seems, on the surface at least, not to fit with the Daruma lineage's image among its critics as an extremist school denying all practice. For instance, Myōan Yōsai's *Kōzen gokoku ron* of 1198 says (T 80:7c26–8a3): "Question: 'Some falsely call the Zen lineage the *Daruma lineage* and say of themselves: "There is neither practice nor cultivation [*mugyō mushu*]; from the outset there are no depravities; and from the beginning it is awakening. Therefore, there is no need to adhere to the precepts and no need to engage in practice. You just need to lie down on your back [and do nothing]. Why trouble yourself over practicing *nenbutsu*, making offerings to sacred relics, giving vegetarian meals, etc.? What is the benefit [of that sort of thing]?"' [Yōsai] answers: 'There is no evil that this type does not commit. These are the people described in the sacred teachings as those of the [extreme] voidness view. You should not talk or associate with these people. You should stay light-years away from them.'"

99. For *Mind Mirror* citations in the *Kōzen gokoku ron*, see T 80:7c2; 7c8; 8a26; and 11b17. On Enni and the *Mind Mirror*, see Carl Bielefeldt, "Filling the Zen shū: Notes on the *Jisshū Yōdō Ki*," in *Chan Buddhism in Ritual Context*, ed. Bernard Faure (London: RoutledgeCurzon, 2003), 191.

100. Ichiki Takeo, *Gozan bungaku yōgo jiten* (Tokyo: Zokugun shorui kansei kai, 2002), 231–32. Bonsen, for instance, in 1342 printed the *Muchū mondō shū* of Musō Soseki (1275-1351), which until the Edo period remained one of the most popular of all Zen works by native Japanese authors.

101. For Myōha's *Chan Prolegomenon*, see Kawase Kazuma, *Gozanban no kenkyū* (Tokyo: Nihon koshosekishō kyōkai [The Antiquarian Booksellers Association of Japan], 1970), 1:404. For a photograph of its first and last pages, see Kawase, *Gozanban no kenkyū*, 2:69. Ishii (1–10) contains this edition. Also see Ishii Shudō, "Daiei toshokan shozō no Gozanban *Zengen shosenshū tojo* ni tsuite," *Indogaku Bukkyōgaku kenkyū* 44, no. 2 (March 1996): 117–24. Komazawa daigaku toshokan, *Shinsan Zenseki mokuroku*, 253, lists an undated woodblock-print edition done by a Tahara Jinzaemon of Kyoto (Komazawa University No. 121–2). Kamata, 373, speculates that this Tahara edition may have been based on Myōha's 1358 edition. For Myōha's *Zongjinglu*, see Kawase, *Gozanban no kenkyū*, 1:398. For photographs of one of the covers, the end, and the beginning, see Kawase, *Gozanban no kenkyū*, 2:77–79. Some of the names of the carvers of this *Zongjinglu* appear to be Chinese (for instance, the craftsmen in charge named Jiangnan Chen and Meng Rong). This edition is listed in Komazawa daigaku toshokan, *Shinsan Zenseki mokuroku*, 224. Shun'oku Myōha was a disciple of the Gozan fountainhead Musō Soseki and a teacher of Zekkai Chūshin (1336–1405), usually considered the greatest of the Gozan poet-monks. Taguchi Akiyoshi of the late Edo period was the first to use the term *Gozanban* ("Gozan editions").

102. Ikkyū's year-by-year biography, the *Tōkai Ikkyū oshō nenpu*, which is attributed to the painter-monk Motsurin Shōtō (Bokusai), records the following event for the year Bummei 12/1480 (Ikkyū's eighty-seventh year): "Hosokawa Yūtenkyū [who could be Hosokawa Masumoto, son of Hosokawa Katsumoto, the leader of one side in the Ōnin War] brought paper and requested [Ikkyū] to write the character 'no' [*muji*]. Beneath it [Ikkyū] wrote a verse and gave it to him. Thereupon [Hosokawa] gave him as a farewell present a copy of the *Sugyōroku*" (Hirano Sōjō, ed. and trans., *Ikkyū oshō zenshū*, vol. 3 [Tokyo: Shunjūsha, 2003], 102 and 74).

103. Tangut=Chinese Dangxiang. For a general treatment, see Ruth W. Dunnell, *The Great State of White and High: Buddhism and State Formation in Eleventh-Century Xia* (Honolulu: University of Hawaii Press, 1996). A classic work on Xixia language and script is: Nishida Tatsuo, *Seikago no kenkyū*, 2 vols. (Tokyo: Zauhō, 1966).

104. K. B. Kepping, "Mi-nia (Tangut) Self-Appellation and Self-Portraiture in Khara Khoto Materials," *Manuscripta Orientalia: International Journal for Oriental Manuscript Research* 7 (2001): 37. Kepping remarks: "But the tradition of using the foreign designations is so stable that, despite the fact that today these indigenous terms are quite familiar to the scholars, the foreign designations are still preferred." Mi-nia=Chinese Miyao=Tibetan Mi nyag. The Chinese literally rendered the name of the state as *Da Baigaoguo*.

105. Nie Hongyin, "Tangutology During the Past Decades," http://bic.cass.cn/ english/infoShow/Arcitle_Show_Forum2_Show.asp?ID=307&Title=The %20Humanities%20Study&strNavigation=Home-%3EForum-%3EEthnography& BigClassID=4&SmallClassID=8.

106. Nishida Tatsuo, *Seika moji* (Tokyo: Kinokuniya shoten, 1967), 39.

107. Shi Jinbo, *Xixia Fojiao shilüe* (Yinchuan: Ningxia renmin chubanshe: 1988), 334 and 336.

108. For a survey of the extant Tangut Buddhist materials, see E. I. Kychanov, *Katalog Tangutskikh Buddiyskikh pamyatnikov Instituta vostokovedeniya Rossiyskoi akademii nauk* (*Catalogue of the Tangut Buddhist Texts from the Collection of the Institute of Oriental Studies, Russian Academy of Sciences*] (Kyoto: Kyoto daigaku, 1999). The following list of Zongmi-related texts is based on K. J. Solonin, "Tangut Chan Buddhism and Guifeng Zong-mi," *Zhonghua Foxue xuebao* 11 (July 1998): 371–95; Xixia, 60; and Nishida Tatsuo, *Seikabun Kegonkyō* (Kyoto: Kyoto daigaku bungaku-bu, 1977), 3:26, 30, 36, and 56. The catalogue numbers are those of the St. Petersburg Institute of Oriental Studies, Russian Academy of Sciences, as given by Solonin (Tangut=Tang.):

1. Tangut 227-735 is a *Zhushuo chanyuanji duxu zhi jie* (*Explanation of the Chan Prolegomenon*), a translation of the first fascicle of the *Chan Prolegomenon* preceded by an *Explanation*. Solonin says it is a woodblock edition and that the *Explanation* is actually Pei Xiu's preface. Nishida 026-091 is a *Zhushuo chanyuanji duxu* listed as Tangut 227, and his 026-093 is a *Zhushuo chanyuanji duxu zhi jie* (*Explanation of the Chan Prolegomenon*) listed as British Museum 2239. See the discussion at Nishida, *Seikabun Kegonkyō*, 1:18–19.

2. Tangut 292-7119 is a *Chanyuan xia* (*Chan Source Second Roll*), a translation of the the first and second part of the last fascicle of the *Chan Prolegomenon*. Solonin says only fragments of this woodblock edition survived. See the discussion at Nishida, *Seikabun Kegonkyō*, 1:18–19.

3. Tangut 227-4736 is a *Zhushuo chanyuanji duxu luewen* (*Outline of the Chan Prolegomenon*), a schematic commentary on the *Chan Prolegomenon*. Solonin says that the extant portion deals with the last fascicle and that it is a woodblock edition. He suggests that the Chinese tradition did not preserve this text, and so it was probably composed at the Guifeng community of Xixia. Nishida 026-092 is a *Zhushuo chanyuanji duxu gangwen* (*Programme of the Chan Prolegomenon*), which Nishida describes as translated from Chinese, a fragment of a printed edition. He lists it as Tangut 227-4736, British Museum 2239.

4. Tangut 227-5172 is a *Zhushuo chanyuanji duxu faju ji* (*Issuing-the-Torch Record of the Chan Prolegomenon*), a *Chan Prolegomenon* commentary. Solonin says it is a woodblock edition of an unknown, probably originally Tangut commentary. Nishida 026-094 is a *Zhushuo chanyuanji duxu zeju ji* (*Selecting-the-Torch Record of the Chan Prolegomenon*), which Nishida describes as translated from Chinese and lists as Tangut 227-5172, 7754.

5. Tangut 421-113 bears the abridged Tangut title *Chart of Passing and Receiving the Teaching*. Solonin says it is a woodblock edition of a translation of the *Chan Letter* and that this text exists in both Chinese and Tangut versions. Nishida 080-119 is a *Zhonghua xindichuan chanmen shizi chengxi tu yijuan* (*Chart of the Master-Disciple Succession of the Chan Gate that Transmits the Mind Ground in China in One Roll*), which Nishida describes as translated from Chinese. See the discussion at Nishida, *Seikabun Kegonkyō*, 1:19–21.

6. Tangut 398 is a *Pei Xiu chanshi suiyuan ji* (*Collection of Encounters of Pei Xiu and the Chan Masters*), an unknown record by Zongmi's disciple and friend Pei Xiu. Solonin says it is a woodblock edition in two fascicles and that it seems extant only in this Tangut version. He describes it as a record of Pei Xiu's travels about Buddhist places and his encounters with various Chan masters, adding that it seems to contain unique information on late Tang Buddhism. Nishida 181-159 is a *Pei Xiu chanshi suiyuan ji* (*Collection of Encounters of Pei Xiu and the Chan Masters*), which Nishida describes as translated from Chinese, middle fascicle and last fascicle fragment, printed edition, and lists as Tangut 398.

7. Tangut 421-113 (not in Nishida) is most of a work entitled *The Mirror* (*Jing*), an exposition of Chan teachings accompanied by the author's critiques. Solonin says it is a woodblock edition with no colophon, and his comments on the Zongmi connection are worth quoting: "The identification of Shenhui as the Seventh Patriarch [*The Mirror* quotes the sixth and seventh patriarchs] seems adequate, since *The Mirror* definitely belongs to the Huayan-Guifeng lineage: the text is abundant in quotations from the Huayan master Chengguan, the former Zongmi teacher, Zongmi himself, especially his *Chan Preface*, and Chan master Huangbo, who could be somehow related to the Zongmi school through Pei Xiu. The structure of *The Mirror* resembles the scheme of Zongmi's *Chan Preface*."

8. Tangut 111-2529 is a *Hongzhou zongshi jiaoyi* (*Teachings and Rituals of the Hongzhou Lineage Masters*), a short dialogue between Daji (Hongzhou Ma) and some of his disciples. See Xixia, appendix 1, for a tentative translation. It serves as the root text for the commentary below. Solonin proposes the native Tangut origin of both the root text and commentary. Nishida 226-291 is a *Hongzhou zongshi jiaoyi* (*Teachings and Rituals of the Hongzhou Lineage Masters*), which he describes as translated from Chinese.

9. Tangut 112-2540 is a *Hongzhou zongqu zhujie minghu ji* (*Record of the Hongzhou Axiom with Commentary and Clarification*), the root text above with the commentary of an unknown figure by the name of Fayong. Solonin describes the Fayong commentary as an attempt to render the Hongzhou teaching through the prism of Huayan and to demonstrate the unity of the teachings of Hongzhou Ma ("everything is the real [*yiqie shi zhen/yiqie jie zhen*]") and Shenhui's "Knowing." See Xixia, appendix 2, for a tentative translation. Solonin proposes the native Tangut origin of both the root text and commentary. Nishida 226-290 is a *Hongzhou zongshi qu zhu kaiming yaoji* (*Essential Record of the Purport of the Hongzhou Lineage*

Masters with Commentary and Clarification), which he describes as translated from Chinese.

10. Tangut 183-2848 (not in Nishida) is a *Jiujing yisheng yuanming xin yi* (*Meaning of the Perfectly Enlightened Mind of the Ultimate One Vehicle*). Xixia, 60, says that it could be another source for research into Zongmi's doctrine in Xixia and that the text still awaits research.

Two other Tangut translations should be noted. Nishida's catalogue lists two versions (Nishida 204-241/Tangut 324 and Nishida 204-242/Tangut 395) of one of Zongmi's Huayan works, the *Commentary on the Huayan Dharma Sphere Discernment Gate* (*Zhu huayan fajie guanmen*; T no. 1884). This is Zongmi's commentary on the *Huayan Dharma Sphere Discernment Gate* attributed to Dushun. The former is described as a manuscript scroll. Solonin, "Tangut Chan Buddhism," 372, mentions that one of these copies originated from the imperial residence of the Xia king. Secondly, Solonin, "Tangut Chan Buddhism," 394, mentions (without catalogue number) a text with the deduced Chinese title *Tang Chang'an guoshi gongnei chuanfa yao* (*Essentials of the Transmission of Dharma Within the Palace of the National Teacher of the Tang [Capital] Chang'an*) and remarks: "This text was also quite widespread, but despite this fact, I [have] failed to identify its authorship and origin." Perhaps it is related to Pei Xiu's *Essentials of the Dharma of Mind Transmission* (*Chuanxin fayao*). All in all, this is an amazing cache of valuable material.

109. Xixia, 58–59.

110. Solonin, "Tangut Chan Buddhism," 365.

111. Xixia, 60. Solonin goes so far as to say: "Even a surface scan of Tangut Buddhist texts reveals the substantial presence of the Chan-Huayan tradition of Zongmi in Xixia, while the doctrinal writings of other Chinese schools are almost completely absent. Further evidence of Huayan popularity is provided by the so-called Tangut 'Odes,' in one of which Huayan is mentioned as a synonym for Buddhism itself. Bearing all this in mind, one is inclined to assume the exclusive role of the Huayan tradition in the formation of a national Tangut Buddhism" (59).

112. See nos. 7, 9, and 10 in note 108. The title of no. 2 here is according to Solonin.

113. This is is a Huayan term. Chengguan's *Da fangguang fohuayan jing suishu yanyi chao* (T 36:615a16–18) says: "This nature origination itself has two aspects. The first is non-substantiality [*asvabhāva*] due to dependence on conditions and so nature origination [*xingqi*]. The second is the dharma nature [*dharmatā*] accords with conditions and so nature origination." The *Chan Prolegomenon* (section 18) explains nature origination as follows: "Grounded in the nature, characteristics are originated [*yixing qi xiang*] through causation." This is the second of Chengguan's two aspects.'

114. I have not traced this quotation.

115. Solonin reconstructs the name of this unknown master as Kaiyuan Ming shi. I have not traced the following quotation.

116. T 32:576a10–13. Zongmi uses this quotation as the caption under *Inexpressible* in the chart of sentient-being mind in the *Chan Prolegomenon* (section 54).

117. T 48:379c15–16; Iriya, *Denshin hōyō*, 6. This quotation from Pei Xiu's *Chuan-xin fayao* (*Essentials of the Dharma of Mind Transmission*) suggests that in Xixia Pei Xiu's work was part of the corpus of Guifeng Chan. If so, this probably reflects the situation in China itself. There is also the unknown Tangut text entitled *Pei Xiu chan-shi suiyuan ji* (*Collection of Encounters of Pei Xiu and the Chan Masters*). See note 108, no. 6.

118. Solonin reconstructs this term as *"xinjing."* Chengguan's *Da fangguang fohuayan jing suishu yanyi chao* (T 36:261c6) says: "Mind's constant calmness [*xin chang jijing*] is the buddha-in-embryo [tathagatagarbha]."

119. Yanagida, *Daruma no goroku*, 25.

120. *"wunian nian zhe ji nian zhenru."* Tōdai goroku kenkyūhan, ed., *Jinne no goroku: Dango* (Kyoto: Zen bunka kenkyūjo, 2006), 169. It is possible that a Tangut translation of Shenhui's *Platform Talks* circulated alongside Zongmi's Chan works in Xixia.

121. T 17:914a21–23; Yanagida, *Engakukyō*, 38; Muller, "The Sutra of Perfect Enlightenment (Yuanjuejing)," 8. This, of course, is Zongmi's favorite sutra.

122. Solonin reconstructs this term as *"xingqi."* Judging from the wording of the *Bodhidharma Anthology* (Yanagida, *Daruma no goroku*, 25) perhaps it should be *"faxing."*

123. Yanagida, *Daruma no goroku*, 25.

124. This Chinese master and commentary are unknown. The reconstructed Chinese title is *Yuanjue zhushu*. This comment suggests that there was a Chinese prototype behind the Tangut formulation of three teachings.

125. Solonin (411 and 415) gives Tangut [mǐou-nwə]=Chinese *zizhi*. These are graphs no. 1245 and 2699 in Li Fanwen, *Xia-Han zidian* (Beijing: Zhonghua shehui kexue chubanshe, 1997), 238 and 508. *The Mirror* shows us that the "Knowing" of Shenhui's *Platform Talks* and Zongmi's Chan works played a role in Xixia Buddhism. Is it possible that this teaching of "Knowing" had reached Tibet somewhat earlier? Xixia acted as a cultural intermediary between China and Tibet and translated many Tibetan Buddhist books into Tangut. The source of Rdzogs chen teachings in Tibet is one of the mysteries of early Tibetan Buddhism—the later Tibetan tradition and Indic-oriented modern scholarship both predictably claim that Rdzogs chen originated in Indian Vajrayāna sources. Judging from two of the earliest extant Rdzogs chen documents, the six verses of the *Rig pa'i khu byug* (*Cuckoo of Knowing*), which is found in the Tibetan Dunhuang manuscript Stein Tibetan 647, and the opening statement of the Rdzogs chen section of the central Tibetan text *Bsam gtan mig sgron* (*Lamp of the Eye of Dhyana*), Rdzogs chen teachings originally centered on spontaneous perfection (*lhun rdzogs pa*) and a "Knowing" (*rig pa*) or spontaneous "Knowing" (*rang rig pa*) that knows the substance (*ngo bo/ngo bo nyid*) directly (*mgon sum*), not through intellection or conceptual thought.

Samten Gyaltsen Karmay, *The Great Perfection (Rdzogs-chen): A Philosophical and Meditative Teaching in Tibetan Buddhism* (Leiden: E. J. Brill, 1988), 41–59 and 106–20, treats these documents as central to early Rdzogs chen. Karmay (56 and photographs at the end) gives a transliteration and reproduction of Stein Tibetan 647, fol. 1a1–3, and at 108 a transliteration of the relevant passage of the *Bsam gtan mig sgron*. For the original of the latter, see Gnubs-chen Sans-rgyas-ye-śes, *Rnal 'byor mig gi bsam gtan or Bsam gtan mig sgron*, Smanrtsis shesrig spendzod 74 (Leh, Ladakh: S. W. Tashigangpa, 1974), fols. 290.6–292.1. The Tibetan Dunhuang manuscript Pelliot Tibetan 116, which is in part an anthology of Chinese Chan materials, contains a chunk (fols. 60.3–63.2) from a work called the *Bsam brtan gyi mkhan po Shinho'i bsam brtan gyi mdo* (*Chan Book of Chan Master Shinho [=Shenhui]*). This extract from the *Chan Book of Chan Master Shinho* also appears in Pelliot Tibetan 813, fol. ka 8b4–ka 9b1 and fol. ka 17b4–5. (See Obata Hironobu, "Pelliot tib. n. 116 bunken ni mieru shozenji no kenkyū," *Zen bunka kenkyūjo kiyō* 8 [August 1976]: 28–30.) Materials like the *Chan Book of Chan Master Shinho* probably circulated in Tibetan-occupied Dunhuang and perhaps made it to central Tibet in one form or another, as many other Chan materials found in Pelliot Tibetan 116 did. The *Chan Book of Chan Master Shinho* as found in Pelliot Tibetan 116 appears to have been a digest of Shenhui's *Platform Talks*, picking up scattered elements of the Chinese original and pasting them together (just as the Xixia *Mirror* quotes from the *Platform Talks*). In the Chinese original the elements are concentrated at: Hu Shih, ed., *Shenhui heshang yiji* (Taipei: Hu Shi jinian guan, 1968), 232–47; Suzuki Daisetsu, *Suzuki Daisetsu zenshū* (Tokyo: Iwanami shoten, 1968), 3:310–13; and Tōdai goroku kenkyūhan, *Jinne no goroku: Dango*, 51–112. Chan Master Shinho (Shenhui) preaches that Knowing/spontaneous Knowing (*rig pa=zhi/rang gis rig pa=ziran zhi*) knows the calm substance (*zhi ba'i ngo bo nyid=jijing ti*) directly (*mngon sum du=zhi*), with no mental activity (*yid la bya ba myed=buzuoyi*), and that the calm substance constitutes spontaneous perfection (*lhun kyis rdzogs pa=benzi juzu?*). One can see that all the major points of early Rdzogs chen teaching as found in both the *Rig pa'i khu byug* (*Cuckoo of Knowing*) and the *Bsam gtan mig sgron* (*Lamp of the Eye of Dhyana*) are found in this *Chan Book of Chan Master Shinho* excerpt. Is it possible that Shenhui's "Knowing" is the prototype of Rdzogs chen's *rig pa*?

126. The tripod simile sounds similar to the *Chan Prolegomenon* (section 20): "[My reasoning is best explained by] reference to the three round marks of the [triangular] letter *i*. Three marks standing apart would not constitute an *i*. If the three [Chan] axioms ran counter to each other, how could they make buddhas?" The three round marks of the letter *i* (*yuanyi san dian*) refers to the short *i* vowel in the Indic script known as *siddham* (*xitan*).

127. I have not been able to trace the following Zongmi quotation, but the same idea is found in the *Chan Letter* (section 22): "Even though you all-at-once awaken to the realization that the true mind of the dharma body is identical to the buddhas, nevertheless, for many eons you have [engaged in] unreal grasping of the four ele-

ments as a self, and the habit energy has become your nature. Because finally this is difficult to eliminate all-at-once [*zu nan dunchu*], you must [engage in] a step-by-step practice grounded in awakening [*yiwu jianxiu*]."

128. My translation of these scattered passages from *The Mirror* is an adaptation from the translation in Solonin, "Tangut Chan Buddhism," 396–409. I have made changes in Solonin's rendering of the Tangut by consulting the Chinese originals.

129. Xixia, appendix 2, pp. 2b and 4a. The Chinese equivalents are: "*yiqie jie zhen*" and "*chulei shi dao.*" Solonin has an erroneous Chinese reconstruction for the second slogan—it comes from Zongmi's *Chan Notes*, section 4. The following discussion is based on Xixia, 61–77 and the translation in Xixia, appendix 2.

130. Xixia, appendix 2, pp. 6a–b, 10b–11a, 14a–b, 15a, 17b, and 19a. The Chinese equivalents are: (1) *ciwai chan/juwai chan*; (2) *cisui chan/jusui chan* [*sic*]; and (3) *da gubaoyin*. Xixia, 75, gives Xixia [gjwi-niow śjā]=Chinese *juwai chan*. These are graphs no. 3195, 1906, and 3504 in Li, *Xia-Han zidian*, 598, 364, and 652. Li's dictionary actually gives two Chinese equivalents for no. 3195, *ci* (*character combination/word*) and *ju* (*phrase/line*), citing an entry in the Xixia lexicon *Sea of Characters* (*Wenhai* 11.222).

131. The metaphor of the open eye and the closed eye may be related to a passage in the *Chan Prolegomenon* (section 35): "The voidness axiom with its unidirectional eye [*yixiang mu*] regards the original source of all dharmas as the [lack of self-]nature [or voidness of self-nature], while the nature axiom with its multiple eyes [*duomu*] regards the original source of all dharmas as mind." Note also *Zongjinglu*, T 48:660a9–12: "Generally, scholars who consult with profundity must possess two eyes [*xu ju er yan*]. One is the eye of self that is enlightened to the axiom, and the second is the eye of wisdom that distinguishes delusions. Therefore, the Chan axiom says: 'Single enlightenment to the self without understanding what is in front of one—this sort of person possesses just one eye [*zhi ju yi yan*]. Principle will be isolated and phenomena scant, and he will never have perfect penetration.'"

132. Xixia, appendix 2, pp. 2a–b, 4a, 6a–7a, 10b, 14b, and 19a. I have adapted Solonin's translation of the Tangut. For the root text standing alone, see note 108, no. 8.

133. "*xu xian yue san zhong fojiao zheng san zong chanxin.*"

134. For a recent edition, see Pojo sasang yŏn'guwon, ed., *Pojo chŏnsŏ* (Seoul: Puril ch'ulp'ansa, 1989), 103–65. For an English translation, see Buswell, *The Korean Approach to Zen*, 262–374.

135. We can surmise that Chinul is here referring specifically to Zongmi's teachings because the phrasing is repeated (with the inclusion of Zongmi's name) near the very end of the *Excerpts* (Pojo sasang yon'guwon, *Pojo chŏnsŏ*, 164): "For this sort of type, it is still better to rely on Master Mi's oral teachings concerning things as they really are [*ŭi Mil sa yŏshil ŏnkyo*] and zealously practice reflection."

136. Pojo sasang yon'guwon, *Pojo chŏnsŏ*, 103. For Buswell's translation of this passage, see Buswell, *The Korean Approach to Zen*, 263–64. For a comparative chart of Zongmi's *Chan Letter* and Chinul's *Excerpts*, see Shūmitsu, 391–410.

137. The *Excerpts* says: "The all-at-once awakening and step-by-step practice that is esteemed at the present time, in terms of the teachings, is the all-at-once of responding to beings of the highest disposition. It is practiced by ordinary beings of superior faculties and sharp intellect. . . . [All-at-once awakening and all-at-once practice] is not as good as the gate of all-at-once awakening and step-by-step practice that has been set up for ordinary beings of great aspiration at the present time" (Pojo sasang yon'guwon, *Pojo chŏnsŏ*, 127 and 132).

138. Daizōkyō, 602.

139. T 19:155a8–9. See note 90.

140. T 48: 1006b23–24 and c11–18; for another English translation, see Buswell, *The Korean Approach to Zen*, 143–44.

141. Kuroda Ryō, *Chosen kyūsho kō* (Tokyo: Iwanami shoten, 1940), 122–25, lists ten Korean editions he personally inspected, three of them in his own collection. Komazawa daigaku toshokan, *Shinsan Zenseki mokuroku*, 253, lists thirteen Korean editions.

142. Kuroda, *Chosen kyūsho kō*, 122.

143. Kamata Shigeo, ed. and trans., *Genninron* (Tokyo: Meitoku shuppansha, 1973), 25. This importance is illustrated by the fact that we have two commentaries on the *Chan Prolegomenon* by eighteenth-century Korean scholars (see Kamata, 374, and Komazawa daigaku toshokan, *Shinsan Zenseki mokuroku*, 254). The two commentaries are (1) *Sŏnwŏnjip tosŏ ch'akpyŏng* (*Grasping the Power of the Chan Prolegomenon*) by Hoeam Chŏnghye (1685–1741): There is a woodblock-print edition in Komazawa University Library (No. 121-4). According to Shūmitsu, 266, it merely divides the text into sections and is not really a detailed commentary. Chŏnghye also did a commentary on Chinul's *Excerpts* entitled *Pyŏrhaeng nok sagi hwajok* (edition in Shūmitsu, 410–32); (2) *Sŏnwŏn jejŏnjip tosŏ kwamok pyŏngip sagi* (*Headings of the Chan Prolegomenon with Inserted Personal Notes*) by Yŏndam Yuil (1720–1799)

This second *Chan Prolegomenon* commentary contains schematics and some useful paraphrases of Zongmi. Yuil aptly sums up the main thread of the *Chan Prolegomenon* (Shūmitsu, 276): "To broadly and clearly bring together the three [Chan] axioms into one taste and resolve all-at-once and step-by-step into one practice is the axiom of the *Prolegomenon*." There is a woodblock-print edition at Seoul University, a handwritten copy (1944) in Komazawa University Library (*kotsu*-1195), and an edition of the Komazawa handwritten copy in Shūmitsu, 267–292. At the end it gives the date of mid-spring 1796. Yuil also did a commentary on Chinul's *Excerpts* entitled *Pŏpchip pyŏrhaeng nok chŏryo kwamok pyŏngip sagi*. According to Buswell, *The Korean Approach to Zen*, 423, there is a woodblock print of Taehŭng-sa dated 1916 in the Tongguk University archives.

144. Robert E. Buswell Jr., *The Zen Monastic Experience: Buddhist Practice in Contemporary Korea* (Princeton, N.J.: Princeton University Press, 1992), 95–99. The *Dahui Pujue chanshi shu* is T 47:916b8–943b4; for a modern Japanese translation, see

Araki Kengo, ed. and trans., *Daie sho*, Zen no goroku 17 (Tokyo: Chikuma shobō, 1969). In these letters to laymen the Song-period Linji master Dahui Zonggao (1089–1163) strongly advocates his method. The *Gaofeng Yuanmiao chanshi chanyao* is ZZ 2.27.4; CBETA *Wan Xuzangjing* vol. 70, no. 1401. It consists of various types of talks by the Song-Yuan-period Linji master Yuanmiao (1238–95) on such subjects as the one doubt. Thus, the Chogye school course of study based on the *Fourfold Collection* is an amalgam of (1) Dahui's practice of gazing at the topic, (2) Yuanmiao's sayings, and (3) Zongmi's "Knowing," that is, suddenly awakening to "Knowing" followed by a gradual practice grounded in "Knowing."

145. A preface to the *Chan Prolegomenon* in the *Taishō Canon* by the otherwise unknown Jia Ruzhou (T 48:398a19–21) states: "The Empress Dowager of Emperor Chong of the Liao court in Qingning 8 [1062] did a printing and promulgated a definitive edition [*dingben*] for all-under-heaven." Connections between Khitan Buddhism and Mi-nia Buddhism remain unclear. Another example of an affinity between the *Chan Prolegomenon* and non-Han peoples of the north centers on the Mongol ruler Khubilai khan and the Buddhist preceptors around him at his court in the Yuan dynasty capital Dadu (modern Beijing). A preface to the *Chan Prolegomenon* in the *Taishō Canon* by Deng Wenyuan (T 48:397c20–22) states: "In Zhiyuan 12 [1275] of the national court [Emperor] Shizu [that is, Khubilai khan] in his Guanghan Hall wished to inquire about the essential meaning of the Chan teaching. The Imperial Teacher [the Tibetan monk 'Phags pa Blo gros rgyal mtshan (1235–1280)] and various venerable worthies took the *Expressions of the Chan Source* [that is, the *Chan Prolegomenon*] as their reply. The emperor was pleased and ordered a woodblock printing to circulate in the world." Jia Ruzhou's preface (398a12–17) also mentions this event. Deng Wenyuan's dates are 1259–1328; for information on him, see Ishii (10), 87.

146. For a study of Shōjō and his *Zenshū kōmoku*, see Shūmitsu, 609–37. Kamata and Tanaka, *Kamakura kyū Bukkyō*, 160–88, is a *kanbun kakikudashi* (without the original text) of the *Zenshū kōmoku*. Shōjō states at the end: "I received personal instruction from the Shōnin [Myōe] over twelve years and transmission of the exoteric and esoteric [teachings], not just one time. Subsequently, in the winter of Jōō 2 [1223], in the Zen dharma he transmitted secret judgments [*hiketsu*] another time. My feelings of doubt melted like ice; my original mind manifested itself like the moon. The purport of his [secret] oral transmission [*kuden*] is not something that can be recorded with brush and ink. Now I am presenting a grand summary and quoting texts for an explanation. Transmitters! Do not even slightly pollute it with other views. Recorded in the third month, late spring of Kenchō 7 [1255]. *Zenshū kōmoku* ends" (187–88).

147. Kamata and Tanaka, *Kamakura kyū Bukkyō*, 160. The five gates are: (1) *kyōzen dōi*, (2) *kyōge betsuden*, (3) *kenshō jōbutsu*, (4) *goshu zenton*, and (5) *shoryū kenge*.

148. Joseph D. Parker, *Zen Buddhist Landscape Arts of Early Muromachi Japan (1336–1573)* (Albany: State University of New York Press, 1999), 11, 18, and 209. For a

peek into the Gozan world via its ink paintings and their inscriptions, see the ground-breaking Shimada Shūjirō and Iriya Yoshitaka, eds., *Zenrin gasan: Chūsei suibokuga o yomu* (Tokyo: Mainichi shinbunsha, 1987).

149. See note 101.

150. This is the first of the "four items" (*si jie*) spoken by Purity Bodhisattva in the *Perfect Awakening Sutra*: "Good sons! All obstructions [such as the one Myōha's teacher Musō had been speaking of] are ultimate awakening. Whether you have obtained mindfulness or lost mindfulness, there is nothing that is not liberation. . . . Good sons! It is just that all the bodhisattvas and sentient beings of the end period, [1] *wherever they are at any time, do not produce false thoughts* [*ju yiqie shi bu qi wangnian*]; [2] *in the midst of false thoughts do not [attempt to] extinguish them* [*yu zhu wangxin yi bu ximie*]; [3] *even while dwelling in sense objects of false thought, do not attempt to understand them* [*zhu wangxiang jing bu jia liaozhi*]; and [4] *do not analyze lack of understanding itself as reality* [*yu wu liaozhi bu bian zhenshi*]" (T 17:917b2–11; Yanagida, *Engakukyō*, 133–37; and Muller, "The Sutra of Perfect Enlightenment [Yuanjuejing]," 23). Yanagida (137) remarks in a note that the four items were popular in Song dynasty Chan circles. These four eight-character sayings seem similar in style to the two eight-character sayings on sudden awakening–gradual practice in the *Heroic Progress Samadhi Sutra*, which were also popular in Song dynasty Chan circles (see note 90). Both suggest the influence of Guifeng-style Chan on Chan in the Song.

151. *Chikaku Fumyō kokushi goroku*, T 80:719a19–21. For Zongmi's similar experience with the *Perfect Awakening* as recounted by Pei Xiu, see note 8.

152. For a biographical treatment of Kiyō, see Parker, *Zen Buddhist Landscape Arts*, 74–77; and Tamamura Takeji, *Gozan Zensō denki shūsei* (Tokyo: Kōdansha, 1983), 70–71. Parker has a portrait of Kiyō from Reiun-in in Kyoto (75).

153. *"zen furi kyō kyō furi zen."* The piece is contained in his literary collection entitled *Funi ikō* (*Non-Duality's Bequeathed Draft Copy*). Kiyō was also known as Man-of-the-Path Non-Duality (*Funi dōjin*). See Uemura Kankō, *Gozan bungaku zenshū* (Tokyo: Teikoku kyōikukai shuppanbu, 1936), 3:950. Among his accomplishments, he did the Japanese reading marks for Shushi's *Shisho shūchū* (*Commentary on the Collection of the Four Books*), which became the core curriculum in schools established by the state during the Tokugawa period, and compiled the *Hekiganroku Funi shō* (*Non-Duality's Extracts from the Blue-Green Cliff Record*). For the last, which because of its scholarly approach (much like that of Zongmi) is still useful to modern Zen studies as a dictionary of Zen words, see Zen bunka kenkyūjo, ed., *Zengo jisho ruiju 3: Hekiganroku Funi shō* (Kyoto: Zen bunka kenkyūjo, 1993).

154. Komazawa daigaku toshokan, *Shinsan Zenseki mokuroku*, 254. These are the Hiranoya Sabē edition done in Kyoto during the Tenna (1681–1684) and Genroku (1688–1704) eras (Komazawa University No. 121-19) and the edition executed in Genroku 11 (1698) at the Sōtō Zen monastery Seishō-ji in Edo by its abbot, Tangai Kiun (Ōtani University and Matsuoka Bunko in Kamakura).

155. Ui Hakuju, ed. and trans., *Zengen shosenshū tojo* (1939; repr., Tokyo: Iwanami shoten, 1943). This pocket volume is no. 1888–1890 in the Iwanami Bunko series.

156. Ui's book was followed three decades later by Kamata Shigeo's edition and translation of the *Chan Prolegomenon* and *Chan Letter* in the Zen no goroku series published in the late 1960s and 1970s: Kamata Shigeo, ed. and trans., *Zengen shosenshū tojo*, Zen no goroku 9 (Tokyo: Chikuma shobō, 1971). Since this series was intended to cover about twenty of the most important texts of Chinese Chan (roughly half Tang and half post-Tang), the inclusion of Zongmi's *Chan Prolegomenon* in the Tang half is significant. During the 1990s Ishii Shudō and Ogawa Takashi published an edition and translation of the *Chan Prolegomenon* in ten installments (abbreviated as Ishii [1–10]). (In 1981 Ishii had published a Kamakura manuscript of the *Chan Letter* that was discovered at Shinpuku-ji in Nagoya.) Interestingly, all these scholars are associated with Sōtō Zen and its university Komazawa. Ui was a Sōtō Zen priest who taught at one point at Sōtōshū University (now Komazawa); Kamata graduated in Buddhist Studies from Komazawa; and Ishii is a professor at Komazawa.

157. Shūmitsu, 50; QTW 16:743.9731a15–16.

158. Shūmitsu, 50; QTW 16:743.9731b2–3.

159. For instance, Zengaku daijiten hensansho, *Zengaku daijiten*, 1:494, uses the term "union of the teachings and Zen" (*kyōzen itchi*) in its Zongmi entry. As an example of the tendency to contextualize him as the last patriarch of the Kegon school there is a set of portraits of Chinese Huayan patriarchal masters preserved at Kumida-dera in Osaka prefecture. The set, which dates to around 1400, includes Dushun, Fazang, Chengguan, and Zongmi (Zhiyan's portrait was missing by the time of a restoration in Meiwa 2 [1765]). For photographs, see Kishiwada-shiritsu kyōdo shiryōkan, *Kumida-dera no rekishi to bijutsu: Butsuga to chūsei bunsho o chūshin ni* (Kishiwada-shi: Kishiwada-shiritsu kyōdo shiryōkan, 1999), 14–15. The four portraits have disparate conventions. While Fazang sits at a low lectern and Chengguan on a small sitting platform, Zongmi sits in a chair, holding a whisk. See frontispiece. The conventions of the Zongmi portrait, from which an inscription at the top may have been cropped, are similar to those of a typical Kamakura-Muromachi Zen *chinzō*, such as the one of Lanxi Daolong (dated 1271) at Kenchō-ji in Kamakura (see Tokyo kokuritsu hakubutsu-kan, *Kenchō-ji: Zen no genryū* [Tokyo: Nihon keizai shinbunsha, 2003], 36) or the one of Kiyō Hōshū at Reiun-in in Kyoto (see Parker, *Zen Buddhist Landscape Arts*, 75). If the inscriptions at the top of these two were cropped off, the remaining proportions would be similar to those of the Zongmi portrait. Further examples of the contextualizing of Zongmi as a Kegon patriarch are found in Japanese Buddhist dictionaries. The venerable Oda Tokuno, ed., *Bukkyō daijiten* (1917; repr., Tokyo: Daizō shuppan, 2005), 820, begins its Zongmi entry by describing him as "a Kegon patriarch of the Tang." The more recent Nakamura, *Iwanami Bukkyō jiten*, 490, begins its Zongmi entry by describing him as "the fifth patriarch of the Kegon lineage." A 1950s handcopy of the *Chan Prolegomenon*—Takamine Ryōshū, ed., *Zengen shosenshū tojo* (Nara: Tōdai-ji

Kangakuin, 1955), postface—states that "Zongmi has come to be designated the fifth patriarch of the transmission of the Kegon lamp in China." The syncretic label "Kegon Zen" is a modern Japanese coinage (it appears as "so-called Kegon Zen" in Mochizuki's entry for "Kegon lineage": Mochizuki Shinkō, ed., *Bukkyō daijiten* [Tokyo: Sekai seiten kankō kyōkai, 1958–1963], 1:870). At every occurrence of the term *"Huayan"* in the *Chan Letter, Chan Prolegomenon*, and *Chan Notes*, it means the *"Huayan Sutra"* or a commentary on that sutra. It is never used to designate the third and highest of the *Chan Prolegomenon*'s three teachings, the nature teaching/nature axiom. If someone had asked Zongmi to label his Chan, he probably would have replied with "Heze Chan" or the "Chan of the Seventh Patriarch" (*Chan Letter*, section 5).

160. For instance, the Zen dictionary of the Sōtō Zen school, Zengaku daijiten hensansho, *Zengaku daijiten*, 1:111, in its Yanshou entry devotes several lines to his fusion of Chan and *nenbutsu* practice: "He concurrently cultivated Zen and *nenbutsu* and at night on another peak took going around doing *nenbutsu* as a constant. King [Wuyi of Wu-yue] built a Hall of the Broad Teachings of [Amitābha's Pure Land in] the West and had him dwell there." But all that this entry says of his imposing *Zongjinglu* is that "it was honored by both monks and lay people." In its entry on the Fayan lineage (2:1127) *Zengaku daijiten* says: "Yongming Yanshou aimed at a union of Pure Land thought and Zen; he also compiled the *Mind Mirror* in one-hundred fascicles, attempting a systematization the various schools." In short, he was a Fayan patriarch and a syncretist, rather than a Bodhidharma Chanist in the broadest sense. Welter, "The Problem with Orthodoxy," 13, mentions meeting with a leading Rinzai Zen academic in Japan and asking why little research was done on Yanshou in Japan. The response was that Zen scholars in Japan paid little attention to Yanshou because he was not a Zen master. The *Zongjinglu*'s actual position on buddha-recitation is the following (T 48:506a10–15): "Question: 'As your previous analysis of principle and phenomena clarifies, outside of the Buddha there is no mind and outside mind no Buddha. Why do the teachings further erect a dharma gate of buddha-recitation [*geng li nianfo famen*]?' Answer: 'It is just for those who do not have faith in "one's own mind is the Buddha [*zhi wei bu xin zixin shi fo*]" and rush around seeking on the outside [*xiangwai chiqiu*]. If they are of medium or inferior faculties, we provisionally make them gaze on a buddha's form body and moor to coarse mindfulness, taking the external to reveal the internal. Step-by-step they awaken to their own minds. If they are of high ability, we make them gaze at the reality mark of the [Buddha] body. Gazing at a buddha is like this.'"

161. In Japan two definitions of pure Zen (*jun Zen*) have been (for the Sōtō school) Kigen Dōgen (1200–1253) and (for the Rinzai school) Ōtōkan, three masters beginning with Nanpo Jōmyō (1235–1308). The case of the Ming-dynasty Linji Chan monk Yinyuan Longqi (Ingen Ryūki; 1592–1673), who arrived in Nagasaki at the age of sixty-three, illustrates the power of this conception of pure Zen in Tokugawa Japan. Nakamura, *Iwanami Bukkyō jiten*, in its Ingen entry says: "There was a movement to wel-

come him as abbot of [the Rinzai Zen monastery] Myōshin-ji in Kyoto, but in Japan there was a tradition of pure Zen [*jun Zen no dentō*] since the Kamakura period, and even then the plan was not implemented due to the opposition of people like Gudō Tōshoku, who called [Ingen's Linji Chan] Ming dynasty "*nenbutsu Zen.*" In 1661 at Uji Ōbakusan Manpuku-ji was erected, and Ingen became the founding patriarch of a [separate] Japanese Ōbaku school" (57–58).

162. The *Record of Linji* says: "Followers of the Way! The great teacher dares to slander the buddhas and patriarchs, pronounce the world right or wrong, discard the teachings of the canon [*paichi sanzang jiao*], curse small children, and, while sometimes going against [the world] and sometimes going along with it, seek out the [upright] person" (T 47:499b24–26; Iriya, *Rinzairoku*, 77–78).

163. T 19:155a8–9. See notes 90 and 139.

164. T 47:920a6–16; Araki, *Daie sho*, 36 (translation follows Araki's text). Dahui's *Letters* repeatedly quotes the *Heroic Progress Samadhi* and *Perfect Awakening Sutras*; for citations, see Araki's index (1 and 4). Chinul's *Susim kyŏl* quotes the first portion of this Dahui passage in defense of the Guifeng-Yanshou sudden awakening–gradual practice model (T 48:1007b25-c7): "Ordinary people from without beginning over expansive eons have arrived at the present day, revolving through the five rebirth paths, coming to be born and going to die. They have firmly grasped the self characteristic, and thought of the unreal, topsy-turvy thinking, ignorance, and various habits have long become their nature. Although, upon arriving at the present life, they all-at-once awaken to the realization that self nature from the outset is void and calm and that they are no different from the buddhas, these old habits at last are difficult to eliminate. Therefore, when they encounter sense objects that go against them or accord with them, anger and joy, right and wrong, rise up and die down like a blaze. And their adventitious depravities are no different than before. If they do no exert effort through wisdom, how will they be able to counteract ignorance and arrive at the stage of great stopping and great rest? . . . And Chan Master [Dahui Zong]gao says: 'Often people of sharp faculties, without expending a lot of effort, send this matter packing. They then produce easy-going thoughts and do not engage in [post-awakening] practice. Days and month pass, and they wander on as before without avoiding the wheel-turning [of the rebirth process].' How could one, because of one phase of awakening, set aside later practice?" For Buswell's translation, see Buswell, *The Korean Approach to Zen*, 148.

165. T 47:930c4–7; Araki, *Daie sho*, 130. This topic (*huatou*) comes from a case (*gong'an*) based on a passage in the *Yunmen Kuangzhen chanshi guanglu* (*Extensive Record of Yunmen*), T 47:550b15: "Question: 'What is the body of Śākyamuni like?' Answer: 'A cylinder of dried shit [*ganshijue*].'" See note 92. Urs App, *Master Yunmen: From the Record of the Chan Teacher "Gate of the Clouds"* (New York: Kodansha International, 1994), 242, remarks that Yunmen cases are more numerous than those of any other master in the major case collections. He provides a table of Yunmen-related cases, including this one (243–45).

166. This all-at-once *laying down* of the self and world (*yi nian fangxia shenxin shijie*) and *lifting up* of this one moment (*ti ci yi nian*) is clearly working from Dahui Zonggao's teachings on his *huatou* method. For example, see T 47:921c2–15; Araki, *Daie sho*, 50–51, where Dahui urges his reader to all-at-once lay down (*yi shi anxia*) the mind of intellection and discrimination and, at just the locus where he has laid down that discriminatory mind, gaze at the topic (*kan ge huatou*) or constantly lift the topic to attention (*shishi tixi*). Deqing mixes the Zongmi true mind/nature axiom with the Dahui *huatou* method, much in the manner of Chinul.

167. "*zhiguan niannian bubu zuo jiangqu.*"

168. *Hanshan laoren mengyouji*, CBETA *Wan Xuzangjing* vol. 73, no. 1456:469c15[00]–18[00] and 557a20[03]–21[01]. See Iwaki Eiki, "Kanzan Tokushō no shisō," *Indogaku Bukkyōgaku kenkyū* 46, no. 1 (December 1997): 223. As in the case of Yanshou, modern Japanese Zen studies chooses to emphasize Deqing's dual practice of Chan and recitation of Amida Buddha's name (*nenbutsu*). For instance, Zengaku daijiten hensansho, *Zengaku daijiten*, 2:951, says: "He advocated the dual practice of *nenbutsu* and gazing at the topic [of the *kōan*] and together with Zhuhong, Zhenke, and Zhixu is called one of the four great Buddhists of the late Ming."

169. Deqing did the *Yuanjuejing zhijie* (ZZ 1.16; CBETA *Wan Xuzangjing* vol. 10, no. 258) and the *Lengyan jing tongyi* (ZZ 1.19; CBETA *Wan Xuzangjing* vol. 12, no. 279).

170. *Yuanjuejing zhijie*, CBETA *Wan Xuzangjing* vol. 10, no. 258:485a14[10]–20[02].

171. Solonin, "Tangut Chan Buddhism," 396 and 400 (for the *Perfect Awakening* quotation, see note 121). It also mentions (403) an unknown commentary on the *Perfect Awakening* (see note 124). According to Xixia, 58, neither the *Perfect Awakening Sutra* nor Zongmi's commentary, the *Yuanjuejing dashu chao* (*Extracts from the Great Commentary on the Perfect Awakening Sutra*), has yet been discovered among the Tangut holdings.

172. For citations of these two sutras in the *Excerpts*, see the index of Buswell, *The Korean Approach to Zen*, 463 and 468. For a quotation from the *Heroic Progress Samadhi* in the *Formula for Cultivating Mind*, see note 139. Chinul's position sounds similar to that of Hanshan Deqing.

173. In the *Gidō oshō goroku* (T 80:523a2–7), Gidō quotes section 11 of the *Chan Prolegomenon* (perhaps via the *Zongjinglu*, T 48:418b6–8) on the identity of the sutras and Zen: "There was a Zen follower who commented: 'Since Hekitan [Shūkō; 1291–1374] came over to our [Zen] lineage, we should just completely hold up the commands of the [Zen] patriarchs. Why should we still employ lecturing [on the sutras and treatises]?' The Preceptor [Gidō] listened and then told this person: 'You fail to see the path. The sutras are buddha word, while Zen is the mind of the buddhas. The words and mind of the buddhas cannot possibly be contradictory. Certainly, among the patriarchal masters of India from Mahākāśyapa through Upagupta all equally propagated the three baskets [of rules of discipline, sutra, and scholasticism].'" Hekitan Shūkō, an offspring of the Kamakura Hōjō family, originally became highly versed in Shingon

secret teachings. During the Genkō Incident of 1331 he fled and entered Musō Soseki's assembly, converting to Zen. In Gidō's diary, the *Abbreviated Collection of Flower-in-the Sky's Everyday Practice (Kūge nichiyō kufū ryakushū)*, Gidō is frequently requested to give lectures on the *Perfect Awakening* or asked questions about it (Kageki Hideo, trans., *Kunchū Kūge nichiyō kufū ryakushū: chūsei Zensō no seikatsu to bungaku* [Kyoto: Shibunkaku, 1982], 25, 47, 110, 215, 220, 238, 272, 275–78, 286, 298–99, 301, and 303). His name, Kūge (Flower-in-the Sky), is a prominent term in that sutra. For references to the *Heroic Progress Samadhi*, see 47, 127, 173, 197, 274, 276, 277–281, 293, 298, 300, 308, 311, 317–18, 337, 350, and 365. The *Mind Mirror (Sugyōroku)* references are 142–44 and 298. See also Parker, *Zen Buddhist Landscape Arts*, 165n. 42. Zekkai Chūshin also often lectured on the *Perfect Awakening* and *Heroic Progress Samadhi* (*Zekkai oshō goroku*, T 80:759b1 and 759c8). The passage in his year-by-year biography (*nenpu*) giving his death poem (760a13–16) mentions that he read both sutras on a daily basis: "Verse of taking leave of the world: 'Sky falls to earth, and Mars flies about in confusion. Toppled, I turn a somersault and suddenly pass beyond the ring of iron [mountains encircling Mt. Sumeru in the Buddhist cosmology].' His everyday course of study was the *Perfect Awakening* and *Heroic Progress Samadhi*. The Master himself said: 'I have experienced the *Heroic Progress Samadhi*—there are parts where I cannot help laughing.'" Chūshin has a quatrain dedicated to Zongmi at 750b17–20.

174. See note 8.

175. For a translation, see Xixia, appendix 2.

176. Yanagida, *Daruma no goroku*, 68; *Zongjinglu*, T 48:939b25–26. The *Bodhidharma Anthology* attributes the saying to Tripitaka Dharma Master (*sanzang fashi*). The *Mind Mirror* gives it as: "The master Bodhidharmatara stated the *Dharma Gate of Quieting Mind [Anxin famen]*: 'When deluded, the person pursues dharmas [i.e., quickens his pace to catch up to dharmas]; when understanding, dharmas pursue the person [*mi shi ren zhu fa jie shi fa zhu ren*]. When understanding, consciousness [*vijñāna*] absorbs forms [*rūpa*]; when deluded, forms absorb consciousness [*jie ze shi she se mi ze se she shi*].'"

177. Shenhui's *Platform Talks*, which dates to 720–730, says: "The sixth-generation patriarchal master [Huineng] had a mind-to-mind transmission because he separated from the written word" (*Tōdai goroku kenkyūhan, Jinne no goroku: Dango*, 47). One scenario would be that Zongmi as a master in the Heze line inherited Shenhui's account, introduced a slight change in the second part, and made the attribution to Bodhidharma. Another early occurrence of the saying is in the *Xuemailun* (T 48:373b3–4), a so-called Bodhidharma apocryphon. Unfortunately, we have no dates for this text, but it probably emerged around Zongmi's time. At the very least we can say that Zongmi was one of the first, if not the very first, to propagate the famous Bodhidharma slogan.

178. "*xianzong pozhi gu you siyan fei li wenzi shuo jietuo ye.*"

179. T 48:660a5–8.

180. *Bai Juyi ji*, 2:31.698. The third couplet in italics is: "*jinli wenzi fei zhongdao / chang zhu xukong shi xiaosheng*." Two other heptasyllabic regulated verse by Bai are of interest to students of Zongmi. The first (2:32.716), which is entitled "On Reading a Chan Sutra," mentions "forgetting words" (*wangyan*) in a way reminiscent of the *Chan Prolegomenon* (section 8) and uses the same quotation from the apocryphal sutra *Jingang sanmei jing* (*Vajrasamadhi Sutra*) that Zongmi uses in section 31 in support of the one-practice samadhi:

> You must know that all characteristics are non-characteristics.
> If you are fixed in [the nirvana] without residue, it is with residue.
> Suddenly to forget words is all-at-once understanding.
> In a dream to speak dream is a twofold falsity.
> With an illusionary flower in the sky why would you simultaneously try
>   to get the fruit?
> With the river willows all ablaze why would you keep looking for river fish?
> Perturbations are Chan—Chan is movement.
> No Chan, no movement—that is tathata.

The second (also 2:31.698), which is entitled "Seeing Off the Four Superior Men Zhao, Mi, Xian, and Shi," celebrates the banquet in 833 that Bai gave at his Luoyang estate for Luoyang Shenzhao, Zongmi, and two of Shenzhao's disciples. The Heze master Shenzhao, a fellow Sichuanese, was a fellow student of Zongmi's master, Daoyuan, under Nanyin/Weizhong (see the chart in the *Chan Letter*, section 7). Bai, who had sought retirement in a "Luoyang assignment" as a court official, that is, a Regency official in the top echelons of the bureaucracy, spoke of himself as "a middle hermit" (*zhongyin*) between the great hermit who dwells at the court and in the market (active service in Chang'an) and the small hermit who retreats to a hut in the mountains (complete withdrawal from public life). See Stephen Owen, *The Late Tang: Chinese Poetry of the Mid-Ninth Century (827–860)* (Cambridge, Mass.: Harvard University Asia Center, 2006), 47–48. After the dinner, Bai muses about what to offer as a gift to the Chan monks:

> A purple-robed court scholar, an old man with white hair,
> Unfamiliar with the conventional world, but in touch with the path.
> With official rank three times down to Luoyang,
> In friendly contacts one half among monks.
> Smelly, old rag of a world—in the end must get out;
> Burning incense, *pratītya-samutpāda* [origination by dependence]—
>   long vowed to unite with them.
> After this vegetarian cuisine, what can I use to serve as an offering?
> The west veranda's spring and rocks, the north window's breeze.

1. TRANSLATION OF THE *CHAN LETTER*

1. This is the title of the text in Kamata, 267. The section numbers are from Kamata; at the beginning of each section I have supplied a summary of its contents in my own words. Passages in italics within parentheses are Zongmi's autocommentary.

2. This official title for a Buddhist monk (*nei gongfeng*) was established in Zhide 1 (=756) of the Tang.

3. This is the title of the text in Shinpuku-ji, 77.

4. In fact, not many years later, in the 840s, Pei did compose a Chan record dealing with the Hongzhou house (actually two), the *Chuanxin fayao* and *Wanlinglu*, but he did not publish this work until 857.

5. Shinpuku-ji, 77, retains more of the epistolary trappings of the original correspondence.

6. There is a question as to whether *zhuanji* is the title of a text (the *Transmission Record*) or simply should be translated as "transmission records." In the former case, the title probably is a lost record of the Shenhui line, and both Kamata, 269, and Ishii Shudō, trans., *Zen goroku*, Daijō butten Chūgoku Nihon hen 12 (Tokyo: Chuōkōronsha, 1992), 293, understand it this way. In the latter case, it could refer to various biographical records in circulation in Zongmi's time, each giving an account *only* of its own line of descent. (Kamata, 279, thinks it is different from the *Zuzong zhuanji* mentioned in section 4.) Nishida Tatsuo, *Seikabun Kegonkyō* (Kyoto: Kyoto daigaku bungaku-bu, 1977), 1:21, gives a Japanese translation of the Tangut translation of this passage that reads: "Previous narrations are histories [that is, genealogies] of the sudden-sudden lineage." I assume "sudden-sudden" refers to the Huineng line. In short, the passage is quite unclear but important.

7. Note the emphasis upon Chan teachings as oral teachings, teachings by word of mouth (*yanjiao*=*pravacana*). This term appears in the *Lotus Sutra* (T 9:5c1–3), where it refers to the preaching of the Buddha: "Śāriputra! Since I have become a buddha, through various conditions and various metaphors I have widely developed oral teachings, and through innumerable teaching devices I have led sentient beings to divorce from attachments."

8. See *Chan Notes*, section 5.

9. Huiyong/Huirong is also known as Fayong/Farong (594–657).

10. Zhiwei (646–722) has an entry in the *Song gaoseng zhuan* (T 50:758b–c). His master Fachi at thirteen heard of Hongren of East Mountain, visited him, and received instruction in his dharma essentials (*Song gaoseng zhuan* Fachi entry, T 50:757c4–5). This may be the beginning of the connection between the East Mountain and Niutou lineages.

11. Masu is also known as Xuansu or Yuansu (668–752). He has an entry in the *Song gaoseng zhuan* (T 50:761c–762b) and an inscription by Li Hua (QTW 7:320.4106b–4108b).

12. Jingshan Daoqin is also known as Faqin (714–793). He has an entry in the *Song gaoseng zhuan* (T 50:764b–765a) and an inscription by Li Jifu (QTW 11:512.6599a–6601a).

13. See *Chan Notes*, section 1.

14. See *Chan Notes*, section 1.

15. Presumably refers to the *Yuanjuejing dashu chao*, ZZ 1.14.3.277b5–6; CBETA *Wan Xuzangjing*, vol. 9, no. 245:532b20[01]. This commentary dates to about 823 or 824, about a decade earlier than the *Chan Letter*.

16. This *Zuzong zhuanji* appears to be a lost transmission record of the Heze lineage, corresponding to the transmission records of other lineages, such as the *Lidai fabao ji*, *Lengjia shizi ji*, etc. Much of this literature, which was probably extensive in the eighth and early ninth centuries, was lost. Some of it was retrieved from the manuscripts found in the Dunhuang cave complex in the early twentieth century.

17. This line (*"zhe shaer zheng gan quci yu"*) contains two elements of old *baihua*, the vernacular-based literary language so prevalent in Chan literature after the time of Zongmi. Jiang Lansheng and Cao Guangshun, eds., *Tang Wudai yuyan cidian* (Shanghai: Shanghai jiaoyu chubanshe, 1997), 436, states of *"zhe"*: "Used as a close indicating pronoun ["this"], pronounced *zhe* [in the falling/fourth tone]." This dictionary goes on to say that in Tang and Song times, three characters read *"zhe"* were used as "this" in a mixed-up way. Iriya Yoshitaka and Koga Hidehiko, *Zengo jiten* (Kyoto: Shibunkaku shuppan, 1991), 195, defines *"quci"* as "random"; "haphazard"; "wild"; "grandstand play"; "playing to the gallery"; "thoughtlessly"; "offhand."

18. Yao and Shun are ancient sage-kings. Yao consulted Shun on all the affairs of state, examined his words, and found that they could be carried into practice. Previously Yao had given Shun his daughters in marriage in order to observe Shun's behavior.

19. "Twenty years" is presumably a cryptic reference to Shenhui's attack on the Northern lineage starting in Kaiyuan 20 (732).

20. The *Sōkei daishi den* (*Biography of the Great Master Caoqi*), a manuscript brought back to Japan by Saichō in 803 and stored at Enryaku-ji on Mt. Hiei, says of Xingtao: "In that year [713] the assembly requested the preeminent disciple Xingtao to guard the transmitted robe. [He did so] for forty-five years." Ishii Shudō, "*Sōkei daishi den* kō," *Komazawa daigaku Bukkyō gakubu kenkyū kiyō* 46 (March 1988): 103; Ishii, *Zen goroku*, 33. The *Sōkei daishi den* embodies the image of Huineng handed down within Xingtao's line. Nothing is known of Chaosu. At its end the Dunhuang manuscript *Platform Sutra* claims Fahai as the compiler: "This *Platform Sutra* was compiled by the head monk Fahai, who on his death handed it over to his fellow student Daocan. After Daocan died it was handed over to his disciple Wuzhen. Wuzhen resides at the Faxing Temple at Mount Caoqi in Lingnan [Guangzhou-Guangxi], and as of now he is transmitting this dharma" (T 48:345b1–4; Philip B. Yampolsky, *The Platform Sutra of the Sixth Patriarch* [New York: Columbia University Press, 1967],

182). The two names in the Fahai line are unidentified. The *Platform Sutra* embodies the image of Huineng handed down within Fahai's line.

21. "Seven temples" refers to the Chou system of state ancestral temples described in the Wangzhi section of the *Book of Rites*. The temple of the founder occupies the central position. Beneath his, the second, fourth, and sixth generations are arranged on the left and called "*zhao*"; the third, fifth, and seventh generations are arranged on the right and called "*mu*."

22. The Wangzhi section of the *Book of Rites* states that the Son of Heaven is encoffined on the seventh day and buried in the seventh month.

23. These are the seven buddhas of the past, Śākyamuni and the six who appeared before him. The first three are said to be the three buddhas of the past adornment kalpa, the last four the four buddhas of the present fortunate kalpa.

24. The *Sukhavati Array Sutra*, T 12:347b, says: "If there is a good son or good daughter who, hearing talk of Amitābha Buddha, holds to the name, whether for one day, two days, three days, four days, five days, six days, or seven days, with one mind undisturbed, for this person, on the verge of the end of life, Amitābha Buddha and the assembly of noble ones will appear before him, and this person's mind at the end will not be topsy-turvy. He will attain rebirth in the land of extreme joy of Amitābha Buddha."

25. When someone is receiving the full precepts, a master to confer the precepts, a master to teach the regulations, a master to teach the ceremonies and forms, and seven ordained monks to serve as authenticators are necessary. These are referred to as the three masters and seven authenticators.

26. Perhaps this refers to the seven usages for governing the monks: censure, expulsion, etc.

27. The *Lotus Sutra*, T 9:61a, says: "They did the ceremony of touching Śākyamuni Buddha's feet to their heads and circumambulated him to the right seven times."

28. Yanagida Seizan, "Goroku no rekishi," *Tōhō gakuhō* 57 (March 1985): 445 and n. 493, cites an inscription for Huijian (719–792), a Shenhui disciple listed by Zongmi in his chart (section 7) as Jian of the western capital. This inscription, the *Tang gu Zhaosheng si dade Huijian chanshi beiming bing xu* by Xu Dai (found in Xi'an beilin, Tuban 103), states: "Also, receiving an imperial command, together with venerables, they distinguished the false and the correct of the buddha-dharma and set in order the two lineages of Southern and Northern." According to Yanagida, this is referring to Zongmi's imperial proclamation setting up Shenhui as the seventh patriarch.

29. Not extant.

30. See *Chan Notes*, section 4.

31. Again Chan teachings as oral teachings, teachings by word of mouth (*yanjiao*).

32. This slogan ("*yi xin chuan xin bu li wenzi*") may have begun with Zongmi. Another early occurrence is in an early-ninth-century work attributed to Bodhidharma, the *Xuemailun* (T 48:373b3–4).

33. This term derives from the *Dasheng qixin lun*, T 32:576b.

34. *Vimalakīrti Sutra*, T 14:543b: "The inexhaustible torch is like one torch lighting up a hundred thousand torches."

35. *Vimalakīrti Sutra*, T 14:538a.

36. See *Chan Prolegomenon*, section 5.

37. According to Jiang and Cao eds., *Tang Wudai yuyan cidian*, 315, *ranshi* = "after this/after that." A synonym is *ranhou*.

38. Again Chan teachings as oral teachings, teachings by word of mouth (*yanjiao*).

39. Zongmi is quoting Shenxiu's verse in the *Platform Sutra*, though he nowhere in his Chan works mentions that text by title. See Yampolsky, *The Platform Sutra*, 130. Chengguan's *Da fangguang fohuayan jing suishu yanyi chao*, T 36:164c, quotes the last two lines of both Shenxiu's verse and Huineng's verse, adding after the latter: "This is the sixth patriarch's directly revealing the original nature and eradicating this gradual practice."

40. Zhiyan's *Da fangguang fohuayan jing souxuan fenji tongzhi fanggui*, T 35:62c25–27, says: "In dharma sphere origination-by-dependence there are many [aspects]. Now, using the gate of essentials, I will reduce them to two. The first is to distinguish origination-by-dependence according to the impure dharmas of the common person. The second is to clarify origination-by-dependence according to the pure portion of awakening."

41. Presumably refers to sections 2 and 3 of the *Chan Notes*.

42. Zongmi has patched together two quotations from the sutra: T 16:510b4–5 and 512b16–17.

43. T 16:480a.

44. T 16:493a27–b1.

45. Following Shinpuku-ji, 85.

46. Corroboration of the vocabulary of Zongmi's appraisal of Hongzhou can be found in two Hongzhou works by Zongmi's lay disciple Pei Xiu, the *Chuanxin fayao* and *Wanlinglu*. For example, in Pei's classic we find: "Do not take mind to pursue mind" (*bu ke jiang xin geng qiu yu xin*), etc.; "as it is everything is right" (*zhixia bian shi*); "give free rein to luck and don't get caught up" (*renyun bu ju*); "all day long give free rein to luck and ascend energetically" (*zhongri renyun tengteng*); and "the mind nature is without difference" (*xinxing bu yi*). See T 48:380c9, 381b1, 382c14, 380b18, 384a17, 386c5–6, and 384b27–28; Iriya Yoshitaka, ed. and trans., *Denshin hōyō Enryōroku*, Zen no goroku 8 (Tokyo: Chikuma shobō, 1969), 20, 30, 61, 19, 90, 135, and 97. There is also a *Jiangxi Mazu Daoyi chanshi yulu* found in the Northern Song collection *Sijia yulu* (ZZ 2.24.5; CBETA *Wan Xuzangjing* vol. 69, no. 1321; Iriya Yoshitaka, ed. and trans., *Baso no goroku* [Kyoto: Zen bunka kenkyūjo, 1984], 1–119), and it also shows parallels to these themes. However, it seems not to have circulated as an independent text and is dated 1085.

47. *Mohe banruo boluomi jing*, T 8:276b.

48. *Banruo boluomiduo xin jing,* T 8:848c.

49. The likely place to look for corroboration of this appraisal of Niutou is the Dunhuang text *Jueguanlun,* which is quoted under Niutou's name in three tenth-century Chan texts: *Zutangji* (Yanagida, *Sodōshū,* 52b–53a); Yanshou's *Zongjinglu* (T 48:463b10–13); and Yanshou's *Wanshan tonggui ji* (T 48:974b5–6). Whether or not we accept this attribution, it is noteworthy that the *Jueguanlun* discusses *wushi* ("having nothing to do"), which Zongmi considered to be the essential idea of the Niutou house. See sections X.7–8 of Tokiwa Gishin and Yanagida Seizan, eds. and trans., *Zekkanron* (Kyoto: Zen bunka kenkyūjo, 1973), 93.

50. The term is *"kanhui."* Ishii, *Zen goroku,* 60, renders this line: "My nature is such that I am not satisfied until I have corroborated something with my own eyes."

51. Chengguan's *Huayan xinyao famen* (ZZ 2.8.4.303a; CBETA *Wan Xuxangjing* vol. 58, no. 1005:426a10[00]–11[00]) opens with: "The ultimate path is rooted in the mind. Mind and dharmas are rooted in the non-abiding. The non-abiding mind substance is a spiritual Knowing that never darkens." Heze Chan according to Zongmi is built on this Knowing, and we find it as Shenhui's most basic teaching in his *Platform Talks (Tanyu):* "The basic substance is void and calm *[benti kongji],* and from that void and calm substance there arises Knowing *[cong kongji ti shang qi zhi]*" (Tōdai goroku kenkyūhan, ed., *Jinne no goroku: Dango* [Kyoto: Zen bunka kenkyūjo, 2006], 84).

52. Shinpuku-ji, 87, reads: "This Knowing of voidness and calm is precisely the mind of purity that Bodhidharma formerly transmitted." In other words, the buddha-in-embryo or intrinsically pure mind of Bodhidharma's teaching is identical to the Knowing of Heze Chan.

53. Chengguan's *Da fangguang fohuayan jing suishu yanyi chao,* T 36:262a5, is an early instance of this slogan. In the background is *Laozi,* 1.

54. The earliest extant Chan cross-legged sitting manual, Zongze's *Zuochan yi,* which is found in his *Chanyuan qinggui* of 1103, incorporates this line (*"nian qi ji jue jue zhi ji wu"*) as the essence of Chan sitting: "If a thought arises, be aware of it; once you are aware of it, it will be lost *[nian qi ji jue jue zhi ji shi].* After you have for a long time forgotten objective supports, you will spontaneously become integrated *[zicheng yipian].* This is the essential art *[yaoshu]* of Chan sitting" (Kagamishima Genryū and others, trans., *Yakuchū Zen'en shingi* [Tokyo: Sōtōshū shūmuchō, 1972], 281).

55. The themes of this section are corroborated by Shenhui's *Platform Talks.* See Tōdai goroku kenkyūhan, ed., *Jinne no goroku: Dango,* 84.

56. *Dasheng qixin lun,* T 32:576a.

57. The following is based on the thought-gem simile in the *Yuanjuejing,* T 17:914c. There the thought gem reflects five colors, and the ignorant ones think that the gem really has the five colors.

58. The mirror knowledge (*dayuan jingzhi*) is the first of the four types of knowledge that emerge from the eight consciousnesses when the defilements are destroyed and awakening attained. Mirror knowledge is the name given to the store-

house consciousness, the eighth consciousness, in the stage of buddhahood when it is free from all possible defilements and is so called because it resembles a mirror that reflects all things in their true state.

59. *Yuanjuejing,* T 17:919b21–22.

60. Following Shinpuku-ji, 89. Jiang and Cao, eds., *Tang Wudai yuyan cidian,* 256, says of the old-*baihua* pronoun "*mouyi*": "The first-person pronoun, equivalent to *moujia,* first appearing during the Tang period."

61. Following Shinpuku-ji, 90.

62. See the *Śrīmālā Sutra,* T 12:221c17–18.

63. Based on *Nirvana Sutra,* T 12:395b–c.

64. Following Shinpuku-ji, 91.

65. Following Shinpuku-ji, 91.

66. *Thunderbolt-Cutter Sutra,* T 8:749a24.

67. Following Shinpuku-ji, 92.

68. Iriya and Koga, *Zengo jiten,* 334–35, defines "*dangti*" as "the very thing-in-itself," adding that it was a technical term much favored from the late Tang to the Song.

69. *Huayan Sutra,* T 10:69a.

70. In Pei Xiu's *Chuanxin fayao* (T 48:381a22–23; Iriya, *Denshin hōyō,* 30) the Hong-zhou master Huangbo Xiyun does use this term "*lingjue*": "This spiritual awakening nature [*ci lingjuexing*] from time without beginning is as old as space. It has never arisen, never disappeared." Also, Yanshou's *Zongjinglu* (T 48:492a19) contains a lengthy Mazu saying with a very similar line: "But the nature of spiritual awakening [*lingjue zhi xing*] really has no arising-disappearing." Obviously, Pei Xiu at this time, the early 830s, is already familiar with and somewhat sympathetic to Hongzhou teachings. This is well before his contact with Xiyun in the 840s after Zongmi's death.

71. The expression "*keti*" is a variant of "*dangti*." See section 20.

72. See note 51.

73. See note 69.

74. Following Shinpuku-ji, 94.

75. These are two of the three sources of knowledge (*san liang*) in Buddhist logic: inference (*biliang*); direct perception (*xianliang*); and buddha word (*foyanliang*).

76. See *Nirvana Sutra,* T 12:617a–b.

77. T 14:549c5.

78. *Nirvana Sutra,* T 12:693a1.

79. This god inhabits the third heaven of the first dhyana in the realm of form.

80. The first ten stages of the fifty-two stages of the bodhisattva path.

81. The *Da zhidu lun,* T 25:134a1–2, lists them as: gold, silver, lapis lazuli, quartz, coral, emerald, and pearl. *Lotus Sutra,* T 9:8c18–19, has a slightly different list.

82. The five precepts are: no killing living things, no stealing, no illicit sexual activity, no speaking false words, and no intoxicants. The ten good actions are: no kill-

ing living things, no stealing, no illicit sexual activity, no speaking false words, no flowery language, no slander, no double-tongued speech, no greed, no hatred, and no false views.

83. For instance, *Lotus Sutra*, T 9:54a.

84. From this point through note 86, the translation is working from Shinpuku-ji, 96.11–97.12.

85. *Laozi*, 48.

86. From this point the translation reverts from Shinpuku-ji (97.12) to Kamata's edition (341.8).

87. Buddhas and bodhisattvas in order to transform sentient beings rely on super-human powers to manifest various forms and activities. Examples include: walking, standing, sitting, and lying in the sky; manifesting a gigantic body that fills the sky; etc. See *Lotus Sutra*, T 9:60a.

88. *Yuanjuejing*, T 17:917c15–16.

89. Shinpuku-ji, 98–104, includes three more sections of questions to Zongmi from three laymen. It concludes with the title *Pei Xiu shiyi wen* (*Imperial Redactor Pei Xiu's Inquiry*).

2. TRANSLATION OF THE *CHAN PROLEGOMENON*

1. This alternate title reflects the continuing influence of the *Bodhidharma Anthology*'s dichotomy of entrance by principle (*liru*) and entrance by practice (*xingru*). See Yanagida Seizan, ed. and trans., *Daruma no goroku*, Zen no goroku 1 (Tokyo: Chikuma shobō, 1969), 31. The Gozan edition of Ishii (2), 51–52, does not have this subtitle. The section numbers are from Kamata; at the beginning of each section I have supplied a summary of its contents in my own words. Passages in italics within parentheses are Zongmi's autocommentary.

2. Mt. Zhongnan, the main summit of the Qinling Range that divides northern China from central China, was about fifteen miles south of the capital Chang'an in Shaanxi. Caotang Monastery was in the neighborhood of Gui Peak (Guifeng), Zongmi coming to be known as Guifeng Zongmi. His teacher Chengguan had done commentarial work at the Caotang.

3. Zongmi assumes that the oral teachings of Chan (*yanjiao*) are eventually transcribed as "written words and lines of verse [*wenzi juji*]." These poetic transcriptions are what he has collected in his *Chan Canon*. The "*ju*" refers to a "line of poetry" or "phrase," the "*ji*" to a gatha, a type of four-line verse common in the sutras and treatises. In regulated verse the five-syllable line was called the "short line" (*duanju*) and the seven-syllable line the "long line" (*changju*). The last couplet of a Bai Juyi poem (Bai Juyi, *Bai Juyi ji* [Beijing: Zhonghua shuju, 1979], 2:28.633) gives us an example of the type of Chan-flavored poetic line Zongmi probably had in mind: "I just chant one

line of a gatha [*yi juji*]: 'No mindfulness is no arising.'" The Gozan edition of Ishii (2), 52, adds "songs and secret formulas [*gejue*]."

4. This criticism seems to be aimed at the Hongzhou lineage. Hongzhou *just* declares that every type of passion, hatred, precept holding, concentration, etc. is the functioning of the buddha nature. Thus, no distinctions exist, and they decline to pick and choose. See *Chan Letter*, section 22.

5. T 24:1003c.

6. The sixteen viewings are found in the *Guan Wuliangshoufo jing*, T 12:342aff. They include the sun visualization, the water visualization, etc. This sutra says one attains the buddha-recitation concentration during the eighth viewing, a visualization of Amitābha's form. The engendered concentration (*banzhou sanmei=pratyutpanna-samadhi*) is a concentration in which all the buddhas are manifested before the practitioner. Tiantai calls it the constantly walking concentration, one of its four concentrations. See *Mohe zhiguan*, T 46:12a.

7. Refers to the non-Buddhist teachings and adherents of ancient India, specifically the six non-Buddhist teachers and ninety-five non-Buddhist views.

8. Nanyue Huisi (515–577) was the second patriarch in the Tiantai lineage. Tiantai Zhiyi (538–592), the third Tiantai patriarch, was responsible for the creation of the main center of Tiantai on Mt. Tiantai in Zhejiang. The three truths are the voidness truth (*kongdi*), the provisional truth (*jiadi*), and the middle truth (*zhongdi*). The three tranquillizations and three viewings refer to Tiantai meditation practice based on the three truths.

9. It is unclear just what standard or proof Zongmi has in mind. Kamata, 29, thinks that it is a copy of the *Platform Sutra*, but I am not convinced. Ishii (2), 67, says that, judging from section 30, "standard" is referring to Shenhui's word "Knowing [*zhi*]." In the two other instances of this word "*ping*" (*you suoping*) in the *Chan Prolegomenon* it means an inked marking string used by a skilled woodworker to determine the false and correct (used as a simile for the sutras in section 13) and buddha word (the sutras), the third of the three sources of knowledge of Buddhist logic (section 15).

10. T 14:545b3–4.

11. In the first month of 821 Zongmi withdrew to Caotang Monastery on Mt. Zhongnan south of Chang'an. He lived there until 832, with the exception of the two-year interval from 828 to 829, when he served at the court of Emperor Wenzong. Thus, the earlier stay lasted seven years and the later about three.

12. The eight classes are: devas (gods); nagas (snakes); yaksas (dwarfs with protuberant bellies); musicians of the gods; asuras (titans); birds with golden wings; singers and musicians of the gods with the body of a man and head of a horse; and demons shaped like snakes.

13. This is a very informative generalization about Chan literature. Chan catches the essence of the teachings of Buddhism as poetry, just as gathas (*ji*) summarize the

prose portions of sutras, and Chan is geared to the temperaments and preferences of China. In short, *Chan literature is a form of Chinese poetry.*

14. The three worthies (*san xian*) are: the ten abodes (*shi zhu*), the ten degrees of conduct (*shi xing*), and the ten diversions (*shi hui*). See Leon Hurvitz, *Chih-I: An Introduction to the Life and Ideas of a Chinese Buddhist Monk*, Mélanges chinois et bouddhiques 12 (Brussels: l'Institut Belge des Hautes Études Chinoises, 1962), 363–66. The ten stages (*shi di*) of the bodhisattva are: joyous, free-from-defilement, illumining, flaming-wisdom, impossible-to-conquer, become-manifest, far-going, immovable, good-wisdom, and dharma-cloud. See Har Dayal, *The Bodhisattva Doctrine in Buddhist Sanskrit Literature* (Delhi: Motilal Banarsidass, 1970), 283–291. The thirty-seven parts of the path (*sanshiqi daopin*) are the thirty-seven practices and principles conducive to the attainment of awakening: four stations of mindfulness (*si nianchu*); four right exertions (*si zhengqin*); four bases of magical power (*si ruyizu*); five faculties (*wu gen*); five powers (*wu li*); seven limbs of awakening (*qi juezhi*); and noble eightfold path (*ba zhengdao*). See Dayal, *The Bodhisattva Doctrine*, 80–164. Four perfections (good skill in means [*fangbian shanqiao*]; vow [*yuan*]; power [*li*]; and knowledge [*zhi*]) were added to the usual six in order to fit with the ten stages. The bodhisattva emphasizes one perfection in each stage. See Dayal, *The Bodhisattva Doctrine*, 248–69.

15. The *Eighty Huayan* or *New Translation Huayan* (T no. 279) is divided into nine assemblies (*jiu hui*) (Daizōkyō, 79–80). The stages are the forty-one stages (*sishiyi wei*) of the bodhisattva.

16. At least one copy of the *Chan Canon* must have been in existence for the questioner to browse through. It is interesting that the questioner says that most of the Chan writings are in the format of question piled upon question (*suiwen fanzhi*). This format, in which the disciple does the questioning and the preceptor gives the answers, is richly represented in the Dunhuang manuscript finds. Examples include the *Jueguanlun*, *Dunwu zhenzong yaojue*, *Dunwu zhenzong lun*, *Dunwu dasheng zhengli jue*, *Wuxinlun*, etc. Apparently this was a preferred genre within Chan virtually from the beginning. The preceptor's answers are always geared to the disposition of the disciple.

17. *Zhuangzi*, Waiwu: "The reason for words lies in the idea. Get the idea and forget the words [*de yi er wang yan*]."

18. Ānanda was the only major disciple who had not become an arhat by the time of the Buddha's complete nirvana. Mahākāśyapa rebuked him and would not allow him to attend the first council. During the night Ānanda achieved knowledge of destruction of the outflows, tantamount to release from the rebirth process, and hence was admitted. He proceeded to recite the discourses of the Buddha from memory.

19. The assumption here is that Chan instruction generally follows a question-and-answer format. Masters-to-be will be able to study the *Chan Canon* and pick up pointers about how to answer questions by reading transcripts of previous dialogues.

20. Zongmi may be critical of Hongzhou and repeat Shenhui's criticism of so-called Northern Chan, but I think it can be said that this sort of tolerance is the core of his response to all the various teachings and practices of the Chan lineages.

21. The questioner's use of the word "present/now [*jin*]" once again supports the conclusion that a copy of the *Chan Canon* was indeed in existence at the time, the early 830s. Given its huge size it is quite possible that very few copies, or even just one, were executed before Zongmi's death in 841.

22. For a table of the Indian patriarchs according to various sources, see Philip B. Yampolsky, *The Platform Sutra of the Sixth Patriarch* (New York: Columbia University Press, 1967), 8–9. Mahākāśyapa is usually listed as the first patriarch. Upagupta, a Sarvāstivādin at the time of King Aśoka, is listed as either the fourth or fifth.

23. Dhrtaka is listed as the fifth or sixth patriarch.

24. Refers to a story in the *Fufa zang yinyuan zhuan*, T 50:321c14–18: "Also there was a monk by the name of Simha. In Kashmir he did great things for Buddhism. At the time that country's king was named Miluojue. His false views were numerous, and his mind lacked faith. In Kashmir he destroyed stupas and monasteries and killed off monks. He then took a sharp sword and beheaded Simha. From the head there was no blood; just milk flowed out. The transmission of the dharma with this was cut off." Thus, Simha was the twenty-third and final patriarch.

25. Asvaghosa is the eleventh or twelfth and Nagarjuna the thirteenth or fourteenth, depending on the Chan source.

26. See *Chan Letter*, note 32.

27. The *Thunderbolt-Cutter Sutra* is closely associated with Huineng in the *Platform Sutra*. See Yampolsky, *The Platform Sutra*, 127, 133, 149, and 151. The sacred history *Lengjia shizi ji* by its very title is a record of the transmission of the *Lanka Descent Sutra*.

28. See the *Chan Notes* for the seven Chan lineages: Jiangxi (=Hongzhou); Heze; Northern (Bei-Xiu); Shen in the South (Nan-Shen=Zhishen of the South=Jingzhong); Niutou; Baotang; and Xuanshi (=South Mountain Buddha–Recitation Gate Chan Lineage). Huichou-Gunabhadra and Tiantai are non-Bodhidharma lineages. Huichou was a disciple of the Central Indian master Buddhabhadra (359–429), who arrived in Chang'an in 408. The South Indian Gunabhadra (394–468) arrived by ship in Guangzhou in 435. He translated many works, including the *Lanka Descent Sutra* (T no. 670). The *Lengjia shizi ji* considers him the first patriarch, with Bodhidharma as the second (T 85:1283c23; Yanagida I, 93). These two lineages are mentioned again in section 22. Tiantai refers to the lineage of Zhiyi (538–592). This is the only mention of the Shitou lineage in Zongmi's Chan works. Shitou Xiqian (700–790) has an entry in the *Song gaoseng zhuan*, T 50:763c–764a. It is said there that early he had contact with Huineng and eventually became the successor of Qingyuan Xingsi, a disciple of Huineng. Apparently, Zongmi knew virtually nothing of this line or its teachings.

29. In the *Heroic Progress Samadhi Sutra* (T 29:124b7–132c26), twenty-five bodhisattvas and arhats attain perfect penetration (*yuantong*) by means of various *upā-
yas*. Among them Avalokiteśvara Bodhisattva, who attains awakening via the ear sense
organ (*ergen*), is considered the highest. The term *"yuantong"* also appears in sections
14 and 58.

30. The term *"kanhui"* also appears in the *Chan Letter* (see note 50), where
Zongmi says by nature he likes "checking and verifying." Kamata, 55, interprets it
here as "checking actual practice against the sutra texts." Ishii (2), 99, glosses it as a
"comparative investigation of the content of the sutras and one's own position."

31. Gozan edition of Ishii (2), 101, reads: *"shi yu zhi"* ("in ten-plus sheets").

32. This refers to the section of transcriptions of sutra passages in the *Chan Canon*.
In section 58 Zongmi remarks that these sutra passages come at the end of the *Chan
Canon*, following the miscellaneous writings of the Chan houses.

33. The term *"kanqi"* refers to the Tang security system for opening and closing
palace gates. There was a fish key (*yuqi*), a piece of wood carved into the shape of a
fish and ornamented with metal fish scales, and a plank of wood with a cavity carved
to the exact shape of the fish. The former was in the possession of the gate functionary
and the latter inside the palace. At the necessary time the lock was activated by placing the fish into the cavity. If they *coincided*, the gate was opened.

34. Three exegetes of Zongmi's time are Shenqing, Duanfu, and Zhixuan. They
have biographical entries in the *Song gaoseng zhuan* (T 50:740c–741a; 741a–c; and
743b–744c). An example of a scholar's doubts about Chan is found in Shenqing's 806
Beishanlu (T 52:612c11–13): "There is a deviant theory [*yishuo*]: 'The origin of sin and
merit is just mind, and that is all. When mind extinguishes, there is no action. The
path lies in having nothing to do. No obeisance and praises, no lecturing and chanting [*bu lizan bu jiangsong*], that is true non-action. No supplications [of the buddhas
and bodhisattvas] and precepts, no guarding against sin [*bu zijie bu huzui*], that is true
freedom from characteristics.'" The target here is probably Baotang Chan, since
Shenqing was associated with Jingzhong.

35. The *Sōkei daishi den* has Huineng telling Shenhui: "If I transmit this robe, the
person to whom the dharma is transmitted will have a short life. If I do not transmit
this robe, my dharma will broadly flourish. Keep the robe protected at Caoqi. Seventy
years after my death bodhisattvas will come from the East. One, a lay bodhisattva,
will repair the temple. A second, a monk bodhisattva, will once again establish my
teaching" (Ishii Shudō, "*Sōkei daishi den* kō," *Komazawa daigaku Bukkyō gakubu
kenkyū kiyō* 46 [March 1988]: 100; Ishii Shudō, trans., *Zen goroku*, Daijō butten
Chūgoku Nihon hen 12 [Tokyo: Chuōkōronsha, 1992], 30). The Dunhuang manuscript *Platform Sutra* has: "The Great Master [Huineng] said: 'The dharma has already been handed over. You need not ask about that. Twenty-plus years after I die a
false dharma will run rampant and will cast doubt on my axiom purport. Someone
will come forward and, at the risk of his life, fix the right and wrong in the teachings

of the buddhas and establish the axiom purport. This will be my true dharma. The robe should not be handed down. In case you do not trust in me, I shall recite the verses of the five previous generations of patriarchs, recited when they transmitted the robe and handed over the dharma. If you depend on the meaning of the verse of the first patriarch Bodhidharma, you should not transmit the robe. Hear the five verses as I recite them to you'" (T 48:344a18–23; Yampolsky, *The Platform Sutra*, 176).

36. See *Chan Letter*, note 32.

37. T 14:539c19–20.

38. In Shenhui works a set of four slogans is criticized as the defective teaching of the "Northern" masters Puji and Xiangmo Zang: "Freeze mind and enter concentration [*ningxin ruding*]; abide in mind and gaze at purity; produce mind and illuminate the external; collect mind and realize the internal." Shenhui says that these slogans constitute an obstruction to awakening. See Hu Shih, ed., *Shenhui heshang yiji* (Taipei: Hu Shi jinian guan, 1968), 133–34; 175–76; 239–40; and 287–88. In time the Northern-Southern context was dropped and new targets provided. Here one half-line is being employed by a Chan follower to criticize Zongmi for his emphasis on sitting.

39. No such passage appears in the *Platform Sutra*. In the *Sōkei daishi den* Huineng strikes the thirteen-year-old novice Shenhui during a dialogue. Ishii, "*Sōkei daishi den* kō," 94; Ishii, *Zen goroku*, 22.

40. *Dasheng qixin lun*, T 32:575c20–21: "As to Mahayana, altogether we speak of the existence of two types. What are the two? The first is dharma and the second is principles."

41. *Wuliangyi jing*, T 9:385c24.

42. *Dasheng qixin lun*, T 32:575c21–23: "The term "dharma" means sentient-being mind [that is, one mind]. This mind includes all mundane and supramundane dharmas. Grounded in this mind, the Mahayana principles are revealed."

43. The nature or dharma-nature axiom is based on the *Huayan Sutra*, *Perfect Awakening Sutra*, buddha-in-embryo sutras, *Lotus Sutra*, *Nirvana Sutra*, etc. The characteristics or dharma-characteristics axiom is Xuanzang's Yogācāra.

44. According to the characteristics axiom, consciousness transformation (*shi suobian*) is of three types: coming-to-fruition (*yishu*=ālaya-vijñāna); intellection (*siliang*=manas); and perception of sense objects (*liaobie jing shi*=six sense consciousnesses). These are the eight consciousnesses. See the characteristics-axiom textbook *Cheng weishi lun*, T 31:1a (Sanskrit equivalents at 60a–b).

45. Considered the compiler of the *Dasheng qixin lun*.

46. See note 42.

47. *Dasheng qixin lun*, T 32:576a.

48. See Rolf Homann, *Die wichtigsten Körpergottheiten im Huang-t'ing ching* (Goppingen: Verlag Alfred Kümmerle, 1971), 1–11. "Lump of flesh" (*routan*) is echoed in the *Linjilu* (T 47:496c10; Iriya, *Rinzairoku*, 20).

49. According to Hirakawa, 937, *yuanlü=adhyālambana* ("acquiring the support"). A late-eighteenth-century Korean commentary on the *Chan Prolegomenon*, the *Sŏnwŏn jejŏnjip tosŏ kwamok pyŏngip sagi* by Yŏndam Yuil remarks (Shūmitsu, 275): "For the *yuanlü* mind there is no Sanskrit." See introduction, note 143. Ishii (2), 119, notes that Zongmi was thinking of the Sanskrit term *"vijñāna."*

50. *Cheng weishi lun,* T 31:10a13–19: "Locus [*chu*] refers to place. It is the vessel world [*qi shijian*] because it is the locus that all sentient beings are grounded in. There are two graspings, the [karmic] seeds [*zhongzi*] and the organ body [*genshen*]. 'Seeds' refers to the habit energy of characteristics, names, and discriminations. 'Organ body' refers to the various sense organs and organ bases. These two are both grasped by the consciousnesses. Because [these two] are subsumed in the self substance [*ziti=ālaya-vijñāna*] as a unified existence, the [two] graspings and the locus both serve as [its] objective supports [*suoyuan*]. When the *ālaya-vijñāna*, because of the power of causes and conditions, arises as a self substance, within it transforms into the seeds and organ body, and without it transforms into the vessel [world]. It then takes these transformations as its own objective supports [*zi suoyuan*]."

51. *Dasheng qixin lun,* T 32:576b.

52. T 16:519a1–2.

53. T 12:221c11.

54. T 16:747a17–20.

55. In other words, both scholiasts lost in endless research in the canonical texts (*kongxun wenju*) and self-indulgent Chanists who trust only their own feelings and inclinations (*xin xiongjin*) fail to comprehend the one mind. Zongmi is saying that some Chan practitioners simply trust what they feel in their heart, without sensing a need to back that up with Buddha word (or perhaps even going so far as to consider the sutras irrelevant). I suspect that this criticism is directed at the Hongzhou practice (as presented by Zongmi) of "just giving free rein to mind" (*dan renxin* in *Chan Notes,* section 4, and *Chan Letter,* section 11) and "indulging the mind nature" (*zongren xinxing* in *Chan Notes,* section 5).

56. In the late eighth and early ninth centuries this was a burning issue not only in the Chinese world of Zongmi but in central Tibet and Tibetan-occupied areas of Central Asia as well. The so-called Council of Tibet is but one theater of this debate. It was certainly Zongmi's intention to dampen the conflict.

57. Refers to the thirty-two marks of the great person: having a head surmounted by an excrescence; body hairs one by one turning to the right, etc. A buddha's enjoyment body, visible only to bodhisattvas, bears these thirty-two marks and the eighty minor signs. See Hurvitz, *Chih-I,* 353–61.

58. See note 14.

59. The *Dasheng qixin lun,* T 32:577a and c, divides characteristics into three subtle and six coarse. The subtle are: the karma of ignorance, seer (subject), and sense objects.

These are root ignorance that is difficult to remove. The coarse are: knowledge, continuity, grasping, calculating names, production of karma, and suffering that results from karma. These are branch ignorance that is easy to eliminate.

60. *Dasheng qixin lun*, T 32:576b11–14.

61. Refers to the struggle between Xiang Yu, who belonged to a family of hereditary generals of the southern state of Chu, and Liu Bang, who received the title king of Han from Xiang Yu in 206 B.C.E. Four years later Liu Bang won out and called his dynasty Han.

62. Refers to washing the feet of previous lives and embarking on a new path. Ui, 257, thinks this metaphor may come from a folklore source. For the blind men and the elephant as a metaphor for mistaken perception, see *Nirvana Sutra*, T 12:556a12–21. A great king summons blind men and has them touch various parts of an elephant. The one who touches the tusk says an elephant is like a Japanese radish (*daikon*); the one who touches the ear says an elephant is like a winnowing basket; the one who touches the head says an elephant is like a stone, etc. The elephant is the buddha nature, and the blind men sentient beings of ignorance.

63. *Nirvana Sutra*, T 12:376c11–17. The three round marks of the letter *i* (*yuanyi san dian*) refers to the short *i* vowel in the Indic script known as *siddham* (*xitan*). According to Shizuka Jien, *Bonji shittan* (Osaka: Toki shobō, 1997), 10–19, there are many interpretations of the word "*siddham*"; in what region of India and in what period this script came into use is not entirely clear. In China "*siddham*" was used in Sanskrit-Chinese glossaries and to ensure the correct pronunciation of incantations. The beginning of *siddham* studies in China is Zhiguang's *Xitan zi ji*. We have no dates for this figure, but his work was brought back to Japan by Kūkai in 806, and many commentaries were compiled (Daizōkyō, 628). See R. H. van Gulik, *Siddham: An Essay on the History of Sanskrit Studies in China and Japan*, Śata-Pitaka Series 247 (1956; repr., New Delhi: International Academy of Indian Culture and Āditya Prakāshan, 2001), 22–36.

64. The term "*miyi*" refers to the secret meaning, the *real* meaning, as opposed to the prima facie or superficial meaning, of a text or teaching. In other words, there is a cryptic or esoteric meaning *behind* the first two teachings here; only the third teaching can be taken at face value. According to the *Cheng weishi lun*, T 31:48a4–6: "When the Buddha said that all dharmas have no self nature [*wu zixing*], it was not that [he meant] self nature is completely non-existent; speaking words of cryptic meaning is to reveal the incomplete teaching."

65. The phrase "*xiwang xiuxin*" involves a double abbreviation. The "*wang*" stands for "*wangxiang*" and the "*xin*" for "*weixin*." According to Hirakawa, 355 and 255, *wangxiang=vikalpa, abhūta-vikalpa*, etc., and *weixin=citta-mātra*. By employing Yogācāra terminology to name this Chan axiom, Zongmi is telegraphing its correspondence to the third subdivision of the first teaching, the teaching that takes consciousness to eradicate sense objects (section 26).

66. Once again we find the association between oral teachings, teachings by word of mouth (*yanjiao*), and Chan.

67. The term *"guanxin"* probably echoes the *Guanxinlun* by Shenxiu. This treatise, done during his Yuchuan Monastery period (676–700), eventually came to be attributed to Bodhidharma and presented as a dialogue between Bodhidharma and Huike. Numerous copies have been found among the Dunhuang manuscripts. See T no. 2833 and Suzuki Daisetsu, *Suzuki Daisetsu zenshū* (Tokyo: Iwanami shoten, 1968), 1:576–645.

68. Zongmi is quoting Shenxiu's verse in the *Platform Sutra.* See Yampolsky, *The Platform Sutra,* 130.

69. For all these lineages, see note 28.

70. This phrase, *"minjue wuji,"* appears under the rubric *"zhenkong guan* [viewing of true voidness]" in Dushun's *Fajie guanmen* as contained in Zongmi's commentary, the *Zhu huayan fajie guanmen,* T 45:684c27–28 and 686c5. A variant at 686c24 is *"jiongjue wuji* [distantly cut off and not leaning on anything]." Dushun/Fashun (557–640) is considered the first patriarch of Huayan. The variant also appears in Chengguan's *Huayan fajie xuanjing,* T 45:675c7. By employing Madhyamaka-style terminology to name this Chan axiom, Zongmi is telegraphing its correspondence to the second teaching, the teaching that eradicates characteristics to reveal the nature.

71. *Jueguanlun:* "All sentient beings are like an illusion, like a dream." Tokiwa Gishin and Yanagida Seizan, eds. and trans., *Zekkanron* (Kyoto: Zen bunka kenkyūjo, 1973), 99. See *Chan Letter,* note 49.

72. *Jueguanlun:* "There is neither buddha nor sentient being." Tokiwa and Yanagida, *Zekkanron,* 101.

73. *Mohe banruo boluomi jing,* T 8:276b7: "I say that even nirvana is like an illusion, like a dream."

74. *Thunderbolt-Cutter Sutra,* T 8:749a: "Whatever has characteristics is unreal."

75. *Jueguanlun:* "Question: 'Does having something to do [imply] having some sort of hindrance?' Answer: 'No hindrance is nothing to do [*wufang ji wushi*]. If you had nothing to do, what sort of hindrance would you have to ask about?'" (Tokiwa and Yanagida, *Zekkanron,* 93).

76. On Shitou, see note 28; on Niutou, see *Chan Notes,* section 5. The chart in *Chan Letter,* section 7, lists Daoqin of Mt. Jing in the Niutou lineage. See *Chan Letter,* note 12.

77. Numerous Daoist works are mentioned in Fayong's biographical entry in the *Xu gaoseng zhuan,* T 50:603c–5b. See Kamata Shigeo, "Sho Tō ni okeru sanronshū to dōkyō," *Tōyō bunka kenkyūjo kiyō* 46 (March 1968): 49–108; and Kamata Shigeo, "Sanronshū gozushū dōkyō o musubu shisō-teki keifu," *Komazawa daigaku Bukkyō gakubu kenkyū kiyō* 26 (March 1968): 79–89.

78. In other words, Heze, Hongzhou, and Tiantai use the *Perfection of Wisdom Sutras* and Madhyamaka terminology and turns of phrase, but these are not their "axiom realization," that is, their *zong/siddhānta.*

79. According to Hirakawa, 462, *xinxing=cittatā, citta-dharmatā, citta-svabhāva,* etc.

80. Corroboration of the following encapsulation of Hongzhou can be found in Pei Xiu's *Chuanxin fayao* and *Wanlinglu*. See *Chan Letter*, n. 46.

81. The *Hanshan shi*, the collection of poems of the (ninth-century?) poet Hanshan, has the following:

> In my house there is a cave.
> In the cave there is not a thing.
> It is clean, empty, and broad.
> The rays of light sparkle like the sun.
> A vegetarian diet nourishes my subtle body.
> A cotton robe covers my illusionary frame.
> Let a thousand noble ones appear before me.
> I have the buddha of the heavenly real [*tianzhen fo*].

(Iritani Sensuke and Matsumura Takashi, *Kanzan-shi*, Zen no goroku 13 [Tokyo: Chikuma shobō, 1970], 227)

82. *Zhuangzi*, Keyi: "Move by taking the conduct of heaven, this is the path of nourishing the spirit [*yangshen*]."

83. *Noble embryo* (*shengtai*) refers to the three worthies (*san xian*) in Tiantai and Huayan. See note 14.

84. Confirmation of the following encapsulation of Heze can be found in Shenhui's *Platform Talks*. See *Chan Letter*, note 55.

85. See *Chan Letter*, note 51.

86. See *Chan Letter*, note 53.

87. See *Chan Letter*, note 54.

88. Fazang's *Huayan jing tanxuan ji*, T 35:347a16–18, in laying out ten theories of consciousness only, says of the fifth: "The fifth takes characteristics back to the nature [*she xiang gui xing=hui xiang gui xing*], and on that basis speaks of consciousness only. This means that these eight consciousnesses are all without self substance; they are just the buddha-in-embryo appearing in sameness. All other characteristics are exhausted." A *Lanka Descent Sutra* quotation follows. The buddha-in-embryo is the basis of the third or final teaching in the Huayan schema of five teachings.

89. In his *Yuanrenlun*, T 45:709a11, Zongmi labels this the Hinayana teaching.

90. *Lotus Sutra*, T 9:14c25.

91. According to Hirakawa, 718, *fashu=dharma-paryāya*. Here "*fashu*" is a synonym of "*famen*," which is also an equivalent of "*dharma-paryāya*," according to Hirakawa, 715. The term "*dharma-paryāya*" means "method, way, means of teaching." Zongmi seems to be referring to the tendency in Hinayana texts to go to great lengths in making fine distinctions. Ishii (3), 47, supports this interpretation when he says that

"*fashu*" refers to classifying all dharmas into such categories as the three realms, four truths, five aggregates, six perfections, etc.

92. *Abhidharma Storehouse Treatise*, T 29:47b27–c1: "There is no self, just the aggregates, created by the depravities and karma [*fannao ye*]. Due to the fact that in the intermediate state between death and rebirth [*zhongyou*] there is the personal continuity series [*xiangxu*], entrance into a womb is like the flame of a lamp [lighting another lamp in succession]. As if stretching, it increases in a series. The personal continuity series, due to depravities and karma, once again proceeds to another life, and so the wheel of existence has no beginning."

93. *Abhidharma Great Explanations Treatise*, T 27:99b23–24: "Individual karma [*bieye*] gives birth to hell beings. Individual karma gives birth to animals. Individual karma gives birth to hungry ghosts. Individual karma gives birth to gods. Individual karma gives birth to humans." Because of individual karma, sentient beings receive individual effects.

94. *Abhidharma Great Explanations Treatise*, T 27:107a1–2: "Mt. Sumeru, etc. [that is, the vessel world consisting of the four continents] is produced by the common karma [*gongye*] of all sentient beings."

95. Following the *Ming Canon* edition of Ui, 60, and the Gozan edition of Ishii (3), 39, both of which read: "*miedao er di*." The 1576 Korean edition of Kamata, 104.6, has the last two truths reversed.

96. According to Hirakawa, 465, *xinshu*=*caitasika, caitta, cetasika*. This is the old translation term, the new translation term being "*xinsuo*." *Abhidharma Storehouse Treatise*, T 29:18c–21c, gives forty-six mentals or mind functions (*xinsuo*=*caitasika*) divided into five kinds plus indeterminate mentals beyond these five: universal dharmas (feeling, thought, volition, touch, desire, intellect, mindfulness, attention, confirmation, and concentration); universal good dharmas (confidence, diligence, indifference, shame, modesty, non-covetousness, non-anger, non-harming, flexibility, and non-negligence); universal depravity dharmas (ignorance, negligence, indolence, non-confidence, depression, and restlessness); universal non-good dharmas (non-shame and non-modesty); lesser depravity dharmas (rage, covering over [conduct], stinginess, jealousy, worry, harming, bearing a grudge, flattery, deception, and arrogance); and indeterminate dharmas ([remorse over] bad actions, sleepiness, investigation, examining, covetousness, anger, pride, and doubt).

97. The four *Āgamas, Dīrghāgama* (*Chang ahan jing*), *Madhyamāgama* (*Zhong ahan jing*), *Samyuktāgama* (*Za ahan jing*), and *Ekottarāgama* (*Zengyi ahan jing*), which are contained in T vols. 1 and 2 (along with numerous individual sutras), correspond to the first four of the five Pāli *Nikāyas*. For detailed information, see Daizōkyō, 3–39. Zongmi's numbers for the fascicle counts here are probably coming from Zhisheng's catalogue *Kaiyuan shijiao lu* of 730 (T 55:610b24–c3): "Hearer [Hinayana] sutra basket: 240 sections, 618 fascicles, 48 cases; hearer rules-of-discipline basket: 54 sections, 446 fascicles, 45 cases; hearer *abhidharma* basket: 36 sections, 698 fascicles, 72 cases."

98. The collection of the *abhidharma* researches of Sarvāstivāda commentators resulted in the *Abhidharma Great Explanations Treatise*, a gigantic encyclopedia of Sarvāstivāda lore in the form of a commentary on the *Abhidharma Setting Forth Knowledge Treatise* (T no. 1544). Its contents include the seventy-five dharmas in the fivefold classification schema, the six causes and four conditions, the real existence of the three times, the twelvefold origination by dependence, classification of the depravities, the sixteen aspects of the four noble truths, etc., as well as the investigation of deviant theories. It was translated by Xuanzang in 656 through 659 as T no. 1545; there is also an old translation, T no. 1546 (Daizōkyō, 422–23).

99. Supplying the title *Jushe* (=*Kośa/Storehouse*) from the *Ming Canon* edition of Ui, 62. The *Abhidharma Storehouse Treatise* dates to the middle of the fifth century (with variant theories placing it earlier). It was compiled by Vasubandhu, who belonged to a faction of the Sarvāstivāda school. It was intended as an outline of the *Abhidharma Great Explanations Treatise* above and as a corrective or supplement to the *Miscellaneous Abhidharma Heart Treatise* (T no. 1552). The translation by Xuanzang done in 651 through 654 (T no. 1558) intentionally introduces changes; there is also an old translation by Paramārtha (T no. 1559; Daizōkyō, 427–28).

100. In his *Yuanrenlun*, T 45:709b26, Zongmi labels this the Mahayana dharma-characteristics teaching.

101. The question is whether or not thusness (*zhenru*=tathata) has a relationship to arising-disappearing (*shengmie*=udaya-vyaya) dharmas. In his *Da fangguang yuanjue xiuduoluo liaoyi jing lueshu zhu*, T 39:525c–526a, Zongmi enumerates ten differences between the dharma-nature and dharma-characteristics teachings. The fourth (525c23–24) is: "[The dharma-characteristics teaching holds that] thusness is frozen [*ningran*]; because the eight consciousnesses arise and disappear, [thusness] does not follow conditions [*fei suiyuan*]. [The dharma-nature teaching holds that thusness] follows conditions [*suiyuan*]; because the eight consciousnesses are grounded in the [tathagata]garbha nature [*yi zangxing*], it is just that thusness follows conditions to be established."

102. See note 50.

103. Following the Gozan edition of Ishii (3), 40, which reads: "*qi yuan ba jian.*" Indian Yogācārins held different opinions on what aspect of the eighth consciousness the seventh, the manas, takes as its objective support. *Cheng weishi lun*, T 31:21c18–22a8, lists four positions: (1) the manas takes as its objective support the storehouse consciousness's substance and yoked dharmas (*caitasika*); (2) the manas just takes as its objective support the storehouse consciousness's seeing and characteristics parts; (3) the manas just takes as its objective support the storehouse consciousness and its seeds; and (4) the manas just takes as its objective support the storehouse consciousness's seeing part (*zangshi jianfen*). The last is the interpretation of Dharmapala and hence of the dharma-characteristics tradition of China. Dharmapala was a resident of Nālandā and one of the ten great masters of Yogācāra during the sixth century.

104. *Cheng weishi lun*, T 31:1b2–9: "Internal consciousness transforms into seeming external sense objects. Because of the power of fumigating habit [energy] that discriminates a self and dharmas, when the various consciousnesses arise, they transform into a seeming self and dharmas. Even though these self and dharma characteristics are in internal consciousness, due to discrimination, they seem to appear as external sense objects. The various sentient-being types, from time without beginning, take these as objective supports, grasping them as a real self and real dharmas. It is like one who is ill or one who is dreaming. Because of the power of the illness or the dream, in the mind the characteristics of various external sense objects seem to arise. [The sick person and the dreamer] take these as objective supports, grasping them as really existent external sense objects. The real self and real dharmas calculated by the stupid ones have no existence at all. It is just that, following feelings of the unreal, they are established, and, therefore, we call them 'provisional' [*shuo zhi wei jia*]. Even though the seeming self and seeming dharmas of internal consciousness transformation [provisionally] exist, they are not of the nature of a real self and dharmas."

105. Xuanzang's disciple Ji (traditional name Kuiji; 632–682) includes this contemplation system in his *Dasheng fayuan yilin zhang*, T 45:258b–259a, and in his *Banruo boluomiduo xin jing yuzan*, T 33:526c–527b. The five tiers, running from shallow to deep, are: (1) the dispatch the empty and preserve the real consciousness (*qianxu zunshi shi*); (2) the discard the overflow and keep the pure consciousness (*shelan liuchun shi*); (3) the hold the branches and revert to the root consciousness (*shemo guiben shi*); (4) the conceal the inferior and reveal the superior consciousness (*yinlie xiansheng shi*); and (5) the dispatch characteristics and realize the nature consciousness (*qianxiang zhengxing shi*).

106. The four articles of attraction (*si she*) are the means by which a buddha or bodhisattva attracts or draws in beings: giving, kind speech, beneficial conduct, and having the same aims (or having the same pleasures and sorrows).

107. *Cheng weishi lun*, T 31:48c6–11: "The depravities hindrance [*fannao zhang*] refers to the 128 basic depravities and the secondary depravities issuing from them, which take as their chief the view of an existent self that grasps the 'real' self of the completely imagined [*bianji suozhi*]. All of these trouble the body-minds of sentient beings and can hinder nirvana, and they are called the depravities hindrance. The objects-of-knowledge hindrance [*suozhi zhang*] refers to the views, doubt, ignorance, love, anger, pride, etc., which take as their chief the view of an existent self that grasps the 'real' dharmas of the completely imagined. They cover the realm of objects of knowledge and the non-topsy-turvy nature and can hinder awakening, and they are called the objects-of-knowledge hindrance."

108. *Cheng weishi lun*, T 31:54b9–10: "As to the ten thusnesses, the first is the thusness that acts everywhere. This is because this thusness is revealed by dual voidness, and there is not one dharma that does not exist in it."

109. *Cheng weishi lun*, T 31:56b1–3: "These four items [the great, perfect mirror knowledge; sameness knowledge; excellent reflection knowledge; and completing what is to be done knowledge] completely subsume all the conditioned merits of the buddha stage, exhausting them all. These [four knowledges] turn over their associated items, the eighth, seventh, sixth, and [the set of] five [sense] consciousnesses that are possessed of the outflows, attaining them one after the other."

110. *Cheng weishi lun*, T 31:51a5–8: "By continually practicing the non-discriminative knowledge one cuts off the two-hindrances depravities within the root consciousness [the storehouse consciousness], and, therefore, is able to turn over and reject the completely imagined that is on top of the arising-through-dependence-on-something-else [*yita qi shang bianji suozhi*] and is able to turn over and attain the completely perfected that is within the arising-through-dependence-on-something-else [*yita qi zhong yuancheng shixing*]. From turning over the depravities one attains great nirvana."

111. The *Unraveling the Deep Secret Sutra*, one of the basic scriptures of the Yogācāra school, seems to have emerged about 300. It opens with the enjoyment-body Buddha Vairocana in a Lotus-womb world, a pure land, speaking dharma to various bodhisattvas and so forth. It discusses the storehouse consciousness and the six consciousnesses, but the seventh consciousness, the manas, is absent. It also discusses the three natures, the three no-natures, and a classification schema of three periods (existence, voidness, and the middle). Xuanzang's translation (T no. 676) was standard for the dharma-characteristics axiom. Other translations are T nos. 675 and 677–79 (Daizōkyō, 205–6).

112. The *Yoga Course Stages Treatise*, one of the basic Yogācāra treatises, dates to about 300 to 350. In the Chinese tradition it is attributed to Maitreya. This enormous encyclopedia summarizes Hinayana and Mahayana and even deals with Veda and the five sciences. It particularly focuses on all aspects of the career of the yoga practitioner, discussing the storehouse consciousness, the three natures and no-natures, consciousness only, etc. The translation is by Xuanzang (T no. 1579; Daizōkyō, 435–36).

113. The *Cheng weishi lun* (T no. 1585) is a commentary on the *Thirty Verses on Consciousness Only* of Vasubandhu (T no. 1586). It is a mixture of numerous Indian commentaries in translation. Xuanzang and his followers were going to translate the commentaries of the ten great masters of Yogācāra in their entirety, but the disciple Ji argued this would lead to confusion and requested that the orthodox opinions of Dharmapala and a judicious selection of the opinions of the other nine be brought together in one book. The result was the *Cheng weishi lun* (Daizōkyō, 438).

114. Ji's *Cheng weishi lun shuji*, T 43:229c28–230a3, cites as authoritative for the dharma-characteristics axiom six sutras and eleven treatises. The name of the school in Chinese, Faxiang, derives from a chapter title in the translation of the *Unraveling the Deep Secret Sutra*, T 16:693a3: "Chapter on All Dharma Characteristics [*yiqie faxiang pin*]."

115. Zongmi is implying that the cultivation of mind of the first Chan axiom tallies with the cultivation of mind of the Mahayana Faxiang teaching, that is, the five-tiered consciousness-only contemplation system of Xuanzang's disciple Ji. See note 105.

116. This term *"kanjing"* appears in a Shenxiu saying found in an early East Mountain work, the *Xiande ji yu Shuangfeng Shan ta ge tan xuanli (Former Worthies Gather at the Mount Shuangfeng Stupa and Each Talks of the Dark Principle)*. This Dunhuang manuscript text is a very short collection of sayings for each of twelve figures at an imaginary memorial gathering for Hongren at his stupa on Mt. Shuangfeng in Hubei. The twelfth saying is that of Shenxiu. See Yanagida Seizan, *"Denbōhōki to sono sakusha:* Pelliot 3559go bunsho o meguru hokushū Zen kenkyū shiryō no satsuki, sono ichi," *Zengaku kenkyū* 53 (1963): 55. The term also appears in Shenhui's works as one element in the four aphorisms criticizing the teaching of Shenxiu's lineage. See note 38.

117. From Shenxiu's verse in the *Platform Sutra*. See *Chan Letter*, note 39.

118. These are elements in Shenhui's four aphorisms. See note 38.

119. T 14:539c20–21: "This sitting is not necessarily quiet sitting. Now, quiet sitting is not to manifest body and mind in the three realms. This is quiet sitting."

120. An inscription for Shenxiu by Zhang Yue (667–730), the *Jingzhou Yuchuan si Tatong chanshi beiming bing xu*, which was compiled sometime after 708, states: "During the Jiushi era [700–701] the Chan Master's years were already high. An imperial edict invited him [to the court at Luoyang], and he came. Sitting cross-legged to have an audience with the sovereign, his palanquin, which was carried on shoulders, ascended the hall. He submitted to [the Son of Heaven] of the ten-thousand-chariot state and bowed his head. He sprinkled water on the nine gates [of the Son of Heaven's residence] and was at ease. As a transmitter of the noble path he did not face north [in the respectful position of a subject]. As a possessor of flourishing virtue he did not observe the ritual of a minister. Subsequently, he was promoted to Dharma Ruler of the Two Capitals and State Master to Three Emperors" (Yanagida Seizan, *Shoki Zenshū shisho no kenkyū* [Kyoto: Hōzōkan, 1967], 499; QTW 5:231.2953b9–11).

121. *Vimalakīrti Sutra*, T 14:545a16–17.

122. Echoing the early sacred history *Lengjia shizi ji* (Yanagida I, 273).

123. The *Bodhidharma Anthology*'s biography of the Dharma Master uses this term *"biguan"*: "Thus quieting mind [*rushi anxin*] is wall viewing" (Yanagida, *Daruma no goroku*, 25). It also appears in a description of Bodhidharma's dhyana style in Daoxuan's *Xu gaoseng zhuan*, T 50:596c9.

124. This quotation may be our earliest extant exegesis of *"biguan."* In Buddhist texts the term *"yuan"* is used as the equivalent of both *"pratyaya"* ("condition") and *"ālambana"* ("objective support"). I think here yuan = ālambana. Zhiguang's *Jushelun ji*, the standard commentary on the *Abhidharma-kośa*, glosses *"ālambana"* as follows (T 41:39b11–12): "The word yuan [*ālambana*] means grab on to [*panyuan*]. Mind and mentals are called grabber [*nengyuan*]. Sense objects are the grabbed [*suoyuan*]." The

term *"chuan"* ("panting, gasping for breath") is a modern term in medicine for asthma. The transmission record *Jingde chuandeng lu* (T 51:219c31–220a4) of 1004 gives this Bodhidharma quotation and some material from section 30 as a quotation from a work called the *Bieji* (*Separate Record*).

125. The Sanskrit title of this work may have been something like *Yogācāra-bhūmi-sūtra* or *Yogācāra-dhyāna-sūtra*. The translation (T no. 618) was done by Buddha-bhadra in 413. Opening with a discussion of breath counting followed by other praxes, such as contemplation on impurity, etc., it is essentially a practice guide. Although taken as a Mahayana sutra, it has a Mainstream/Hinayana orientation (Daizōkyō, 185–86). Zongmi seems to be getting his information here from an apocryphal story in the Baotang sacred history *Lidai fabao ji*, which links the title of the sutra, *Da-moduoluo chan jing*, to the first patriarch of Chan (T 51:180c3–15; Yanagida II, 67–68): "The first patriarch of the Liang Dynasty, Chan Master Putidamoduoluo [Bodhi-dharmatāra], was the third son of the king of a South Indian state. When young he left home. As soon as he attached himself to a master, he suddenly awakened. He did transforming work in South India and accomplished great things for Buddhism. At the time he ascertained that the sentient beings of the land of Han were of a Ma-hayana nature. He then dispatched his two disciples Buddha and Yaśas to go to the land of Qin and speak the dharma of all-at-once awakening. When the great worthies in Qin first heard of it, they were suspicious, and none would believe or accept it. They were chased out and ended up at the Donglin Monastery on Mt. Lu. At the time there was the Dharma Master Yuan Gong who asked: 'Great Worthies! What dharma did you bring that you were chased out?' At that the two Indians stretched out their hands and told Yuan Gong: 'The hand becomes a fist. The fist becomes a hand. It's quick, isn't it?' Yuan Gong said: 'Very quick.' The two Indians said: 'This is not quick. The depravities *are* awakening—that is quick.' Yuan Gong, fathoming this, immedi-ately realized that awakening and the depravities from the outset are not different. He then asked: 'Over there [in India] who did you follow to study this dharma?' The two Indians answered: 'Our master Dharmatara.' Yuan Gong, having gained deep confi-dence in them, immediately had them do the translation *Chanmen jing* in one roll."

126. Zongmi is probably drawing again from the *Lidai fabao ji* (T 51:181c10–11; Yanagida II, 86): "[Daoxin] day and night sat constantly without lying down. For more than sixty years he did not touch his ribs to a mat [*xie bu zhi xi*]." This, in turn, is based on a story about how Monk Pārśva got his name in the *Fufa zang yinyuan zhuan* (T 50:314c5–7). The sacred history *Chuan fabao ji* by Du Fei, which dates to shortly after 713, also emphasizes the East Mountain patriarch Daoxin's single-minded focus on sitting with a pithy exhortation he favored (Yanagida I, 380): "Strive dili-gently at sitting. Sitting is the root [*zuo wei genben*]. If you can do it for three to five years, you will be able to prevent hunger and sores with one mouthful of food. Shut the door and sit. Do not read the sutras and do not talk with others. The one who can do this will be worthy to be used for a long time. It is like the monkey who takes the

meat in the chestnut and eats it. Rare is the person who sits, investigates, and takes [the essence]."

127. *Zhonglun,* T 30:33b13–14.

128. See note 74.

129. *Banruo boluomiduo xin jing,* T 8:848c7–10.

130. The mother ship of this enormous sutra literature is the *Great Perfection of Wisdom Sutra* in six hundred fascicles (T no. 220) translated by Xuanzang from 660 through 663. It is composed of sixteen *Perfection of Wisdom Sutras.* The first assembly corresponds to the *One Hundred Thousand Perfection of Wisdom;* the second to the *Twenty-Five Thousand;* the third to the *Eighteen Thousand;* the fourth and fifth to the *Eight Thousand,* etc. It fills T volumes 5 to 7 (Daizōkyō, 65). T vol. 8 contains individual translations of these *Perfection of Wisdom Sutras.* Two of the most important have been T no. 223, the *Mohe banruo boluomi jing* translation of the *Twenty-Five Thousand* done by Kumarajiva in 404 (also known as the *Dapin* or *Large Version*), and T no. 227, the *Xiaopin banruo boluomi jing* (*Small Version*) translation of the *Eight Thousand* done by Kumarajiva in 408. As for content, there is an enormous amount of overlap and repetition (Daizōkyō, 66–67).

131. The *Zhonglun* (*Madyamaka-śāstra?;* T no. 1564) is composed of 445 verses of Nagarjuna and the prose commentary of the Indian Mādhyamika known in Chinese as Qingmu (=Pingala?), who is not listed among the commentators in the Indian and Tibetan traditions. Kumarajiva did the translation in 409. It is divided into four fascicles and twenty-five chapters (Daizōkyō, 430–31).

132. The *Bailun* (*Śataka-śāstra;* T no. 1569) is a work by Nagarjuna's disciple Aryadeva that under the banner of *no-svabhāva/*voidness criticizes the theories of outsider schools. Kumarajiva did the *Bailun* translation in 404. It includes the commentary of someone known in Chinese transliteration as Posoukaishi. There is a *Four Hundred Verses* by the same Aryadeva, which is nearly identical in contents. There are three theories: the first half of the *Four Hundred Verses* corresponds to the *Bailun;* the *Bailun* was compiled as a summary of the *Four Hundred Verses;* and the *Four Hundred Verses* is an expansion of the *Bailun* (Daizōkyō, 433).

133. The *Shi'er men lun* (*Dvādaśa-nikāya-śāstra?;* T no. 1568) is attributed to Nagarjuna, but there are doubts. Kumarajiva did the translation in 409. In the style of the *Zhonglun* (seventeen verses are taken from that work) it propounds no-*svabhāva/* voidness. In substance it is a summary of the *Zhonglun* (Daizōkyō, 432–33).

134. The *Guang bailun ben* (T no. 1570) is a work by Nagarjuna's disciple Aryadeva. Xuanzang did the translation in 650. It corresponds to the second half of the *Four Hundred Verses.* To distinguish it from the *Bailun* (T no. 1569) it is called the *Guang bailun* or *Expanded Bailun* (Daizōkyō, 433).

135. Tradition presents Kumarajiva's hundred-fascicle *Da zhidu lun* (T no. 1509) as the translation of a commentary by Nagarjuna on the *Twenty-Five Thousand Perfection of Wisdom Sutra.* The theory that it is by someone else has been dominant for

some time. It includes so many quotations from sutras and treatises, running from the treatises of the Mainstream schools to Mahayana sutras such as the *Lotus* and *Huayan*, that it is known as a magical incantation of the whole of Buddhism. Its explanations of Buddhist terminology make it a sort of encyclopedia (Daizōkyō, 409–10).

136. Zongmi is saying that, whereas in the *Zhonglun* Nagarjuna exhibits only the side of negativistic denial of *svabhāva*, in the *Da zhidu lun* he advances a step and develops the side of positivistic affirmation of the true nature (*tattva*). Therefore, the *Da zhidu lun* actually is identical to the third teaching that "openly shows," that is, does not show solely by eradicating characteristics.

137. In this section Zongmi looks to Huayan lore on the compatibility between Indian Mādhyamikas and Yogācārins as a device to dampen contemporary conflicts, including the one between all-at-once and step-by-step Chan adepts. The gist is that in the words of their texts they conflict, but in their intentions they confirm each other. Here he is drawing from Fazang's *Shi'er men lun zhiyi ji* (T 42:218b8–15): "Even though Nagarjuna and others spoke of a voidness that exhausts existence [*jin you zhi kong*], they were not awaiting the extinguishing of existence [*bu dai mie you*]. Since it does not destroy existence [*bu sun you*], it is a voidness that does not go against existence [*bu wei you zhi kong*]. Therefore, Nagarjuna spoke of a voidness that is free of both existence and non-existence. This is true voidness [*zhenkong*]. Even though Asanga and others spoke of an existence that exhausts voidness [*jin kong zhi you*], it does not destroy true voidness [*bu sun zhenkong*]. Since it does not destroy true voidness [*bu sun kong*], it is an existence that does not go against voidness [*bu wei kong zhi you*]. Therefore, it is an illusion-like existence [*huanyou*] free of both existence and non-existence. How do they go against each other? You should know that the two theories take part in each other as a complete whole [*quanti xiangyu*]. In terms of limits there is nothing left behind. Although each writes of one principle, they form a perfect whole [*juti yuanju*]. That is why they do not go against each other."

138. Here Zongmi is drawing from Fazang's *Shi'er men lun zhiyi ji* (T 42:218b22–c3) or his *Huayan yisheng jiaoyi fenqi zhang* (T 45:501a12–29). I will give the latter: "Question: If, because there are two principles to the dependent-on-something-else, treatise masters of the previous period [such as Nagarjuna and Asanga] each write of one principle, fusing the dependent-on-something-else and not going against each other, why do treatise masters of the later period, such as Bhavaviveka and others, each grasp one principle and eradicate each other? Answer: These confirm each other; they do not eradicate each other [*xiangcheng fei xiangpo*]. Why? The faculties of sentient beings during the final phase [of the dharma] are gradual and dull, and, when they hear it said that the dependent-on-something-else is the principle of existence, they do not comprehend that that is an existence no different from voidness. Therefore, they grasp it as an existence like the one talked about. Therefore, Bhavaviveka and others eradicate the dependent-on-something-else in order to enable them to arrive at non-existence. When they arrive at ultimate non-existence [*bijing wu*], they immediately

attain the existence of that dependent-on-something-else [*bi yita zhi you*]. If they did not arrive at this thoroughgoing voidness of nature, then they would not be able to confirm the existence of the dependent-on-something-else. Therefore, in order to confirm existence [*cheng you*], there is eradication towards existence [*po yu you*]. Also, when those sentient beings hear it said that the dependent-on-something-else is ultimately devoid of nature, they do not comprehend that that is a voidness no different from existence, and, therefore, they grasp it as a voidness like the one talked about. Therefore, Dharmapala and others eradicate the voidness they talk about in order to preserve illusion-like existence. Because illusion-like existence is established, one immediately attains the voidness no different from existence [*bi bu yi you zhi kong*]. If there is extinction [of illusion-like existence], it is not true voidness, and, therefore, in order to confirm voidness, there is eradication towards voidness. By 'forms are voidness' [*se jishi kong*] Bhavaviveka's principle is established; by 'voidness is form' [*kong jishi se*] Dharmapala's principle is preserved. The two principles fuse [*rongrong*] and are subsumed as a perfect whole [*juti quanshe*]. If there were no treatise masters of the later period to interlace these two principles and have them completely snatch each other up [*quanti xiangduo*], there would be no way to reveal the exceedingly deep dependent-on-something-else nature of origination by dependence." Bhavaviveka (Bhavya), a sixth-century Mādhyamika, has two translations in T. The *Banruodeng lun shi* (T no. 1566) is a commentary on Nagarjuna's *Madhyamaka Verses*. The *Dasheng zhangzhen lun* (T no. 1578) is an exegesis of voidness (Daizōkyō, 431–32 and 435). Dharmapala is one of the ten great masters of Yogācāra of the sixth century. He criticizes Madhyamaka at the beginning of the *Cheng weishi lun* (T 31:1a11–12). See Sebun Fukaura, "Controversy Between Dharmapāla and Bhāvaviveka," *Ryūkoku daigaku ronshū* 345 (1952): 11–25.

139. After the Buddha's complete nirvana, the first 1,000 (or 500) years is called the true dharma, the next 1,000 years the imitation dharma, and the last 10,000 years the final or end phase of the dharma (*modai=mofa*). In this final phase all that remains is the teachings of Buddhism, but there is neither practice nor realization.

140. Fazang's *Shi'er men lun zhiyi ji* (T 42:218c4–9): "This is because, due to the dharma of origination by dependence, there are two principles to excellent existence and true voidness. The first is mutual agreement in the extreme [*ji xiangshun*]. This means that they mysteriously fuse into one characteristic [*minghe yi xiang*], and the whole substance is completely taken in [*juti quanshe*]. The second is mutual contradiction in the extreme [*ji xiangwei*]. This means that they each clash [*ge huxiang hai*] and are completely snatched up and eternally exhausted [*quanduo yongjin*]. If they did not snatch each other up and completely exhaust each other, there would be no way for the whole substance to be completely drawn in. Thus, contradiction in the extreme [*jiwei*] *is* agreement in the extreme [*jishun*]. Because Nagarjuna and Asanga accorded with the gate of agreement in the extreme, there was no eradication of each other. Because Bhavaviveka and Dharmapala are based on the gate of contradiction

in the extreme, it was necessary for them to eradicate each other. Contradiction and agreement are unobstructed [*wei shun wuai*], and, therefore, it is origination by dependence."

141. A very similar line appears in a commentary on a tantric sutra, the *Da Pilu-zhena chengfo jing shu* (T 39:709b28–c1): "In the present in discussing this dharma of self-realization [*zizheng zhi fa*] it is not the sphere of those followers of the two vehicles and outside paths. Within this dharma there is no possibility of metaphor, and therefore we say it is incomparable. It is like someone's drinking water—he himself knows whether it is cold or hot."

142. According to Hirakawa, 876, *zhenxing=tattva*.

143. T 31:830c15–16.

144. T 12:222c4–5.

145. T 10:272c5–273a2.

146. Chengguan's *Da fangguang fohuayan jing suishu yanyi chao* (T 36:261b16–17): "Now directly stating that spiritual Knowing [*lingzhi*], the true mind [*zhenxin*], is different from a tree or a stone [implies that it] penetrates both the realizer and the realized [*nengsuo zheng*]." Zongmi is making the point that Knowing is not an insentient thing but a dynamically active awareness.

147. *Dasheng qixin lun* (T 32:579a12–16): "Also, next, as to the characteristic of the self substance of thusness [*zhenru ziti xiang*], in all common persons, hearers, private buddhas, bodhisattvas, and buddhas it is without increase or decrease. It does not arise in the past, nor does it disappear in the future. It is ultimately constant. From the outset the nature is spontaneously perfect with all merits, because the so-called self-substance has the aspect of the radiance of great wisdom [*da zhihui guangming yi*], because of its aspect of pervasively illuminating the dharma sphere [*bianzhao fajie yi*], because of its aspect as the Knowing of reality [*zhenshi shizhi yi*]."

148. T 10:162c1: "Thusness takes illlumination as its substance [*zhenru zhaoming wei ti*]."

149. Here Zongmi is drawing from Chengguan's subcommentary, the *Da fang-guang fohuayan jing suishu yanyi chao* (T 36:261b18–26): "[The *Huayan jing*] *shu* [has the line] 'understanding by differentiating is not true Knowing,' etc. I will bring together the pair of the Southern and Northern lineages of Chan in order to penetrate the sutra's idea. This line jettisons the disease of the Southern lineage. It means that consciousness takes understanding-by-differentiating as its principle. [The Southern lineage's] seeing the mind nature [*liaojian xinxing*] is not true Knowing [*zhenzhi*]. The *Vimalakīrti* says: 'Rely on wisdom, not on consciousness.' This means that discrimination is called 'consciousness,' and non-discrimination is called 'wisdom.' Now, because there is a consciousness that understands by differentiating, it is not true Knowing. True Knowing is only seen in no mindfulness [*wei wunian fang jian*]. The *Shu* [has the line] 'if even for a split second it is produced, it is not true Knowing.' I will explain this second line and jettison the disease of the Northern lineage. Because the Northern

lineage takes non-production of mind as the profound excellence, it refers to the accumulation [of conditions and consequent] production as 'mind.' [However, Northern] producing mind and gazing at mind [*qixin kanxin*] are thought of the unreal and, therefore, are not true Knowing. Therefore, true Knowing necessarily forgets mind and jettisons illumination, and the path of speech and thought is cut off." It is noteworthy that Chengguan criticizes Southern Chan as a whole, something that Zongmi certainly does not do anywhere in his Chan works.

150. *Heroic Progress Samadhi Sutra*, T 19:124c24.

151. *Dasheng qixin lun*, T 32:577b19.

152. This saying ("*nixin ji cha*") does not seem to appear in any of Shenhui's extant works. It is one of those sayings attributed to Shenhui, such as the four slogans, that stayed alive as a stock line in Chan literature after Zongmi's time. For instance, we find it in Pei Xiu's *Chuanxin fayao* (T 48:381b3); the *Record of Linji* (T 47:501b9–10); the *Zutangji* (Yanagida Seizan, ed., *Sodōshū*, Zengaku sōsho 4 [Kyoto: Chūbun shuppansha, 1974], 101a3); the *Jingde chuandeng lu* (T 51:365a17); and even in Shōjō's *Zenshū komoku* (Kamata Shigeo and Tanaka Hisao, eds., *Kamakura kyū Bukkyō*, Nihon shisō taikei 15 [Tokyo: Iwanami shoten, 1971], 170). In all cases Shenhui's name is missing. The related term "*niyi*" ("never implementing, never putting into practice; being hesitant, dawdling, shilly-shallying; wondering what should I do") is ubiquitous in the *Record of Linji* (496b19, 496c7, 496c13, 496c25, 497a3, 497a16, 503a29, 503c24, and 504a28), and those who exhibit *niyi* fare badly at the hands of the master Linji.

153. T 10:69a3–26. This quotation from the "Chapter on [the Bodhisattvas'] Questions About Enlightenment" begins above with the nine bodhisattvas' asking Mañjuśrī "What is the wisdom of the buddha realm?"

154. T 9:7a22–25: "Śāriputra! Why is it said that the buddhas, just because of the one great task of causes and conditions, appear in the world? Because the buddhas want to enable sentient beings to open up buddha Knowing-seeing and have them attain purity, they appear in the world."

155. T 45:144a22–23. This treatise is attributed to Kumarajiva's disciple Sengzhao (374–414), but it is a Tang work showing Lao-Zhuang influence (Daizōkyō, 541).

156. This section is based on quotations from the *Da fangguang fohuayan jing* translation made from 695 through 699 by the Khotanese Siksananda (T no. 279). This version is also called the *Eighty Huayan, New Translation Huayan Sutra*, and *Tang Sutra*. Each chapter originally circulated as an independent sutra, and they were brought together around the fourth century. The final chapter (the ninth assembly) is the Jeta Grove Assembly, constituting about one-quarter of the entire sutra. It is the story of the youth Sudhana's cultivating the stages of the bodhisattva practice. Beginning with Mañjuśrī and ending with Samantabhadra, in between he receives instruction from fifty-three good friends and progresses in his realization of the dharma sphere. Chengguan wrote his commentary, the *Huayan jing shu* (T no. 1735), and subcommentary, the *Yanyi chao* (T no. 1736), on this version. T no. 278 is a translation

done by Buddhabhadra from 418 through 420. It is also known as the *Sixty Huayan, Old Translation Huayan Sutra*, and *Jin Sutra*. Fazang's commentaries are on this version. T no. 293 is a translation done by Prajna from 795 through 798. This rendering, also known as the *Forty Huayan, Puxian xingyuan pin*, etc., is an enlargement of the last chapter, the "Entrance into the Dharma Sphere," in the versions above (Daizō-kyō, 78–80 and 83).

157. This is a comparatively late Mahayana sutra, thought to have been compiled around 600. There are two translations, T no. 681, made by Divakara between 680 and 688 and T no. 682 by Amoghavajra (705–774). The following description applies to the second. When the Buddha is in the land called Secret Array, the bodhisattva Vajragarbha asks him about the dharma nature and the highest meaning, and the Buddha answers with the non-arising and non-disappearing of the buddha-in-embryo. Vajragarbha explains the buddha-in-embryo, storehouse consciousness, etc., to bodhisattvas above the first stage and at the end shows why the buddha-in-embryo, the storehouse consciousness, and the secret array are different names for the same thing (Daizōkyō, 207).

158. See introduction, note 8.

159. Zongmi always refers to this sutra as the *Foding* (Buddha Top-knot), but it is commonly known as the *Shoulengyan jing* (Heroic Progress [Samadhi] Sutra). It is T no. 945, the *Da foding rulai miyin xiuzheng liaoyi zhupusa wanxing shoulengyan jing*. This sutra is associated with India's Nālandā Monastery. The translation during the Tang is by Paramiti, but it is an apocryphon in part. The Buddha's disciple Ānanda, because of the incantation power of an outcast woman, falls into evil ways and is rescued by the magical power of the Buddha. It extols the power of dhyana and the merit power of the incantation of the white umbrella, a metaphor for the pure or white compassion that covers sentient beings everywhere (Daizōkyō, 279).

160. T no. 353, the *Shengman shizihou yisheng da fangbian fangguang jing*, is a translation by Gunabhadra (394–468). Śrīmālā, the daughter of King Prasenajit of Kosala, receives a prediction of buddhahood from the Buddha and through the supernatural power of the Buddha discourses on dharma. The two main topics are the reality of the one vehicle and the buddha-in-embryo possessed by all sentient beings. There is also a translation in T no. 310 (no. 48) by Bodhiruci, who arrived in Luoyang in 693 (Daizōkyō, 97 and 87).

161. T no. 666, the *Da fangdeng rulaizang jing*, is a translation by Buddhabhadra done in 420. It says that though all sentient beings are in the midst of the depravities in the various rebirth paths, they still have the buddha-in-embryo that is never impure. There is also T no. 667, a translation by Amogavajra (705–774) (Daizōkyō, 201–2).

162. T no. 262, the *Miaofa lianhua jing*, is a translation by Kumarajiva done in 406. The core chapter is the second, in which the Buddha rises from concentration and says that the provisional teaching of the three vehicles is originally just the one vehicle (*yisheng*) and the reason a buddha appears in the world is just the one great task (*yi*

dashi) of saving sentient beings. There are two other extant translations, T nos. 263 and 264 (Daizōkyō, 74–76).

163. T no. 374, the *Da banniepan jing*, is also known as the *Large Edition Nirvana* and *Northern Edition Nirvana*. It is also called the *Mahayana Nirvana Sutra* to distinguish it from the sutra of the same name in the Āgamas (T no. 7, etc.). The three main points in the sutra are: the buddha body abides permanently; nirvana is permanent, possessing pleasure, self-like, and pure (*chang le wo jing*); and all sentient beings have the buddha nature. Other translations are: T no. 375 (also called the *Northern Edition Great Complete Nirvana Sutra*); T no. 376; and T no. 377 (also called the *Latter Part Nirvana Sutra*) (Daizōkyō, 106–7).

164. T no. 1611, the *Jiujing yisheng baoxing lun* (*Ratnagotra-vibhāga-mahāyānottara-tantra-śāstra*) is a systematic exposition of buddha-in-embryo teachings. The author is not recorded in the text, but the Chinese tradition attributes it to Jianhui (Saramati), who is thought to antedate Sthiramati in the sixth century. The translation is by Ratnamati (arrived in Lo-yang in 508) (Daizōkyō, 450–51).

165. T no. 1610, the *Foxing lun*, is attributed to Vasubandhu. It discusses the meaning of the buddha nature and the buddha-in-embryo. The first of four parts explains the Buddha's teaching that all sentient beings have the buddha nature. The translation is by Paramartha (499–569), and his interpretations are included in the text as we have it (Daizōkyō, 449–50).

166. In the *Chan Prolegomenon* Zongmi relies heavily on the *Dasheng qizin lun*, a treatise based on buddha-in-embryo teachings. No Sanskrit version or Tibetan translation is extant, and it is not quoted in Indian treatises. In Japanese scholarship Mochizuki Shinkō propounded the theory that it was a Chinese composition, while Tokiwa Daijō, Ui Hakuju, and others held to a theory of Indian origins. It is attributed to Asvaghosa (first to second century). In terms of content it is thought to date to the fifth to sixth centuries. There are two "translations," T nos. 1666 and 1667 (Daizōkyō, 467–68).

167. T no. 1522, the *Shidi jing lun* (*Daśabhūmika-sūtra-śāstra*), is a commentary by Vasubandhu (fifth century) on the *Ten Stages Sutra*, that is, the "Ten Stages Chapter" of the *Sixty Huayan* (T no. 278) and *Eighty Huayan* (T no. 279). The translation is by Bodhiruci (arrived in Luoyang in 508) and others (Daizōkyō, 414).

168. The *Dasheng fajie wuchabie lun* (*Mahayana Dharma Sphere Without Difference Treatise*) is a treatise by Saramati explicating the fifth chapter, "All Sentient Beings Possess the Buddha-in-Embryo," of his own *Ratnagotra-śāstra* (see note 164). The aim is to reveal the supreme, calm nirvana sphere of the Buddha by means of the twelve aspects of the thought of awakening. T no. 1626 is a translation done by Devaprajna in 691. T no. 1627, also known as the *Buddha-in-Embryo Treatise*, is said to be a translation by the same Devaprajna in 692, but this is doubtful (Daizōkyō, 456).

169. T no. 1527, the *Niepan lun*, is attributed to Vasubandhu, but there is a theory that it was composed in China. It attempts to show the main points of the *Nirvana Sutra* by interpreting the versified questions of the bodhisattva Kāśyapa found in the

third fascicle of T nos. 374 and 375 (see note 163). The translation is attributed to Dharmabodhi, who was active in the Northern Wei (386–534) (Daizōkyō, 416).

170. In the *Dasheng qixin lun*, T 32:575c21–23.

171. In the "Chapter on [the Bodhisattvas'] Questions About Enlightenment" of the *Huayan Sutra*. See note 153.

172. See note 123.

173. This question and answer and the next set as well, plus a Bodhidharma quotation in section 26, are found in the *Jingde chuandeng lu* as a Bodhidharma-Huike dialogue. The whole thing is presented as a quotation from an unknown work called the *Bieji*. See note 124.

174. See *Chan Letter*, section 4.

175. See *Chan Letter*, note 53.

176. It is noteworthy that this section associates cross-legged Chan sitting (*zuochan*) with the first teaching and associates the one-practice concentration (*yixing sanmei*), the practice that is a non-practice, with the third teaching. The four sources cited in support of the latter, the *Dasheng qixin lun*, *Jingang sanmei jing*, *Fajujing*, and *Vimalakīrti Sutra*, are much quoted in Chan texts.

177. The earliest reference to the one-practice concentration in Chan literature appears to be the *Lengjia shizi ji* (c. 719–720). It associates the one-practice concentration with the fourth patriarch Daoxin and Shenxiu (T 85:1286c22–23 and 1290b2–3; Yanagida I, 186 and 298). Daoxin says: "This dharma essence of mine relies on the 'mind of the buddhas is the first' in the *Lanka Descent Sutra* [T 16:481c2] and relies on the one-practice concentration of the *Mañjuśrī Speaks of Wisdom Sutra* [T 8:731a25–27]." The author Jingjue, after a lengthy quotation from the *Mañjuśrī Speaks of Wisdom Sutra*, adds that "all behavior and activity [*shiwei judong*] is awakening." He is making the point that the highest dhyana is not static and is carried out in the midst of movement and activity.

178. T 32:582a16–22.

179. T 9:368a14. This sutra, a Chinese or Silla (Korean) apocryphon of the first half of the seventh century, shows influence from the entrance by principle of the *Bodhidharma Anthology* (Daizōkyō, 77). See Robert E. Buswell Jr., *The Formation of Ch'an Ideology in China and Korea: The* Vajrasamādhi-Sūtra, *a Buddhist Apocryphon* (Princeton, N.J.: Princeton University Press, 1989). This particular line from the sutra must have been quite popular, since it is found in a couplet of a Bai Juyi poem entitled "On Reading a Chan Sutra" (*Bai Juyi ji*, 2:32.716). Another Bai poem (2:18.392) has the line "just using the thunderbolt samadhi" and appends a note: "In my early years I and Mr. Qian practiced reading the *Jingang sanmei jing*, and thus my poem." The strong connection between this sutra and Chan led to its translation into Tibetan. It is no. 253 ('*Phags rdor je'i ting nge 'dzin gyi chos kyi yi ge*) in the *Ldan dkar ma dkar chag (Denkar [Palace] Catalogue)*, the oldest extant catalogue of Buddhist canonical texts in Tibetan (c. 824). For a transcription of this catalogue, see Yoshimura Shūki, *Indo daijō Bukkyō*

shisō kenkyū (Kyoto: Hyakkaen, 1976), 140. The *Jingang sanmei jing* is also found among the Tibetan Dunhuang manuscripts: a translation of the preface and first chapter in Pelliot Tibetan 623 (from fol. 1.1) and a quotation in Pelliot Tibetan 116 (fol. verso 24.2–4). See Obata Hironobu, "Chibetto no Zenshū to Zōyaku gigyō ni tsuite," *Indogaku Bukkyōgaku kenkyū* 23, no. 2 (1975): 170–71.

180. T 85:1435a21–22. Once again we have the emphasis on active practice and the denigration of passive, static cross-legged Chan sitting. The *Fajujing* is a Chinese apocryphon of the seventh century, and, judging from its numerous quotations in Chan texts, it was probably created by someone connected to Chan (Daizōyō, 841).

181. T 14:539c20–22.

182. Based on *Zhuangzi*, Qiushui.

183. Iriya Yoshitaka and Koga Hidehiko, *Zengo jiten* (Kyoto: Shibunkaku shuppan, 1991), 141–42, defines *"keti"* as "the very thing-in-itself." See *Chan Letter*, notes 68 and 71.

184. In the "Chapter on [the Bodhisattvas'] Questions About Enlightenment" of the *Huayan Sutra*. See note 153.

185. The four immeasurable minds (*si deng=si wuliang*) are: friendliness (*ci*); compassion (*bei*); joy (*xi*); and indifference (*she*). The four unobstructed understandings (*si [wuai] bian*), which buddhas and bodhisattvas have in speaking dharma, are: understanding of the dharma; understanding of the meanings; understanding of the words; and understanding of becoming clear. The ten powers (*shi li*) are the ten knowledge powers possessed by a buddha. See Dayal, *The Bodhisattva Doctrine*, 20.

186. T 10:89a2–3.

187. T 32:577b16–19.

188. Zongmi has patched together three quotations from two translations of the sutra: T 16:519a1–2, 510b4–5, and 512b16–17.

189. Note that the word *"duxu* [prolegomenon]" is missing. Sometimes the *Chan Prolegomenon* went under abbreviated titles. For instance, Yanshou's *Zongjinglu*, T 48:627a9, quotes from sections 45 and 46 under the title *Chanyuan ji* (*Chan Source Collection*), which makes it sound like a quotation from the *Chan Canon*.

190. Zongmi inherited Fazang's discussion of the opposition between existence (*you=bhava*) and voidness (*kong=sunyata*). Fazang's *Dasheng qixin lun yiji* (T 44:242a29–b27) relates that he got his information on this topic from questioning the Central Indian master Divakara, who worked in Chang'an and Luoyang from 680 to 688. Divakara responded that at India's Nālandā Monastery in the recent period there were simultaneously two great treatise masters, Silabhadra (Jiexian) and Jnanaprabha (Zhiguang). Silabhadra was in the line of Maitreya/Asanga and Dharmapala/Nanda. He set up three types of teachings, taking the dharma-characteristics Mahayana (*faxiang dasheng*) as the real, complete meaning. Toward dependently originated dharmas, the first (Hinayana) just says they exist and falls into the extreme of existence. The

second (*Perfection of Wisdom Sutras*) just says they are void and falls into the extreme of voidness. Since each falls into an extreme, neither of them is the complete meaning. In the last period the *Unraveling the Deep Secret Sutra*, etc., say that the imagined nature is void, but the other two, the dependent-on-something-else and the completely perfected, are existent. This accords with the middle path and hence is the complete meaning. Jnanaprabha was in the line of Mañjuśrī/Nagarjuna and [Arya]deva/ Bhavaviveka. He set up three teachings in order to clarify that the no-characteristics Mahayana (*wuxiang dasheng*) is the real, complete meaning. The Buddha, at first at Deer Park for the sake of those of small faculties, spoke of the four truths, clarifying that mind and sense objects are both existent (*xin jing ju you*). Next, in the middle period, for the sake of those of medium faculties, he spoke the dharma-characteristics Mahayana, clarifying the consciousness-only principle in which sense objects are void but mind is existent (*jing kong xin you*). Because their faculties were still inferior and they were not yet able to enter the true voidness of sameness, he spoke this teaching. In the third period, for the sake of those superior faculties, he spoke the no-characteristics Mahayana, distinguishing that mind and sense objects are both void (*xin jing ju kong*). It has the one flavor of sameness and is the real, complete meaning. The three-teachings schema in the *Chan Prolegomenon* shows a structural similarity to the Jnanaprabha's schema.

191. Zongmi in his *Da fangguang yuanjue xiuduoluo liaoyi jing lueshu zhu*, T 39:525c10–526a10, probably drawing from Chengguan's *Huayan jing gangyao* (ZZ 1.12–14), outlines ten differences between the dharma-nature axiom (*faxing zong*) and the dharma-characteristics axiom (*faxiang zong*):

1. The characteristics axiom holds to the three vehicles because the natures of sentient beings are fivefold (those who will become bodhisattvas; those who will become private buddhas; those who will become hearers; those of an indeterminate nature; and those who lack the nature, that is, cannot be transformed); the three vehicles are the complete meaning on the basis of the *Unraveling the Deep Secret Sutra*. The nature axiom holds to the one vehicle because beings are one; only the one vehicle is the complete meaning on the basis of the *Lotus Sutra*, etc.

2. The characteristics axiom holds to the five natures of sentient beings on the basis of the *Lanka Descent Sutra*, etc. The nature axiom holds to one nature because the *Lotus*, *Lanka Descent*, and *Nirvana* speak of just one nature.

3. The characteristics axiom holds that mind only is unreal, because the eight consciousnesses arise from the depravities and karma. The nature axiom holds that mind only is real, because the eight consciousnesses pervade the buddha-in-embryo (*tong rulaizang*).

4. The characteristics axiom holds that thusness is frozen (*zhenru ningran*); because the eight consciousnesses arise and disappear, (thusness) does not follow condi-

tions (*fei suiyuan*). The nature axiom holds that thusness follows conditions (*suiyuan*); because the eight consciousnesses are grounded in the (tathagata)garbha nature (*yi zangxing*), thusness' following conditions is established.

5. The characteristics axiom holds that the voidness or existence of each of the three natures separates them; the completely imagined is void, but the dependent and perfect exist. The nature axiom holds that the three natures are identical; having no nature is the perfect.

6. The characteristics axiom holds that living buddhas neither increase nor decrease because those of an indeterminate nature and those without the (buddha) nature cannot possibly become buddhas. The nature axiom holds the sentient-being sphere does not decrease; because the one principle is level, there is neither increase nor decrease.

7. The characteristics axiom holds that the voidness or existence of the two truths separates them; the real and worldly truths are regular. The nature axiom holds that the two truths are identical; the highest meaning, voidness, is possessed of both the real and the unreal (*gaitong zhenwang*).

8. The characteristics axiom holds that the four conditioned characteristics (coming into being, abiding, changing, and disappearing) are sequential; after the manifestation extinguishes, there is nothing. The nature axiom holds that the four conditioned characteristics are simultaneous; the substance is identical to the extinguishing.

9. The characteristics axiom holds that the one who cuts off and realizes and what is cut off and realized are separate; the sense organs take sense objects as objective supports to cut off the depravities, and one takes conditioned wisdom to realize the unconditioned principle. The nature axiom holds that the one who cuts off and realizes and what is cut off and realized are identical; the depravities *are* awakening, and seeing *is* thusness.

10. The characteristics axiom holds that a buddha body is conditioned; because the four knowledges are grounded in the consciousness seeds that arise and disappear, the enjoyment body is conditioned. The nature axiom holds that a buddha body is unconditioned; because the knowledges are grounded in the buddha-in-embryo, the transformation body of a buddha is constant, is dharma, and does not fall into the various mental functions. How much more so the enjoyment body?

192. In the schema of the *Chan Prolegomenon* this is tantamount to saying that people are confused about the difference between the second and third Chan axioms, that is, in concrete terms, the difference between Niutou Chan and the Chan of Hongzhou and Heze. By emphasizing in the following sections ten differences between the voidness and nature teachings, Zongmi is by implication emphasizing the differences between Niutou and Hongzhou-Heze.

193. Zongmi in his *Da fangguang yuanjue xiuduoluo liaoyi jing lueshu zhu*, T 39:526a12–27, lists five differences between the eradicating-characteristics axiom (*poxiang zong*) and the dharma-nature axiom (*faxing zong*):

1. The eradication-of-characteristics axiom holds to no nature (*wuxing*) and takes the naturelessness of all dharmas to be thusness. The nature axiom holds to the original nature (*benxing*) and takes the constantly abiding true mind (*changzhu zhenxin*) as thusness.

2. The eradication-of-characteristics axiom holds to true wisdom (*zhenzhi*), which can understand naturelessness. The nature axiom holds to true Knowing (*zhenzhi*); the one-mind reality from the outset has the spontaneous potentiality for Knowing, pervading both principle and wisdom and penetrating both impurity and purity, as the "Chapter on Questions on Enlightenment" of the *Huayan* says.

3. The eradication-of-characteristics axiom holds to the two truths; forms are the worldly, and voidness is the real. The nature axiom holds to the three truths (*san di*), adding the highest-meaning truth (*di-yi yi di*). This means that the one true mind nature is neither voidness nor form but has the potentiality to be void and the potentiality to be form (*nengkong nengse*), like the brightness of a mirror.

4. Concerning the voidness or existence of the three natures, for the voidness [eradication-of-characteristics] axiom existence means the dependent and imagined, and voidness means the completely perfected. For the nature axiom the completely imagined exists in feelings but not in principle; the dependent-on-something-else exists in characteristics but not in the nature; and the completely perfected does not exist in feelings but does in principle, does not exist in characteristics, but does in the nature.

5. The eradication-of-characteristics axiom holds that the buddha qualities are void (*fode kong*). Even though we speak of a buddha body, if you seek it in terms of the five aggregates, you will not obtain it. What you obtain will be unreal; no obtaining is the real. Divorcing from all characteristics is called "buddha qualities." The nature axiom holds that the buddha qualities exist. The buddhas all possess permanence, joy, self, purity, and real merits (*zhenshi gongde*). The wisdom of a buddha body is like limitless shafts of light. The nature has existed from the outset; it does not wait for a karmic nexus.

These five correspond to the third, fourth, eighth, ninth, and tenth differences in the *Chan Prolegomenon*.

194. *Da zhidu lun*, T 25:246a23–b9.

195. *Wuliangyi jing*, T 9:385c24.

196. T 10:202c24–203a11.

197. For instance, T 12:222c4.

198. T 32:576a11–13.

199. T 16:481c3.

200. *Dasheng qixin lun*, T 32:576b5–6: "As to *non-void [bu kongzhe]*, because it is already revealed that the dharma substance is void and without the unreal, it is the true mind, constant and unchanging, filled with pure dharmas, and therefore it is called 'non-void.'"

201. In the background here is the Heze Chan teaching of Knowing. By implication it is higher than the limited wisdom (prajna) of the Niutou house of Chan.

202. See note 148.

203. See note 147.

204. T 12:617b11.

205. T 12:617a20 and 27–28.

206. T 12:617c3–6.

207. T 12:618c10.

208. This terminology of "*zhequan* [negativistic explanation]" and "*biaoquan* [expressive explanation]" appears in Chengguan's *Da fangguang fohuayan jing shu*, T 35:766a29–b1.

209. See note 183.

210. The target here may be voidness Chan, that is, Niutou and perhaps Shitou, though the latter seems to be completely outside Zongmi's sphere.

211. *Da zhidu lun*, T 25:293c2–3 or 297b26.

212. The term "*gongneng*" refers to the *vāsanā* power latent in the storehouse consciousness. *Cheng weishi lun*, T 31:8a6: "[The seeds] inside the root consciousness produce their own effects [*ziguo*], having the [latent] power of differentiation [*gongneng chabie*]."

213. See note 183.

214. Chengguan's *Da fangguang fohuayan jing shu*, T 35:612b28: "Knowing is the mind substance [*zhi ji xinti*]."

215. These two phrases probably refer to Niutou Chan and Hongzhou Chan respectively. See sections 23 and 24.

216. Echoing the slogan "the one word 'Knowing' is the gate of all excellence [*zhi zhi yi zi zhongmiao zhi men*]." See section 24.

217. The quotation is from the Hongzhou sacred history *Baolinzhuan*, compiled by Zhiju/Huiju and dated 801. Of its original ten fascicles only seven are extant. The full quotation is: "I point to one word to speak directly of 'mind is buddha' [*zhi yi yan yi zhi shuo jixin shi fo*]." Yanagida Seizan, ed., *Hōrinden Dentō gyokuei shū*, Zengaku sōsho 5 (Kyoto: Chūbun shuppansha, 1975), 140b10. Zongmi is here criticizing Hongzhou's "mind is buddha" and proclaiming Heze's "Knowing" as Bodhidharma's one word. In section 30 Zongmi says that Bodhidharma's silent transmission of mind actually refers to the fact that Bodhidharma was silent about the word "Knowing," not that he did not say anythng at all.

218. The most famous is probably that of the *Zhonglun*, T 30:32c16–17: "The buddhas rely on the two truths to speak dharma for sentient beings. One is the worldly truth [*shisu di*], and the second is the truth of the highest meaning [*di-yi yi di*]."

219. According to Hirakawa, 475 and 993, *xing=dharmatā* and *ziti=svabhāva*. These correlate respectively to the real truth (voidness) and the highest meaning of the middle path (the one true mind substance) discussed below.

220. T no. 1485, the *Pusa yingluo benye jing*, discusses the main thread of the bodhisattva practice (Daizōkyō, 402–3). It says (T 24:1018b21–22): "The Buddha said: 'Buddha sons! The so-called existence truth, non-existence truth, and truth of the highest meaning of the middle path are the mother of the wisdom of all the buddhas and bodhisattvas.'"

221. See note 130.

222. T no. 281, the *Foshuo pusa benye jing*, corresponds to the seventh and eleventh chapters of the *Sixty Huayan* and the eleventh and fifteenth chapters of the *Eighty Huayan*. See note 156. The translation is by Indo-Scythian Zhiqian, who worked from 220 through 252 in China (Daizōkyō, 80–81).

223. See note 8.

224. This could refer to the three buddha bodies. Vasubandhu's *She dasheng lun shi*, T 31:257c13–14: "The three bodies are the three virtues. The dharma body is the virtue of cutting off [the depravities]; the response body is the virtue of wisdom; and the transformation body is the virtue of kindness [for sentient beings]." Kamata, 176, thinks they are dharma body, wisdom, and liberation, and Ishii (6), 102, wonders if they refer to the three truths of Tiantai.

225. The three natures are a trademark of the Mahayana dharma-characteristics axiom. Xuanzang's *Cheng weishi lun*, T 31:45c14–18: "Because it calculates everywhere, it is called the 'completely imagined' [*bianji*]. Speaking of a multitude of types, it makes them into this and that, meaning it is the discrimination of the unreal of the complete imaginer. Because of discrimination of this and that unreal [item], it completely imagines various completely imagined things. This means that falsely grasped aggregates, sense fields, and psycho-physical elements become essence-like differentiations of dharmas or self. These falsely grasped essence-like differentiations in their totality are called the 'completely imagined self nature [*bianji suozhi zixing*].'"

226. *Cheng weishi lun*, T 31:46a18–19: "The substance that the two [grasped and grasper] are grounded in really arises in dependence on conditions. This nature is not non-existent and is called the 'arising-through-dependence-on-something-else [*yita qi*].'"

227. *Cheng weishi lun*, T 31:46b10: "The completely accomplished [*yuanman chengjiu*] real nature of all dharmas that is revealed by dual voidness is called the 'completely perfected [*yuan chengshi*].'"

228. Zongmi is drawing from Fazang's *Huayan yisheng jiaoyi fenji zhang* (T 45:499a10–17): "Within the previous each of the three natures has two aspects [*er yi*].

Within the real [*zhen zhong*] the two aspects are the immutable aspect [*bubian yi*] and the following-conditions aspect [*suiyuan yi*]. The two aspects of the dependent-on-something-else are the seems-to-exist aspect [*siyou yi*] and the has-no-nature aspect [*wuxing yi*]. The two aspects within the grasped are the exists-in-feelings aspect [*qingyou yi*] and the does-not-exist-in-principle aspect [*liwu yi*]. Due to the immutable within the real, the no-nature of the dependent-on-something-else, and the does-not-exist-in-principle of the grasped, due to these three aspects, the three natures are of one limit, identical, without difference. These [three], without destroying the branches, are a permanent root. The sutra says: 'Sentient beings are nirvana. There is no further extinguishing.' Also, according to the following-conditions of thusness, the seems-to-exist of the dependent-on-something-else, and the exists-in-feelings of the grasped, due to these three aspects, there also is no difference."

229. *Thunderbolt-Cutter Sutra*, T 8:749a21–25.

230. *Thunderbolt-Cutter Sutra*, T 8:751c22–23.

231. *Thunderbolt-Cutter Sutra*, T 8:752a17–18.

232. T 30:29c8–9.

233. *Thunderbolt-Cutter Sutra*, T 8:750b9.

234. *Nirvana Sutra*, T 12:617a16–b16.

235. *Eighty Huayan*, T 10:266c5–10: "Buddha sons! The Tathagata's skin pores one after the other radiate thousands of shafts of light like this. Five hundred shafts of light illuminate the lower region. Five hundred shafts of light illuminate the various lands, the various buddha locales, and the assemblies of the bodhisattvas of the upper region. These bodhisattvas, etc., see these shafts of light, and simultaneously they all attain the realm of the Tathagata. The ten heads, the ten eyes, the ten ears, the ten noses, the ten tongues, the ten bodies [*shi shen*], the ten hands, the ten feet, the ten stages, and the ten knowledges [*shi zhi*] are all purified."

236. See note 57.

237. Following the Gozan edition of Ishii (6), 108: "*yi wu daiqing.*"

238. The source of this quotation has not been identified. Kamata, 184, notes that the Hiranoya Sabē woodblock-print edition of Kyoto dating to the Tenna (1681–1684) to Genroku (1688–1704) eras (Komazawa University No. 121-19) has an inserted notation to the effect that these are the words of Miaole, the ninth Tiantai patriarch Zhanran (711–782), who is known as the Great Master Miaole. A passage in the *Da banniepan jing* (T 12:631c17–22) has both "boils and warts" and "excellent medicine." See also T 12:632a9. Furthermore, a commentary on this version of the sutra entitled *Da banniepan jing shu*, which was compiled by Guanding and revised by Zhanran, mentions "warts" in the same context (T 38:92b12–13 and 92c19–20). Ishii (6), 110, suggests this might directly point to Zhanran as the source of this saying. Ui, 276, however, thinks it is probably a Chan saying.

239. It is unclear what the "*san ban* [three kinds]" indicates. Kamata, 188, thinks it is the three kinds of prajna: reality-mark prajna (*shixiang banruo*); perceiving prajna

(*guanzhao banruo*); and teaching-devices prajna (*fangbian banruo*). I think it refers to the three types of teachings, and Ishii (7), 73, also says it probably refers to the three types of teachings. Yŏndam Yuil's commentary *Sŏnwŏn jejŏnjip tosŏ kwamok pyŏngip sagi* concurs (Shūmitsu, 284).

240. For the three periods of the Indian dharma-characteristics Mahayana, see note 190. Many Chinese scholars from the time of the Northern and Southern dynasties onward, including Zhiyi, held to a five-periods (*wu shi*) schema. An example is that of Huiguan (354–424), which does include the *Huayan* in its two major categories: all-at-once teaching (*Huayan*) and step-by-step teaching. The latter is divided into five periods: (1) the three vehicles separate teaching (*Āgamas*); (2) the three vehicles common teaching (*Perfection of Wisdom Sutras*); (3) the restraining and raising up teaching (*Vimalakīrti*); (4) the return to identity teaching (*Lotus*); and (5) the permanently abiding teaching (*Nirvana*). See Hurvitz, *Chih-I*, 214–44.

241. This terminological pair is adapted from Fazang's *Huayan yisheng jiaoyi fenji zhang* (T 45:482b18–c8): "The teachings arise in a sequence. Within it there are two. First, I will clarify the root teaching of proclaiming dharma [*chengfa benjiao*=Zongmi's *huayi dun*/all-at-once of the rite of transforming beings] and, second, clarify the branch teaching of responding to [beings of the highest] disposition [*zhuji mojiao*=Zongmi's *zhuji dun*/responding to beings of the highest disposition]. The first means the one vehicle of the separate teaching [*biejiao yisheng*]. The Buddha, on the fourteenth day after first completing the path, beneath the tree of enlightenment, like the sun emerging to illumine the high mountains, in the midst of the ocean-seal concentration [*haiyin sanmei*], simultaneously gave discourses on hundreds of dharma gates. . . . The second is the branch teaching of responding to [beings of the highest] disposition. This means that the three vehicles have two aspects. One is spoken simultaneously with the one vehicle but at a different place. The second is spoken at a different time and a different place. Because the first aspect is the same teaching [as the one vehicle], the branch is not divorced from the root and comes into being grounded in the root. Because in the latter aspect the root and branch are apart from each other, it is not one with the root."

242. T 10:89a1–2.

243. This line is not found in T no. 842.

244. See *Chan Letter*, note 37.

245. For Zongmi, all-at-once awakening followed by step-by-step practice is the formula of Heze Chan. The practice gates of the first two teachings include Hinayana practices, the five-tiered consciousness-only viewing of the dharma-characteristics Mahayana, and so forth.

246. T 32:578a7–13.

247. The phrase "*Huayan yifen* [one part of the *Huayan*]" is perplexing. One possibility is that it refers to the *Huayan* line quoted above: "When one first raises the

thought [of awakening], one attains unexcelled, perfect awakening." This line appears in the "Chapter on the Holy Life" of the *Eighty Huayan* (T 10:88b1–89a3). Yŏndam Yuil's commentary, *Sŏnwŏn jejŏnjip tosŏ kwamok pyŏngip sagi*, remarks (Shūmitsu, 284) that the phrase generically refers to "when one first raises the thought, one attains awakening."

248. For all of these sutras, see section 29.

249. Chengguan's *Da fangguang fohuayan jing suishu yanyi chao* (T 36:3b15–17): "If [this sutra the *Huayan*] says that causes suffuse the sea of effects [*yin gai guohai*], effects penetrate to the source of causes [*guo che yinyuan*], and the two mutually penetrate each other [*er hu jiaoche*], then it reveals depth. When one first raises the thought [of awakening], one completes perfect awakening. Causes suffuse effects."

250. The one sutra is the last chapter of the *Eighty Huayan* entitled "Entrance into the Dharma Sphere" (T 10:319a1–444c29).

251. See note 167.

252. The ten profundities (*shi xuan*) in Fazang's *Huayan yisheng jiaoyi fenji zhang* (T 45:503a16–509a3) are called the old ten profundities and those in Fazang's *Huayan jing tanxuan ji* (T 35:123a27–125a11) are called the new ten profundities. Chengguan and Zongmi received the new ten profundities.

253. Chengguan's *Da fangguang fohuayan jing suishu yanyi chao* (T 36:7b29–c3) in explaining a line from his *Huayan jing shu*, says: "This correctly reveals the purport. Within it there are two. First it clarifies that principle and phenomena are unobstructed [*li shi wuai*]. Later it reveals that phenomenon and phenomenon are unobstructed [*shi shi wuai*]. Even though in this [*Huayan*] sutra it extensively speaks of phenomena and extends to speaking of principle, both are unobstructed, and, therefore, it takes the unobstructed dharma sphere [*wuzhangai fajie*] as its purport."

254. Below, Zongmi appears to be drawing from Chengguan's *Da fangguang fohuayan jing suishu yanyi chao* (T 36:164c8–17): "All-at-once also has many aspects. The first is all-at-once awakening and step-by-step practice [*dunwu jianxiu*]. It is like seeing a nine-storied platform [*jiu ceng zhi tai*]. You might see it all-at-once, but you must tread up the staircase later to reach the top. Now, also, in this manner one all-at-once understands the mind nature. 'Mind is buddha,' and there is no dharma not possessed, but one must accumulate merit and everywhere cultivate the myriad practices. This is in conformity with [intellectual] understanding awakening [*jiewu*]. The second is all-at-once practice and step-by-step awakening. This is like rubbing a mirror [*mo jing*]. At one time you rub it all over, but [the restoration of] the brightness and purity is step-by-step. The myriad practices are all-at-once practiced, but awakening is victorious step-by-step. This is in conformity with [direct] realization awakening [*zhengwu*]. The third is all-at-once practice and all-at-once awakening. This is like a sharp sword cutting silk. A thousand threads are evenly cut, and at one time they are evenly severed. This is also like dying a thousand silk threads. At one time they are evenly dyed, and at one time

they become the color. Therefore, the myriad practices are evenly cultivated, and at one time there is bright awakening. The fourth is step-by-step practice and step-by-step awakening. This is like cutting bamboo sections. If the sections are not identical, they are of no use right now."

255. The poem is by Wang Zhihuan (688–742), a man of of Puyang in Bingzhou (Taiyuan in Shanxi). At the beginning of the Kaiyuan era (713–742) he served as a Keeper-of-the-Registers of Hengshui county in Jizhou (Hebei) but retired and held no official post for fifteen years. In his late years he took a post in Henan. His poetic fame was high, and it is said that people loved to chant his poetry. The poem is entitled "Climbing Crane Tower." This three-storied tower was located at the southwest city wall of Hezhong superior prefecture (Shanxi) and was famous as a site for viewing the Yellow River. It is the first of six poems by Wang in the *Complete Tang Poems* (*Quan Tangshi*, 8:253.2849):

> The bright sun disappears behind the mountains.
> The Yellow River flows to the sea.
> Wanting to investigate with the eye of a thousand *li*,
> I went up one more story.

256. Hirakawa, 1096, gives *zhengwu=adhigama* (*spiritual realization*). I have adopted "[direct] realization awakening." It is the unexcelled, perfect awakening of a buddha.

257. Hirakawa, 1068, gives *jiewu=mata* (*learned* or *understood*). I have adopted "[intellectual] understanding awakening."

258. T 10:89a1–2.

259. See note 14.

260. The sutra has not been identified.

261. This seems to be a generalized statement of Buddhist attainment. Compare *Vimalakīrti Sutra*, T 14:539a8–10: "At that time in the great city of Vaiśālī there was a venerable named Vimalakīrti, who had already made offerings to immeasuable buddhas, deeply planted good roots, obtained the non-arising patience, of unimpeded skill in debate, playful among the superknowledges, having attained 'the dharanis [*zhu zongchi*]."

262. This saying is found in a section entitled "Sayings of the Great Master Heze Shenhui of Luojing" in the *Jingde chuandeng lu*, T 51:439c1.

263. The source has not been identified.

264. T 9:367a14–15. See note 179.

265. T 9:47c17.

266. See *Chan Notes*, section 5.

267. Yampolsky, *The Platform Sutra*, 137: "Good friends, in the dharma there is no sudden or gradual, but among people some are keen and others dull."

268. Following the *Ming Canon* edition of Ui, 112, and the Gozan edition of Ishii (7), 77, both of which read: *"fei qiang chuanzao."*

269. *Lanka Descent Sutra*, T 16:485c26–486a18, gives four similes for step-by-step (the mango fruit step-by-step ripens; potters making various pieces complete them step-by-step; the great earth step-by-step produces the myriad things; and people studying various skills such as music and painting bring them to completion step-by-step) and four similes for all-at-once (a bright mirror all-at-once manifests all the colored images without characteristics; the solar and lunar disks all-at-once illuminate to reveal all colored images; the storehouse consciousness all-at-once knows one's own mind and the sense objects; and buddha radiance all-at-once illuminates). Chengguan's *Da fangguang fohuayan jing suishu yanyi chao* (T 36:164b11–c3) correlates these eight with the ten faiths, ten abodes, etc.

270. Following the *Ming Canon* edition of Ui, 112: *"renwu."*

271. Following the *Ming Canon* edition of Ui, 114: *"fangde."*

272. This phrase (*"Damo yi zong"*) echoes the description of entrance by principle in the two-entrances section of the *Bodhidharma Anthology*: "Entering by principle means that by relying on the teachings one awakens to the axiom [*wu zong*] and comes to have deep confidence that living beings, common and noble, are identical to the true nature; that it is just because of the unreal covering of adventitious dust that [the true nature] is not revealed" (Yanagida, *Daruma no goroku*, 31–32).

273. This line seems to imply that the *Chan Prolegomenon* was composed before the compilation of the *Chan Canon*.

274. This presumably refers to section 45's step-by-step teaching (the first two teachings); all-at-once of responding to beings of the highest disposition (third teaching); and all-at-once of the rite of transforming beings (third teaching). Kamata, 199, suggests it could also refer to: section 46's all-at-once/step-by-step of instructional devices; all-at-once/step-by-step of ability for awakening; and all-at-once/step-by-step of willpower for practice.

275. Following the punctuation of the *Ming Canon* edition of Ui, 114, and the Gozan edition of Ishii (8), 18.

276. This quotation has not been traced.

277. T 9:7a21–b6. This section is a complicated patchwork of sutra quotations and paraphrases, mainly from the *Huayan* and *Lotus*. Some passages are only distillations of the sense and context of the original.

278. T 10:275a19–21.

279. T 10:1b23–c4.

280. T 10:275a19–20.

281. T 16:457b29–c3.

282. T 10:272c5–273a1.

283. T 9:8b4–5.

284. T 10:5b25–c1. On the four articles of attraction, see note 106.

278 TRANSLATION OF THE CHAN PROLEGOMENON

285. This portion appears to be Zongmi's condensation. The *Huayan's* chapter entitled "Entrance into the Dharma Sphere" opens at the Jeta Grove (T 10:319a4) with the World-honored-one entering into the lion's sport concentration (320a12).

286. Near the beginning of the *Huayan's* chapter entitled "Entrance into the Dharma Sphere," T 10:322c19, it says: "The great hearers, at the Jeta Grove, did not see the Tathagata's divine powers. . . ."

287. This quotation has not been traced.

288. In the *Lotus Sutra*, T 9:28b26–27, the Buddha tells Mahākāśyapa: "These twelve-hundred arhats, I now will give them, one after the other, predictions of unexcelled, perfect awakening."

289. *Huayan Sutra*, T 10:272a7 and 16–17.

290. T 9:9c5–10a6.

291. This is not a quotation by any means, but it is based on *Lotus Sutra*, T 9:13b18–29.

292. The crossroads and white ox occur at *Lotus Sutra*, T 9:12c14 and 22.

293. T 12:767a28–29.

294. T 12:1110c13–15.

295. Refers to the line that cites the *Great Expanded Dharma Sphere*.

296. This short line (*"chanzong li jiao"*) is a quintessential expression of Zongmi's stance on the relationship between Chan and the teachings. The teachings, the sutras and treatises, serve as *li*, that is, precedents, regulations, customary practices, institutions, and traditions that *underpin and legitimize* the three Chan axioms. His emphatic tone here is revealing.

297. See notes 278 and 290.

298. The following is based on *Dasheng qixin lun*, T 32:576a5–c4.

299. *Neither Increasing nor Decreasing Sutra*, T 16:467b6–8.

300. The following is based on *Dasheng qixin lun*, T 32:576b7–16 and 577a7–21.

301. *Dasheng qixin lun*, T 32:576b15–16.

302. *Dasheng qixin lun*, T 32:577a7.

303. Fazang's *Dasheng qixin lun yiji bieji* (T 44:292a12): "Overturn the unreal stain [*fangdui wang ran*] to reveal one's own true quality [*xian zi zhen de*]."

304. See note 59.

305. *Banrujo boluomiduo xin jin*, T 8:848c3–4.

306. *Dasheng qixin lun*, T 32:578b10.

307. *Dasheng qixin lun*, T 32:581c8–13.

308. *Dasheng qixin lun* (T 32:581c14–16): "Of practices there are five gates that can perfect this faith. What are the five? The first is the gate of giving; the second the gate of precepts; the third the gate of forbearance; the fourth the gate of striving; and the fifth the gate of stopping-viewing."

309. *Dasheng qixin lun*, T 32:580c6–9.

310. Echoes the *Bodhidharma Anthology*'s description of the fourth of the four practices of Bodhidharma, according with dharma (*chengfa*): "In the dharma substance there is no stinginess" (Yanagida, *Daruma no goroku*, 32).

311. *Banruo boluomiduo xin jing*, T 8:848c4–5.

312. *Ratnagotra-śāstra* (T 31:821b24–25): "For bodhisattvas in the eighth stage the ten masteries are foremost [*shi zizai wei shou*]." The second is mastery over mind; mastery over forms, however, does not appear in the list.

313. *Dasheng qixin lun* (T 32:576b24–26): "Full of teaching devices [*manzu fangbian*], in a moment he is in conjunction [*yi nian xiangying*]. Aware of the first arising of mind, mind has nothing to be characterized as *first*. Because one is far divorced from subtle thoughts, he is able to see the mind nature. Mind is then eternally abiding, and it is called ultimate awakening."

314. *Dasheng qixin lun* (T 32:576c1–4): "If one attains no mindfulness, then one knows the arising, abiding, changing, and disappearing of mind characteristics. Because they are equal to no mindfulness [*wunian*], in reality there is no such thing as initial awakening's changing [*wu you shijue zhi yi*]. This is because the four characteristics simultaneously exist; none of them is erected on its own; and from the outset it is equally one, identical awakening."

315. Zongmi once again echoes the two-entrances portion of the *Bodhidharma Anthology* (Yanagida, *Daruma no goroku*, 32): "If one rejects the unreal and reverts to the real and frozenly abides in wall viewing, then self and other, common man and noble one, are identical; firmly abiding without shifting, no longer following after the written teachings, this is mysteriously tallying with principle [*yu li mingfu*]. It is nondiscriminative, quiescent, and inactive. We call it entrance by principle."

316. Actually, these are the three minds of the second level. The three minds of the fourth level are: straight mind, deep mind, and mind of great compassion.

317. See note 249.

318. T 12:838a4.

319. T 10:89a1–2.

320. Kamata, 232, understands "*hao* [labels]" as "*fuhao* [symbols; signs; marks]" and remarks that there are no symbols, by which he means the various drawings of circles, in his root edition, the Wanli 4 (1576) Korean edition. Ui, 280, says: "These *gō* [*hao*] and *ten* [*dian*], that is, *fugō* [*fuhao*] and *futen* [*fudian*], were dropped off in the process of transmission by copying. The Tahara edition [see introduction, note 101] shows the red writing in a single line and the black writing in a double line, and the Korean edition jettisons these differences altogether." Ishii (9), 68, notes: "The *Ming Canon* edition has the o symbol [*kigō*] in red and the ● symbol [*kigō*] in black. In comparing the various lineages of editions, *one can only reach the conclusion that these symbols were added at the* Ming Canon *edition*." The italics are mine, since this conclusion has implications for the position of these circles in the history of Chinese

thought. Much suggests that there were no circles in Zongmi's original text and that they were added later. Ishii (9), 68, adds that the word "ten" (*dian*), which appears toward the end of this section, seems to refer to the explanatory text in the chart. In my translation the *hao*/labels are "Sentient-Being Mind," "Real," "Unreal," etc., which in the 1576 Korean edition and in the Dunhuang manuscript fragment are written in large script, and the *dian* are the passages in *small script*, that is, the captions under the labels in smaller graphs in the Korean edition and the Dunhuang fragment.

321. Kamata, 232, suggests that the term "*yishuo* [discussion of principles]" might refer to Fazang's *Dasheng qixin lun yiji* (T no. 1846). However, Yŏndam Yuil's commentary *Sŏnwŏn jejŭnjip tosŏ kwamok pyŏngip sagi* (Shūmitsu, 289) remarks: "The line "discussion of principles in the text of the treatise" refers to discussion of principles in the text of the root treatise [that is, the *Awakening of Faith*]."

322. The residual warmth of the heart is a metaphor for the residual pure seeds that have always been attached to the storehouse consciousness. *Cheng weishi lun* (T 31:45b29–c5): "From without beginning attached to the root consciousness [*yifu benshi*] there are no-outflows seeds [*wulou zhong*]. Due to the repeated perfumings of the revolving consciousnesses, they are gradually augmented, up to and including the ultimate. Upon becoming a buddha, it turns over to eject the consciousness seeds that are impure from the outset and turns over to apprehend the pure seeds arisen from the beginning, maintaining the seeds of all [good] qualities. Due to the power of the original vow, it exhausts the limit of the future and produces all the excellent functions, continuing without end."

323. See note 14.

324. A metaphor for something that is easy to see or easy to know. *Book of Rites*, Zhongni yanju: "Governing the state is like laying the finger on the palm, and that is all." *Analects*, Bayi: "Someone asked for an explanation of the imperial sacrifice. The master said: 'I do not know. He who knows the explanation could deal with all-under-heaven as easily as laying this here.' He laid his finger upon his palm."

325. Following the *Ming Canon* edition of Ui, 148, and the Dunhuang manuscript of Tanaka Ryōshō, *Tonkō Zenshū bunken no kenkyū* (Tokyo: Daitō shuppansha, 1983), 432, both of which read "*xudong*." The Gozan edition of Ishii (10), 65, reads "*zhi xudong*."

326. Based on *Chunqiu Zuoshi zhuan*, Chenggong, eighteenth year. Not making a distinction between beans and barley is a metaphor for stupidity.

327. These are called the eight winds (*ba feng*), mentioned below. The term appears in a poem by Hanshan saying that the no-outflows cliff of Cold Mountain "is unmovable even when the eight winds blow" (Iritani and Matsumura, *Kanzan-shi*, 401).

328. Once again we encounter one of Zongmi's two favorite themes, all-at-once awakening followed by step-by-step practice. The other is that the teachings serve as precedents for the Chan axioms.

329. The closest thing in the *Platform Sutra* is a saying in section 31 of the Dunhuang manuscript version: "As to the dharma of no mindfulness, one sees all dharmas

but does not attach to all dharmas; makes a circuit of all loci, but does not attach to any locus" (Yampolsky, *The Platform Sutra*, 153). We do find this saying in the *Chuan-xin fayao* (T 48:381b6–7; Iriya Yoshitaka, ed. and trans., *Denshin hōyō Enryōroku*, Zen no goroku 8 [Tokyo: Chikuma shobō, 1969], 30) and the *Wanlinglu* (T 48:384b 21–22; Iriya, *Denshin hōyō*, 97). In neither case is the saying attributed to the sixth patriarch Huineng.

330. Iriya and Koga, *Zengo jiten*, 169, defines "*zhime*" as "just; merely; solely; only" and mentions that the "*-me*" is a suffix without meaning. The word "*zhime*" occurs three more times in the remainder of this section.

331. The Gozan edition of Ishii (10), 70, reads: "What need is there to go further and collect the *Chan Canon*, which in number surpasses one hundred rolls (one hundred sixty rolls)?"

332. Eighty thousand stands for eighty-four thousand, referring to the eighty-four thousand Buddhist teachings (*famen=dharma-paryāya*) intended to extinguish the eighty-four thousand depravities. *Da zhidu lun* (T 25:222c17–20): "Furthermore, dharma has two types. The first is the three baskets, twelve sections, and eighty-four thousand dharma aggregates expounded by the Buddha. The second is the dharma principles spoken of by the Buddha, that is, holding to the precepts, dhyana, wisdom, the eightfold noble path, up to the fruit of liberation, nirvana, etc."

333. This suggests the possibility that Zongmi included in the *Chan Canon* a genealogical chart of the Chan houses similar to the one in the *Chan Letter* (section 7).

334. In other words, even teachings that Zongmi himself finds somewhat disturbing have been included in the *Chan Canon* without editorial revision.

335. This suggests that the critiques (*ping*) of the *Chan Notes* and *Chan Letter* became a structural element of the Chan Canon.

336. *Huayan Sutra* (T 10:314c11–12): "Contemplate the great sea of the three types of existence [in the three realms of desire, form, and non-form], pinch up the gods, humans, and serpents, and place them on the shore of nirvana."

337. This appears to refer to a work that is quoted in the first letter of the *Bodhidharma Anthology* (Yanagida, *Daruma no goroku*, 47): "Moreover, I reveal the *Verses on Teaching Devices for Entering the Path* [*Rudao fangbian ji*], to be used as an admonition to those who have the conditions for the same type of awakening. If you have time, unroll and read it. Through cross-legged sitting dhyana in the end you necessarily see the original nature." A four-line verse follows. (It is unclear where the quotation begins and ends.) A work with a similar title (*Rudao anxin yao fangbian famen*) and description is attributed to the fourth patriarch Daoxin at the beginning of his lengthy entry in the sacred history *Lengjia shizi ji* (T 85:1286c21; Yanagida I, 186). And this title is clearly linked to the teaching devices for entering the path (*rudao fangbian*) that Daoxin showed his student Shanfu according to the Shanfu entry in Daoxuan's *Xu gaoseng zhuan* (T 50:603a7–8). Just why Zongmi thought of arranging his *Chan Canon* according to the dictates of this verse work is unclear.

338. See *Chan Letter,* note 21.

339. Refers to the four practices of the *Bodhidharma Anthology.* See introduction, note 46.

340. See note 28.

341. Zongmi seems to regard Wolun as a non-Bodhidharma-lineage figure who lived during the eighth century. We have no biographical information on Wolun beyond this. We do have two works attributed to him, both found among the Dunhuang manuscripts: a very brief treatise entitled *Wolun chanshi kanxin fa* (Stein Chinese 646 and 1494 plus a Ryūkoku University manuscript); and three verses entitled *Wolun chanshi ji* (Stein Chinese 5657 and 6631 plus Beijing *guo*-41). Editions of both are to be found in Wu Qiyu, "Wolun chanshi yi yu Dunhuang Tufanwen (Pelliot 116 hao) yi ben kaoshi," *Dunhuang xue* 4 (1979): 44–46. Also, Suzuki, *Suzuki Daisetsu zenshū,* 2:452–53, has an edition of the former. Both the treatise and the verses echo through a number of Chan texts. A quotation from the *Wolun chanshi kanxin fa* appears in Yanshou's *Zongjinglu,* T 48:942c16–19. The sacred history *Lengjia shizi ji* (T 85:1284a10–11; Yanagida II, 93) has a line in common with the *Wolun chanshi kanxin fa,* though the history may be quoting directly from the sutra source. The *Jueguanlun* (Tokiwa and Yanagida, *Zekkanron,* 101) has a passage in common with the *Wolun chanshi kanxin fa.* There is a quotation of one verse of the *Wolun chanshi ji* in the Ming Canon edition of the *Platform Sutra* (T 48:358a26–28) and the quotation of the same verse in *Jingde chuandeng lu* (T 51:245b6–8). In addition, Wolun's teachings were known among the Tibetans, both at Dunhuang and in central Tibet. Obata Hironobu, "Pelliot tib. n. 116 bunken ni mieru shozenji no kenkyū," *Zen bunka kenkyūjo kiyō* 8 (August 1976): 5 and 21, provides transliterations of the Tibetan Wolun material. Wolun's name is either transliterated into Tibetan as Hgvalun, etc., or translated as Nyal ba'i 'khor lo.

342. Huiwen is considered the founding patriarch of the Tiantai lineage. The *Xu gaoseng zhuan* entry on his disciple Huisi (515–577), T 50:563a12, says that Huisi attained the Lotus concentration under his tutelage. Huisi is honored as the second patriarch of Tiantai.

343. Zhi Gong (418–514) is also known as Baozhi. *Gaoseng zhuan,* T 50:394a15–395b4, has an entry for him. His career combines dhyana practice, eccentricity, strangeness, and the composition of poetry. *Jingde chuandeng lu,* T 51:449a26–451c24, contains three short collections of verse attributed to him, but they are probably products of the middle Tang. He became a figure in Chan literature via the memorable exchange between Emperor Wu of the Liang and Bodhidharma. After Emperor Wu is frustrated by Bodhidharma's answers to his questions and Bodhidharma has departed for the north, there is an exchange between Baozhi and the emperor. The earliest account we have of this dialogue is in the Bodhidharma entry of the *Baolinzhuan,* which is dated 801 (Yanagida, *Hōrinden,* 133a1–10): "Later Śākya Baozhi asked the Liang Emperor: 'Formerly I heard that Bodhidharma arrived in the country. Why did the great king not look up to him in reverence and keep him here?' Emperor Wu said: 'I did not yet know

that this person's ambition lay in the purport of the highest vehicle, calmly distant from common feelings. I was unsympathetic and because of this slandered him. Therefore, I did not detain him.' Baozhi said: 'Though the king encountered, he did not encounter.' Emperor Wu said: 'Who was he?' Baozhi said: 'This was the great master who transmits the buddha mind, the noble one Avalokiteśvara.' The king for a long time was frightened and remorseful. He then despatched the messenger Zhao Guangwen to go and get him. Baozhi said: 'Of course, a Guangwen can get that one, but even if you exhaust the power of your whole country, this person will not return.'" For the version in the *Zutangji*, see Yanagida, *Sodōshū*, 36b2–8.

344. The only early mention we have of the strange layman Fu Xi (also known as Fu dashi, etc.) is in the *Xu gaoseng zhuan* entry for the thaumaturge Huiyun (T 50:650b1–6): "At the time of Emperor Xuan of the Chen [r. 569–583] the Shuanglin Great Scholar Fu Hong of Wushang county of Dongyang prefecture [in Zhejiang], embodying the provisional and responding to the path, tread as a successor of Vimalakīrti. Sometimes he changed into various forms in order to fulfill his responsibility of saving beings. He stayed at Shuanglin and led both monks and lay people. Sometimes a golden color emanated from his breast, and an unusual scent flowed from his palms. Sometimes he manifested a bodily height of ten feet plus, and his arms went beyond his knees. His feet were two feet in length and his fingers six inches. His two eyes were bright and shone outward like a double sunrise. His appearance was towering with the form of a giant." Among the Dunhuang manuscripts there are many copies of a work attributed to Fu, the *Liangchao Fu dashi song Jingang banruo jing*. This set of verses on the *Thunderbolt-Cutter Sutra* is said to have been composed by Fu at the request of Emperor Wu of the Liang, but it is probably an eighth-century apocryphon. There is also the *Shanhui dashi yulu* (ZZ 2.25.1; CBETA/Wan Xuzangjing vol. 69, no. 1335) compiled by Lou Ying, a scholar of the Tianbao era (742–756). It contains a biography of Fu dashi, his sayings, and his works. On the basis of this late and very detailed biography his dates are usually given as 497–569. Fu dashi and Baozhi are incorporated into Chan literature as a duo. The preface to the *Liangchao Fu dashi song Jingang banruo jing* (T 85:1a2–9) starts off with the following story: "Emperor Wu first requested Zhi Gong to lecture on the sutra. Zhi Gong replied: 'There is Great Scholar Fu who is good at interpreting and lecturing on it.' The emperor asked: 'Where is this person now?' Zhi Gong replied: 'Now at a fish shop.' At just that moment the Great Scholar [Fu] entered the hall. The emperor asked: 'Great Scholar! I want to request you to lecture on the *Thunderbolt-Cutter Sutra*. What sort of high seat do you require?' The Great Scholar replied: 'I need no high seat. I just need an oak plank.' The Great Scholar got a plank, and then chanted forty-nine songs on the sutra. When done, he left. Zhi Gong asked Emperor Wu: 'Did you understand him?' The emperor said he did not understand [*bu shi*]. Zhi Gong told the emperor: 'This is Maitreya Bodhisattva changed into another form.'" This story is reworked into the sixty-ninth case of the *Xuedou songgu* of Mingjue Zhongxian (980–1052): "Emperor Wu of the

Liang requested Great Scholar Fu to lecture on the sutra. The Great Scholar ascended the seat and swept the desk once. He then got down from the seat. Emperor Wu was startled. Zhi Gong asked: 'Does Your Highness understand?' The emperor said: 'I don't understand [*bu hui*].' [Zhi] Gong said: 'The Great Scholar's lecture on the sutra is over'" (Iriya Yoshitaka, Kajitani Sōnin, and Yanagida Seizan, eds. and trans., *Secchō juko*, Zen no goroku 15 [Tokyo: Chikuma shobō, 1981], 195).

345. Baotang Wuzhu quotes the poems of Wang Fanzhi in the sacred history *Lidai fabao ji* (T 51:193a19–20; Yanagida II, 270). Since that history was compiled some time after Wuzhu's death in 774, the *Wang Fanzhi shiji* was circulating by the Dali era (766–779). Many copies are found among the Dunhuang manuscripts (see T no. 2863). The poems encourage good actions and are directed toward a popular audience, containing many examples of old *baihua* (Daizōkyō, 834). See Iriya Yoshitaka, "Ō Bonji shishū kō," in *Kanda hakushi kanreki kinen shoshigaku ronshū*, ed. Kanda hakushi kanreki kinen kai (Tokyo: Heibonsha, 1957), 491–501.

346. There is an entry for Huiyuan/Yuan Gong (334–416) in the *Gaoseng zhuan* (T 50:357c20–361b13). He was a disciple of Dao'an and founded the White Lotus Society on Mt. Lu in Jiangxi in 403. See Erik Zurcher, *The Buddhist Conquest of China: The Spread and Adaptation of Buddhism in Early Medieval China* (Leiden: E. J. Brill, 1972), 204–53.

347. The *sheng* is a type of wind instrument consisting of nineteen or thirteen bamboo pipes bundled together into a vertical column, their feet shod in a single bowl made from a gourd. The *huang*-s are the thin elastic reeds made of bamboo or copper within each of the pipes. Such a wind instrument was played via a single mouthpiece set into the bowl; its overall notes and chords were modulated using the finger-holes on the individual pipes.

348. This refers to Tiantai Zhiyi's works on the *Lotus Sutra* and his great meditation compendium: *Miaofa lianhua jing xuanyi* (T no. 1716); *Miaofa lianhua jing wenju* (T no. 1718); and *Mohe zhiguan* (T no. 1911).

349. See note 308. The one gate is the fifth, stopping-viewing.

350. See notes 18 and 22.

351. The *Ming Canon* edition of Ui, 156, and the Gozan edition of Ishii (10), 74, both read: "*xia zuzhuan xu zhong* [in the preface to the *Patriarch Transmission* below]" rather than the "*liuzuzhuan xu zhong* [in the preface to the *Sixth Patriarch Transmission*]" in the 1576 Korean edition (Kamata, 254). The former is probably an error. This title appears to be a "clip" of the title of the lost *Zuzong zhuanji* (*Patriarch Lineage Transmission Record*) quoted in section 4 of the *Chan Letter* (see *Chan Letter*, note 16).

352. See note 272.

353. The line "*yin zong shengjiao* [noble teachings that seal the Chan axioms]" is a variant of the line at note 296.

354. This is, as far as I know, the earliest application of a legal metaphor to Chan literary materials, well before the term "*gong'an*" appears in Chan literature. In fact,

the term here, "*guansi wen'an* [lawsuit document]," is a synonym of "*gong'an*." With Zongmi the final judgment rests with the noble teachings, the sutras and treatises.

355. Thus, if the *Chan Canon* was on the order of one hundred rolls, the canonical extracts constituted about 10 percent of the whole. In section 14 it is mentioned that the *Chan Canon* includes twenty-plus sheets (*ershi yu zhi*) of sutra passages.

356. See *Chan Letter*, note 21.

357. T 14:545b5–6.

358. Unidentified source.

3. TRANSLATION OF THE *CHAN NOTES*

1. I have supplied the section numbers and at the beginning of each section a summary of its contents in my own words. Passages in italics within parentheses are Zongmi's autocommentary.

2. The slogan is "*fuchen kanjing fangbian tong jing.*" "Sweeping away dust" echoes Shenxiu's verse in the *Platform Sutra*. See *Chan Letter*, note 39. On the connection between "gazing at purity" and Shenxiu, see *Chan Prolegomenon*, note 116. The term "teaching devices [*fangbian*]" is found in the titles of two so-called Northern school texts found among the Dunhuang manuscripts: *Dasheng wusheng fangbian men* and *Dasheng wu fangbian beizong.* They show the same five rubrics as Zongmi's summary here. See T no. 2834; Suzuki, Suzuki Daisetsu, *Suzuki Daisetsu zenshū* (Tokyo: Iwanami shoten, 1968), 3:161–235; and Ui Hakuju, *Zenshū-shi kenkyū* (1935; repr., Tokyo: Iwanami shoten, 1966), 1:449–68.

3. Among the Dunhuang manuscripts we have two sacred histories dealing with the line of Shenxiu, the *Chuan fabao ji* and the *Lengjia shizi ji*, both compiled in the north during the first two decades of the eighth century, about forty years after Hongren's death in 675 or 674. The second incorporates a long quotation from the lost *Lengjia renfa zhi* in its Hongren entry. The *Lengjia renfa zhi* has Hongren saying (T 85:1289c10; Yanagida I, 273): "Those who will henceforth transmit my path are only about ten [*zhi ke shi er*]." The list of ten that follows begins with Shenxiu, thus presenting him as Hongren's most prominent successor, corresponding to Śāriputra in the list of the Buddha's ten major disciples. This list includes Huineng of Shaozhou in Guangdong as the eighth of the ten, not, as Zongmi has it, as the central or orthodox successor outside the ten. In fact, Huineng is explicitly relegated to the second tier of Hongren successors. The ninth is a foreigner, the Korean monk Chidok of Yangzhou in Jiangsu, and the seventh is Faru of Luzhou in Shanxi, for whom the *Lengjia shizi ji* evinces a definite antipathy. These three are lumped together and condescendingly labeled mere regional teachers: "They are all worthy to become teachers of men, but they are just personages of one direction [*dan yi fang renwu*]." Both the *Chuan fabao ji* and the *Lengjia shizi ji* show Shenxiu as central to Hongren's East Mountain line

and include biographical entries for Shenxiu (T 85:1290a–c; Yanagida I, 396–407 and 295–320). In addition, an inscription for Shenxiu by Zhang Yue (667–730), which was compiled sometime after 708, has Hongren exclaiming: "The dharma of East Mountain is exhausted in Xiu [*jin zai Xiu yi*]!" (Yanagida Seizan, *Shoki Zenshū shisho no kenkyū* [Kyoto: Hōzōkan, 1967], 498; QTW 5:231.2953a19–b1). The *Lengjia shizi ji* lists four successors of Shenxiu, with Chan Master Puji of Mt. Song outside the capital of Luoyang as the first (T 85:1290c; Yanagida I, 320–21). Also, an inscription for Puji by Li Yong, a son of Emperor Xuanzong, that was erected in 742 has Puji referring to himself as the "seventh leaf" (*qi ye*) of the lineage (QTW 6:262.3362a11). Li Yong's inscription for Songyue Monastery also makes Puji Shenxiu's successor (QTW 6:263.3380a19). From these sources we must conclude that what Zongmi refers to as Northern (Beizong) *was not a collateral lineage, as he asserts, but the main line of Hongren's East Mountain school, and Huineng was originally not the sixth patriarch, but a relatively obscure follower at Hongren's East Mountain.* In other words, there was a Huineng at East Mountain, but he was far overshadowed during the heyday of East Mountain and for some time thereafter by other figures, particularly Shenxiu. But Huineng was not a later creation out of nothing.

4. See *Chan Letter*, note 39.

5. See *Chan Letter*, note 40.

6. *fangbian tong jing=wu fangbian.*

7. This slogan ("*san ju yongxin wei jie ding hui*") centers on the three topics of Musang (Wuxiang). The sacred history *Lidai fabao ji* in its Musang entry (T 51:185b6–8; Yanagida II, 144) has Musang attributing the formula of the three topics to Bodhidharma himself: "[Musang] also said: 'This three-topics formula of mine is a teaching originally transmitted by the patriarchal master Bodhidharma. Do not say that [the three topics] were something [originally] spoken by Preceptor [Zhi]shen and Preceptor Tang.'"

8. The list of ten major disciples of Hongren in the *Lengjia shizi ji* (actually within the incorporated material from the *Lengjia renfa zhi*) has Zhishen as the second, suggesting his great prestige in the East Mountain tradition (T 85:1289c11–12; Yanagida I, 273). The Dunhuang manuscript sacred history *Lidai fabao ji*, which was compiled after 774, in its Zhishen entry gives his place of origin as Runan in Henan and says that as a child he followed his grandfather to an official post in Sichuan, returning to Dechun Monastery there after training under Hongren (T 51:184b; Yanagida II, 137). It goes on to say that in 702 Zhishen handed over the robe of faith (*xin jiasha*), Bodhidharma's robe, which Empress Wu had given him, to his disciple Chuji. The subsequent entry for Chuji has Chuji in 736 summoning Chan Master Musang of Korea and handing over to Musang, that is, Preceptor Kim (Jin heshang), the dharma and the robe of faith (T 51:184c10–12; Yanagida II, 140). The subsequent entry for Musang of Jingzhong Monastery in the superior prefecture of Chengdu in Jiannan (Sichuan) states that he taught at the Jingzhong for more than twenty years (T 51:185a1–2; Yanagida II, 142). Also, an in-

scription for Chengyuan, another student of Chuji, by Lü Wen, who was active in the early ninth century, mentions a lineage running from Hongren of East Mountain to Shen Gong (that is, Zhishen) of Zizhou to Chan Master Tang (that is, Chuji) of Sichuan (QTW 13:630.8074b17–18). Zongmi seems reliable on Jingzhong, and perhaps he was even working from some version of the materials in the *Lidai fabao ji*.

9. Mt. Changsong is in Jianzhou, Sichuan. Zhuzhou is Suizhou, Sichuan. Tongquan county is southeast of Shehong county, Sichuan.

10. The *Lidai fabao ji* Musang entry (T 51:185a11–15; Yanagida II, 143) says that at his great convocations Musang initially taught a singing buddha-recitation: "Preceptor Kim, annually in the twelfth and first months, for thousands of monks, nuns, and laypeople, [held a ceremony] of receiving conditions [that is, conferring the precepts]. At the ornamented practice site he took the high seat [on the platform] and spoke dharma. He first taught chanting buddha-recitation as a gentle song, exhausting one breath in the recitation [*xian jiao yin sheng nianfo jin yi qi nian*]. Just when the sound died down and the buddha-recitation had stopped, he said: 'No remembering [*wuyi*], no mindfulness [*wunian*], and do not forget [*mowang*]. No remembering is the precepts. No mindfulness is concentration. Do not forget is wisdom. These *three topics* are the dharani gate [*zongchi men*].'"

11. Zongmi's description of a Musang convocation is more detailed than that contained in the *Lidai fabao ji* Musang entry (see note 10). The only divergence is that, whereas the *Lidai fabao ji* says these assemblies were annual, Zongmi says below that they were sometimes once in a year, sometimes once in two or three years.

12. This slogan ("*jiaoxing bu ju er mie shi*") means that Baotang is not constrained or restricted by either the teachings of the sutras and treatises or the traditional range of Buddhist practices. The second or practice part of the slogan ("*mie shi*") seems to anticipate the *Chan Prolegomenon's* classification of Baotang into the first Chan axiom, which involves turning away from sense objects and extinguishing thought of the unreal (*ximie wangnian*). See *Chan Prolegomenon*, section 22. Wuzhu raised a slogan of his own: "Lively like a fish waving its tail, at all times everything is Chan [*huo bobo yiqie shi zhong zong shi chan*]." This catchy line in variant forms appears numerous times in the *Lidai fabao ji's* Wuzhu entry (T 51:191c12, 193a23, 194c14–15, 195a28–29, and 195b2–3; Yanagida II, 245, 270, 291, 304, and 307).

13. The *Lengjia shizi ji* in its list of ten Hongren disciples gives Old An (Lao'an) of Mt. Song as the sixth (T 85:1289c13; Yanagida I, 273).

14. These three seem to have been part of Mt. Song's world of spirits, recluses, Daoist immortals, hermits, shamanesses, and alchemists at their stoves. Teng Teng was associated with inner alchemical works on the golden pill. Pozao Duo spoke dharma to a fearful shamaness and converted her. Thereupon the tiles of her alchemical stove spontaneously loosened and broke apart. This action gave him his name.

15. The foundation of the *Lidai fabao ji* is its Wuzhu entry. The following is a synopsis of that entry (T 51:186a21–187c7, 187c19–23, and 188b21–189a24; Yanagida II, 168–72,

189, and 198–200): Wuzhu suddenly encountered the white-robed layman Chen Chu-zhang, whose origins are unknown. People of the time called him a magical-creation body of Vimalakīrti. Vimalakīrti Chen spoke the all-at-once teaching. On the very day Preceptor Wuzhu met him, they secretly meshed in mutual knowing, and Vimalakīrti Chen silently transmitted the mind dharma (*mo chuan xinfa*). Wuzhu arrived at the Jingzhong Monastery in Chengdu superior prefecture in 759, with Musang extraordinarily pleased to see him. That very night, at a communal assembly, Wuzhu received the precepts. On each of the three days and nights of this great assembly Musang asked in a loud, singing voice: "Why do you people not go off into the mountains? Of what benefit is it to remain here for so long?" Musang's attendants became alarmed at these words, but Wuzhu silently entered the mountains. At Wuzhu's mountain retreat a Master Daoyi practiced chanting, doing obeisance, and buddha-recitation, but Wuzhu intently cut off thoughts (*yixiang jue si duan*) and entered the realm of self-realization (*ru zizheng jingjie*). When Daoyi and other young masters asked Wuzhu's permission for a twenty-four-hour session of obeisance to the buddhas and confession, his response included: "No mindfulness [*wunian*] is seeing the buddhas!" Daoyi disagreed and left, going to Jingzhong Monastery and complaining that Wuzhu did not allow obeisance, confession, buddha-recitation, and chanting, but just sat in voidness and quietude (*zhi kongxian zuo*). Some in Musang's entourage were aghast. But when this shocking report on Wuzhu was conveyed to Musang, he scolded the reporters: "You should retreat! When I was in the training stage, I did not even eat but just sat in voidness and quietude." Wuzhu asked a messenger to take a gift of bud tea (*chaya*) to Musang as a sign of faith. In 762 the messenger arrived at the Jingzhong and was received by Musang, who, upon seeing the tea, was extraordinarily pleased. Musang said that he in turn had a gift of faith for Wuzhu. On the day the messenger was to return to the mountains Musang sent all of his personal attendants outside the hall and showed the robe (*jiasha yi ling*) to the messenger, telling him to take it secretly to Wuzhu with the following message: "Wait three to five years, until there is an important person to welcome you, and then come out." Musang died in sitting posture that year. Following the prediction, in the spring of 766 Vice-Generalissimo, Vice-President of the Yellow Gate (Imperial Chancellery), Minister Du Hongjian (709–769) arrived in Chengdu, and in a matter of months Wuzhu was invited down from Mt. Baiya and received Du as a visitor. Du eventually heard from his attendants that Wuzhu had obtained the robe from Musang and was his successor. That same year a delegation, presumably sent by Du, went up into the mountains and invited Wuzhu to come down. Minister Du then visited Wuzhu, and Wuzhu, in cross-legged sitting posture, did not even rise to welcome him (*bu ying bu qi*). Minister Du, as the new disciple, asked about Musang's teaching.

The details in the above account betray a heavy-handed straining on the part of the compilers, students of Wuzhu at the Baotang Monastery in Chengdu after his death, to forge a link between Musang and Wuzhu and in the process to downplay the role of the Jingzhong disciples in Chengdu as the true inheritors of Musang. Zongmi presents Jingzhong Shenhui, whom he calls Yizhou Shi, as the successor of Musang. He presents Baotang Wuzhu as essentially an inheritor of the layman Vimalakīrti Chen. For Zongmi Jingzhong and Baotang are two distinct lineages with completely different instructional styles, and this perspective sounds more reliable than the *Lidai fabao ji*'s Wuzhu entry.

16. The *Lidai fabao ji* shows that this complete avoidance of the practice of the phenomenal characteristics of Buddhism (*shimen shixiang yiqie bu xing*) perplexed some lay adherents around Wuzhu. In the following excerpt from the *Lidai fabao ji* (T 51:193b2–19; Yanagida II, 273) italicized portions are strikingly close to Zongmi's phraseology in his summary of Baotang in the *Chan Notes*, suggesting the high level of accuracy in Zongmi's reports on the Chan houses: "One day when the Preceptor [Wuzhu] was drinking tea, thirty secretaries and imperial functionaries of the military government happened to come by for an audience. Having taken their seats, they inquired: 'Does the Preceptor have a great liking for tea?' The Preceptor said: 'Yes.' He then recited the *Verses on Tea*:

> "Luminous plants grow in dark valleys,
> Fit to be a catalyst for entering the path.
> Mountain dwellers pick the leaves;
> Exquisite flavor flows into cups.
> In quietude false consciousness is settled;
> Enlightened mind illuminates the platform of understanding.
> Without expenditure of human energy and strength,
> Immediately the dharma gate swings open.

"The secretaries at this point asked: 'Why does the Preceptor *not teach people to read the sutras, practice buddha-recitation, and do obeisance [bu jiao ren dujing nianfo libai]*? [≈ *Chan Notes*: "When it comes to doing obeisance and confession, turning and reading [the sutras], making paintings of buddhas, and copying out sutras, they revile all such things as thought of the unreal (*zhi yu lichan zhuandu huafo xiejing yiqie hui zhi jie wei wangxiang*)."] We disciples do not understand.' The Preceptor said: 'Having realized the ultimate of nirvana, I teach people to do likewise. I do not utilize the Tathagata's incomplete teachings. I send around liberation of self in order to awaken beginning trainees, who are already people who have attained true concentration.' Having finished speaking, the Preceptor became stern and immobile. The secretaries and functionaries in unison said: 'There has never been such a thing!' Question: 'Why does the preceptor *not teach a dharma of phenomenal characteristics [bu jiao shixiang fa]*?' [≈ *Chan Notes*: "practices none of the phenomenal characteristics of the Sakya gate (*shimen shixiang yiqie bu xing*)"] The Preceptor replied: 'The excellent principle of the Mahayana is the extreme principle of voidness and brightness. Sentient beings that are engaged in mental activities cannot awaken to the teachings of the sutras. If you point to the original nature of sentient beings and have them see the nature, then they achieve the buddha path. If they attach to characteristics, then they sink into the wheel [of the rebirth process]. When mind arises, then various dharmas arise; when mind disappears, then the various dharmas disappear. *Turning the sutras and doing obeisance are all production of mind [jie shi qixin]. Production of mind is the rebirth process; non-production [of mind] is seeing the Buddha'.* [≈ *Chan Notes*: "All wheel turning in the rebirth process is the production of mind (*qixin*). The production of mind is the unreal. No matter whether good or bad, not producing (mind) is the real."] Another question to the Preceptor: 'Is it alright to teach people in this way?' The Preceptor said: 'Alright. Production of mind is sense-object fatigue; setting thoughts in motion is the Evil One's net. All conditioned dharmas are like a dream, illusion, bubble, shadow, like dew or like lightning. You should contemplate them this way.' When the officials heard these words, their net of doubt was all-at-once destroyed, and they all said they would become disciples."

17. One question Du Hongjian put to Wuzhu concerned Musang's three topics. The *Lidai fabao ji* (T 51:189a14–21; Yanagida II, 200) records: "The Minister asked: 'Preceptor Kim spoke of no remembering, no mindfulness, and do not forget. Is that so?' The Preceptor replied: 'Yes.' The Minister also asked: 'In this three-topics slogan, is it one or three?' The Preceptor replied: 'It is one, not three. No remembering [*wuyi*] is precepts. No mindfulness [*wunian*] is concentration. Do not [allow the] unreal [*mowang*] is wisdom.' He also said: 'Non-production of thoughts [*nian buqi*] is the precepts gate. Non-production of thoughts is the concentration gate. Non-production of thoughts is the wisdom gate. No mindfulness [*wunian*] is precepts, concentration, and wisdom complete.' The Minister also asked: 'In [writing] this "*wang*" character, is it the woman radical beneath the "*wang*" [in the graph for "unreal"] or is it the mind radical beneath the "*wang*" [in the graph for "forget"]?' The Preceptor replied: 'Woman beneath the "*wang*."'"

18. Probably those around Shenhui of Jingzhong Monastery, that is, Yizhou Shi, were continuing to transmit the no-forgetting (*mowang*) form of the three topics. There were tensions between Jingzhong and Baotang over the Musang legacy. Shenqing, who was associated with the Jingzhong faction, criticizes Baotang's lack of practice in his *Beishanlu*. See *Chan Prolegomenon*, note 34.

19. The *Lidai fabao ji* (T 51:188c26–189a4; Yanagida II, 199) records that Wuzhu flabbergasted everyone in the hall when he did not rise from sitting posture to welcome the very high-status Generalissimo Du Hongjian: "[A large group of officials] came ahead and addressed the Preceptor: 'The Minister is coming to visit the Preceptor.' [Wuzhu] replied: 'If coming, then *follow other* in coming [*lai ji cong ta lai*].' [≈ *Chan Notes*: "In all things they give free rein to other (*yiqie ren ta*)."] The imperial guard captain and others addressed the Preceptor: 'The Minister is a distinguished guest, and you must go out to welcome him.' The Preceptor replied: 'I should not welcome him. Welcoming is human feeling, and non-welcoming is buddha dharma.'

As the imperial guard was about to speak again, the Minister entered the hall and saw that the Preceptor's facial expression did not change, [a countenance] of stern composure. The Minister bent deeply at the waist, descended the stairs, bowed, did [the greeting of respect] with his palms pressed together, and inquired about how they were getting along. The secretaries and officials had never seen such a thing. They watched as the Preceptor *did not welcome him, did not even rise [bu ying bu qi]*. [≈ *Chan Notes*: "If someone enters their halls, regardless of whether he is of high status or low status, in no case do they go out to welcome him, not even rising (*dou bu feng-ying yi bu qidong*) when he enters."] By pairs they looked at each other and asked: 'Why does he not rise and welcome [the minister]?'"

20. On the second element of this slogan, see the introduction, note 24.

21. Three sources retain very early snapshots of an unadorned Huineng before he was transformed into the renowned sixth patriarch with an extensive biography, that is, the *Platform Sutra's* biography of the young commoner from the deep South (*Xinzhou baixing*), a member of the short-muzzled dog people known as the Lao (Gelao) and an illiterate (*bu shi zi*), who dazzles the abbot of East Mountain Hongren and subsequently bests Shenxiu's mind verse with one of his own (T 48:337a–338a; Yampolsky, *The Platform Sutra*, 126–33). The first such source is the list of ten Hongren disciples in the *Lengjia shizi ji* (T 85:1289c13–15; Yanagida I, 273), where Huineng is portrayed as a minor, regional teacher. The second source is the *Xiande ji yu Shuangfeng Shan ta ge tan xuanli (Former Worthies Gather at the Mount Shuangfeng Stupa and Each Talks of the Dark Principle)*, a very short collection of sayings for each of twelve figures at an imaginary memorial gathering for Hongren at his stupa on Mt. Shuangfeng in Hubei. The eighth saying is by Huineng, the twelfth by Shenxiu. These two sayings lack any sudden-gradual/Southern-Northern patina and clearly antedate the literary creation of the legendary sixth patriarch Huineng. See *Chan Prolegomenon*, note 116. Lastly, an inscription for a Jingzang, which was compiled sometime after 746 and lacks the compiler's name, states that Jingzang trained under Hui'an (Lao'an), another name on the list of ten, and, after Hui'an's death in 708 or 709, went to the deep south to visit Huineng: "[The Great Master Jingzang] came to Mount Song [in Henan], met the Great Master [Hui']an, and personally received consultation and [answers to his] questions for more than ten years. After the Great Master [Hui'an] passed away [in 708 or 709, Jingzang] subsequently went to Shao district [in Guangdong] to visit Preceptor [Hui]neng [*sui wang Shaojun yi Neng heshang*]. He consulted [with Huineng] about the origin and asked about the path. Suddenly his tears flowed" (QTW 20:997.13059b5–7; this inscription is also found in Wang Shu'an, ed., *Jinshi cuibian* [Taipei: Tailian guofeng chubanshe, 1964 and 1973], 3:87.1524a12–14). Once again there is nothing about Huineng's status as the sixth patriarch.

22. As for Zongmi's assertion that early in his career the Sichuanese Ma was a disciple of Preceptor Kim/Musang, the *Song gaoseng zhuan* in its Daoyi entry at T 50:766a16 mentions that Ma "cut his hair under Preceptor Tang [Chuji] of Zizhou [in

Sichuan]." Two epigraphical pieces with no axe to grind likewise have not deleted the Jingzhong background of the fountainhead of Hongzhou. An inscription for Daoyi by Quan Deyu (759–818), without explicitly mentioning Chuji, says that Daoyi "first had his hair cut off in Zizhong [county in Sichuan]" (QTW 11:501.6466a15). (According to the *Lidai fabao ji* [T 51:184c9–10; Yanagida II, 140], Chuji taught at the Dechun Monastery in Zizhou, which is just north of Zizhong county, for more than twenty years.) The poet Li Shangyin in 853 wrote an inscription for the Hall of the Four Realized Ones (*Si zheng tang*) within the Southern Chan Temple of Huiyi Monastery in Zizhou. Zizhou on the Fu River was to the northwest of Guozhou, Zongmi's birthplace, and the Huiyi Monastery was once the residence of Shenqing, the Jingzhong compiler of the *Beishanlu*. According to this inscription, the Hall of the Four Realized Ones contained on its walls the portraits of four masters: Great Master Musang of the Jingzhong lineage of Yizhou; Great Master Baotang Wuzhu; Great Master Daoyi of Hongzhou; and Great Master Zhizang of the West Hall (a disciple of Daoyi) (QTW 16:780.10281a4–7; for a discussion, see Yanagida, *Shoki Zenshū shisho no kenkyū*, 339–40). Such a set of portraits shows that in Sichuan at least there remained the memory of a linkage between the local monk Daoyi and the Jingzhong line. It is certain that early in his career Daoyi was a disciple of either Musang or Chuji. In time Hongzhou must have downplayed this connection, exclusively emphasizing the subsequent connection between Daoyi and Huairang, disciple of the "sixth patriarch." The set of four portraits in Sichuan, if we take it as Musang and two of his disciples plus a disciple of the second, tends to reinforce Zongmi's claim of Musang as Daoyi's teacher.

23. See *Chan Letter*, note 42.

24. See *Chan Letter*, note 43.

25. See *Chan Letter*, note 44.

26. See *Chan Letter*, note 46.

27. The "*wushi*" of this slogan ("*ben wushi er wang qing*") is not a Buddhist term per se and is best interpreted in the wider context of Tang literature. Iriya Yoshitaka, ed. and trans., *Rinzairoku* (Tokyo: Iwanami shoten, 1989), 47, says that "*wushi*" was a popular expression in the later years of the Tang and cites the work of two poets. The late Tang poet Du Xunhe (d. 904/905) uses the term rather often. One example (*Quan Tangshi* 20:691.7935) is:

> The old man of the stream lives in a quiet place,
> The stream's birds flying into his gate.
> He rises early to go fishing,
> Deep in the night riding the moon on home.
> I see you, old man of nothing to do [*wushi lao*],
> And you make me aware that my seeking is bad.
> You never say the wind and frost are painful,
> Having had but one straw coat for three winters.

28. The *Xu gaoseng zhuan* entry for Huiyong/Huirong (=Fayong/Farong; T 50:603c-605b) does not connect him to the East Mountain lineage. Modern scholars have held various opinions on the connection, beginning with the Chinese Hu Shih, who held that in the eighth century, Niutou followers felt to the need to make a link to the sixth patriarch Huineng via the fourth Daoxin. The Japanese Ui Hakuju, working from epigraphy, affirmed the historical link to the Daoxin. See Hu Shih, "Ch'an (Zen) Buddhism in China: Its History and Method," in *Ko Teki Zengakuan*, ed. Yanagida Seizan (Kyoto: Chūbun shuppansha, 1975), 680; Ui, *Zenshū-shi kenkyū*, 1:94–96. See also John R. McRae, "The Ox-head School of Chinese Ch'an Buddhism: From Early Ch'an to the Golden Age," in *Studies in Ch'an and Hua-yen*, ed. Robert M. Gimello and Peter N. Gregory (Honolulu: University of Hawaii Press, 1983), 169–252. The connection to Daoxin is probably not as important as the connection to the *Perfection of Wisdom Sutras* and Madhyamaka, which Zongmi stresses.

29. See *Chan Letter*, note 48.

30. See *Chan Letter*, note 49.

31. This encapsulation (*"fu xin mie wang"*) again suggests the connection Zongmi makes in the *Chan Prolegomenon* (section 22) between Baotang and Yogācāra teachings, which aim at extinguishing thought of the unreal (*wangnian=wangxiang=abhūta-vikalpa*).

32. This encapsulation (*"zongren xinxing"*) is Zongmi's critique of Hongzhou in a nutshell.

33. This encapsulation (*"xiu xin bu qi"*) leaves us wondering about the difference between Baotang's "subduing mind [*fu xin*]" and Niutou's "giving mind a rest [*xiu xin*]."

34. The key element of this slogan (*"ji chuanxiang er zun fo"*) is the last graph. Its reading (in Tang pronunciation probably something like *"fhut"* [as in *"boot"*]) was the vocalization of the musical buddha-recitation of this school.

35. Xuanshi does not appear in the list of ten Hongren disciples in the *Lengjia shizi ji*. In fact, nothing is known of any of these figures. Beyond Zongmi we have no other reference to this lineage. Xuanshi and Preceptor Wei were active in Guozhou, Zongmi's native prefecture (see Xuanshi in chart of *Chan Letter*, section 7), and that is probably the reason Zongmi knows of them.

36. See *Chan Letter*, note 21.

37. On Jingzhong's nighttime convocations at a Mahayana practice site, which lasted for weeks, see section 2.

38. *yi chuanxiang wei zishi zhi xin*. Incense was not the only instrument employed as a seal of faith in eighth-century Chan circles. The *Lidai fabao ji* (T 51:187a27–b6; Yanagida II, 171) reports that Wuzhu ordered a layman to take a seal of faith consisting of bud-tea (*jiang ci chaya wei xin*) as an offering to Musang.

39. The description of this singing buddha-recitation is strikingly similar to the *Lidai fabao ji*'s description of Musang's singing buddha-recitation. See note 10. In

both cases the chanting of the incantation began as a slow song and eventually dwindled down to silence.

40. Zongmi is usually precise in his use of Buddhist technical terminology, and portions of the *Chan Prolegomenon* show his deep familiarity with the terminology of Xuanzang's dharma-characteristics axiom. My guess—and it is only a guess—is that the remainder of this section hinges on a distinction between the technical terms "*yi*" and "*xin*" in a dharma-characteristics (Yogācāra) context. The former is the standard equivalent for manas, the seventh consciousness (*Cheng weishi lun*, T 31:19b7–12); in section 18 of the *Chan Prolegomenon*, which discusses the four types of mind, the *ālaya-vijñāna*, the eighth consciousness, is referred to by a transliteration of "*citta*" and by the translation equivalent "*xin*." Thus, Zongmi seems to be saying that the South Mountain house sends the "*fhut*" sound (a reconstruction of the pronunciation of the eighth century) first to the manas, where it remains coarse, and eventually further down to the *citta* or *ālaya-vijñāna*. They continued practicing until this sound was stabilized in the *citta*, leading to no thought (*wuxiang*). The translation of the remainder of this section remains tentative.

41. Refers to the meditative concentration called the no-thought concentration (*wuxiang ding*), which serves as a cause for rebirth into the no-thought heaven (fourth dhyana of the realm of form).

42. On the Knowing of this slogan ("*jizhi zhi ti wunian wei zong*"), see *Chan Letter*, note 51.

43. See *Chan Letter*, sections 4–5.

44. Perhaps this statement of Heze practice is related to the one at *Chan Letter*, note 54.

APPENDIX 2. PEI XIU'S PREFACE TO THE *CHAN PROLEGOMENON*

1. Pei's title here is *Hongzhou cishi jian yushi zhongcheng* ("Hongzhou Prefect Concurrently Vice-President of the Tribunal of Censors"). The *Ming Canon* edition of Ui, 4, gives his title as *Tang Mianzhou cishi* ("Mianzhou Prefect of the Tang"); the Gozan edition of Ishii (2), 39, makes it *Mianzhou cishi* ("Mianzhou Prefect"). It is not certain exactly when Pei Xiu held these titles. According to Ishii (2), 48, Pei became Hongzhou Prefect sometime after 832 and before Zongmi's death in 841, and his time as Mianzhou Prefect was after 838. A preface to the *Chan Prolegomenon* by Deng Wenyuan (1259–1328) found in the *Ming Canon* edition in the *Taishō Canon* dates Pei's composition of this preface to some years after Zongmi's death: "During the Dazhong era [847–860] of the Tang Minister Pei Xiu did a preface for it" (T 48:397c18). For information on Deng Wenyuan, see Ishii (10), 87. In the following Pei imitates the style of the *Chan Prolegomenon* and uses its vocabulary freely. Passages in italics within parentheses are Pei's autocommentary.

2. Ishii (2), 48–49, makes an interesting remark about this line, one with which I am in complete agreement: "Pei Xiu had interactions with numerous Buddhists. Beyond Zongmi, his interactions with Huangbo Xiyun and Weishan Lingyu were particularly deep. But, even in this context, he valued Zongmi highly and was greatly influenced by him. Thus, we can probably raise Zongmi to the position of number one [in Pei Xiu's estimation]."

3. This is one of the ten epithets of a buddha.

4. See *Chan Prolegomenon*, note 8.

5. From the *Wenxin diaolong* (*Literary Mind and the Carving of Dragons*) by Liu Xie (c. 465–522): Vincent Yu-chung Shih, trans., *The Literary Mind and the Carving of Dragons: A Study of Thought and Pattern in Chinese Literature* (New York: Columbia University Press, 1959), 99–100: "Prior to the six states [or Warring States] period, writers were not very far removed in time from the Sage, so that they could discourse in high style over the heads of their contemporaries, and each could open up a new vista [='doors-and-windows'] for himself." It is a metaphor for sectarian groupings of scholars.

6. *Zhou Rites*, Dongguan kaogongji. Ishii (2), 49, points out that Kamata, 3, has incorrectly transcribed the Korean edition's "*yin han* (pronunciation '*han*')."

7. Mencius, Gongsun Chou.

8. *Xunzi*, Quanxue.

9. *Zhouyi Lueli*, Mingtuan. This work is by Wang Bi (226–249), a Wei dynasty scholar.

10. *Analects*, Bayi.

11. An *icchantika* is a being destitute of the buddha nature.

12. Based on the *Shijing*, Xiaoya, Gufeng, Liao'e.

13. From here onward Pei Xiu quotes several lines from Chengguan's final testament: "On the sixth day of the third month of Kaicheng 3 [April 4, 838] the Monastic Administrator Chengguan, National Teacher Qingliang, being about to die, said to his follower Haian and others: 'I have heard that accidental luck is not meritorious. . . . Don't [fall into] the trap of delusions with false thought. Don't be in the prison of fighting and quarreling. The great brightness cannot eradicate the darkness of the long night; a compassionate mother cannot protect her child after its death. You should take your faith from the Buddha and not take your faith from people . . .'" (*Fozu lidai tongzai*, T 49:643c10–16). Since Pei was in possession of this testament, his preface to the *Chan Prolegomenon* must date to sometime after early 838. See Yoshikawa Tadao, "Hai Kyū den: Tōdai no ichi shidaifu to Bukkyō," *Tōhō gakuhō* 64 (March 1992): 140.

14. *Changes*, Xici shang.

15. Also *Changes*, Xici shang.

16. According to the *Zhou Rites*, Diguan, Caishi, the *dadu* is the public land around the capital owned by the king. The term can also mean "great gist." It is possible that Pei

is making a pun based on the title *Prolegomenon* (*dadu=duxu*): "Even though the Tathagata never made a great *Prolegomenon* . . ."

17. This and the following quotation are based on T 12:630b23 and b3–5. The *Da banniepan jing jijie*, T 37:433a, has collected the glosses of a number of commentators on this sutra passage. The gist seems to be that the Buddha sometimes spoke with a cryptic intention. For instance, when beings receptive to the teaching of permanence had not yet arrived, he preached the teaching of impermanence, but his secret intention lay in the teaching of permanence. These are *secret words*. But the Buddha was not like a magician who wants to keep the audience from knowing (from "getting it"). The Buddha always wanted people to come to a knowing. He never had a *secret storehouse*.

18. *Laozi*, 38.

19. The Gozan edition of Ishii (2), 43 reads "*xin* [faith]" rather than "*zheng* [proof]."

20. *Shijing*, Xiaoya, Gufeng, Liao'e.

21. The Gozan edition of Ishii (2), 43, reads "*jie zhe* [understanding]" rather than "*bei gan* [sense of compassion]."

APPENDIX 3. SONG DYNASTY COLOPHON TO THE *CHAN PROLEGOMENON* AS REPRODUCED IN THE WANLI 4 (1576) KOREAN EDITION (KAMATA, 260)

1. This undated Song colophon appears in large characters, six lines on one page, each line ten characters. The *Chan Prolegomenon* text is ten lines to the page, each line twenty characters. For a reproduction, see Kamata, frontispiece, and Kuroda Ryō, *Chosen kyūsho kō* (Tokyo: Iwanami shoten, 1940), 122. The Song colophon does not appear in either the *Ming Canon* edition of Ui or the 1358 Gozan edition of Ishii (1–10). It does appear, however, in the Hongzhi 6 (1493) Korean reprint, which is identical to the 1576 Korean edition. See Yanagida Seizan, ed., *Kōrai-bon*, Zengaku sōsho 2 (Kyoto: Chūbun shuppansha, 1974), 149. A preface by Deng Wenyuan (1259–1328) found in the *Ming Canon* edition incorporates some of the information found in this Song colophon. Deng's preface, T 48:397c18–20, says: "During the Dazhong era [847–860] of the Tang Minister Pei Xiu wrote a preface for it. Furthermore, in his own hand he copied out this *Chart* [*shou shu shi tu*; *Chart=Chan Prolegomenon*] and handed it over to Yanchang Monastery in Jinzhou [in Shaanxi]. Later it was transmitted to Master Weijing. He again transmitted it to Master Xuanqi [=Qixuan], and the *Chart* circulated within Min [Fujian], Hu [Hunan], Wu [southern Jiangsu and northern Zhejiang], and Yue [eastern Zhejiang]." Note that the *Chan Prolegomenon* is referred to as the *Chart*, which may have been a common designation. For information on Deng Wenyuan, see Ishii (10), 87.

2. Could mean "old monks."

3. Weijing is Nanyue Weijing, a disciple of Xuefeng Yizun (822–908). Nanyue Weijing has entries in *Song gaoseng zhuan*, T 50:818b20–c10; *Zutangji* (Yanagida Seizan, ed., *Sodōshū*, Zengaku sōsho 4 [Kyoto: Chūbun shuppansha, 1974], 222); and *Jingde chuandeng lu*, T 51:360b2–16. He studied a Huayan work by Fazang entitled the *Mirror Lamp* (*Jing deng*) and wrote a work entitled *Five Chapters of Five-Word Verses* (*Wuzi song wu zhang*).

4. Nothing is known of Qixuan.

5. Both son and father are unknown.

6. We have no date for this woodblock printing of the *Chan Prolegomenon* in Hangzhou organized by the low-level local official Yan Kai. Yan Kai's printing must date to sometime after 955, perhaps the early eleventh century. It may be the very first printing of the *Chan Prolegomenon*. From Hangzhou, a hub for the printing of Chan literature, the text ultimately traceable to Pei Xiu's handcopy subsequently radiated to various places in East Asia, and Korean editions seem to stem quite directly from this Song edition.

GLOSSARY OF CHINESE CHARACTERS

Includes Korean and Japanese readings

Anxin famen 安心法門
ba feng 八風
baihua 白話
Bai Juyi 白居易
bang 傍
banzhou sanmei 般舟三昧
Baolinzhuan 寶林傳
Baotang (lineage/house) 保唐宗/家
Baotang Monastery 保唐寺
Baotang Wuzhu 保唐無住
Baoyue Chan Master 寶月禪師
bei gan 悲感
Beizong (Northern lineage) 北宗
benjue 本覺
benti kongji 本體空寂
ben wushi er wang qing 本無事而忘情
benzhi 本旨
benzi juzu 本自具足

bian bu xiuxing 便不脩行 [T=便不修行]

bianji suozhi zixing 遍計所執自性

biaoquan 表詮

biaozong zhang 標宗章

Bieji 別記

bieye 別業

biguan 壁觀

biliang 比量

bi zong houxue 彼宗後學

Bodhidharma, the first 達磨第一

bu de li 不得力

bugao zhi zui 不告之罪

bu jiao ren dujing nianfo libai 不教人讀經念佛禮拜

bu jiao shixiang fa 不教事相法

bujue 不覺

bu ke jiang xin geng qiu yu xin 不可將心更求於心

buliaoyi 不了義

bu liao zixin 不了自心

bu lizan bu jiangsong 不禮讚不講誦

bu xi 不習

bu ying bu qi 不迎不起

bu ying yu wenzi er ze ye 不應於文字而責也

bu zhu yiqie 不住一切

bu zijie bu huzui 不祈戒不護罪

buzuoyi 不作意

Caotang chanshi jianyao 草堂禪師牋要

Caotang Monastery 草堂寺

cehui 厠穢

cekong 厠孔

chang zhu xukong 長住虛空

chan jishi dong bu dong bu chan shi wusheng chan 禪即是動不動不禪是無生禪

chanli 禪理

chanmen yanjiao 禪門言教

chanshi shou yu Qixuan gui Min 禪師授於契玄歸閩

[chan]wen 禪文

Chanyuan xia 禪源下

Chanyuan zhuquanji 禪源諸詮集

Chanyuan zhuquanji duxu 禪源諸詮集都序

chanzang 禪藏

chanzong li jiao 禪宗例教

Chen Chuzhang (=Chen Qige) 陳楚章 (=陳七哥)

Cheng of Zhangjing Monastery north of western capital mountains 西京山北章敬
寺澄

chi (Korean) 知

Chinul 知訥

Chi of Jiangning 江寧持

Chogye school 曹溪宗

chŏmsu 漸修

Chonggyŏng nok 宗鏡錄

Chongmil 宗密

Chuanxin fayao 傳心法要

Chuji of Zizhou 資州處寂

Chūka denshinji zenmon shiji shōshū zu 中華傳心地禪門師資承襲圖

chulei shi dao 觸類是道

chulei shi dao er renxin 觸類是道而任心

Ch'ungch'ŏng-do 忠清道

ci ge shi 此箇事

ci lingjuexing 此靈覺性

cisui chan/jusui chan (sic) 詞隨禪/句隨禪

ciwai chan/juwai chan 詞外禪/句外禪

ci xin 此心

ci xin ji fo 此心即佛

cong kongji ti shang qi zhi 從空寂體上起知

cuolue 撮略

Da Baigaoguo 大白高國

dade 大德

dadu 大都

Da fangguang yuanjue xiuduoluo liaoyi jing lueshu zhu 大方廣圓覺修多羅了義經略
疏註

Da foding rulai miyin xiuzheng liaoyi zhupusa wanxing shoulengyan jing 大佛頂如
來密因修證了義諸菩薩萬行首楞嚴經

da gubaoyin 大古寶印

Dahui Pujue chanshi shu 大慧普覺禪師書

Dahui yulu 大慧語錄

Dahui Zonggao 大慧宗杲

Dai-honzan Myōken-ji 大本山妙顯寺

Dainichi Nōnin 大日能忍

Daji (=Mazu Daoyi of Hongzhou) 大寂 (=洪州馬祖道一)

Damo yi zong 達磨一宗

dan dao zhi ru 單刀直入

dan de wunian zhi xin 但得無念之心

dangti 當體

Dangxiang 黨項

dan renxin 但任心

dan yi zhizi 但一知字

Daoqin of Mt. Jing 徑山道欽

Daosu chouda wenji 道俗酬答文集

[Dao]wu of Jiangling 江陵道悟

Daoxin, the fourth 道信第四
Daoyu 道育
Daoyuan of Suizhou 遂州道圓
Dasheng qixin lun 大乘起心論
dayuan jingzhi 大圓鏡智
Dayun Monastery 大雲寺
Dayuan of the western capital 西京大願
Deng Wenyuan 鄧文原
de yi er wang yan 得意而忘言
de zhi 得之
Dharani Nun 尼總持
dian 點
diaokai ban 雕開板
dingben 定本
Dinghui chanshi 定慧禪師
Dongshan famen 東山法門
Dongshan jingmen 東山淨門
dōshin 道心
dou bu fengying yi bu qidong 都不逢迎亦不起動
duanhuo mieku jiao 斷惑滅苦教
dunjiao 頓教
dunmen 頓門
dunwu 頓悟
dunwu zhi zong 頓悟知宗
duomu 多目
duxu ("prolegomenon") 都序
ergen 耳根
ershi yu zhi 二十餘紙
Fachi, the fourth 法持第四
Fahai of the western capital 西京法海
Fajing 法淨
famen 法門
fangbian tong jing 方便通經
fangde 訪得
fang yan zhenzhi shi 方驗真實是
fannao zhang 煩惱障
Fa of Yezhou 業州法
Faru of Luzhou 潞州法如
fashu 法數
[Fa]xian of Jingzhou 荊州法顯
faxiang zong 法相宗
faxing ("generating practice") 發行
faxing zong ("dharma-nature axiom") 法性宗
Fayan (*fayan*="dharma eye") 法眼

fayi 法意

Fayi of Xiangzhou 襄州法意

Fazang (Huayan) 法藏

Fazang of Shuzhou 舒州法藏

fei qiang chuanzao 非強穿鑿

fei suiyuan 非隨緣

fei zong bu yan 非總不言

Foding jing 佛頂經

[fo]jing 佛經

fo[xin] 佛心

foyanliang 佛言量

foyi 佛意

fu 符

fuchen kanjing fangbian tong jing 拂塵看淨方便通經

fu Digang 夫帝鋼未張千璎焉覿宏鋼忽舉萬目自開

fuji 拂跡

Fujiang 涪江

Funi dōjin 不二道人

Funi ikō 不二遺稿

furyū monji kyōge betsuden 不立文字教外別傳

fu xin 伏心

fu xin mie wang 伏心滅妄

fu yu 付與

gakumon 学問

gang 綱

ganlituoye 乾栗陀耶

ganlu 甘露

Gan of Tongde Monastery of the eastern capital 東京同德寺幹

ganshijue 乾屎橛

ganxin 甘心

Gaofeng Yuanmiao chanshi chanyao 高峰原妙禪師禪要

gejue 歌訣

geng li nianfo famen 更立念佛法門

geteng chan 葛藤禪

Gidō Shūshin 義堂周心

gongcheng 宮城

gongguo zhuang 功過狀

gongneng 功能

gongye 共業

goshu zenton 悟修漸頓

goudang 勾當

Gozanban 五山版

Gozan Zen 五山禪

guancha 觀察

Guangyao of Taiyuan　太原光瑤
guan hu renqing yi　管乎人情矣
guansi wen'an　官司文案
guanxin　觀心
gu baihua　古白話
Guifeng　圭峰/峯
Guifeng chanshi beiming bing xu　圭峯禪師碑銘并序
Guifeng da Pei Xiangguo zongqu zhuang　圭峰答裴相國宗趣狀
Guifeng houji　圭峯後集
Guifeng Zongmi　圭峰宗密
Guishan da Pei Xiu wenshu　圭山答裴休問書
Guozhou　果州
Hai Kyū shūi mon　裴休拾遺問
Hanshan Deqing　憨山德清
Hanshan laoren mengyouji　憨山老人夢游集
hao　號
haojia　豪家
hehui　和會
helituoye　紇利陀耶
Hengguan of the eastern capital　東京恒觀
He *shi*　何氏
he yao xiuli　何要修理
Heze (lineage/house)　荷澤宗/家
Heze Monastery　荷澤寺
Heze Shenhui　荷澤神會
hiketsu　秘決
Hiranoya Sabē　平野屋佐兵衛
Hoeam Chǒnghye　晦庵定慧
hǒji　虛知
Hongji of Luzhou　潞州弘濟
Hongren, the fifth　弘忍第五
Hongzhi 6 (1493 Korean edition of *Chan Prolegomenon*)　弘治六年
Hongzhou cishi jian yushi zhongcheng　洪州刺史兼御史中承
Hongzhou (lineage/house)　洪州宗/家
Hongzhou zongqu zhujie minghu ji　洪州宗趣注解明護記
Hongzhou zongshi jiaoyi　洪州宗師教儀
Hongzhou zongshi qu zhu kaiming yaoji　洪州宗師趣註開明要記
houji ("colophon")　後記
[Huai]hai of Baizhang　百丈懷海
[Huai]hui of Zhangjing　章敬懷暉
[Huai]kong of Heyang　河陽懷空
[Huai]rang of Nanyue　南嶽懷讓
huamen zhi shuo　化門之說
Huangbo Xiyun　黃檗希運

Huangting jing 黃庭經

huatou 話頭

Huaxian Layman 華閑居士

Huayan Commentary Master (Qingliang Chengguan) 華嚴疏主 (清凉澄觀)

Huayan yifen 華嚴一分

huayi dun 化儀頓

Huichou-Gunabhadra 慧稠求那

Huifang, the third 惠方第三

[Hui]jian of the western capital 西京慧堅

Huijue of Jingzhou 荊州惠覺

Huike, the second 慧可第二

Huineng, the sixth 慧能第六

hui xiang gui xing 會相歸性

Huiyong [Huirong] of Mt. Niutou 牛頭山慧融

hui zhi ji jie shi 會之即皆是

Huizhong 惠忠

huo bobo yiqie shi zhong zong shi chan 活鱍鱍一切時中總是禪

Hyujŏng 休靜

Ikkyū Sōjun 一休宗純

inkyo osim 因教悟心

jia 家

Jia Dao 賈島 (Epigraph: 哭宗密禪師: 鳥道雪岑巔/師亡誰去禪/几塵增滅後/樹色改
　　生前/層塔當松吹/殘蹤傍野泉/唯嗟聽經虎/時到壞菴邊)

jiang ci chaya wei xin 將此茶芽為信

jiangshi pojing jiao 將識破境教

Jiangxi (=Hongzhou) 江西 (=洪州)

jianjiao 漸教

jianmen 漸門

jianxiu 漸修

jianzhao 鑒照

jiao 教

jiaomen 教門

jiaowai biechuan 教外別傳

jiaowai biexing 教外別行

jiaoxing bu ju er mie shi 教行不拘而滅識

Jia Ruzhou 賈汝舟

Ji chanyuan zhulun guanyao 集禪源諸論關要

ji chuanxiang er zun fo 藉傳香而存佛

jie shi qixin 皆是起心

Jietuo of Fengxiang 鳳翔解脫

jiewu 解悟

Jiexian 戒賢

jie ze shi she se mi ze se she shi 解則識攝色迷則色攝識

jie zhe 解者

ji jiao wu zong 籍教悟宗

jijing ti 寂淨體

jin 今

Jing 鏡

jing kong xin you 境空心有

Jingang sanmei jing 金鋼三昧經

Jingde chuandeng lu 景德傳燈錄

qing yu tingxue 輕於聽學

Jingzhong (lineage/house) 淨眾宗/家

Jingzhong Monastery 淨眾寺

Jingzhong Shenhui 淨眾神會

Jingzong of Xiazhou 陝州敬宗

jinli wenzi fei zhongdao / chang zhu xukong shi xiaosheng 盡離文字非中道/長住虛空是小乘

jinri geteng 今日葛藤

Ji of Tongquan county 通泉縣季

Ji of Weizhou 魏州寂

Ji of Zhuzhou 逐州季

jiongjue wuji 迥絕無寄

ji ru foxing 即汝佛性

jiujing dao 究竟道

Jiujing yisheng yuanming xin yi 究竟一乘圓明心義

jiujiu chunshu 久久純熟

ji wei yi zu 即謂已足

Jiyun of Xiangzhou 襄州寂芸

jizhi zhi ti wunian wei zong 寂知指體無念為宗

Jōtōshōgakuron 成等正覺論

Jueguanlun 絕觀論

Juehui 覺慧

Jue of Yangzhou 揚州覺

juji 句偈

jun Zen no dentō 純禅の伝統

Jushe 俱舍

ju yiqie shi bu qi wangnian 居一切時不起妄念

ju yixin wei zong 舉一心為宗

kaishi benxing 開示本性

Kaiyuan Ming shi 開源明師

kan ge huatou 看箇話頭

kanhui 勘會

kanhwa (Korean) 看話

kanjing 看淨

kanqi 勘契

Keizan tō Hai Kyū monsho 圭山答裴休問書

kenmitsu Bukkyō 顕密仏教

kenshō jōbutsu 見性成佛
keti 尅體
Kihwa 己和
Kim/Jin of Yizhou 益州金
Kiyō Hōshū 岐陽方秀
Kōben 高辨
kong 空
kongji zhi 空寂知
kongxun wenju 空尋文句
kong you xiangdui 空有相對
kongzhong 空中
kongzong 空宗
kotsuzen utoku 忽然有得
kuden 口傳
Kūge nichiyō kufū ryakushū 空華日用工夫略集
Kumida-dera 久米田寺
Kuroda Toshio 黒田俊雄
Kwanŭm Monastery of Sokri Mountain 俗離山觀音寺
kyōge betsuden 教外別傳
kyōzen dōi 教禪同異
kyōzen itchi 教禪一致
lai ji cong ta lai 來即從他來
Lang of Fuzhou 涪州朗
Lang of Huangmei Chan Master 黄梅朗禪師
Lao'an 老安
lao su 老宿
Leidai zushi xuemai tu 累代祖師血脈圖
Lengjia shizi ji 楞伽師資記
Lengyan jing tongyi 楞嚴經通議
liaoyi 了義
Lidai fabao ji 歷代法寶記
Li Liaofa of Baotang (=Baotang Wuzhu) 保唐李了法 (=保唐無住)
ling 領
lingjue 靈覺
lingjue zhi xing 靈覺之性
lingzhi 靈知
lingzhi bumei 靈知不昧
Linjianlu 林間録
Linjilu 臨濟錄
liru 理入
liuxing bu jue 流行不絕
liuzuzhuan xu zhong 六祖傳序中
li xian yu xinyuan 理現於心源
Li Xun 李訓

li yue jian xue 禮樂漸學

li ze dunwu chengwu bingxiao 理則頓悟乘悟併銷

li zong ding zhi 立宗定旨

li zushi ta 禮祖師塔

Ma of Mt. Changsong 長松山馬

Masu 馬素

Ma[zu Daoyi] of Hongzhou 洪州馬祖道一

Mianzhou cishi 綿州刺史

miaoer men 妙耳門

Miaole 妙樂

miaoyuan zhenxin 妙圓真心

miedao er di 滅道二諦

milǔi sangchǒn ch'ǒ 密意相傳處

mingfu 冥符

mingming bumei liaoliao changzhi 明明不昧了了常知

minjue wuji 泯絕無寄

minjue wuji zong 泯絕無寄宗

mi shi ren zhu fa jie shi fa zhu ren 迷時人逐法解時法逐人

Miyao 彌藥

miyi 密意

miyi poxiang xianxing jiao 密意破相顯性教

miyi yixing shuoxiang jiao 密意依性說相教

miyu 密語

mo chuan xinyin 默傳心印

Moguja 牧牛子

Moheyan 摩訶衍

mohua 墨畫

moni zhu 摩尼珠

moran wuyan 默然無言

moujia 某甲

mouyi 某乙

mowang 莫妄

mugyō mushu 無行無修

Myōe Shōnin 妙慧聖人

Nanshan nianfomen chanzong 南山念佛門禪宗

Nan-Shen (=Zhishen of the South=Jingzhong lineage/house) 南侁
   (=智侁[詵]=淨衆宗/家)

Nanyin of Yizhou (=Weizhong=Zhang) 益州南印 (=惟忠=張)

Nanyue Weijing 南嶽惟勁

nei gongfeng 內供奉

neiwai hu 內外護

nei xin wu chuan 內心無喘

nenbutsu Zen 念仏禪

nengyuan 能緣

nian qi ji jue jue zhi ji shi 念起即覺覺之即失
nian qi ji jue jue zhi ji wu 念起即覺覺之即無
niman laoseng 擬瞞老僧
ningran 凝然
ningxin ruding 凝心入定
Niutou (lineage/house) 牛頭宗/家
nixin ji cha 擬心即差
niyi 擬議
oni ni kanabō 鬼に金棒
ou ye 偶謁
paichi sanzang jiao 排斥三藏教
panyuan 攀緣
Pei Xiu 裴休
Pei Xiu chanshi suiyuan ji 裴休禪師隨緣集
Pei Xiu shiyi wen 裴休拾遺問
ping ("critique") 評
ping ("standard") 憑
Pŏpchip pyŏrhaeng nok chŏryo kwamok pyŏngip sagi 法集別行錄節要科目並入私記
Pŏpchip pyŏrhaeng nok chŏryo pyŏngip sagi 法集別行錄節要並入私記
poxiang zong 破相宗
Pozao Duo 破竈墮
Puji (seventh) 普寂七
Puping of Jingzhu 淨住普平
Puril Pojo 佛日普照
putixin 菩提心
Pyŏrhaeng nok sagi hwajok 別行錄私記畫足
qin bi xieben 親筆寫本
Qingliang Chengguan 清凉澄觀
Qinglian zhi ta 青蓮之塔
qin zheng qi ti 親證其體
qishu renxin 棄術任心
qixin 起心
Qixuan 契玄
qi yuan ba jian 七緣八見
Quan fa putixin wen 勸發菩提心文
quci 取次
ranhou 然後
ranshi 然始
rentian yinguo jiao 人天因果教
renwu 人物
renxin 任心
renyun bu ju 任運不拘
renyun zizai 任運自在
rongtong fei li wenzi jietuo 融通非離文字解脫

rongyi xin 容易心

Rudao fangbian ji 入道方便偈

ruseng 儒僧

Ruyi of Yizhou 益州如一

Sajip 四集

san ban 三般

san ju yongxin wei jie ding hui 三句用心為戒定慧

san liang 三量

sanshiqi daopin 三十七道品

Santai shi (San ti shi) 三體詩

san xian 三賢

san yi 三義

sanzang fashi 三藏法師

san zhong jiao 三種教

san zong 三宗

Seishō-ji 青松寺

Sengcan, the third 僧璨第三

Sengrui 僧睿

shan zhishi 善知識

sheng huang 笙簧

shengmie 生滅

shengmo 繩墨

Shengshou Monastery 聖壽寺

shengtai 聖胎

Shenhui, the seventh 神會第七

Shenxiu of the Northern lineage (sixth) 北宗神秀六

Shenzhao of the eastern capital 東京神照

she xiang gui xing 攝相歸性

shi 屎

shi bujing guzhi 拭不淨故紙

shi di 十地

shi fei dunchu yin cidi jin 事非頓除因次第盡

shijue 始覺

shikeng li 屎坑裏

shi li 十力

shili wuai men 事理無礙門

shimen shixiang yiqie bu xing 釋門事相一切不行

Shinpuku-ji 真福寺

Shi of Yizhou (=Jingzhong Shenhui) 益州石 (=淨眾神會)

Shi Shanren 史山人

shi shen 十身

shishi tixi 時時提撕

shishi wuai men 事事無礙門

shishuo 師說

Shitou (lineage/house) 石頭宗/家

shi xuan 十玄

Shiye 實葉

shi yu zhi 十餘紙

shi zhi 十智

Shōjō 證定

shoryū kenge 諸流見解

Shoulengyan jing 首楞嚴經

shou yu 授於

Shūmitsu 宗密

Shun'oku Myōha 春屋妙葩

shuo geteng 說葛藤

shuxie shixing yi 書寫施行矣

si deng=si wuliang 四等＝四無量

si jie 四節

Siming zunzhe jiaoxinglu 四明尊者教行錄

si she 四攝

si [wuai] bian 四無礙辯

sŏno husu 先悟後修

Sŏnwŏn jejŏnjip tosŏ 禪源諸詮集都序

Sŏnwŏn jejŏnjip tosŏ kwamok pyŏngip sagi 禪源諸詮集都序科目並入私記

Sŏnwŏnjip tosŏ ch'akpyŏng 禪源集都序着柄

Sugyōroku 宗鏡錄

suiwen fanzhi 隨問反質

suiyuan 隨緣

suiyuan yingyong 隨緣應用

Suizhou 遂州

suojian/jianjie 所見/見解

suojie/jie 所解/解

suowu li 所悟理

suoxiu zhi dao 所修之道

suoyuan 所緣

suozhi zhang 所知障

Susim kyŏl 修心訣

suyu 俗語

Taguchi Akiyoshi 田口明良

Tahara Jinzaemon 田原仁左衛門

taiken 体験

Taiyi Yanchang Monastery on Mt. Wudang in Jinzhou 金州武當山太一延昌寺

Tangai Kiun 丹崖喜雲

Tang Chang'an guoshi gongnei chuanfa yao 唐長安國師宮内傳法要

Tang Mianzhou cishi 唐縣州刺史

Tanyu 壇語

Teng Teng 騰騰

ti 體

ti ci yi nian 提此一念

Tong of Xiangzhou 襄州通

tongyi zhenxing 同一真性

tongyi zong 同一宗

tongzu 同祖

tono 頓悟

ŭi Mil sa yŏshil ŏnkyo 依密師如實言教

ŭi yŏshil ŏnkyo 依如實言教

wanfa lin jing 萬法臨鏡

wang 網

wangnian 妄念

wangqing ("feelings of the unreal") 妄情

wangqing ("forget feelings") 忘情

wangxiang 妄想

wangyan 忘言

wangyan renti 忘言認體

Wang Zhihuan 王之渙

Wanli 4 (1576 Korean edition of *Chan Prolegomenon* executed at Kwanŭm
    Monastery on Sokri Mountain) 萬曆四年

Wanlinglu 宛陵錄

wei du xinglu 未覩行錄

Weijing (of Pei Xiu's preface) 唯勁

[Wei]kuan of Xingshan 興善惟寬

wei ping 為憑

Wei Preceptor of Guozhou 果州未和上

wei shi yixin 唯是一心

weixin 唯心

Weizhong 惟忠

wei zhun 為準

wenda zhang 問答章

Wen Shangshu 溫尚書

wenyan 文言

wenzi chan 文字禪

wenzi juji 文字句偈

wu fangbian 五方便

wu jianci 無漸次

wuming 無明

Wuming of Fucha 浮查無名

wunian 無念

wunian nian zhe ji nian zhenru 無念念者即念真如

wushi 無事

wuxiang 無想

wuxing 無性

wuyi 無憶

wuzhangai fajie 無障礙法界

wu zixing 無自性

wuzong zhi zong 無宗之宗

Xiang Layman 向居士

xiangwai chiqiu 向外馳求

xiangzong 相宗

xian jiao yin sheng nianfo jin yi qi nian 先教引聲念佛盡一氣念

xianliang 現量

xianshi zhenxin jixing jiao 現示真心即性教

xianzong pozhi gu you siyan fei li wenzi shuo jietuo ye 顯宗破執故有斯言非離文字
　說解脫也

Xiao Xianggong 蕭相公

xia zuzhuan xu zhong 下祖傳序中

Xichong *xian* 西充縣

xie bu zhi xi 脅不至席

xiepi 邪僻

ximie wangnian 息滅妄念

xin ("faith") 信

xin ("mind") 心

xin chang jijing 心常寂靜

xing 性

Xingfu *tayuan* 興福塔院

xingmen 行門

xingqi ("arising of practice") 行起

xingqi ("nature origination") 性起

xingru 行入

xing xiang ji ziti 性相及自體

xingzong 性宗

xinjing 心靜 ("mind calmness")

xinjing 心鏡 ("mind mirror")

xin jing ju kong 心境俱空

xin jing ju you 心境俱有

Xinjinglu 心鏡錄

xinshu 心數

xinxing 心性

xinxing bu yi 心性不異

xin xiongjin 信胷襟

xishen yangdao 息神養道

Xiude *fang xibei yu* Xingfu *si* 脩德坊西北隅興福寺

xiu xin bu qi 休心不起

xiuxing/xing/xiu 修行/行/修

xiuxi zhi men 修習之門

xiwang xiuxin 息妄修心

xiwang xiuxin zong 息妄修心宗

Xixia 西夏

xiye yangshen 息業養神

Xuanshi of Guo[zhou] and Lang[zhou] 果閬宣什

xuantong bi zai wangyan 玄通必在忘言

Xuanya of Jianyuan 建元玄雅

xudong 須洞

Xuefeng Yizun 雪峰義存

Xuemailun 血脈論

xu ju er yan 須具二眼

xunxi 熏習

xu xian yue san zhong fojiao zheng san zong chanxin 須先約三種佛教證三宗禪心

Yamamoto Genpō 山本玄峰

yangshen 養神

yanjiao 言教

Yan Kai 嚴楷

Yan Ming 嚴明

Yan of Jingzhou 荊州衍

yanxia bu liu qi ji 言下不留其迹

yaoshu 要術

yi ("idea") 意

yi ("principle/aspect") 義

yi chuanxiang wei zishi zhi xin 以傳香為資師之信

yi dai shanqiao 一代善巧

[Yi]fang of Yuezhou 越州義方

yi fen 一分

yijiao 依教

yi lingxin 一靈心

yinben jianzun 印本見存

yingjing yuanming 瑩淨圓明

yin han 音含

yi nian fangxia shenxin shijie 一念放下身心世界

yinxin yu 印心於

yin zhai ci 因齋次

yinzheng zhang 引證章

Yinzong Dharma Master 印宗法師

yin zong shengjiao 印宗聖教

yiping you ju 依憑有據

yiqie faxiang pin 一切法相品

yiqie jie zhen 一切皆真

yiqie ren ta 一切任他

yiqie shi zhen 一切是真

yiran 怡然

Yisheng Nun of Xiangru county 相如縣尼一乘

yi shi anxia 一時按下
yishuo ("deviant theory") 異説
yishuo ("discussion of principles") 義說
yita qi 依他起
yiti qi xing xiu er wu xiu 依體起行修而無修
yi wu daiqing 亦勿滯情
yiwu jianxiu 依悟漸修
yixiang mu 一向目
yixin 一心
yi xin chuan xin bu li wenzi 以心傳心不立文字
yi xin chuan xin li wenzi gu 以心傳心離文字故
yixing qi xiang 依性起相
yixing sanmei 一行三昧
yixing xiuchan 依性修禪
Yixueyuan 義學院
yi zangxing 依藏性
yizong 依宗
Yǒndam Yuil 蓮潭有一
yong 用
yǒngji pulmae 靈知不昧
Yongming Yanshou 永明延壽
you suoping 有所憑
yuan 緣
yuan chengshi 圓成實
yuanjiao 圓教
Yuanjuejing 圓覺經
Yuanjuejing *dashu chao* 圓覺經大疏鈔
Yuanjuejing *zhijie* 圓覺經直解
Yuanjue *zhushu* 圓覺註疏
Yuanjue Zongyan 圓覺宗演
yuanlü 緣慮
yuantong 圓通
yuanyi san dian 圓伊三點
Yunmen *guanglu* 雲門廣錄
Yunyu of Langzhou 閬州蘊玉
yuqi 魚契
yu wu liaozhi bu bian zhenshi 於無了知不辨真實
yu zhu wangxin yi bu ximie 於諸妄心亦不息滅
zangshi 藏識
zangshi jianfen 藏識見分
Zekkai Chūshin 絕海中津
zen furi kyō kyō furi zen 禪不離教教不離禪
Zengen shosenshū tojo 禪源諸詮集都序
Zenshū kōmoku 禪宗綱目

Zhao of that monastery (Zhao misprint for Shi=Jingzhong Shenui) 當寺召
    (召＝石＝淨衆神會)

zhao wanfa ru jing 照萬法如鏡

zhe 遮

zheng ("correct/central/orthodox") 正

zheng ("proof") 證

zhengwu 證悟

zhengzong 正宗

zhenru 真如

zhenxin 真心

zhenxing 真性

zhequan 遮詮

zhe shaer zheng gan quci yu 遮沙彌爭敢取次語

zhi ("directly") 直

zhi ("Knowing"=Sanskrit *jñāna*) 知

zhiduoye 質多耶

zhiguan niannian bubu zuo jiangqu 只管念念步步做將去

Zhiguang 智光

zhi huan 知幻

zhi ju yi yan 只具一眼

zhime 只麼

Zhiru of Cizhou 磁州智如

[Zhi]shen of Zizhou 資州智侁[詵]

zhi shi konghua 知是空華

zhi wei bu xin zixin shi fo 只為不信自心是佛

Zhiwei, the fifth 智威第五

zhixia bian shi 直下便是

zhixian xinxing zong 直顯心性宗

zhixin 直心

zhi xudong 直須洞

Zhiyan, the second 智巖第二

zhi yu lichan zhuandu huafo xiejing yiqie hui zhi jie wei wangxiang 至於禮懺轉讀畫
    佛寫經一切毀之皆為妄想

[Zhi]zang of Xitang 西堂智藏

zhi zhi yi zi zhongmiao zhi men 知之一字衆妙之門

zhongchen 忠臣

Zhonghua chuanxindi chanmen shizi chengxi tu 中華傳心地禪門師資承襲圖

Zhonghua xindichuan chanmen shizi chengxi tu yijuan 中華心地傳禪門師資承襲圖
    一卷

Zhongnan Shan 終南山

zhongri renyun tengteng 終日任運騰騰

zhongyin 中隱

zhongyuan 衆緣

zhuanji 傳記

zhuhua 朱畫

zhujia zashu 諸家雜述

zhuji dun 逐機頓

Zhushuo chanyuanji duxu 諸說禪源集都序

Zhushuo chanyuanji duxu faju ji 諸說禪源集都序發炬記

Zhushuo chanyuanji duxu gangwen 諸說禪源集都序綱文

Zhushuo chanyuanji duxu luewen 諸說禪源集都序略文

Zhushuo chanyuanji duxu zeju ji 諸說禪源集都序擇炬記

Zhushuo chanyuanji duxu zhi jie 諸說禪源集都序之解

zhuti 珠體

zhu wangxiang jing bu jia liaozhi 住妄想境不加了知

Zhuxian Fanxian (Jikusen Bonsen) 竺仙梵僊

zhuzhi 主旨

zhuzong suoshuo 諸宗所說

zhuzuyu yibai ershi ben 諸祖語一百二十本

zicheng bifa 自成筆法

zicheng yipian 自成一片

zi chunshu 自純熟

ziran zhi 自然知

ziti 自體

zixin 自心

zixing benyong 自性本用

Zizai 自在

zizhi 自知

zong 宗

zongchi men 總持門

Zongjianlu 宗鑑錄

zong-jiao 宗教

Zongjinglu 宗鏡錄

zongren xinxing 縱任心性

zong-shuo 宗說

zongtong ji shuotong 宗通及說通

zongzhi 宗旨

zu nan dunchu 卒難頓除

zuozhu 座主

Zutangji 祖堂集

[zu]yi 祖意

Zuzong zhuanji 祖宗傳記

BIBLIOGRAPHY

Aichi daigaku Chū-Nichi daijiten hensansho, ed. *Chū-Nichi daijiten.* 2nd ed. Tokyo: Taishūkan shoten, 1999.

App, Urs, ed. *Concordance to the "Preface" by Zongmi.* Hanazono Concordance Series 11. Kyoto: International Research Institute for Zen Buddhism Hanazono University, 1996.

——. *Concordance to the Record of Linji (Rinzai).* Kyoto: International Research Institute for Zen Buddhism Hanazono University, 1993.

——. *Concordance to the Record of Yunmen.* Hanazono Concordance Series 15. Kyoto: International Research Institute for Zen Buddhism Hanazono University, 1996.

——. "The Making of a Chan Record." *Zen bunka kenkyūjo kiyō* 17 (1991): 1–90.

——. *Master Yunmen: From the Record of the Chan Teacher "Gate of the Clouds."* New York: Kodansha International, 1994.

Araki Kengo, ed. and trans. *Daie sho.* Zen no goroku 17. Tokyo: Chikuma shobō, 1969.

Bai Juyi. *Bai Juyi ji.* 4 vols. Beijing: Zhonghua shuju, 1979.

Bielefeldt, Carl. "Filling the Zen shū: Notes on the *Jisshū Yōdō Ki.*" In *Chan Buddhism in Ritual Context,* ed. Bernard Faure, 179–210. London: RoutledgeCurzon, 2003.

Buswell, Robert E., Jr. *The Formation of Ch'an Ideology in China and Korea: The Vajrasamādhi-Sūtra, a Buddhist Apocryphon.* Princeton, N.J.: Princeton University Press, 1989.

——. *The Korean Approach to Zen: The Collected Works of Chinul.* Honolulu: University of Hawaii Press, 1983.

——. *The Zen Monastic Experience: Buddhist Practice in Contemporary Korea.* Princeton, N.J.: Princeton University Press, 1992.

CBETA Chinese Buddhist Electronic Text Association. http://www.cbeta.org.

Chen, Ping. *Modern Chinese: History and Sociolinguistics.* Cambridge: Cambridge University Press, 1999.

Dai Nippon zoku-zōkyō (Manji zokuzō). 150 cases. Tokyo: Zōkyō shoin, 1905–12.

Daizōkyō gakujutsu yōgo kenkyūkai, ed. *Taishō shinshū daizōkyō sakuin shoshūbu 3,* vol. 27. Tokyo: Daizōkyō gakujutsu yōgo kenkyūkai, 1983.

Dayal, Har. *The Bodhisattva Doctrine in Buddhist Sanskrit Literature.* Delhi: Motilal Banarsidass, 1970.

DeFrancis, John. *ABC Chinese-English Comprehensive Dictionary.* Honolulu: University of Hawai'i Press, 2003.

Dunnell, Ruth W. *The Great State of White and High: Buddhism and State Formation in Eleventh-Century Xia.* Honolulu: University of Hawaii Press, 1996.

Faure, Bernard. "The Daruma-shū, Dōgen, and Sōtō Zen." *Monumenta Nipponica* 42, no. 1 (Spring 1987): 25–55.

Fukaura, Sebun. "Controversy Between Dharmapāla and Bhāvaviveka." *Ryūkoku daigaku ronshū* 345 (1952): 11–25.

"Genpō Rōshi no meigen sono ichi, monku kei." http://www.marino.ne.jp/%7Erendaico/kuromakuron/genpo.htm.

Gnubs-chen Sans-rgyas-ye-śes. *Rnal 'byor mig gi bsam gtan or Bsam gtan mig sgron.* Smanrtsis shesrig spendzod 74. Leh, Ladakh: S. W. Tashigangpa, 1974.

Gregory, Peter N. *Tsung-mi and the Sinification of Buddhism.* Princeton, N.J.: Princeton University Press, 1991.

Gu Zuyu, ed. *Dushi fangyu jiyao.* 6 vols. Taipei: Hongshi chubanshe, 1981.

Hirakawa Akira, ed. *Bukkyō Kan-Bon daijiten/Buddhist Chinese-Sanskrit Dictionary.* Tokyo: The Reiyūkai, 1997.

Hirano Sōjō, ed. and trans. *Ikkyū oshō zenshū.* Vol. 3. Tokyo: Shunjūsha, 2003.

Hiraoka Takeo. *Chōan to Rakuyō: Shiryō.* Tōdai kenkyū no shiori 6. Kyoto: Kyoto daigaku jinbun kagaku kenkyūjo, 1956.

Homann, Rolf. *Die wichtigsten Körpergottheiten im Huang-t'ing ching.* Goppingen: Verlag Alfred Kümmerle, 1971.

Hu Shih. "Ch'an (Zen) Buddhism in China: Its History and Method." In *Ko Teki Zengakuan,* ed. Yanagida Seizan, 689–98. Kyoto: Chūbun shuppansha, 1975.

——, ed. *Shenhui heshang yiji.* Taipei: Hu Shi jinian guan, 1968.

Hurvitz, Leon. *Chih-I: An Introduction to the Life and Ideas of a Chinese Buddhist Monk.* Mélanges chinois et bouddhiques 12. Brussels: l'Institut Belge des Hautes Études Chinoises, 1962.

Ichiki Takeo. *Gozan bungaku yōgo jiten.* Tokyo: Zokugun shorui kansei kai, 2002.

Iritani Sensuke and Matsumura Takashi. *Kanzan-shi.* Zen no goroku 13. Tokyo: Chikuma shobō, 1970.

Iriya Yoshitaka, ed. and trans. *Baso no goroku.* Kyoto: Zen bunka kenkyūjo, 1984.

——, ed. and trans. *Denshin hōyō Enryōroku.* Zen no goroku 8. Tokyo: Chikuma shobō, 1969.

——. "*Ō Bonji shishū kō.*" In *Kanda hakushi kanreki kinen shoshigaku ronshū,* ed. Kanda hakushi kanreki kinen kai. Tokyo: Heibonsha, 1957.

——, ed. and trans. *Rinzairoku.* Tokyo: Iwanami shoten, 1989.

Iriya Yoshitaka, Kajitani Sōnin, and Yanagida Seizan, eds. and trans. *Secchō juko.* Zen no goroku 15. Tokyo: Chikuma shobō, 1981.

Iriya Yoshitaka and Koga Hidehiko. *Zengo jiten.* Kyoto: Shibunkaku shuppan, 1991.

Iriya Yoshitaka, Ruth F. Sasaki, and Burton F. Watson. "On Some Texts of Ancient Spoken Chinese with Comments and Emendations." Photocopy, Kyoto, 1954.

Ishii Shudō. "Daiei toshokan shozō no Gozanban *Zengen shosenshū tojo* ni tsuite." *Indogaku Bukkyōgaku kenkyū* 44, no. 2 (March 1996): 117–24.

——. *Dōgen Zen no seiritsushi-teki kenkyū.* Tokyo: Daizō shuppan, 1991.

——. "Shinpuku-ji bunko shozō no *Hai Kyū shūi mon* no honkoku." *Zengaku kenkyū* 60 (1981): 71–104.

——. "*Sōkei daishi den kō.*" *Komazawa daigaku Bukkyō gakubu kenkyū kiyō* 46 (March 1988): 79–127.

——, trans. *Zen goroku.* Daijō butten Chūgoku Nihon hen 12. Tokyo: Chūōkōronsha, 1992.

Ishii Shudō and Ogawa Takashi. "*Zengen shosenshū tojo* no yakuchū kenkyū (1)." *Komazawa daigaku Bukkyō gakubu kenkyū kiyō* 52 (March 1994): 1–53.

——. "*Zengen shosenshū tojo* no yakuchū kenkyū (2)." *Komazawa daigaku Bukkyō gakubu kenkyū kiyō* 53 (March 1995): 37–125.

——. "*Zengen shosenshū tojo* no yakuchū kenkyū (3)." *Komazawa daigaku Bukkyō gakubu kenkyū kiyō* 54 (March 1996): 19–55.

——. "*Zengen shosenshū tojo* no yakuchū kenkyū (4)." *Komazawa daigaku Bukkyō gakubu ronshū* 27 (October 1996): 39–73.

——. "*Zengen shosenshū tojo* no yakuchū kenkyū (5)." *Komazawa daigaku Bukkyō gakubu kenkyū kiyō* 55 (March 1997): 19–39.

——. "*Zengen shosenshū tojo* no yakuchū kenkyū (6)." *Komazawa daigaku Bukkyō gakubu ronshū* 28 (October 1997): 81–110.

——. "*Zengen shosenshū tojo* no yakuchū kenkyū (7)." *Komazawa daigaku Bukkyō gakubu kenkyū kiyō* 56 (March 1998): 67–86.

——. "*Zengen shosenshū tojo* no yakuchū kenkyū (8)." *Komazawa daigaku Bukkyō gakubu ronshū* 29 (October 1998): 17–56.

——. "*Zengen shosenshū tojo* no yakuchū kenkyū (9)." *Komazawa daigaku Bukkyō gakubu kenkyū kiyō* 57 (March 1999): 51–113.

——. "*Zengen shosenshū tojo* no yakuchū kenkyū (10)." *Komazawa daigaku Bukkyō gakubu ronshū* 30 (October 1999): 59–97.

Iwaki Eiki. "Kanzan Tokushō no shisō." *Indogaku Bukkyōgaku kenkyū* 46, no. 1 (December 1997): 222–26.

Jackson, Roger. "Terms of Sanskrit and Pāli Origin Acceptable as English Words." *The Journal of the International Association of Buddhist Studies* 5, no. 2 (1982): 141–42.

Jan Yün-hua. "Tsung-mi chu *Tao-su ch'ou-ta wen-chi* te yen-chiu." *Hwakang Buddhist Journal* 4 (1980): 132–66.

———. "Two Problems concerning Tsung-mi's Compilation of *Ch'an-tsang.*" *Transactions of the International Conference of Orientalists in Japan* 19 (1974): 37–47.

Jiang Lansheng and Cao Guangshun, eds. *Tang Wudai yuyan cidian.* Shanghai: Shanghai jiaoyu chubanshe, 1997.

Kagamishima Genryū and others, trans. *Yakuchū Zen'en shingi.* Tokyo: Sōtōshū shūmuchō, 1972.

Kageki Hideo, trans. *Kunchū Kūge nichiyō kufū ryakushū: chūsei Zensō no seikatsu to bungaku.* Kyoto: Shibunkaku, 1982.

Kamata Shigeo. *Chūgoku Kegon shisō-shi no kenkyū.* Tokyo: Tokyo daigaku shuppankai, 1965.

———, ed. and trans. *Genninron.* Tokyo: Meitoku shuppansha, 1973.

———. "Sanronshū gozushū dōkyō o musubu shisō-teki keifu." *Komazawa daigaku Bukkyō gakubu kenkyū kiyō* 26 (March 1968): 79–89.

———. "Sho Tō ni okeru sanronshū to dōkyō." *Tōyō bunka kenkyūjo kiyō* 46 (March 1968): 49–108.

———. *Shūmitsu kyōgaku no shisō-shi teki kenkyū.* Tokyo: Tokyo daigaku shuppankai, 1975.

———, ed. and trans. *Zengen shosenshū tojo.* Zen no goroku 9. Tokyo: Chikuma shobō, 1971.

Kamata Shigeo and others, eds. *Daizōkyō zen-kaisetsu daijiten.* Tokyo: Yūzankaku shuppan, 1998.

Kamata Shigeo and Tanaka Hisao, eds. *Kamakura kyū Bukkyō.* Nihon shisō taikei 15. Tokyo: Iwanami shoten, 1971.

Karmay, Samten Gyaltsen. *The Great Perfection (Rdzogs-chen): A Philosophical and Meditative Teaching in Tibetan Buddhism.* Leiden: E. J. Brill, 1988.

Kawase Kazuma. *Gozanban no kenkyū.* 2 vols. Tokyo: Nihon koshosekishō kyōkai [The Antiquarian Booksellers Association of Japan], 1970.

Kepping, K. B. "Mi-nia (Tangut) Self-Appellation and Self-Portraiture in Khara Khoto Materials." *Manuscripta Orientalia: International Journal for Oriental Manuscript Research* 7 (2001): 37–47.

Kimura Ryūtoku. "Tonkō Chibettogo Zen bunken mokuroku shokō." *Tōkyō daigaku bungakubu bunka kōryū kenkyū shisetsu kenkyū kiyō* 4 (1980): 93–129.

Kirchner, Thomas Yuho, ed. *The Record of Linji.* Honolulu: University of Hawai'i Press, 2008.

Kishiwada-shiritsu kyōdo shiryōkan. *Kumida-dera no rekishi to bijutsu: butsuga to chūsei bunsho o chūshin ni.* Kishiwada-shi: Kishiwada-shiritsu kyōdo shiryōkan, 1999.

Komazawa daigaku toshokan, ed. *Shinsan Zenseki mokuroku.* Tokyo: Komazawa daigaku toshokan, 1962.

Kuroda Ryō. *Chōsen kyūsho kō.* Tokyo: Iwanami shoten, 1940.

Kychanov, E. I. *Katalog Tangutskikh Buddiyskikh pamyatnikov Instituta vostgokovedeniya Rossiyskoi akademii nauk* [*Catalogue of the Tangut Buddhist Texts from the Collection of the Institute of Oriental Studies, Russian Academy of Sciences*]. Kyoto: Kyoto daigaku, 1999.

Lancaster, Lewis R., and others, eds. *The Korean Buddhist Canon: A Descriptive Catalogue*. Berkeley: University of California Press, 1979.

Lessing, Ferdinand D., and Alex Wayman, eds. and trans. *Mkhas grub rje's Fundamentals of the Buddhist Tantras*. The Hague: Mouton, 1968.

"Library of Congress Pinyin Conversion Project: New Chinese Romanization Outlines." http://www.loc.gov/catdir/pinyin/romcover.html.

Li Fanwen. *Xia-Han zidian*. Beijing: Zhonghua shehui kexue chubanshe, 1997.

Li Jingde, ed. *Zhuzi yulei*. Vol. 8. Beijing: Zhonghua shuju, 1986.

Lin Shitian and others, eds. *Dunhuang Chanzong wenxian jicheng*. 2 vols. Beijing: Quanguo tushuguan wenxian suowei fuzhi zhongxin, 1998.

Liu Xu and others, comps. *Jiu Tangshu*. 8 vols. Beijing: Zhonghua shuju, 1975.

Maspero, Henri. "Sur quelques textes anciens de chinois parlé." *Bulletin de l'École Française d'Estrème-Orient* 14, no. 4 (1914): 1–36.

McRae, John R. "The Ox-head School of Chinese Ch'an Buddhism: From Early Ch'an to the Golden Age." In *Studies in Ch'an and Hua-yen*, ed. Robert M. Gimello and Peter N. Gregory, 169–252. Honolulu: University of Hawaii Press, 1983.

Mochizuki Shinkō, ed. *Bukkyō daijiten*. 10 vols. Tokyo: Sekai seiten kankō kyōkai, 1958–1963.

Muller, Charles. "The Sutra of Perfect Enlightenment (Yuanjue jing)." http://www.acmuller.net/bud-canon/sutra_of_perfect_enlightenment.html.

Nakamura Hajime and others, eds. *Iwanami Bukkyō jiten*. 2nd ed. Tokyo: Iwanami shoten, 2002.

Nie Hongyin. "Tangutology During the Past Decades." http://bic.cass.cn/english/infoShow/Arcitle_Show_Forum2_Show.asp?ID=307&Title=The%20Humanities%20Study&strNavigation=Home-%3EForum-%3EEthnography&BigClassID=4&SmallClassID=8.

Nishida Tatsuo. *Seikabun Kegonkyō*. 3 vols. Kyoto: Kyoto daigaku bungaku-bu, 1977.

——. *Seikago no kenkyū*. 2 vols. Tokyo: Zauhō, 1966.

——. *Seika moji*. Tokyo: Kinokuniya shoten, 1967.

Obata Hironobu. "Chibetto no Zenshū to Zōyaku gigyō ni tsuite." *Indogaku Bukkyōgaku kenkyū* 23, no. 2 (1975): 170–71.

——. "Pelliot tib. n. 116 bunken ni mieru shozenji no kenkyū." *Zen bunka kenkyūjo kiyō* 8 (August 1976): 1–31.

Obigane Mitsutoshi. *Sairai: Yamamoto Genpō den*. Tokyo: Daihōrin kaku, 2002.

Oda Tokuno, ed. *Bukkyō daijiten*. 1917. Reprint, Tokyo: Daizō shuppan, 2005.

Ōkubo Dōchū, ed. *Dōgen zenji zenshū*. 2 vols. 1970. Reprint, Kyoto: Rinsen shoten, 1989.

Ouyang Xiu and others, comps. *Xin Tangshu*. 20 vols. Beijing: Zhonghua shuju, 1975.

Owen, Stephen. *The Late Tang: Chinese Poetry of the Mid-Ninth Century (827–860)*. Cambridge, Mass.: Harvard University Asia Center, 2006.

Parker, Joseph D. *Zen Buddhist Landscape Arts of Early Muromachi Japan (1336–1573)*. Albany: State University of New York Press, 1999.

Pei Xiu. *Tang Pei Xiu shu Guifeng chanshi bei*. Taipei: Xinshi chubanshe, 1981.

Poceski, Mario. *Ordinary Mind as the Way: The Hongzhou School and the Growth of Chan Buddhism*. New York: Oxford University Press, 2007.

Pojo sasang yŏn'guwon, ed. *Pojo chŏnsŏ*. Seoul: Puril ch'ulp'ansa, 1989.

Quan Tangshi. 25 vols. Beijing: Zhonghua shuju, 1979.

Quan Tangwen. 20 vols. Imperial edition, 1814. Reprint, Taipei: Datong shuju, 1979.

SAT Daizōkyō Text Datatbase. http://21dzk.l.u-tokyo.ac.jp/SAT/.

Shi Jinbo. *Xixia Fojiao shilüe*. Yinchuan: Ningxia renmin chubanshe, 1988.

Shih, Vincent Yu-chung, trans. *The Literary Mind and the Carving of Dragons: A Study of Thought and Pattern in Chinese Literature*. New York: Columbia University Press, 1959.

Shimada Shūjirō and Iriya Yoshitaka, eds. *Zenrin gasan: Chūsei suibokuga o yomu*. Tokyo: Mainichi shinbunsha, 1987.

Shinohara Hisao and Tanaka Ryōshō. eds. *Tonkō butten to Zen*. Tonkō kōza 8. Tokyo: Daitō shuppansha, 1980.

Shizuka Jien. *Bonji shittan*. Osaka: Toki shobō, 1997.

Solonin, K. J. "Hongzhou Buddhism in Xixia and the Heritage of Zongmi (780–841): A Tangut Source." *Asia Major* 16, no. 2 (2003): 57–103.

——. "Tangut Chan Buddhism and Guifeng Zong-mi." *Zhonghua Foxue xuebao* 11 (July 1998): 365–424.

Suzuki Daisetsu. *Suzuki Daisetsu zenshū*. Vols. 1–3. Tokyo: Iwanami shoten, 1968–71.

Suzuki gakujutsu zaidan, ed. *Dai Nihon Bukkyō zensho*. Vol. 63. Tokyo: Suzuki gakujutsu zaidan, 1972.

Takada Takeyama, ed. *Gotai jirui*. 3rd ed. Tokyo: Nigashi-higashi shobō, 2002.

Takakusu Junjirō and Watanabe Kaigyoku, eds. *Taishō shinshū daizōkyō*. 100 vols. Tokyo: Taishō issaikyō kankōkai, 1924–34.

Takamine Ryōshū, ed. *Zengen shosenshū tojo*. Nara: Tōdai-ji Kangakuin, 1955.

Tamamura Takeji. *Gozan Zensō denki shūsei*. Tokyo: Kōdansha, 1983.

Tanaka Ryōshō. *Tonkō Zenshū bunken no kenkyū*. Tokyo: Daitō shuppansha, 1983.

Tōdai goroku kenkyūhan, ed. *Jinne no goroku: Dango*. Kyoto: Zen bunka kenkyūjo, 2006.

Tokiwa Gishin and Yanagida Seizan, eds. and trans. *Zekkanron*. Kyoto: Zen bunka kenkyūjo, 1973.

Tokyo kokuritsu hakubutsukan. *Kenchō-ji: Zen no genryū*. Tokyo: Nihon keizai shinbunsha, 2003.

Uemura Kankō. *Gozan bungaku zenshū*. Vol. 3. Tokyo: Teikoku kyoikukai shuppanbu, 1936.

Ui Hakuju, ed. and trans. *Zengen shosenshū tojo*. 1939. Reprint, Tokyo: Iwanami shoten, 1943.

——. *Zenshū-shi kenkyū*. 3 vols. 1935. Reprint, Tokyo: Iwanami shoten, 1966.

van Gulik, R. H. *Siddham: An Essay on the History of Sanskrit Studies in China and Japan*. Śata-Pitaka Series 247. 1956. Reprint, New Delhi: International Academy of Indian Culture and Āditya Prakāshan, 2001.

Wang Shu'an, ed. *Jinshi cuibian*. 5 vols. Taipei: Tailian guofeng chubanshe, 1964 and 1973.

Wang Tsui-ling. "Yōmei Enju no Zenshū-kan ni tsuite." *Indogaku Bukkyōgaku kenkyū* 47, no. 1 (December 1998): 201–4.

Watanabe Toshirō, Edmund R. Skrzypczak, and Paul Snowden, eds. *Kenkyusha's New Japanese-English Dictionary*. 5th ed. Tokyo: Kenkyūsha, 2003.

Wayman, Alex. "Nāgārjuna: Moralist Reformer of Buddhism." In *Untying the Knots in Buddhism: Selected Essays*, 59–88. Buddhist Tradition Series 28. Delhi: Motilal Banarsidass, 1997.

Welter, Albert. "The Formation of the *Linji lu*: An Examination of the *Guangdeng lu/ Sijia yulu* and *Linji Huizhao Chanshi yulu* Versions of the *Linji lu* in Historical Context." www.skb.or.kr/2006/down/papers/o63.pdf.

——. *The Linji Lu and the Creation of Chan Orthodoxy: The Development of Chan's Records of Sayings Literature*. Oxford: Oxford University Press, 2008.

——. "The Problem with Orthodoxy in Zen Buddhism: Yongming Yanshou's Notion of Zong in the Zongjing lu (Records of the Source Mirror)." *Studies in Religion/ Sciences Religieuses* 31, no. 1 (2002): 3–18.

Wu Qiyu. "Wolun chanshi yiyu Dunhuang Tufan wen (Pelliot 116 hao) yi ben kaoshi." *Dunhuang xue* 4 (1979): 33–46.

Wylie, Turrell. "A Standard System of Tibetan Transcription." *Harvard Journal of Asiatic Studies* 22 (December 1959): 261–67.

Yampolsky, Philip B. *The Platform Sutra of the Sixth Patriarch*. New York: Columbia University Press, 1967.

Yanagida Seizan, ed. and trans. *Chūgoku senjutsu kyōten 1 Engakukyō*. Bukkyō kyōten-sen 13. Tokyo: Chikuma shobō, 1987.

——. *"Denbōhōki to sono sakusha: Pelliot 3559go bunsho o meguru hokushū Zen kenkyū shiryō no satsuki, sono ichi."* *Zengaku kenkyū* 53 (1963): 45–71.

——. "Goroku no rekishi." *Tōhō gakuhō* 57 (March 1985): 211–663.

——, ed. *Hōrinden Dentō gyokuei shū*. Zengaku sōsho 5. Kyoto: Chūbun shuppansha, 1975.

——, ed. *Kōrai-bon*. Zengaku sōsho 2. Kyoto: Chūbun shuppansha, 1974.

——. *Shoki Zenshū shisho no kenkyū*. Kyoto: Hōzōkan, 1967.

——, ed. *Sodōshū*. Zengaku sōsho 4. Kyoto: Chūbun shuppansha, 1974.

——, ed. and trans. *Daruma no goroku*. Zen no goroku 1. Tokyo: Chikuma shobō, 1969.

——, ed. and trans. *Shoki no Zenshi I*. Zen no goroku 2. Tokyo: Chikuma shobō, 1971.

——, ed. and trans. *Shoki no Zenshi II*. Zen no goroku 3. Tokyo: Chikuma shobō, 1976.

Yi-Hsun Huang. *Integrating Chinese Buddhism: A Study of Yongming Yanshou's Guanxin Xuanshu*. Series of the Chung-Hwa Institute of Buddhist Studies 43. Taipei: Dharma Drum Publishing Corporation, 2005.

Yoshikawa Tadao. "Hai Kyū den: Tōdai no ichi shidaifu to Bukkyō." *Tōhō gakuhō* 64 (March 1992): 115–277.

Yoshimura Shūki. *Indo daijō Bukkyō shisō kenkyū*. Kyoto: Hyakkaen, 1976.

Yoshizu Yoshihide. *Kegon Zen no shisō-shi teki kenkyū*. Tokyo: Daitō shuppansha, 1985.

Zen bunka kenkyūjo, ed. *Zengo jisho ruiju 3: Hekiganroku Funi shō*. Kyoto: Zen bunka kenkyūjo, 1993.

Zengaku daijiten hensansho, ed. *Zengaku daijiten*. Tokyo: Taishūkan shoten, 1978.

Zhang Yisun and others, eds. *Bod-Rgya tshig mdzod chen mo*. 1993. Reprint, Beijing: Minzu chubanshe, 2000.

Zurcher, Erik. *The Buddhist Conquest of China: The Spread and Adaptation of Buddhism in Early Medieval China*. Leiden: E. J. Brill, 1972.

INDEX

TRANSLATIONS FROM THE ASIAN CLASSICS

Major Plays of Chikamatsu, tr. Donald Keene 1961

Four Major Plays of Chikamatsu, tr. Donald Keene. Paperback ed. only. 1961; rev. ed. 1997

Records of the Grand Historian of China, translated from the Shih chi of Ssu-ma Ch'ien, tr. Burton Watson, 2 vols. 1961

Instructions for Practical Living and Other Neo-Confucian Writings by Wang Yang-ming, tr. Wing-tsit Chan 1963

Hsün Tzu: Basic Writings, tr. Burton Watson, paperback ed. only. 1963; rev. ed. 1996

Chuang Tzu: Basic Writings, tr. Burton Watson, paperback ed. only. 1964; rev. ed. 1996

The Mahābhārata, tr. Chakravarthi V. Narasimhan. Also in paperback ed. 1965; rev. ed. 1997

The Manyōshū, Nippon Gakujutsu Shinkōkai edition 1965

Su Tung-p'o: Selections from a Sung Dynasty Poet, tr. Burton Watson. Also in paperback ed. 1965

Bhartrihari: Poems, tr. Barbara Stoler Miller. Also in paperback ed. 1967

Basic Writings of Mo Tzu, Hsün Tzu, and Han Fei Tzu, tr. Burton Watson. Also in separate paperback eds. 1967

The Awakening of Faith, Attributed to Aśvaghosha, tr. Yoshito S. Hakeda. Also in paperback ed. 1967

Reflections on Things at Hand: The Neo-Confucian Anthology, comp. Chu Hsi and Lü Tsu-ch'ien, tr. Wing-tsit Chan 1967

The Platform Sutra of the Sixth Patriarch, tr. Philip B. Yampolsky. Also in paperback ed. 1967